Sports Car Racing

IN CAMERA 1980–89

Sports Car Racing
I N C A M E R A 1980–89

First published in September 2018

Behemoth Publishing
59 High Street
Wincanton
Somerset BA9 9JZ
UK

www.behemothpublishing.co.uk

A catalogue record for this book is available from the British Library

ISBN 978-0-9928769-7-5

Printed and bound in the EU by GPS Group

Designed by Richard Parsons

Image credits:
Getty Images '*Getty*'
Grand Prix Library '*GPL*'
LAT Images '*LAT*'
The Revs Institute for Automotive Research, Inc. '*Revs*'

Acknowledgements
My thanks to LAT Photographic (Kevin Wood and Kathy Agar), Sir Paul Vestey and Doug Nye (Grand Prix Library), Jessica Bright (Revs Institute), Getty Images, Tony Dron, Peter Twitchen, my long-suffering publisher Derek Smith and, of course, Sarah Joslin Parker without whom my world would stop rotating.

	Author's introduction	6
	Foreword	8
1980	An erratic start for a new era	10
1981	Much more stuff going on	36
1982	More change as if it were needed	62
1983	Weissach ist wunderbar	88
1984	Yet more change without consultation	116
1985	Jaguar returns but tragedy intrudes	146
1986	The times they are a changin' (well almost)	174
1987	Jaguar on top whilst Porsche reneges	198
1988	TWR celebrates whilst the rest do their best	226
1989	Sauber scintillates or rather Mercedes does	256
	Final thoughts	284
	Bibliography	285
	Index	286

Following on from the mid to late 1970s, when sports/prototype/GT racing was the victim of regulatory diktats and the inevitable consequences, the 1980s began with a largely non-manufacturer base.

The cars were, with exception, all leftovers from the previous decade and without the omnipresent and diverse customer Porsche 911s, 930s and 935s, plus some almost vintage but modified 908s, it would have been even worse. Such was the degeneration of the Championship series that teams and individual racers were choosing what and where they would attend, as Wimpfenn notes in his huge tome *Time and Two Seats*, "the World Manufacturers' Series was less of a true series than it had ever been."

At this point only Lancia were brave enough to dive in the virtual pool and they won some races in 1980/81 and thereafter the odd victory, but they were a team in perpetual chaos and scored inconsistent results. This was a pity in more ways than one, given the proud Ferrari and Maserati history of the 1950s/60s. Lancia's last race was at the Silverstone 1000km in 1986 after which they abandoned motor racing in favour of rallying. The cars were sold on and updated LC85s were still in evidence, notably the Mussato Action Car.

Porsche meanwhile decided to attend Le Mans in 1981 and duly finished 1st. Otherwise the status quo remained with the teams/individuals, but it all changed in 1982 with the emergence of the

Porsche 956 at Silverstone. Thereafter the Weissach cars and later their customer teams dominated the genre until the advent of Tom Walkinshaw's Jaguar XJR team in August 1985. However, Porsche were to effectively pull out of racing with occasional forays later in the decade. Presumably it was costing too much.

Amongst their myriad successes they won at Le Mans seven times, five by the works team and twice with Reinhold Joest's customer 956. There were several serious Porsche customer teams: the aforementioned, the Kremer Brothers, Walter Brun, John Fitzpatrick, Richard Lloyd/GTi Engineering et al. and many others in the USA.

The evolving Jaguars from the XJR-5 onwards were the only

serious threat to Porsche hegemony over time and they were championship winners in 1987/88, but after this the 1989 XJR-9 was ultimately wanting. Walkinshaw hired Ross Brawn to create a new turbocharged car, the XJR-11, but this faltered post its first outing at Brands Hatch. It would improve in the following years with the XJR-14 but never as much as the original V12 cars.

Having taken on and faced down the Porsche dynasty, TWR were threatened by the Sauber Mercedes team from 1988 onwards. This had begun as the Kourus-sponsored C8 in 1986 after a terrifying accident during practice at Le Mans in 1985. Peter Sauber's team had originally been part of the Seger & Hoffman Aerospace company, but he had parted company with them and eventually Mercedes-Benz took over in 1988 with the new C9.

This proved to be very fast from day one and they won five races, finishing 2nd to the TWR Jaguars in the championship. It was followed by seven victories in 1989 and the makes' and drivers' championship. This was well deserved and really fulfilled the premise of German superiority. Amidst the Anglo/German cabal were the French interests that inevitably centred upon Le Mans, notably the Rondeaus, WM Peugeot and Cougar, but only Jean Rondeau won here, in 1980 and finished 2nd and 3rd in 1981. Otherwise the only other French intrusion during this decade was Yves Courage's Cougar C20 Porsche that finished 3rd in 1987.

Meanwhile the lower-capacity classes, C Junior, later C2, were a constant factor with myriad teams and entrants during the period from 1983 onwards with Alba, URD, ADA, Lola, Ecosse, Gebhardt, Spice, Mazda, Argo, Tiga, Ceekar et al. The Italian Alba team were the heroes for a while but Gordon Spice's Spice Engineering was the ultimate C2 champion until the advent of the FISA 3.5-litre 750kg C1 class, which brought about a premature end to the C2 category.

Next time round we will look at these lower classes with more detail but for now I hope you enjoy the latest *In Camera* book.

Paul Parker
June 2018

← A modest smile from Jean Rondeau and a full-on assault of overwhelming joy and passion by Jean-Pierre Jaussaud as they celebrate their victory at the 1980 Le Mans 24 Hours with teammates Gordon Spice/Jean-Michel Martin/Philippe Martin finishing 3rd in the Rondeau M379Bs. Le Mans above all other long-distance races was not only the most famous but also the most revered and at times tragic stage, as 17th century French tragedian and dramatist Pierre Corneille (Rouen, 6 June 1606 – Paris, 1 October 1684) wrote of another era, "A vaincre sans peril, on triomphe sans gloire." ("To win without risk is a triumph without glory.") *LAT*

As an avid motor-racing enthusiast, endurance racing and the Le Mans 24 Hour race in particular shaped my life and left me with wonderful memories that cannot ever be replaced or bettered.

Fellow enthusiast Richard Cleare had a passion and the drive to set up a team to take on the might of factory and sponsored privately entered teams, some whose budgets were almost unlimited as they chased brand-name success.

As Richard's team manager, I rose from an unpaid volunteer to a salaried position within his company, R.H Cleare & Co Ltd. From 1980 to '82 being RC Racing's team manager was my 'other' job, my main employment being stores manager with Porsche Specialists Autofarm and then TIGA Racing cars.

In 1982 I joined R.H. Cleare & Co Ltd as the team's racing manager. A converted Bedford coach served as car transporter, parts truck and mobile home, and before that we trailered the 934 round Europe behind a variety of tow vehicles and mostly camped out at the circuits.

Competing at International level, Richard's first purchase was a four-year-old ex Evertz/Leim Porsche 934. Before racing in 1980 the car had to be completely stripped and rebuilt. It was driven swiftly but with the utmost care to aid reliability by Richard and Tony Dron, remaining competitive for a further three years culminating in a Group-4 Class win at Le Mans in 1982.

This small amateur team punched way above its weight and was finally recognised by the Porsche factory, in 1982 concluding an agreement with Richard to breathe new life into the 934 engine as an alternative to the underperforming 924 Carrera project. Many rounds of the Championship saw the two drivers, myself and two or at most three other personnel travel to races all over Europe.

After the 1982 season the highly successful 934 was sold to the States where it still dwells today. The new Group-C regulations were introduced in 1982 and by 1983 Group-4, -5 or -6 cars were not allowed to participate in the World Endurance Championship. Undaunted, Richard found a car with which to enter the Group-C category, travelling to Cologne and returning with Kremer CK5-01, which had made its debut at the 1982 Le Mans race.

Extra bodywork, windscreens and vital mechanical spares were ordered through Kremer as well as a second Porsche 935-based engine purchased in England, but with no major sponsorship only the two British rounds and Le Mans were planned for the season. A race-car transporter had also been acquired so the faithful converted Bedford coach became just a home from home at the circuits.

Minor sponsorship was found which allowed the car to start at Monza but retirement followed, although not before Tony Dron had the CK5 pass two of the customer 956 cars, proving once again the team had the credentials to compete in this top-level category. This was followed by an excellent 6th place at Silverstone, behind five of the now dominant 956 models and but for an error on my behalf –

gambling to start the car on slick tyres on a still predominately wet track – may well have seen the car finish in the top five.

Le Mans this year gave us no happy ending, the CK5 retiring in the first hour when a Porsche factory rebuilt engine failed due to faulty case-hardened components. Brands Hatch proved even worse with retirement through another engine failure and this was the last race for Tony Dron as Richard's co-driver.

In 1984 and 1985 time was spent completely transforming the CK5 from a basic Porsche 936/917 space-frame design with flat-bottom aerodynamics to that of a fully designed ground-effect chassis, overseen by freelance designer Val Dare-Bryan. This took a very long time to complete and the car raced twice during 1984/85, both times at the Brands Hatch round of the Championship, but alas lack of development testing resulted in retirement on both occasions.

With RC Racing contesting so few races, with Richard's permission I performed the race-day team-management duties for both Charles Ivey Racing [Porsche 930T] and Costas Los. [Lyncar Hart C2] as well as a delightful trip to Australia to look after Barry Robinson's Rover SD1 in the race at Bathurst.

Having exhausted the potential of the CK5, Richard contemplated whether to carry on. To compete in Group C1 as a private entrant now required substantial sponsorship and purchase of a factory-backed car such as the Porsche 956/962 or its equivalent (neither Lancia or Jaguar raced with customer sales in mind).

March did produce competitive cars for the IMSA races in the USA and when Richard decided to still follow his goal of repeating the team's Le Mans success, it was to the IMSA-class cars that he turned rather than consider an entry in the fast-developing C2 category where a great many similarly organised teams had settled and were to prove so successful.

Richard sold off the CK5 project and headed for the USA with chief mechanic Michael Negline to look at various Porsche-engined March cars. Thus, a March Porsche 85G [chassis 06] was purchased from John Kalagian and shipped to England, arriving at Burnham in early 1986.

Michael oversaw the initial and subsequent race preparation whilst the body panels were repainted and the necessary store of spares was organised. Again, the team failed to attract a major sponsor so an IMSA GTP category win at Le Mans was the main aim for the 1986 season. However, this required that the car had to comply with the World Endurance Championship fuel allowances for C1 cars.

The car had been bought with a powerful but less than economic Andial 3.2-litre mechanically injected engine, and so, to increase fuel economy and reliability, Richard purchased a factory-built IMSA 962 single-turbo engine [No. 125], which included a Motronic engine management system.

The first event at Silverstone saw retirement with the loss of both the team's engines. The 3.2 litre during practice and the new 2.8-litre

→ Tony Dron in the pits at Brands Hatch with the immaculate Autofarm-entered Richard Cleare Porsche 934 (930 670 0155) that retired with suspension failure in the race. It was the first outing for the team with the car, and Team Manager Peter Twitchen is leaning against the screen at right, the two in the driver's door are possibly mechanic Geoff O'Connor and Autofarm Director/Partner Steve Carr, at the rear is David Woodward (re-fueller) whilst the man at left could be engine builder and Chief Mechanic Jack Phillips. *LAT*

factory engine during the race, which had been fitted overnight with help from the Porsche customer services mechanics. However, a new IMSA lap record for the car was very encouraging.

For Le Mans the regular team personnel were expanded again to include another Australian mechanic, a New Zealander, a Gulf Oil executive, a transport company owner and my own son who were invaluable to the team effort.

The Porsche factory could only rebuild one of our two broken engines before Le Mans. Therefore, our plans to out-qualify the Mazda opposition using the 3.2-litre engine had to be dropped and it was the 2.8-litre engine that had to be used throughout the whole Le Mans practices and race.

To help financially balance what was becoming a very expensive sport at competitive level, Richard accepted two drivers who could contribute acceptable budgets. Frenchman Lionel Robert and IMSA competitor Jack Newsum from the USA.

In the race, during the night, a broken exhaust manifold allowed hot gasses to burn out the starter-motor wiring, requiring a long stop to replace both manifold and wiring. The Mazda opposition had retired way before dark, so if we finished, the class win was assured but we at least wanted a top-ten finish.

Sadly, a cracked front brake disc meant Richard had to drive the last hour using the gearbox to decelerate and touching the brakes very gently. The reduced pace denied the top-ten aspirations but winning the IMSA GTP class and finishing 14th overall was most rewarding.

The rest of the season saw retirements at the Nürburgring, Spa and Brands Hatch. Once again, Val Dare-Bryan undertook some modifications to the March for the 1987 season. A new under-floor section was designed and produced, the rear wing moved forward and the rear bodywork shortened. These modifications were designed to move the centre of gravity nearer to the mid-section of the car and improve the handling.

Unfortunately, the 1987 Silverstone round of the Championship was the only one the team contested. Without major sponsorship and with Porsche unable to offer any further development on the Motronic fuel-management system to allow better consumption without reduced engine performance for the IMSA engines, the level at which the team could function was no longer viable. Financial constraints and company pressure finally brought Richard's, and therefore my own, dreams to a premature end.

RC Racing closed its doors before Le Mans in 1987, the entry for that year's race being withdrawn. I would go on to team-manage the Charles Ivey Racing TIGA Porsche GC287 for Le Mans and again at Brands Hatch. Nonetheless, I could not sense the same enthusiastic feelings and drive. Not working for a driven enthusiast such as Richard Cleare left me feeling empty and at the end of 1987 I decided to retire. Time to get a proper job!

Peter Twitchen
Richard Cleare Racing Team Manager 1980–87

1980

AN ERRATIC START
FOR A NEW ERA

Porsche victories in 1980 were nearly all achieved by Group-5 935s. They won at Daytona, Sebring, Mosport and Dijon whilst Reinhold Joest triumphed at the Nürburgring with his superannuated 908/3. For Le Mans he created a Group-6 936 lookalike, which was not allowed to use the official factory nomenclature; instead it was called a 908/80. This finished 2nd after assorted problems.

Other Group-6 cars included the Rondeaus, one of which won at Le Mans, plus Alain de Cadenet's well-travelled De Cadenet Lola LM which Alain and Desiré Wilson drove to victory at Monza and Silverstone. There were two Porsche 908s, one as mentioned above plus Siegfried Brunn's car which performed quite well, finishing 2nd at Silverstone and Mugello.

As ever there were oddities such as the DFV-engined Ford Cosworth Japanese Dome and Chevalley's ill-fated ACR, which was based upon the Lola T380. Another close T380 clone was Marco Capoferri's Capoferri Cosworth DFV that was fastest at Monza but retired driven by Renzo Zorzi.

Lancia and director Cesare Fiorio improved upon their 1979 car with the 1.4-litre turbocharged Beta Montecarlo run by the factory together with the privately entered Jolly Club entry. It was a successful season with the cars winning at Brands Hatch, Mugello and Watkins Glen, together with several class wins. This was one of their best years, but there was a lack of consistency and numerous failures that would hamper the team for the years to come.

Meanwhile the GT class was back in favour and Porsche 934s proliferated whilst in America the Mazda RX-7 became the favourite choice in the under 2-litre GTU category. At this point Daytona was still in the FIA World Championship for Makes but they would leave this after 1981, something Sebring had done way back after 1972.

There was an aura of fading interest within the FIA Championship. Porsche had withdrawn, their customers were busy racing elsewhere and France was dependent upon Jean Rondeau's small and essentially modest team albeit with first-class machinery and drivers. Of course Le Mans offered an interesting variety of cars and drivers, and more importantly the Rondeau win as noted above.

However, the majority of races were largely inhabited in the upper echelons by privately entered Porsches of one sort or another plus Lancia and the occasional factory BMW M1 in Europe. The final race of the season at Dijon was essentially a privateer event won by the Sportwagen 935 driven by Pescarolo/Barth.

The World Championship for Makes over-2,000cc was won by Porsche (160 points) with Lancia a distant second (40 points) and the rest headed by Ferrari (12 points) with BMW on 4 and Opel 3. Lancia was equally dominant in the under-2,000cc class with 160 points followed by BMW on 59 points and Porsche with a modest 15.

For now, the status quo was out of balance, not helped by the growing and intrusive presence of authority and later F1, which would ultimately wreck Sports/Prototype racing post 1989.

Brands Hatch 6 Hours, 16 March 1980 Edgar Dören's Porsche 935 K3 (Kremer) with the inevitable flames on overrun, the fastest of the 935s present with Jürgen Lässig/Gerhard Holup, retired with engine problems on lap 72, denying Holup a drive. Dören (6 October 1941 – 2 April 2004, cancer) mostly drove Porsches throughout his long career, but he also raced a 962, BMW M1s, Ferrari 512 BB LM, TOJ SC205, URD C81, Audi/VW and even a Nimrod Aston Martin. In the background are a Ford Transit blood wagon and the pit-road entrance. *LAT*

Daytona 24 Hours, 3 February 1980 The Daytona 24 Hours started the calendar for 1980 and this is Preston Henn's Ferrari 512 BB (26683) entered under the name of Henn's Thunderbird Swap Shop (a drive-in theatre and later a flea market in Fort Lauderdale, Florida, founded in 1963). He shared the car with Belgian racer/journalist Pierre Dieudonné whose career over 25 years included Super Vee, F3, touring cars and racing for Mazdaspeed in the sports/prototype class for seven seasons. The 512 BB was too heavy and the gearbox sat under the hefty 5-litre, flat-12 motor, which did not help the weight distribution or the handling. Preston B. Henn (20 January 1931 – 30 April 2017) retired from racing in 1986. *GPL*

Daytona 24 Hours, 3 February 1980 Following the demise of the BMW M1 Procar series of 1979 the M1 became a regular in the American IMSA series and in the European theatre. March built the M1C with their own chassis based upon BMW engineer Raine Bratenstein's ideas and French designer/engineer Max Sardou's ground-effect underbody. Two were entered at Daytona (it was never a success and March eventually lost interest in it). This is the Michael Korten/Patrick Nève/Ian Grob car entered by March, the faster of the two, the other being Jim Busby's entry, which he shared with Bruce Jenner and Rick Knoop. They both retired due to driveshaft failures, at 260 laps and 139 laps respectively. German racer Korten, a successful Formula Vee and 1979 German F3 champion, raced until 1986. Patrick Marie Ghislain Pierre Simon Stanislas Nève, sometime F2 and F1 driver from 1975 to 1983, was born on 13 October 1949 and died on 12 March 2017. Ian Grob, a regular sports/prototype racer in period, was the son of Ken Grob who was the *ken* in the To*ken* F1 project of 1974. March designer Robin Herd leans into the driver's side during practice. *GPL*

➡ Daytona 24 Hours, 3 February 1980 Long after the Ferrari 365GTB/4, aka Daytona, ended production still these impressive, front-engined 4.4-litre V12 cars were raced at Daytona, Sebring and occasionally elsewhere. This is the Nicholas/McRoberts car (16407) that had finished 2nd here in 1979 and was running 5th after 20 hours in 1980 before it retired due to a broken axle. It was driven by ex-Shelby mechanic John Morton and Tony Adamowicz (2 May 1941 – 10 October 2016) whose myriad successes made him one of only five FIA International-rated American drivers in period. That looks like Tony pointing at John Morton at the gasoline stop just off circuit. *GPL*

➡ Daytona 24 Hours, 3 February 1980 Chevrolet Corvettes were a given at Daytona and Sebring year after year, and by 1980 they were looking ever more extreme. Alas its iron soul and concomitant weight were always against it in its various configurations down the decades. This is the Joe and John Chamberlain car (Markle) shared with Richard J. Valentine. It finished but was non-classified. Just look at the incredibly wide rear tyres, let alone the front end and rear wing. Successful entrepreneur Richard Valentine had a long career in motor racing, which started in the mid 1970s and appears to have ended in 2011. *GPL*

⬆ **Daytona 24 Hours, 3 February 1980** Assorted variants of Porsche's 935 dominated practice at the Daytona 24 Hours, taking the first eight places. The most numerous were the Kremer-built cars, which included the Whittington Brothers, Dick Barbour Racing, Preston Henn (Thunderbird Swap Shop), Racing Associates (Mendex/Woods/Akin), Andial Racing and Interscope Racing (Ted Field). These were accompanied by the Reinhold Joest car and several more that were Porsche factory specification. This is the winning 935J (for Joest) of Stommelen/Joest/Merl, which qualified second fastest and outlasted the opposition after the Whittington entry stopped with a broken distributor on circuit and was then disqualified, presumably for outside assistance. Henn's car finished 2nd (John Paul Sr/Al Holbert) and Ted Field's 935 K3 3rd for Field/Ongais/Minter. *GPL*

↗ **Brands Hatch 6 Hours, 16 March 1980** The next round, at a cold Brands Hatch, included a plethora of sub 2-litre machinery. Lella Lombardi leans over the Osella BMW PA8 entered by Enzo Osella with Marco Rocca in the car. (*Lana Gatto* is a luxury knitting brand, *Tollegno* an upmarket supplier of yarns and fabrics whilst *Alpilatte* seems to be a tile manufacturer.) They were 10th on the grid, but their race ended in tragedy. Firstly, Lombardi collided with Martin Raymond's Chevron B36 early on and then later a Porsche collided with Rocca and both cars hit Raymond who was on track after his Chevron had spun off, poor Raymond dying instantly. The race was halted and then restarted finishing after 3 hours 51 minutes and 57 seconds. Maria Grazia 'Lella' Lombardi, born 26 March 1941 and died 3 March 1992 of cancer, also raced in F5000 and F1 (17 starts from the British GP 1974 to the Austrian GP 1976). Marco Rocca from Turin, born 1953, later ran endurance events for karts and also worked as a driver, coach, administrator and promoter. *LAT*

➡ **Brands Hatch 6 Hours, 16 March 1980** Amongst the grid were two Tigas in the Sports 2000 class, powered by the Ford Pinto L4 motor: one an SC79 entered by Ian Taylor Racing for Ian Taylor/Neil Crang/Mario Hytten, and this one, an SC80 entered by Brands Hatch Racing for Divina Galica MBE (seen here) and Mark Thatcher. They finished 16th and 11th respectively. A successful skier, Galica became a regular in the Shell Sport F1 series and briefly in F1 but failed due to obsolete machinery. Between 1977 and 1980 she had some outings in the European F2 Championship and later in truck racing. Divina eventually moved to America to join Skip Barber's Racing team where she rose to senior vice president. In 2005 she resigned and joined iRacing as a director. *LAT*

← **Brands Hatch 6 Hours, 16 March 1980** Two works Lancia Beta Montecarlos were entered here for Riccardo Patrese/ Walter Röhrl and Eddie Cheever/ Michele Alboreto, and they duly finished 1/2 in that order. This is the winning car (chassis 1002) which qualified 2nd fastest whilst the Jolly Club entry of Facetti/Finotto finished 4th. Lancia were to have a successful season although they did not grace Le Mans with their presence. *LAT*

← **Brands Hatch 6 Hours, 16 March 1980** A brace of Porsche 908s came to Brands Hatch. The first was a twin-turbo 908/03 (008) entered by Reinhold Joest for him and Volkert Merl that was over 2 seconds faster than the Patrese/Röhrl Lancia. They led with ease but after the race restarted, with Merl driving, the gearbox linkage failed. The second one, 908/03 (012), driven by Siegfried Brunn with Albert Obrist, was 4th fastest in practice and raced in the first three but ultimately finished 10th and 14 laps behind due to clutch problems. This is Brunn, an Eberbach-based dentist, making his international racing debut, whose career ended after finishing 6th at Le Mans with a Porsche 936C in 1986 with Ernst Schuster and Rudolf Seher. *LAT*

➡ **Sebring 12 Hours, 22 March 1980** Bob Akin and Swap Shop king Preston Henn at Sebring. Team owner Henn was racing his Porsche 935 K3 with John Paul Sr and Al Holbert and they finished 4th while Bob Akin with Roy Woods and Skeeter McKitterick finished 5th in the Mendez/Woods/Akin Porsche 935. Bob Akin was a successful IMSA team owner and twice won the Sebring 12 Hours. His grandfather formed the Hudson Wire Company in 1902 and Akin inherited the presidency in 1974 after which under his auspice it became a successful supplier to the electronic and aviation industries. He was fatally injured on 25 April 2002 while testing a 1988 Nissan GTP ZX-Turbo at Road Atlanta and died four days later having suffered a broken neck, left shoulder, left leg and right arm, as well as third-degree burns. Robert Macomber 'Bob' Akin, III (6 March 1936 – 29 April 2002). *Revs*

➡ **Sebring 12 Hours, 22 March 1980** In 1980 Kenper Miller and Dave Cowart became partners in a racing team sponsored by the seafood chain Red Lobster. They bought a BMW Procar M1 (WBS59910004301040) and had it rebuilt to the GTO regulations of the IMSA. At Sebring their third driver was Derek Bell and at one point the car was in 5th place but then Bell had to abandon the M1 on circuit due to electrical problems. He made it back to the pits to get the necessary spares and then returned to the car. They eventually finished 30th. *Revs*

↑ **Sebring 12 Hours, 22 March 1980** Bruce Leven's Brumos Porsche 935-77A (930 890 0018) was driven by Hurley Haywood, Peter Gregg and Leven at Sebring. They duelled with Dick Barbour's Kremer 935 K3 (shared with John Fitzpatrick) which was faster but the owner was somewhat slower than his meteoric partner. Leven gave up his seat leaving Haywood and Gregg to pump out consistently fast laps, and they could have won but Haywood was penalised for cutting corners and using the verges. Later they suffered transmission problems, which dropped them to 10th at the finish whilst the Barbour car won the race from the Interscope 935 K3 of Ted Field/Danny Ongais, followed by the Whittington Brothers' similar 935 K3. The only intruders to the Porsche hegemony were the Group 44 Triumph TR8 (Tullius/Adam), 5th, and the Mandeville Racing Mazda RX-7 (Roger Mandeville/Jim Downing/Brad Frisselle), 9th. *Revs*

↗ **Monza 6 Hours/1000km, 27 April 1980** Marco Capoferri (1943 – 1995), son of trade unionist Pietro Capoferri, entered this Cosworth DFV Capoferri M1 (based upon the Lola T380) driven by Renzo Zorzi (12 December 1946 – 15 May 2015) and Claudio Francisci. Zorzi, in car, was fastest in practice and in the race but retired due to a water leak, leaving Francisci without a drive. Renzo was an engineer for Pirelli in 1972 when he began racing and a lucky win at the 1975 Monaco F3 support race landed him a drive for Frank Williams at the Italian GP Monza and the 1976 Brazilian GP, after which his sponsorship ended and he was dropped in favour of Michel Leclère. In 1977 he joined Shadow Racing courtesy of their sponsor Franscesco Ambrosio and was indirectly involved in the tragic incident at Kyalami in 1977 that cost the lives of a marshal and Tom Pryce. He later lost his drive after falling out with Ambrosio post the Spanish GP. His final professional appearance was at the 1985 Monza 1000km where he finished 6th in a Brun Motorsport Porsche 956 with Oscar Larrauri and Massimo Sigala. He later returned to Pirelli. *GPL*

→ **Monza 6 Hours/1000km, 27 April 1980** Two weeks before Monza Lancia Corse finished 1st (Patrese/Cheever) and 2nd (Alboreto/Röhrl) with their Lancia Beta Montecarlos and 'Gimax'/Gallo 3rd in Gallo's Osella PA7 BMW at the Mugello 6 Hours with no other major manufacturers. At Monza, despite the 37-car grid, it was the same and Lancia again entered their Beta Montecarlos. Chassis 1005 was driven by Eddie Cheever and Piercarlo Ghinzani and finished 5th, handicapped by fuel pressure problems, whilst teammates Patrese/Röhrl finished 3rd. *LAT*

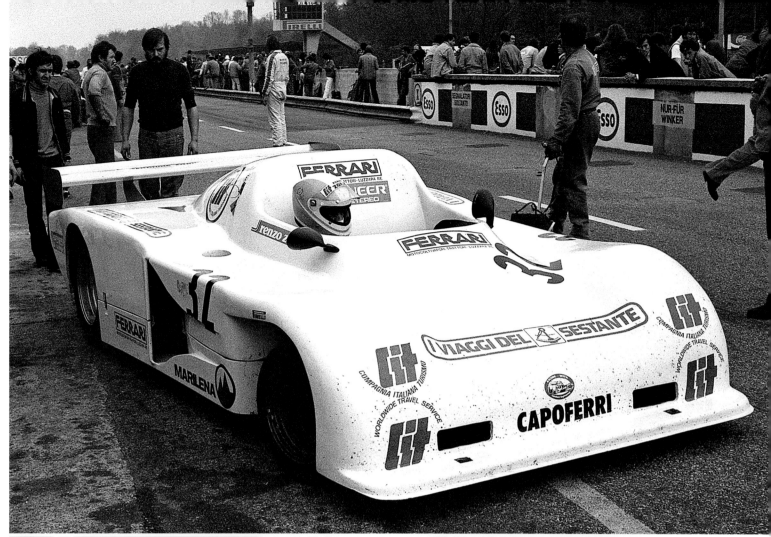

Monza 6 Hours/1000km, 27 April 1980 The Ferrari 512 BB LM Bellancauto (Rome Ferrari Dealership) (28601) with its Pininfarina long nose and tail was aerodynamically modified in an attempt to make it more competitive. It was driven by the Italian duo of Spartaco Dini and Fabrizio Violati but retired with engine problems. Born in 1943, Dini's career included winning the 1,600cc class in the 1969 ETC. Later he lost his licence after a road accident and was briefly incarcerated but returned using a Spanish licence. He retired in 1981. His co-driver Violati (17 June 1935 – 22 January 2010) started by racing Vespa scooters aged 16 and moved on to Fiats, Abarths and later Ferraris, which included the purchase of a Ferrari 250 GTO (3851) in 1965. He had a close friendship with Enzo Ferrari, who asked him to form the Ferrari Club Italia. The bearded Violati can be seen in front of the pit counter behind the car during a pit stop. *LAT*

Monza 6 Hours/1000km, 27 April 1980 Alain de Cadenet is looking pleased, as well he might. He has managed to reach 3rd place after starting 13th in his de Cadenet Lola LM. His co-driver, South African Desiré Wilson, is being strapped in and she worried the leading Lancia of Patrese and Pescarolo in the Sportwagen Porsche 935 K3 during the closing stages. Then it rained and the leading duo decided to pit for 'wet' tyres, leaving Wilson in the lead tiptoeing around on 'dry' tyres (a cash-strapped de Cadenet had no rain tyres) and Pescarolo retook the lead. However, he had to pit again for more fuel as the team had apparently misjudged the race distance and a chastened Frenchman with Jürgen Barth finished 2nd behind a brave Desiré. *LAT*

Silverstone 6 Hours, 11 May 1980 Silverstone was hosting an IMSA (International Motor Sport Association) round and the now controversial John Paul Sr attended in his GTX-configured Porsche 935 JLP2 partnered by Brian Redman. They finished 3rd. *LAT*

↑ **Silverstone 6 Hours, 11 May 1980** At Silverstone de Cadenet/Wilson won again, starting from 6th on the grid and after the demise of the pole-position Kremer Porsche 935 K3-80 of Edwards/Fitzpatrick/Plankenhorn their race was against the Brunn/Barth Porsche 908/3 (012). Once again Desiré outpaced the opposition, but a faulty fuel pump and a trip off-circuit cost her a lap and the 908 took the lead. However, it too had problems and Wilson relentlessly pursued the Porsche, unlapping herself with less than an hour to go. Then Barth had to stop for fuel and Brunn took over but he was delayed by another car and with little time left Wilson caught and passed the Porsche, going on to win by 18 seconds. *LAT*

← **Silverstone 6 Hours, 11 May 1980** The new Kremer-entered Porsche 935 K3-80 (000 00011), which featured aerodynamic and ground-effects tweaks for Edwards/Fitzpatrick/Plankenhorn), was the fastest car at Silverstone by some margin. John Fitzpatrick was 2.4 seconds quicker than the Swiss-entered Ford Cosworth DFV-powered ACR (André Chevally Racing), which was second quickest but had not even been tested and lasted only 25 laps. The Porsche led convincingly but piston failure ended its race on lap 128. *LAT*

⬆ **Silverstone 6 Hours, 11 May 1980** Richard Cleare and Tony Dron had a successful partnership for several years with various Porsches. This is the 934 (930 670 0155) entered by Autofarm/Cleare that finished 8th and 1st in the GT class. Here the 934 is being pursued by the Z&W Enterprises Mazda RX-7 of Ernesto Soto (YV)/Pierre Honegger (USA)/Mark Hutchins (USA) that finished 9th and 3rd in the IMSA category. Note the mesh fencing that was actually quite good at stopping a car without too much damage, allowing for the speed of impact. *LAT*

➡ **Nürburgring 1000km, 25 May 1980** Zakspeed, founded in 1968 by Erik Zakowski, were close to the Nürburgring in Niederzissen and renowned for their modified Ford saloon cars. This is their version of the Ford Capri driven by Jochen Mass and Klaus Ludwig, with a 4-cylinder 1,725cc turbocharged motor avec alloy block. It weighed circa 890kg and produced over 400bhp. They started 4th and raced in the top three until the engine failed with Mass at the wheel. Mass is seen here on the famous Karussel. *LAT*

← **Nürburgring 1000km, 25 May 1980**
Hans Stuck and Nelson Piquet drove this IMSA-specification BMW M1 to an impressive 3rd place and 1st in the GTX class. Stuck qualified 6th fastest and at one point Piquet occupied 2nd place overall. *LAT*

↓ **Nürburgring 1000km, 25 May 1980**
Having lost a certain victory at Brands Hatch, Reinhold Joest won the Nürburgring 1000km with his Porsche 908/03 Turbo (008) but this time driven by Rolf Stommelen and Jürgen Barth. They were fastest in practice and won the race, beating the Fitzpatrick/Plankenhorn/Barbour Porsche 935 K3-80, which set fastest race lap (Fitzpatrick). The 935s of Wollek and Fitzpatrick led early on whilst the heavily fuelled Stommelen bided his time before letting rip. The organisers had allowed Group-6 cars such as Joest's 908 to race otherwise the Group-5 935 K3-80 entered by Dick Barbour would have won. Here Stommelen passes by the caravans and campers that graced every major race of the 14.2-mile (22.835km) circuit then, and note where the basic Armco barrier ends. *LAT*

Le Mans 24 Hours, 15 June 1980
There were six Ferrari 512 BB/LMs at Le Mans, three of them entered by Charles Pozzi, the Paris importer. No.75 (26885) for Lucien Guitteny (F)/Gérard Bleynie (F), no.76 (32129) for Hervé Regout (B)/Jean Xhenceval (B)/Pierre Dieudonné (B) and no.77 (31589) for Jean-Claude Ballot-Léna (F)/Jean-Claude Andruet (F). No.75 retired but no.76 finished 10th and 3rd in the IMSA class whilst no.77 was the fastest of the trio and in the race, after an early delay with spark-plug problems, Ballot-Léna (4 August 1936 – 9 November 1999, cancer) regained many places, but the car ultimately retired due to a broken distributor after 129 laps. He was a successful all-rounder, winning the 1969 Spa 24 Hours and the 1983 Daytona 24 Hours, whilst formidable racer and rally specialist Andruet had a long and varied career including assorted BMWs, Ferraris, Alfa Romeo, Osella, Lancia, Alpine, WM-Peugeot, Ford, Spice, Cougar et al. *LAT*

Le Mans 24 Hours, 15 June 1980
The three factory-entered Porsche 924 Carreras (a precursor for their homologation in 1981) with their 2-litre turbocharged 4-cylinder motors suffered burnt-out pistons during qualifying and also lost two drivers pre-race. Günter Steckkönig was hospitalised with kidney failure, and many-times IMSA champion, four-times winner of the Daytona 24 Hours and owner of Brumos Porsche Peter Gregg had a road accident. The tragic consequence was that he suffered double vision thereafter and had his competition licence withdrawn, leading him to commit suicide that December. Peter Holden Gregg (4 May 1940 – 15 December 1980). So the drivers were Andy Rouse/Tony Dron (no.2), Derek Bell/Al Holbert (no.3) and Jürgen Barth/Manfred Schurti (no.4). The first two suffered more burnt pistons in the race but carried on with three cylinders whilst the German-driven car was fed a richer fuel mix and avoided the problem, finishing 6th (3rd Le Mans GTP) with Rouse/Dron 12th (5th Le Mans GTP) and Bell/Holbert 13th (6th Le Mans GTP). *LAT*

Le Mans 24 Hours, 15 June 1980 A busy pit stop for the Rondeau M379 (003) Ford Cosworth DFV of Jean Rondeau/Jean-Pierre Jaussaud that won at Le Mans – a French car with French drivers and French entrant. Rondeau's victory at Le Mans was the first and so far only victory for a car named after its driver. They suffered some problems during practice and started 5th, ultimately seeing off the challenge of the Ickx/ Joest Porsche 936 copy, of which more in the next caption. Rondeau also entered Gordon Spice with Philippe and Jean-Michel Martin, which was sponsored by a Belgian cigarette producer. Pescarolo/Ragnotti were fastest in practice and raced 3rd after one hour, 6th at 3 hours, 2nd at 5 hours, 1st at 6/7 hours and then 4th at 9 hours before retiring with head-gasket failure. Meanwhile the Belgian car finished 3rd and 1st LM-GTP entry. *LAT*

Le Mans 24 Hours, 15 June 1980 Reinhold Joest's Porsche 936 was a facsimile, and his team near Karlsruhe was approved by Porsche who had withdrawn their works cars at the end of 1979. However, they denied the use of the 936 model number so it was entered as a 908/80. It made use of leftover factory components and the twin-turbo 2-valve motor produced circa 550bhp. Finished in Martini colours, it was co-driven by former factory Porsche driver Jacky Ickx (who had no other offers to race from anybody in 1980) and started 4th but would surely have won had it not been delayed by a failed injection-pump belt and much later a fifth-gear failure, which took 25 minutes to fix. Finally, a decision to stop for rain tyres when Ickx was catching the leading Rondeau backfired as the road began to dry and Jaussaud ultimately finished 1st with Ickx 2nd. Reinhold Joest rounds Mulsanne corner with the Mulsanne escape road in the background. *LAT*

Le Mans 24 Hours, 15 June 1980 There were 15 Porsche 935s of various specifications racing at Le Mans of which four were the latest Kremer K3/80 models. This is the Dick Barbour-entered chassis no.000 00023 driven by John Fitzpatrick, Brian Redman and Barbour, which was fastest in qualifying. In his book *Fitz My Life at the Wheel* Fitzpatrick recalled that they led the race in the pouring rain until early on Sunday morning when the car developed a misfire. Their engine guru Jerry Woods recognised a burnt piston and disconnected the cylinder after which they raced on, eventually finishing 5th and 1st in the IMSA class. *LAT*

◀ **Le Mans 24 Hours, 15 June 1980** The ACR (Andre Chevalley Racing) Ford Cosworth DFV had qualified 2nd fastest at Silverstone but missed the start, joining in later before retiring. It was based upon a Lola T286 and was entered at Le Mans after some modifications, for Patrick Gaillard (F)/François Trisconi (CH)/André Chevalley (CH), posting 13th fastest. However, in the race a variety of other problems caused it to spend over 6 hours in the pits before finally retiring at around 6.20am on Sunday. A thoroughly fed up Trisconi sits in the cockpit in company with the inevitable gendarmes and course marshals as the car sits on the beginning of the Mulsanne escape road facing up the circuit. It reappeared here in 1981 much modified, faster and heavier but retired again, this time with an engine failure after clutch problems. *LAT*

◀ **Le Mans 24 Hours, 15 June 1980** Three of the pleasingly attractive WM (Welter/Meunier) P79/80s, with much modified production-car PRV (Peugeot Renault Volvo) turbocharged V6 engines, were entered and finished 4th (no.5) Guy Fréquelin (F)/Roger Dorchy (F) and 11th (no.6) Max Mamers (F)/Jean Daniel Raulet (F) while this one, no.7 Serge Saulnier (F)/Denis Morin (F)/Jean-Louis Bousquet (F), retired from 5th place after Bousquet crashed following a suspension failure late Sunday morning. They first entered Le Mans in 1976 and the entire operation was run from a small workshop by Peugeot's bodywork designer Gérard Welter (20 October 1942 – 31 January 2018) and engineer Michel Meunier. *LAT*

Le Mans 24 Hours, 15 June 1980 Mark Thatcher shared the very fast stubby Scuderia Torino Corse Osella (Enzo Osella) P8 BMW with Lella Lombardi who suffered electrical problems, including a dead battery, due to the wet conditions early in the race. After taking over, Mark had a stub-axle failure, causing more delays. A subsequent off by Thatcher (seen here) after spinning off at Tertre Rouge on lap 157 with minor damage ended their race as he could not restart the car due to another battery failure. In his book *Le Mans 1980-89* Quentin Spurring tells us that the Osella had a short-stroke 2-litre motor engineered for endurance racing by Paul Rosche at BMW Munich, which gave 290bhp @ 8,600rpm and could reach 198mph. *LAT*

Watkins Glen 6 Hours, 5 July 1980 Forty cars started for the Watkins Glen 6 Hours and this is the pole sitter, Bobby Rahal in Dick Barbour's Porsche 935 K3 (009 00030) shared with Jürgen Barth and Bob Garretson. Bobby Rahal was in 2nd place behind the Ralph Townsend 935 driven by Harald Grohs on lap 6 when the engine self-destructed. Note the *Apple Computers* writ large across the nose and sides of the Porsche. Behind is one of the nine Corvettes that raced here. The winners were the two Lancia Beta Montecarlos of Hans Heyer/Riccardo Patrese and Michele Alboreto/Eddie Cheever, several laps ahead of the Dick Barbour 935 K3 driven by Fitzpatrick/Redman, and five weeks later at Mosport they won the race ahead of the John Pauls and Field/Ongais, all in Porsche 935s of course. *Getty*

Vallelunga 6 Hours, 7 September 1980 Vallelunga, some 20 miles (32km) from Rome, was the third Italian race for the championship in 1980. It began as a 1.02-mile sand circuit in 1959 and was later taken over by the Automobile Club d'Italia (ACI). In 1980 it was a tight, twisty, near 2-mile tarmac circuit that suited the under 2-litre Group 6 category. Thirty-three cars started and 15 finished, the winner being the Osella BMW P8 of Giorgio Francia/Roberto Marazzi. There were two other P8s for Vittorio Brambilla/Lella Lombardi and Claudio Francisci /Carlo Franchi ('Gimax') and they dominated practice in that order. Brambilla took the lead and led the race by an increasing margin but retired after 50 laps with a broken driveshaft whilst the third P8 of Francisci/Franci ultimately finished 6th. The winning car is greeted on the start/finish line 4 and 5 laps ahead of the 2nd- and 3rd-placed cars. *LAT*

Vallelunga 6 Hours, 7 September 1980 Siegfried Brunn certainly made good use of his old Porsche 908/03 (012) in 1980 and finished 2nd here with Derek Bell. They were four laps adrift of the winners, the 908 having suffered a puncture with Brunn driving, but a determined Bell forced the car back up the field although he was unable to challenge the faster Osellas on a very hot day. Siegfried is seemingly warning Derek to stop or proceed with caution in the pits whilst behind the car a pit member is giving a thumbs up. *LAT*

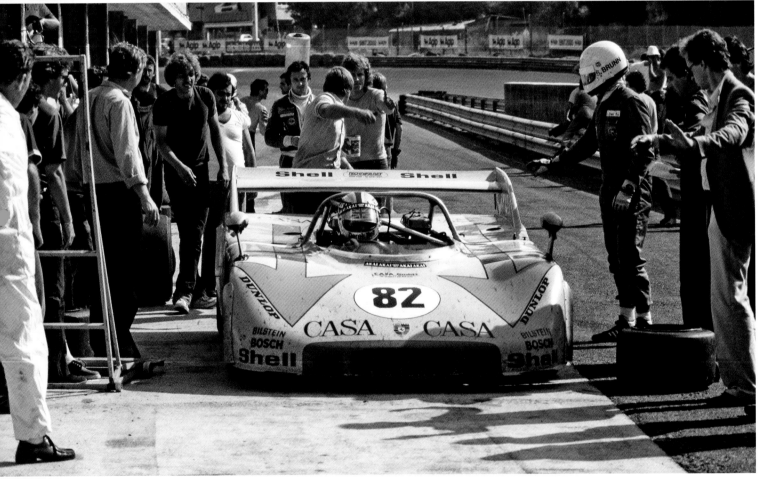

↑ **Dijon 1000km (reduced to 684km due to fog), 28 September 1980** The last race of the season was at Dijon. Lancia did not attend and there were just 26 starters for the 2.361-mile (3.8km) circuit. The shortened race was delayed by foggy conditions with the Lombardi/Brambilla Osella BMW P8 on pole, but after a tardy start Lombardi lost control on the third lap whilst trying to pass Pescarolo's Porsche; both spun but Lella's engine stopped and would not restart. Pescarolo dropped to 7th whilst Dören's Porsche 935 K3 took the lead followed by Brunn in his Porsche 908. The latter retired early on due to broken front suspension. Ultimately the three 935s of Pescarolo/Barth, Haldi/Beguin and Dören/Lässig/Holup led the race, but the last retired after gearbox problems and then ran over a kerb which broke its transmission. This is the Pescarolo/Barth Sportwagen 935 on its way to victory with just a touch of opposite lock. *LAT*

→ **Dijon 1000km (reduced to 684km due to fog), 28 September 1980** Richard Jenvey with Lawrie Hickman had raced his Lotus Esprit S1 in the Group 5 category at the Nürburgring and here at Dijon with backing from Jan Odor. Alas they only completed 84 laps having qualified 19th, faster than all of the Porsche 934s bar one, a very good effort. *LAT*

ENTRANTS

**ACBH Bad Honnef e. V. im ADAC
– VW Golf GTI**
Hans-Jörn Ley (D) NUR
Josef Rietmann (D) NUR

A.S.A. Cachia – Porsche 934
Christian Bussi (F) LM
Bernard Salam (F) LM
Cyril Grandet (F) LM

**Herb Adams V.S.E – Chevrolet Camaro,
Pontiac Firebird Trans-Am**
Herb Adams (USA) DAY (*DNS*), SEB
Kenny Roberts (USA) DAY (*DNS*)
Walker Evans (USA) DAY (*DNS*)
Jerry Thompson (USA) SEB
Richard Valentine (USA) MOS

**All Canadian/Peerless Racing/
Maurice Carter/Carter Racing
– Chevrolet Camaro**
Maurice Carter (CDN) DAY, SEB, WG, MOS
Craig Carter (USA) DAY, SEB
Murray Edwards (CDN) DAY, SEB
Tony DeLorenzo (USA) WG

**Alt & Wiborg Ltd – Aston Martin AM V8,
Gipfast Aston Martin Special**
Robin Hamilton (GB) SIL
Derek Bell (GB) SIL (*DND*)
David Preece (GB) SIL
Simon Phillips (GB) SIL (*DND*)

**American Racing Team (Glen Kalil)
– Porsche 935**
Jack Refenning (USA) DAY
Ray Mummery (USA) DAY
Ren Tilton (USA) DAY

**Pasquale Anastasio – Osella PA6-BMW,
Osella PA7-BMW**
Pasquale Anastasio (I) MUG
Giampaolo Ceraolo (I) MUG

Andial Racing – Porsche 935K3
Elliot Forbes-Robinson (USA) DAY
Randolph Townsend (USA) DAY, SEB, WG
Howard Meister (USA) DAY
John Morton (USA) SEB
Bruce Jenner (USA) WG (*DNS*)

Aquilante/Wolpert – Chevrolet Corvette
David Wolpert (USA) WG
Tom Aquilante (USA) WG
Wade White (USA) WG

Arrow Heating Co. – Chevrolet Corvette
Joe Chamberlain (USA) DAY
John Chamberlain (USA) DAY
Richard Valentine (USA) DAY

Scuderia Ateneo – Osella PA7-BMW
'*Amphicar*' (Eugenio Renna) (I) MUG, MZA
Luigi Moreschi (I) MUG, MZA
Mario Casoni (I) MUG, MZA

Atlas Van Lines – Chevrolet Corvette
John Brandt (USA) WG
Mark Pielsticker (USA) WG (*DND*)
Keith Feldott (USA) WG (*DND*)

Auto Barn – Chevrolet Corvette
Bob Baechle (USA) WG
David Laughlin (USA) WG

**Autofarm Ltd/ Richard Cleare Racing
– Porsche 934**
Tony Dron (GB) BH, SIL, VAL, DIJ
Richard Cleare (GB) BH, SIL,VAL, DIJ

**Automobile International
– Lancia Stratos HF**
Anatoly Arutunoff (USA) DAY, SEB
José Marina (USA) DAY (*DND*), SEB (*DND*)
George Drolsom (USA) DAY (*DND*)

AutosebioRacing – Ferrari 308 GTB
Felice Besenzoni (I) MZA
Luciano Dal Ben (I) MZA (*DND*)

**BASF-Glysantin/Team GS Sport
– BMW 320i**
Hans-Georg Bürger (D) NUR
Bernd Brutschin (D) NUR

**BMW Motorsports France
– BMW M1**
Dieter Quester (A) MUG, LM
Didier Pironi (F) MUG, LM
Marcel Mignot (F) LM

BMW March Racing GB – BMW M1
Michael Korton (D) DAY, BH, SIL, LM
Patrick Neve (B) DAY, BH, SIL, LM
Ian Grob (GB) DAY
Manfred Winkelhock (D) LM (*DND*)

**BMW Motorsports GmbH
– BMW M1**
Hans-Joachim Stuck (D) NUR
Nelson Piquet (BR) NUR

BMW North America – BMW M1
Hans-Joachim Stuck (D) WG
David Hobbs (GB) WG (*DND*)

BMW Zol-Auto – BMW M1
François Servanin (F) MUG, MNZ, LM, DIJ
Laurent Ferrier (F) MUG (*DND*), MNZ,
LM, DIJ
Pierre-François Rousselot (F) LM

**Pasquale Barberio
– Osella PA6 BMW**
Pasquale Barberio (I) VAL
Paolo Giangrossi (I) VAL

**Dick Barbour /Dick Barbour
– Wynn's International, Dick
Barbour Racing/Sachs USA, Dick
Barbour Racing/Apple Computers
– Porsche 935, Porsche 935 K3**
Skeeter McKitterick (USA) DAY, MOS
Bob Garretson (USA) DAY, SEB, LM,
WG (*DND*), MOS
John Fitzpatrick (GB) DAY, SEB, LM,
WG, MOS
Manfred Schurti (FL) DAY
Dick Barbour (USA) DAY, SEB, LM
Bobby Rahal (USA) SEB, LM, WG, MOS
Kees Nierop (CDN) SEB
Buzz Marcus (USA) SEB
Bob Harmon (USA) SEB, LM (*DND*)
Marty Hinze (USA) SEB
Brian Redman (GB) LM, WG, MOS
Allan Moffat (AUS) LM
Michael Sherwin (USA) LM
Robert Kirby (USA) LM (*DND*)
Jürgen Barth (D) WG (*also in second 935 K3
which retired before he could drive it*)
Volkert Merl (D) WG
Rick Mears (USA) MOS

**Bard Boand Racing – Chevrolet
Corvette Sting Ray C2**
Bard Boand (USA) SEB
Robert Kivela (USA) SEB
Ray Irwin (USA) SEB

**Ezio Baribbi (team name not listed)
– Osella PA7 Ford Cosworth**
Ezio Baribbi (I) MZA
'*Pal Joe*' (Ganfranco Palazzoli) (I) MZA

**Bavarian Motors International
– BMW CSL**
Alf Gebhardt (USA) DAY, SEB
Bruno Beilcke (USA) DAY, SEB

**Bayside Disposal Racing – Porsche
935-77A, Porsche 935/80**
Peter Gregg (USA) DAY
Hurley Haywood (USA) SEB, MOS
Bruce Leven (USA) SEB, MOS

**Domenico Bazzani
– Chevron B36 Ford-Cosworth**
Domenico Bazzani (I) MUG
Ettore Bogani (I) MUG

Heinz Becker – Mazda RX-7
Heinz Becker (D) NUR
Theo Körner (D) NUR

**Bell & Colvill
– Lola T492-Ford-Cosworth**
John Sheldon (GB) BH
John Brindley (GB) BH
Juliette Slaughter (GB) BH

**Mario Benusiglio
– Osella PA5 Ford Cosworth**
Mario Benusiglio (I) MZA
Luigi de Angelis (I) MZA

Jacques Berenger – BMW 320
Pierre-François Rousselot (F) VAL
Jacques Berenger (F) VAL
Charles Geeraerts (B) VAL

**Alain-Michel Bernard – Porsche 911
Carrera RSR**
Georges Bourdillat (F) BH
Roland Ennequin (F) BH

Roland Binder – Lola T390-BMW
Roland Binder (D) NUR (*Interseries entry 7
laps only*)

**Bytzek/Litens Automotive – Porsche
911 Carrera RSR**
Klaus Bytzek (CDN) MOS
Rudy Bartling (CDN) MOS

John Blanckley – Chevron B31-BMW
Rolf Götz (D) NUR
John Blanckley (GB) NUR

Bob's Speed Products – AMC-AMX
Bob Lee (USA) SEB
Rick Kump (USA) SEB
Jim Leo (USA) SEB

Furio Boccalero – Osella PA8-BMW
Furio Boccalero (I) MUG
Leonardo Cavallo (I) MUG

**Mennato Boffa – Osella BMW PA5,
Osella BMW PA6**
Mennnato Boffa (I) MUG, VAL
Alessandro Fracastoro (I) MUG
Roberto Arfe (I) VAL (*DND*)

**Boricua Racing – Porsche 911 Carrera
RSR**
Bonky Fernandez (PR) DAY, SEB
Tato Ferrer (PR) DAY, SEB
Kees Nierop (CDN) DAY
Ulrich Lange (D) SEB

Rick Borlase – Porsche 911
Rick Borlase (USA) DAY, SEB
Don Kravig (USA) DAY, SEB
Michael Hammond (USA) DAY, SEB

**Botero Racing
– Porsche 911 Carrera RSR**
Honorata Espinosa (CO) DAY, SEB
Jorge Cortes (CO) DAY, SEB
Francisco Lopez (CO) DAY

Giuseppe Bottura – March 75S-BMW
Giuseppe Bottura (I) MNZ
Giuseppe Pellin (I) MNZ

Georges Bourdillat – Porsche 934
Georges Bourdillat (F) LM, DIJ
Roland Ennequin (F) LM, DIJ
Alain-Michel Bernard (F) LM, DIJ

Brands Hatch Racing – Tiga SC80-Ford
Divina Galica (GB) BH
Mark Thatcher (GB) BH

**Brauneiser Renntechnik Köln
– Ford Escort (2 cars shared
by drivers)**
Franz-Josef Bröhling (D) NUR
Peter Prang (D) NUR
Axel Felder (D) NUR
Paul Hulverscheid (D) NUR

**Group Bruckmann
– Porsche 911 Carrera RSR**
Volker Bruckman USA) DAY
David Goodell (USA) DAY
Rug Cunningham (USA) DAY

**Brumos Porsche Audi
– Porsche 935-79**
Peter Gregg (USA) DAY
Hurley Haywood (USA) DAY
Bruce Leven (USA) DAY

**Karl-Ernst Brune
– Alfa Romeo 2000 GTV**
Karl-Ernst Brune (D) NUR
Gerhard Hennemann (D) NUR

Siegfried Brunn/Casa – Porsche 908/3
Siegfried Brunn (D) BH, MUG, MNZ, SIL,
VAL, DIJ
Albert Obrist (CH) BH
Jürgen Barth (D) BH, SIL
Herbert Müller (CH) MNZ
Derek Bell (GB) VAL, DIJ (*DND*)
Steve O'Rourke (GB) DIJ (*DND*)

Buist/Syfert – Chevrolet Corvette
Catherine Kyzer (USA) WG
Jack Broomall (USA) WG

**Jim Busby Racing/Industries
– BMW M1 (March)**
Jim Busby (USA) DAY, SEB
Bruce Jenner (USA) DAY, SEB
Rick Knoop (USA) DAY

Christian Bussi – Porsche 935
Christian Bussi (F) BH, MUG, SIL, DIJ
Bernard Salam (F) BH, MUG (*DND*), DIJ
Jacques Guérin (F) SIL
Fréderic Alliot (F) SIL

**Alain de Cadenet – de Cadenet
Lola Ford-Cosworth LM**
Alain de Cadenet (GB) BH, MNZ, SIL, LM
Desiré Wilson (ZA) BH, MNZ, SIL
François Migault (F) LM

**Caribbean AMC/Jeep
– AMC Spirit AMX**
Lou Statzer (VI) SEB
Amos Johnson (USA) SEB
Dennis Shaw (USA) SEB

Frank L. Carney – Datsun 280ZX
Don Devendorf (USA) DAY
Dick Davenport (USA) DAY
Frank Carney (USA) DAY

Case Racing – Porsche 911
Dave Panaccione (USA) SEB
Ron Case (USA) SEB (*DND*)
Jack Rynerson (USA) SEB (*DND*)

**André Chevally Racing
– ACR 80-Ford Cosworth**
Patrick Gaillard (F) SIL
André Chevally (CH) SIL (*DND*)
François Triconi (CH) SIL (*DND*)

**Angelo Chiapparini
– Alfa Romeo Alfetta GTV**
Ademaro Massa (I) MZA
Giancarlo Galimberti (I) MZA
Angelo Chiapparini (I) MZA

Tim Chitwood – Chevrolet Nova
Tim Chitwood (USA) SEB
Sam Fillingham (USA) SEB (*DND*)
Vince Gimondo (USA) SEB (*DND*)

**Scuderia Colonia e. V. im ADAC
– Ford Escort**
Gunter Wohlfahrter (D) NUR
Karl Pathe (D) NUR

**Condor Racing (Racing Associates)
– Porsche 935**
Ralph Kent-Cooke (USA) DAY, SEB
Gerard Bleynie (F) DAY
Claude Ballot-Lena (F) DAY
Lyn St. James (USA) SEB

**Chris Cord Racing
– Chevrolet Monza**
Chris Cord (USA) DAY, WG
Jim Adams (USA) DAY, WG

**Climax Racing
– Porsche 911 Carrera RSR**
Ludwig Heimrath Jr (CDN) MOS
Brian Hardacre (CDN) MOS
John Reski (CDN) MOS

Joe Cotrone – Chevrolet Corvette
Joe Cotrone (USA) SEB
Emory Donaldson (USA) SEB
Phil Currin (USA) SEB

**The Cummings Marque
– Shelby GT350**
Don Cummings (USA) DAY
Guido Levetto (USA) DAY

**David Deacon
– Porsche 911 Carrera RSR**
David Deacon (CDN) DAY, SEB
Peter Moennick (CDN) DAY, SEB
Jacques Bienvenue (CDN) DAY

Dei Fiori – Porsche 911 Carrera RSR
Franco Berruto (I) MZA
Franco Bizzato (I) MZA
Michele Licheri (I) MZA

Der Klaus Haus – Porsche 911
Klaus Bitterauf (USA) SEB
James Oxley (USA) SEB
Vicki Smith (USA) SEB

**DeNarvaez Enterprises
– Porsche 911 Carrera RSR**
Mauricio DeNarvaez (CO) DAY, SEB, MOS
Albert Noon (USA) DAY
Ricardo Londono (CO) DAY, SEB
Tony Garcia (CO) MOS

Deren Automotive – BMW M1
Kemper Miller (USA) DAY
David Cowart (USA) DAY
Christine Beckers (B) DAY

DiLella Racing – Porsche 914/6
Vince DiLella (USA) SEB
Manuel Cueto (USA) SEB

Dome Co. Ltd. – Dome Zero RL 80
Chris Craft (GB) LM
Bob Evans (GB) LM

**Dorset Racing Associates
– Lola T297/T290-Ford
Cosworth BDG/Richardson**
Leon Walger (RA) BH
Peter Clark (GB) BH (*DND*), SIL, LM
Nick Faure (GB) SIL
Nick Mason (GB) SIL, LM
Martin Biranne (IRL) LM

Chris Doyle – Mazda RX-7
Chris Doyle (USA) SEB
Charles Guest (USA) SEB
Mike Meyer (USA) SEB

Drolsom Racing – Porsche 911
George Drolsom (USA) SEB, MOS
Bill Johnson (USA) SEB
Robert Hoskins (USA) SEB
Hugh Davenport (USA) MOS

Dynasales – Chevrolet Corvette
John Carusso (USA) SEB (*withdrawn*) (*no second driver listed*), MOS
Phil Currin (USA) MOS

Murray Edwards – Chevrolet Corvette
Murray Edwards (CDN) MOS
Craig Carter (USA) MOS

Paul Edwards – Porsche 911 Carrera RSR
Paul Edwards (GB) BH
Barry Robinson (GB) BH

Eggenberger Motorsport – BMW 320i
Enzo Calderadi (CH) SIL, VAL
Marco Vanoli (CH) SIL, VAL (*DND*)
Willi Spavettti (I) VAL (*DND*)

Electrodyne Racing – Porsche 935, Porsche 934
Gianpiero Moretti (I) DAY, SEB, WG
Fernando Cazzaniga (I) DAY (*DND*)
Bruce Canepa (USA) DAY (*DND*)
Giorgio Pianta (I) SEB
Renzo Zorzi (I) SEB
Bruce Jenner (USA) WG
Chester Vincenz (USA) WG
Bob Garretson (USA) WG
Reinhold Joest (D) WG

Michel Elkoubi - Primagaz (F) – Lola T298 BMW M12
Patrick Perrier (F)
Pierre Yver (F)

Equipe Alméras Freres – Porsche 934
Jacques Alméras (F) LM
Jean-Marie Alméras (F) LM
Marianne Hoepfner (F) LM

Peter Ernst (Team name not listed) – BMW 320i
Peter Ernst (D) NUR
Raine Zweibäumer (D) NUR

Escolette (see also Renzo Zorzi) – Osella P8 BMW, Capoferri M1Ford Coswoth DFV, Chevron B31 Ford Cosworth,
Claudio Francisci (I) VAL
'Gimax' (Carlo Franchi) (I) VAL
Renzo Zorzi (I) VAL
Luigi Moreschi (I) VAL
'Menes' (Maurizio Cavalla) (I) VAL
Franco Forini (CH) VAL
Arcadio Pezzali (I) VAL
Francesco Cerulli-Irelli (I) VAL

Fassler-Mullen Racing – Porsche 911 Carrera RSR
James Mullen (USA) SEB
Paul Fassler (USA) SEB
Craig Siebert (USA) SEB

Nick Faure/Vandervell – de Cadenet Lola Ford-Cosworth LM
Richard Jones (GB) DIJ
Nick Faure (GB) DIJ

Diego Febles Racing (PR) (See also Coco Lopez Racing) – Porsche 934
Mandy Gonzalez (PR) LM
Francisco Romero (YV) LM
Diego Febles (PR) LM

Fenstermann Rennsport – VW Scirocco
Hans-Werner Hilger (D) NUR
Wolfgang Jacobs (D) NUR (*DND*)

Bill Ferran – Porsche 911 Carrera RSR
Bill Ferran (USA) SEB
Rusty Bond (USA) SEB
Jack Refenning (USA) SEB

Fifth Essence Racing – Chevrolet Corvette
Eppie Wietzes (CDN) MOS
Jacque Bienvenue (CDN) MOS

Ford Berkenkamp Racing – Ford Escort RS 2000, Ford Capri (3 cars)
Dieter Selzer (D) NUR
Günther Braumüller (D) NUR
Lili Reisenbichler (D) NUR
Bernhard Mangold (D) NUR
Mathias Schneider (D) NUR

Ford Team Zakspeed – Ford Capri Turbo
Klaus Ludwig (D) NUR
Jochen Mass (D) NUR

Forrest/Leifheit – Chevrolet Corvette
Herb Forrest (USA) WG
Craig Leifheit (USA) WG

Format Küchen – Ford Escort
Herbert Kummle (D) NUR
Karl Mauer (D) NUR

Formel Rennsport Club der Schweiz FRC – Porsche 934, Lola T297-BMW, Lola T212-BMW
Peter Zbinden (CH) SIL
Edi Kofel (CH) SIL
Eugen Grupp (CH) NUR
Ralf Walter (CH) NUR
Urs Neukomm (CH) NUR

Framm Promotions – Porsche 911 Carrera RSR
Roger Schramm (USA) SEB
Rudy Bartling (CDN) SEB

Giorgio Francia – Osella P8-BMW
Giorgio Francia (I) MZA, VAL
Remo Ramanzini (I) MZA
Roberto Ramazzi (I) VAL

Brad Frisselle Racing – Mazda RX-7
Brad Frisselle (USA) MOS
Roger Mandeville (USA) MOS

Full Time Racing – Chevrolet Corvette
Phil Currin (USA) DAY
(*no second driver listed*)

Enrico Gagliotto – Osella PA7 BMW
Enrico Gagliotto (I) MZA
Willi Lovato (I) MZA

Marco M. Gallo (see also 'Gimax') – Osella-BMW PA7
'Gimax' (Carlo Franchi) (I) MUG
Marcello Gallo (I) MUG

George Garcia – Chevrolet Corvette
George Garcia (USA) SEB
Vic Shinn (USA) SEB
Daniel Vilarcao (USA) SEB

Maurizio Gellini – Chevron B31 Ford Cosworth
Maurizio Gellini (I) VAL
Luigino Grassi (I) VAL

Gelo Racing Team – Porsche 935/80
Bob Wollek (F) NUR, LM
Manfred Schurti (FL) NUR
Helmut Kelleners (D) LM

Duilio Ghislotti – Lola T296-BMW
Duilio Ghislotti (I) MZA
Luigi Colzani (I) MZA DND

Gilden Kölsch Racing Team – Opel Monza 3E
Herbert Herler (D) NUR
Hanno Schumacher (D) NUR
Johann Weisheidinger (D) NUR

'Gimax' (Carlo Franchi, see also Marco M.Gallo) – Osella PA8-BMW
'Gimax' (Carlo Franchi) (I) MNZ
Marcello Gallo (I) MNZ

Gozzy Kremer Racing (D) – Porsche 935 K3/80
Rolf Stommelen (D) LM
Axel Plankenhorn (D) LM
Tetsu Ikuzawa (J) LM

Chuck Graemiger/Yacco – Cheetah G602 BMW
Daniel Brillat (F) DIJ
Valentin Bertapelle (F) DIJ

Jean-Philippe Grand – Chevron B36 BMW
Yves Courage (F) LM
Jean-Philippe (F) LM (*DND*)

Green Racing – Porsche 911 SC
John Bauer (USA) WG
Larry Green (USA) WG

Group 44 – Triumph TR8
Bob Tullius (USA) DAY, SEB
John McComb (USA) DAY
John Kelly (USA) DAY
Bill Adam (CDN) SEB

Jacques Guérin – Porsche 934
Jacques Guérin (F) BH, MUG
Marcel Gastaretti (F) BH, *at Mugello the third driver is listed as Franco Gasparetti (I)*
Jean-Louis Schlesser (F) BH, MUG

Hahn Sportwagen GmbH – Porsche 911SC
Armin Jahn (D) NUR
Klaus Utz (D) NUR

Hamilton House Racing – Porsche 911S
Robert Overby (USA) SEB
Joseph Hamilton (USA) SEB (*DND*)
Herb Forrest (USA) SEB (*DND*)

Heimrath Racing – Porsche 935
Ludwig Heimrath (CDN) DAY, SEB, WG, MOS
Carlos Moran (ES) DAY (*DND*), SEB
Johnny Rutherford (USA) DAY (*DND*), SEB, WG, MOS

Herman Racing – Mazda RX-7
Chris Doyle (USA) DAY
Charles Guest (USA) DAY
Mike Meyer (USA) DAY

Kurt Hild – Toj S306-Ford Cosworth
Kurt Hild (D) NUR
Kur Lotterschmid (D) NUR

Marty Hinze – Porsche 935
Marty Hinze (USA) WG
Dale Whittington (USA) WG

Fritz Hochreuter – Porsche 911 S
Fritz Hochreuter (CDN) MOS
Rainer Brezinka (CDN) MOS
Norm Ridgely (CDN) MOS

Peter Hoffman – McLaren M8F, Sauber C5-Chevrolet
Peter Hoffman (D) NUR
Norbert Dombrowski (D) NUR
(*Both drivers listed for both cars but only Dombrowski drove the Sauber which may have been an Interseries entry restricted to 7 laps only*)

Holley & LaGrow – Chevrolet Camaro
Kenneth LaGrow (USA) SEB
William Boyer (USA) SEB
Jack Turner (USA) SEB

Hector Huerta – Porsche 911 Carrera RSR
Francisco Romero (YV) DAY
Jean-Paul Libert (B) DAY
Ernesto Soto (YV) DAY, SEB
Luis Rodriguez (YV) SEB
Luis Mendez (DR) MOS
Mandy Gonzalez (PR) MOS (*DND*)

John E. Hulan – Porsche 914/6
John Hulan (USA) SEB
Ron Coupland (USA) SEB

IFM Efector – Audi 80GTE
Hagan Arlt (D) NUR
Peter Kuhlmann (D) NUR
Klaus Bieler (D) NUR (*DND*)

Independent Personalized (Wayne Baker) – Porsche 914
Wayne Baker (USA) DAY
Dan Gilliland (USA) DAY
Jeff Scott (USA) DAY

Interscope Racing – Porsche 935K3
Ted Field (USA) DAY, SEB, WG, MOS
Danny Ongais (USA) DAY, SEB, WG, MOS

Intrepid, Inc. – Porsche 911
Joe Dibattista (USA) DAY
Tom Ciccone (USA) DAY
Alan Howes (USA) DAY

Charles Ivey Racing – Porsche 935K3
John Cooper (GB) BH, SIL, LM, DIJ
Peter Lovett (GB) BH, SIL, LM
Dudley Wood (GB) BH, SIL, LM, DIJ

JLC Racing – Mazda RX-7
Allan Moffat (AUS) DAY
Amos Johnson (USA) DAY
Stu Fisher (USA) DAY

JLP Racing – Porsche 935 JLP-2
John Paul Sr. (USA) SIL, NUR (*DND*), LM, WG, MOS
Brian Redman (GB) SIL, NUR
Preston Henn (USA) NUR, WG
John Paul Jr. (USA) LM, WG, MOS
Guy Edwards (GB) LM

JRT/Quaker State – Triumph TR8
Bob Tullius (USA) MOS
Bill Adam (CDN) MOS

Jägermeister Racing Team – BMW 320i, Porsche 935
Eckhard Schimpf (D) NUR
Anton Fischhaber (D) NUR
Mario Ketterer (D) NUR
Erich Schiebler (D) NUR
Anton Fischhaber (D) NUR
Rick Köhler (D) NUR

Bruce Jennings – Porsche 911
Bruce Jennings (USA) SEB
Bill Bean (USA) SEB
Tom Ahby (USA) SEB

Reinhold Joest (Liqui Moly Equipe) – Porsche 935J, Porsche 908/4
Reinhold Joest (D) DAY, BH
Rolf Stommelen (D) DAY, NUR
Volkert Merl (D) DAY, BH
Jürgen Barth (D) NUR

Jolly Club/Jolly Club Milano/Lancia Corse – Lancia Beta Montecarlo Turbo, Lola T296 Ford-Cosworth, Ferrari 308 GTB
Carlo Facetti (I) DAY, BH, MUG, MNZ, SIL, LM, WG, MOS, VAL
Martino Finotto (I) DAY, BH, MUG, SIL, NUR, LM, WG, MOS, VAL
Gianfranco Ricci (I) MNZ
Manfred Mohr (D) NUR, VAL
'Gero' (Cristiano Del Bazo) (I) VAL
Carlo Giorgio (I) VAL
Antonio Bernardini (I) VAL
Sergio Rombolotti (I) VAL
Claudio Magnani (I) VAL

Jones Industries Racing – Buick Skylark
Herb Jones Jr (USA) SEB
Steve Faul (USA) SEB
Kent Combs (USA) SEB

KWS Motorsport – Ford Escort (3 cars)
Hartmut Bauer (D) NUR
Helmut Gall (D) NUR
Detlef Deege (D) NUR
Thomas von Löwis (D) NUR
Rolf Rosenkranz (D) NUR
Rudolf Dötsch (D) NUR

Keirn Garage – Chevrolet Corvette
Philip Keirn (USA) DAY, WG
Larry Trotter (USA) DAY
Ed Errington (USA) DAY, WG

Kirby-Hitchcock Racing – Porsche 911 Carrera RSR
Robert Kirby (USA) SEB
Freddy Baker (USA) SEB
Michael Sherwin (USA) SEB

Karl-Adolf Kneip – KMW SP30-Porsche
Peter Hardt (D) NUR
Karl-Adolf Kneiper (D) NUR (*DND*)

William Koll/Koll Motor Sport – Porsche 914/6, Porsche 911
William Koll (USA) DAY, MOS
Jim Cook (USA) DAY, MOS
Greg La Cava (USA) DAY

Bruce Kulczyk – Triumph TR8
Peter Bulkowski (CDN) MOS
Bruce Kulczyk (CDN) MOS

Dominique Lacaud – BMW M1
Hans-Joachim Stuck (D) LM
Hans-Georg Bürger (D) LM
Dominique Lacaud (F) LM

Lancia Corse/Lancia Italia – Lancia Beta Montecarlo Turbo
Riccardo Patrese (I) BH, MUG, MNZ, SIL, NUR, WG, VAL
Walter Röhrl (D) BH, MUG, MNZ, SIL, MOS
Eddie Cheever (USA) BH, MUG, MNZ, SIL (*DND*), NUR, WG, VAL
Michele Alboreto (I) BH, MUG, SIL, WG
Piercarlo Ghinzani (I) MNZ, NUR, LM, MOS, VAL
Hans Heyer (D) NUR, LM, WG, MOS
Gianfranco Brancatelli (I) LM (*DND*)
Markku Alén (SF) LM (*DND*)
Bernard Darniche (F) LM (*DND*), MOS, VAL
Teo Fabi (I) LM (*DND*)
Giorgio Pianta (I) VAL
Andrea de Cesaris (I) VAL

Karl Langjahr – Tecno Eigenbau Spyder-Porsche (Interseries entry 7 laps only)
Karl Langjahr (D) NUR

Klaus Ligensa (Team name not listed) – VW Scirocco
Klaus Ligensa (D) NUR
Horst Bonefeld (D) NUR

Little Foreign Car Shop – Chevrolet Corvette
Michael Oleyar (USA) WG
Bill Craine (USA) WG

Walter Löffler (Team name not listed) – Opel Monza
Walter Löffler (D) NUR
Hugo Nückel (D) NUR
Günter Filthaut (D) NUR

Lopez Brothers – Porsche 911
Juan Lopez (DR) SEB
Jose Arzeno (DR) SEB

Coco Lopez-Pina Colada (See also Diego Febles Racing) – Porsche 911 Carrera RSR, Porsche 934
Diego Febles (PR) DAY, SEB
Chiqui Soldevila (PR) DAY (*DND*), SEB
Armando Gonzalez (PR) DAY (*DND*), SEB

Jeffrey Loving – Chevrolet Camaro
Ralph Noseda (USA) SEB
Jeff Loving (USA) SEB (*DND*)
Richard Small (USA) SEB (*DND*)

**MSC Wahlscheid e. V. im ADAC
– VW Golf GTI**
Heinrich Sprungmann (D) NUR
Gerhard Mennecken (D) NUR

MSTC Erbach e. V. – BMW 2002
Hans Weissgerber (D) NUR
Hermann-Josef Nett (D) NUR

Claudio Magnani – Lancia Stratos HF
Claudio Magnani (I) MZA
Sergio Rombolotti (I) MZA

**Malardeau Kremer Racing (D)
– Porsche 935 K3/80**
Xavier Lapeyre (F)
Anny-Charlotte Verney (F)
Jean-Louis Trintignant (F)

Roger Mandeville – Mazda RX-7
Roger Mandeville (USA) DAY, SEB
Jim Downing (USA) DAY, SEB
Brad Frisselle (USA) DAY, SEB

Malaya Garage – Porsche 911 SC
Barrie Williams (GB) BH, SIL
Adrian Yates-Smith (GB) BH, SIL
Mike Wilds (GB) SIL

**Martini Racing-Liqui Moly
– Porsche 908/80 Turbo**
Jacky Ickx (B) LM
Reinhold Joest (D) LM

**Meccarillos Racing Team/ Haldi
– Porsche 935/77A**
Claude Haldi (CH) NUR, LM, DIJ
Derek Bell (GB) NUR
Bernard Béguin (F) NUR (*DND*), LM, DIJ
Volkert Merl (D) LM

**Mendiz/Woods/Akin
– Porsche 935K3**
Bob Akin (USA) SEB
Roy Woods (USA) SEB
Skeeter McKitterick (USA) SEB
Charles Mendiz (USA) SEB
Brian Redman (USA) SEB
Paul Miller (GB) SEB

David Mercer – Vogue SP2-Ford
David Mercer (GB) BH, SIL, DIJ
Richard Jenvey (GB) BH
Mike Chittenden (GB) SIL (*DND*), DIJ
Richard Jones (GB) SIL (*DND*)

Metalcraft Racing – Porsche 914/6
Bob Zulkowski (USA) SEB, WG
Denis Brisken (USA) SEB
Gary Nylander (USA) SEB
Gary Pullyblank (CDN) WG
Bernie Storc (USA) WG (*DND*)

**Lothar Mich Opel Tuning
– Opel Kadett**
Toni Ochs (D) NUR
Karl-Heinz Schäfer (D) NUR

**Maurizio Micangeli – De Tomaso
Pantera**
Maurizio Micangeli (I) VAL
Carlo Pietromarchi (I) VAL (*DND*)

**Moana Corp.
– Porsche 911 Carrera RSR**
Robert Kirby (USA) DAY
John Hotchkis Sr (USA) DAY
John Hotchkis Jr (USA) DAY

Mogil Motors Ltd – Chevron B36-Ford
Martin Raymond (GB) BH
 (*fatal accident lap 103*)
Tony Charnell (GB) BH

**Montura Racing
– Porsche 911 Carrera RSR**
Tony Garcia (USA) DAY, SEB
Alberto Vadia Jr (USA) DAY
Terry Herman (USA) DAY, SEB, MOS
Albert Noon (USA) SEB
Albert Naon (USA) MOS

Moran Construction – Porsche 911 SC
Marion L. Speer (USA) DAY, SEB
Ray Ratcliff (USA) DAY, SEB
Terry Wolters (USA) DAY, SEB

**Georges Morand – Lola T296 Ford
Cosworth**
Jacques Boillat (F) MZA
Georges Morand (CH) MZA

Tim Morgan – Chevrolet Corvette
Vince Muzzin (USA) SEB
Marcus Opie (USA) SEB (*DND*)
Tim Evans (USA) SEB (*DND*)

NTS Racing – Datsun 240Z
Bob Earl (USA) DAY
William Coykendall (USA) DAY
Fred Stiff (USA) DAY, SEB, MOS
Sam Posey (USA) SEB, MOS (*DND*)
George Aldrman (USA) SEB

National Jets – Chevrolet Corvette
Russ Boy (USA) SEB
Tom Hunt (USA) SEB

Tom Nehl – Chevrolet Camaro
Tom Nehl (USA) DAY
Peter Kirill (USA) DAY
Kathy Rude (USA) DAY

Dick Neland – Chevrolet Camaro
Dick Neland (USA) DAY
Bill Ferran (USA) DAY
Jo Cotrone (USA) DAY

Mauro Nesti – Lola T298-BMW
Mauro Nesti (I) MUG
Arcadio Pezzali (I) MUG

**Nicholas/McRoberts Racing
– Ferrari 365GTB/4 Daytona**
John Morton (USA) DAY
Tony Adamowicz (USA) DAY

**Norddeutscher Automobil Club e.V.
– Porsche 930**
Matthias Lörper (D) NUR
Karl-Josef Römer (D) NUR
Joachim Oppermann (D) NUR

**OBI Team Deutschland
– Alfa Romeo 2000 GTV**
Bernd Knipper (D) NUR
Wolfgang Balzar (D) NUR

**Jan Odor/Richard Jenvey
– Lotus Espirit S1**
Richard Jenvey (GB) NUR, DIJ
Lawrie Hickman (GB) NUR, DIJ

Oftedahl Trucking – Chevrolet Camaro
David Heinz (USA) DAY, SEB
Gerry Wellik (USA) DAY
Bob Young (USA) DAY, SEB
Bob Lazier (USA) SEB
Bob Nagel (USA) SEB

Marco Onori – OsellaPA5-BMW
Marco Onori (I) MUG
Sivano Cecchi (I) MUG

Steve O'Rourke – Ferrari 512 BB/LM
Steve O'Rourke (GB) LM
Richard Down (GB) LM
Simon Phillips (GB) LM

Robert Overby – Porsche 911 SC Targa
Robert Overby (USA) WG
Frank Harmstad (USA) WG

**Angelo Pallacivini /Lubrifilm Racing
Team – Porsche 934**
Angelo Pallavicini (I) BH, NUR, VAL, DIJ
Herbert Müller (CH) BH, NUR
Peter Bernhard (CH) VAL
Neil Crang (AUS) DIJ

Robert Parker – Lola T492-Ford
Robert Parker (GB) BH
Nick Faure (GB) BH
Jorge Kochelin (PE) BH

**Ruggero Parpinelli (see also Torino
Corse) – Osella PA6-Ford Cosworth**
Ruggero Parpinelli (I) MNZ
Dilvano Frisori (I) MNZ

**Salvatore Pellegrino – Osella PA-7
Ford-Cosworth**
Salvatore Pellegrino (I) VAL
Vito Carone (I) VAL

Performance Marine – Chevrolet Camaro
Ford Smith (USA) SEB
Bruce Jernigan (USA) SEB

Thierry Perrier – Porsche 911 SC
Thierry Perrier (F) BH
Roger Parmillet (F) BH

Personalized Porsche – Porsche 914/4
Wayne Baker (USA) SEB
Dan Gilliland (USA) SEB
Jeff Scott (USA) SEB

Arcadio Pezzali – Osella P8 BMW
Mauro Nesti (I) MZA
Arcadio Pezzali (I) MZA

**Simon Phillips
– Porsche 911 Carrera RSR**
Ray Mallock (GB) BH
Richard Jones (GB) BH
Simon Phillips (GB) BH

Giuseppe Piazzi – Fiat X1 (Dallara)
Renzo Zorzi (I) BH, MUG
Giuseppe Piazzi (I) BH (*DND*), MUG (*DND*),
 MZA, NUR, VAL, DIJ
Sandro Cinotti (I) MZA, VAL, DIJ
Leandro La Vecchia (I) NUR, VAL, DIJ

**Porsche-Audi Northwest
– Porsche 911 SC**
Monte Shelton (USA) WG
Bruce Leven (USA) WG

**Porsche Kremer Racing
– Porsche 935 K3/80**
Guy Edwards (GB) SIL
John Fitzpatrick (GB) SIL
Axel Plankenhorn (D) SIL

**Porsche Montecarlo Dominican
Republic – Porsche 911 Carrera RSR**
Luis Mendez (DR) SEB
Jaime Rodriguez (DR) SEB
Ernesto Soto (YV) SEB

**Porsche System
– Porsche 924 Carrera GT Turbo**
Jürgen Barth (D) LM
Manfred Schurti (FL) LM
Andy Rouse (GB) LM
Tony Dron (GB) LM

Hervé Poulain – Porsche 935
Dany Snobek (F) MUG, LM
Pierre Destic (F) MUG, LM
Hervé Poulain (F) LM

**Charles Pozzi-JMS Racing
– Ferrari 512 BB**
Pierre Dieudonné (B) LM
Jean Xhenceval (B) LM
Hervé Regout (B) LM
Claude Ballot-Léna (F) LM
Jean-Claude Andruet (F) LM

**Pier Giorgio Provolo
– AMS Ford Cosworth**
Piergiorgio Provolo (I) MZA
Francesco Cerulli-Irelli (I) MZA

**Norbert Przybilla
– TOJ SC302-Ford Cosworth**
Norbert Przybilla (I) NUR
Klaus Walz (D) NUR

R&H Racing – Porsche 914/6
Gary Hirsch (CDN) SEB
Rainer Brezinka (CDN) SEB
Peter Aschenbrenner (CDN) SEB

**Racing Associates (see also
Condor Racing) – Porsche 935 K3**
Charles Mendez (USA) DAY, LM, WG
Brian Redman (GB) DAY
Paul Miller (USA) DAY, LM, MOS
Bob Akin (USA) DAY, SEB, LM, WG, MOS
Roy Woods (USA) DAY, SEB, WG
Bobby Rahal (USA) DAY
Ralph Kent-Cooke (USA) LM
Skeeter McKitterick (USA) LM (*DND*), WG
Leon Walger (RA) LM (*DND*)
Kees Nierop (CDN) MOS

Racing Beat – Mazda RX-7
Walt Bohren (USA) DAY, MOS (*DND in
 second car crashed by Downing*)
Dennis Aase (USA) DAY (*DND*)
Jeff Kline (USA) DAY (*DND*), MOS (*DND in
 second car crashed by Downing*)
John Morton (USA) MOS
Jim Downing (USA) MOS

**Rallye Gemeinschaft Ulm
– Lola T297-BMW**
Eugen Grupp (D) NUR
Ralf Walter (D) NUR

**Mike Ramirez Racing
– Porsche 911**
Mike Ramirez (PR) DAY, SEB
Manuel Villa (PR) DAY, SEB
Luis Gordillo (PR) DAY, SEB

Luigi Rampa – Alfa Romeo GTA
Luigi Rampa (I) VAL
Luciana Galluzzo (I) VAL

Raytown Datsun – Datsun 280ZX
Dick Davenport (USA) MOS
Frank Carney (USA) MOS

Red Lobster Racing – BMW M1
David Cowart (USA) SEB, WG
Kenper Miller (USA) SEB, WG
Derek Bell (GB) SEB

**Siegfried Rieger – McLaren
M8 Special –Chevrolet
(Probably an Interseries
entry 7 laps only)**
Siegfried Rieger (D) NUR

Gerhard Reiss – BMW 320 Turbo
Albrecht Krebs (D) BH, MUG, MZA
Gerhard Reiss (D) BH, MUG, MZA

**Renngemeinschaft Bergisch-Gladbach
e.V. im ADAC – BMW 2002**
Jürgen Möhle (D) NUR
Richard Bremmekamp (D) NUR
Ernst Thierfelder (D) NUR

**Renngemeinschaft Sieglar e. V. im
– VW Scirocco**
Klaus Bornschein (D) NUR
Jochen Schramm (D) NUR (*DND*)
Alexander Nickisch (D) NUR (*DND*)

**Revolution Wheels (USA)
(Alan L. Johnson) – Mazda RX-2**
Robert Giesel (USA) DAY
Bruce Nesbitt (USA) DAY, SEB
Alan Johnson (USA) DAY, SEB

Dino Ridolfi – Lola T284-BMW
Guido Cappelletto (I) MUG
Secondo Ridolfi (I) MUG (*DND*), MZA
Pasquale Barberio (I) MZA

**Rocky Mountain Performance
– Chevrolet Camaro (2)**
Bob Raub (USA) WG
Roy Woods (USA) WG
Bob Young (USA) WG
Bob Lazier (USA) WG

**Rödler, Sport Dienst
– Opel Kadett (2 cars)**
Michael Dagenhardt (D) NUR
Christoff Esser (D) NUR
Winfried Esser (D) NUR
Wolfgang Offermann (D) NUR
Wolf-Dieter Mantzel (D) NUR

**Jean Rondeau
– Rondeau M379B Ford Cosworth**
Jean Rondeau (F) LM
 Jean-Pierre Jassaud (F) LM
Gordon Spice (GB) LM
Jean-Michel Martin (F) LM
Philippe Martin (F) LM

**Rosso Ltd (Steve O'Rourke).
– Ferrari 512 BB/LM**
Steve O'Rourke (GB) SIL
Chris Craft (GB) SIL
Vic Norman (GB) SIL

Tom Rynone – Chevrolet Corvette
David Kicak (USA) WG
Tom Eastham (USA) WG

**Sachs Sporting Dick Barbour Team
Kremer – Porsche 935 K3/80**
John Fitzpatrick (GB) NUR
Axel Plankenhen (D) NUR
Dick Barbour (USA) NUR

William Sala – De Tomaso Pantera
Carlo Pietromarchi (I) MZA
Marco Micangeli (I) MZA
Massimo Faraci (I) MZA

**Joachim Scheefeldt (D) – (No team
name listed) BMW 2002**
Joachim Scheefeldt (D) NUR
Robert Heckenbach (D) NUR

Erich Schiebler – Porsche 935
Anton Fischhaber (D) MNZ
Ralf Walter (D) MNZ
Erich Shiebler (D) MNZ

Fred Schuler – Datsun 280X
David Schuler (USA) WG
Robert Schuler (USA) WG

**Scorpio Racing (Enrique Molins)
– Porsche 911 Carrera RSR**
'Jamsal' (Enrique Molins) (ES) DAY, SEB
Carlos Pineda (ES) DAY, SEB
Eduardo Barrientos (ES) DAY

**Secula Veltman Tuning
– Opel Ascona B SR 2000**
Wolfgang Walter (D) NUR
Werner Prinz (D) NUR

François Servanin – Lola T298 ROC
François Servanin (F) VAL
Laurent Ferrier (F) VAL

**Shulnburg Scrap Metal
– Chevrolet Corvette**
R. V. Shulnburg (USA) SEB
Michael Keyser (USA) SEB
Tim Morgan (USA) SEB

Fabio Siliprandi – Lucchini BMW
Fabio Siliprandi (I) VAL
Arcadio Pezzali (I) VAL (*DND*)
Mario Casoni (I) VAL (*DND*)

Snowmobile Racing
– Porsche 911S
Joseph Hamilton (USA) DAY
Tom Cripe (USA) DAY
Fred Snow (USA) DAY

Sociétié ROC Yacco/ Sociétié ROC – Lola T298 ROC Simca, Chevron B36 ROC Simca
Michel Dubois (F) LM
Florian Vetsch (CH) LM
Christian Debias (F) LM
Marc Sourd (F) LM, DIJ
Bernard Verdier (F) LM
Jean-Claude Justice (F) DIJ
Victor Chelli (F) DIJ
Noël del Bello (F) DIJ
René Boccard (F) DIJ
Bruno Sotty (F) DIJ
Gérard Cuynet (F) DIJ
Xavier Mathiot (F) DIJ

'Spiffero' – De Tomaso Pantera
'Baronio' (Aldo Ceruti) (I) VAL
'Spiffero' (Marco Curti) (I) VAL

Sportwagen – Porsche 935-77A
Jürgen Barth (D) MNZ, VAL, DIJ
Henri Pescarolo (F) MNZ, VAL, DIJ

Sports Ltd Racing – Mazda RX-7
Bob Bergstrom (USA) DAY, SEB
Pat Bedard (USA) DAY, SEB

Maurice Stapleton Morgan – Morgan Plus 8
Bill Wykeham (GB) BH, SIL (DND)
Brian Classic (GB) BH
Bruce Stapleton (GB) BH, SIL
Richard Down (GB) SIL

Hubert Striebig/BP – TOJ SM01BMW
Hubert Striebig (F) DIJ
Anny-Charlotte Verney (F) DIJ

Werner Struck (No team name listed) Ford Escort
Werner Struck (D) NUR
Kennerth Persson (S) NUR (DND)
Josef Kaufmann (D) NUR (DND)

Scuderia Supercar Bellancauto – Ferrari 512BB/LM
Spartaco Dino (I) MNZ, LM
Fabrizio Violati (I) MNZ, LM
Maurizio Micangeli (I) LM

TDC Trailers and Rigids Ltd. – Lola T492-Ford
Syd Fox (GB) BH
Mike Ford (GB) BH

T & R Racing – Porsche 911 Carrera RSR, Chevrolet Corvette (Protofab)
Luis Mendez (DR) DAY
Tico Almeida (USA) DAY, SEB
Rene Rodriguez (USA) DAY, SEB
Gabriel Riano (USA) SEB

Ian Taylor Racing – Tiga SC79-Ford
Ian Taylor (GB) BH
Neil Crang (AUS) BH
Mario Hytten (CH) BH

Janis Taylor – Alfa Romeo Alfetta GTV
Del Taylor (USA) SEB
Janis Taylor (USA) SEB
Dave Cavenaugh (USA) SEB

Guy Thomas – Chevrolet Camaro
North Northam (USA) DAY
Hugh Davenport (USA) DAY
Guy Thomas (USA) DAY (DND)

Thunderbird Swap Shop/ Thunderbird Racing – Porsche 935 K3, Ferrari 512 BB
John Paul Sr (USA) DAY, SEB
Al Holbert (USA) DAY, SEB
Preston Henn (USA) DAY, SEB, MOS
Pierre Dieudonné (B) DAY
Dale Whittington (USA) MOS

Tom's/Dome/Kegel Enterprises – Dome-Toyota Celica Turbo
Nobuhide Tachi (J) SEB
Bill Koll (USA) SEB (DND)
Tim Sharp (USA) SEB (DND)

Tom's Mechanical Emporium – Chevrolet Camaro
Tom Roberts (USA) WG
Paul Schulte (USA) WG

Torino Corse/Lella Lombardi/Enzo Osella – Osella-BMW PA8, Osella-Ford-Cosworth PA6,
Lella Lombardi (I) BH, MUG, MZA (DND), SIL, NUR, LM, VAL (DND), DIJ
Marco Rocca (I) BH
Gerardo Vatielli (I) MUG
Paolo Giangrossi (I) MUG
Vittorio Brambilla (I) MUG, MZA, SIL, NUR, VAL, DIJ (DND)
Ruggero Parpinelli (I) MUG
Danilo Tesini (I) MUG
Mark Thatcher (GB) LM
Silvano Frisori (I) VAL
Ruggero Parpinelli (I) VAL

Tortilla Flats Racing – Porsche 911 Carrera RSR
Warwick Henderson (AUS) SEB
Bob Copeman (USA) SEB
John Humphreys (USA) SEB

Raymond Touroul/Total – Porsche 911 Carrera RS
Raymond Touroul (F) DIJ
FrancisBondil (F) DIJ

Toyota Village – Porsche 934
Werner Frank (USA) DAY, SEB
Rudy Bartling (CDN) DAY (DND)
Angelo Pallavicini (CH) DAY (DND)
James Brolin (USA) SEB

Trinity Racing – Mazda RX-7
Lyn St. James (USA) DAY
Mark Welch (USA) DAY, SEB
Tom Winters (USA) DAY, SEB
John Casey (USA) DAY, SEB
Steve Dietrich (USA) DAY, SEB
Lee Mueller (USA) DAY, SEB
Jim Cook (USA) SEB

Tuff-Kote Dinitrol Racing/Lundgardh – Porsche 935 L1
Jan Lungardh (S) BH, NUR, VAL, DIJ
Kurt Simonsen (S) BH
Preben Kristoffersen (DK) BH
Kenneth Persson (S) NUR (DND)
Eberhard Braun (D) VAL, DIJ
'James Bald' (Friedrich Glatz) (A) DIJ

University of Pittsburgh – AMC Javelin
Bob Fryer (USA) WG
Don Yenko (USA) WG (DND)

USA Racing – Chevrolet Corvette
Dave Heinz (USA) WG
Bob Nagel (USA) WG
Richard Valentine (USA) WG

Valvoline Deutschland – Porsche 935
Erich Schiebler (D) MUG
Fritz Müller (D) MUG

Valvoline Racing – BMW 320i, BMW 2000 RS
Peter Valder (D) NUR
Paul Strohle (D) NUR
Kurt Müller (D) NUR
Dieter Kraft (D) NUR (DND)
Alexander Géttes (D) NUR (DND)

Van Every Racing – Porsche 911 Carrera RSR
Lance Van Every (USA) SEB
Ash Tisdelle (USA) SEB

Pasquale Vecchione – Osella PA8 Ford-Cosworth
'Peppers' (I) MUG
Pasquale Vecchione (I) MUG, VAL (DND)
Ciro Nappi (I) VAL

Gerardo Vatielli – Osella PA6-FordCosworth
Gerardo Vatielli (I) MZA
Paolo Giangrossi (I) MZA (DND)

Vegla Racing Team Aachen – Porsche 935-77A
Dieter Schornstein (D) BH, MNZ, SIL, NUR, LM
Harold Grohs (D) BH, MNZ, SIL, NUR
Götz von Tschirnhaus (D) LM

Vito Veninata – Osella PA7-BMW (listed as a PA6 at Monza and Vallelunga)
Vito Veninata (I) MUG, MZA, VAL
Giovanni Cascone (I) MUG, MZA, VAL

Scuderia Vesuvio – Osella PA8-Ford Cosworth
Roberto Marazzi (I) MNZ
Pasquale Vecchione (I) MNZ

Veytal-Tuning – VW Golf GTI
Helmut Sanden (D) NUR
Michael Sanden (D) NUR

'Victor' (Victor Coggiola) – Porsche 935
'Victor' (Victor Coggiola) (I) MNZ
Giorgio Schön (I) MNZ

Welter/Meunier Esso/Welter Meunier Secateva Esso – WM-Peugeot P79/80
Guy Fréquelin (F) LM
Roger Dorchy (F) LM, DIJ
Max Mamers (F) LM
Jean-Daniel Raulet (F) LM, DIJ
Serge Saulnier (F) LM
Denis Morin (F) LM
Jean-Louis Bousquet (F) LM

Weralit-Elora Racing Team – Porsche 935K3
Edgar Dorën (D) BH, SIL, NUR, VAL, DIJ
Jürgen Lässig (D) BH, SIL, NUR, VAL, DIJ
Gerhard Holup (D) NUR, DIJ

Whittington Brothers – Porsche 935K3, Porsche 935/79
Bill Whittington (USA) DAY, SEB
Don Whittington (USA) DAY, SEB, LM, WG
Dale Whittington (USA) DAY, SEB, LM, WG
Axel Plankenhorn (D) DAY
Hurley Haywood (USA) LM, WG

Willy F. Racing Team – BMW 320i
Preben Kristoffersen (DK) NUR, DIJ
Kurt Simonsen (SWE) NUR
Kurt Elgaard (S) DIJ

Tony Wingrove – Porsche 911 Carrera
Tony Wingrove (GB) SIL
Barry Robinson (GB) SIL (DND)

Yale Stapler Team – BMW 2002, Porsche 911SC
Kurt Hens (D) NUR
Peter Biewald (D) NUR
Hans Schell (D) NUR
Helge Probst (D) NUR

Knuth Mentel (D) NUR
Wolfgang Walter (D) NUR

Yenko Chevrolet-Honda – Chevrolet Corvette
Kim Mason (USA) DAY
Don Yenko (USA) DAY (DND)
Jerry Thompson (USA) DAY (DND)

Z&W Enterprises (Pierre Honegger) – Mazda RX-7
Mark Hutchins (USA) DAY, SEB, SIL, NUR, LM
Pierre Honegger (USA) DAY, SEB, SIL, NUR, LM, MOS
Fred Apgar (USA) DAY
Walt Boren (USA) SEB
Carlos Ramirez (USA) SEB
Neale Messina (USA) SEB (DND)
Chester Vincentz (USA) SEB (DND)
Ernest Soto (YV) SIL, NUR, LM, MOS

Renzo Zorzi – Capoferri M1 Ford Cosworth DFV
Renzo Zorzi (I) MZA
Claudio Francisci (I) MZA (DND)

Zotz Garage – Porsche 914/6
Harro Zitza (USA) DAY
John Belperche (USA) DAY (DND)
Doug Zitza (USA) DAY (DND)

RESULTS

Daytona 24 Hours, 3 February, USA
World Manufacturers' Championship
Started 68, finished 28, classified 14
1st Reinhold Joest (D) Rolf Stommelen (D) Volkert Merl (D) Porsche 935J (77003/0016) (IMSA GTX/Gp 5) Liqui Moly 715 laps
2nd John Paul Sr (USA) Al Herbert (USA) Porsche 935/77A (9308900024) (IMSA GTX/Gp 5) Thunderbird Swap Shop 682 laps
3rd Ted Field (USA) Donny Ongais (USA) Milt Mintner (USA) Porsche 935 K3/80 ((000 00017) (IMSA GTX/Gp 5) Interscope Racing 664 laps

Brands Hatch 6 Hours, 16 March, GB
World Manufacturers' Championship
Started 32, finished 22, classified 21 (Race stopped due to fatal accident to Martin Raymond and restarted to complete 70% of the race distance)
1st Riccardo Patrese (I) Walter Röhrl (D) Lancia Beta Montecarlo Turbo (1002) (Gp 5) Lancia Corsa Italy 147 laps
2nd Eddie Cheever (USA) Michele Alboreto (I) Lancia Beta Montecarlo Turbo (1003) (Gp 5) Lancia Corsa Italy 146 laps
3rd Alain de Cadenet (GB) Desiré Wilson (ZA) Thompson (78/1) de Cadenet Lola LM Ford-Cosworth (S+2000) 145 laps

Sebring 12 Hours, 22 March, USA
World Challenge for Endurance Drivers and round 2 Endurance Triple Crown
Started 79, finished 34, classified 23
1st John Fitzpatrick (GB) Dick Barbour (USA) Porsche 935 K3 (Kremer) (000 0009) (GTX) Dick Barbour 253 laps
2nd Ted Field (USA) Donny Ongais (USA) Porsche 935 K3 (Kremer) (000 00017) (GTX) Ted Field 250 laps
3rd Don Whittington (USA) Bill Whittington (USA) Dale Whittington (USA) Porsche 935 K3 (000 00015) (GTX) Whittington Brothers 247 laps

Mugello 6 Hours, 13 April, Italy
World Manufacturers' Championship
Started 26, finished 11, classified 11
1st Riccardo Patrese (I) Eddie Cheever (I) Lancia Beta Montecarlo (1004) (Gp 5) Lancia Corsa Italy 177 laps
2nd Michele Alboreto (I) Walter Röhrl (D)

Lancia Beta Montecarlo (1005) (Gp 5) Lancia Corsa Italy 176 laps
3rd Carlo Franchi ('Gimax') (I) Marcello Gallo (I) Osella-BMW PA7 (Sports 2000) Marcello M. Gallo 173 laps

Monza 6 Hours, 27 April, Italy
World Manufacturers' Championship and World Challenge for Endurance Drivers
Started 37, finished 13, classified 13
1st Alain de Cadenet (GB) Desiré Wilson (ZA) de Cadenet Lola LM Ford-Cosworth (Thompson) (78/1) (S+2000) de Cadenet 183 laps
2nd Jürgen Barth (D) Henri Pescarolo (F) Porsche 935 K3 (Kremer) (000 00012) (Gp 5) Sportwagen 183 laps
3rd Riccardo Patrese (I) Walter Röhrl (D) Lancia Beta Montecarlo (1004) (Gp 5) Lancia Corsa Italy 182 laps

Silverstone 6 Hours, 11 May, GB
World Manufacturers' Championship and World Challenge for Endurance Drivers
Started 26, finished 11, classified 11
1st Alain de Cadenet (GB) Desiré Wilson (ZA) de Cadenet Lola LM Ford-Cosworth (Thompson) (78/1) (S+2000) de Cadenet 236 laps
2nd Jürgen Barth (D) Seigfried Brunn (D) Porsche 908/3 (0009) (S+2000) Siegfried Brunn 236 laps
3rd John Paul Sr (USA) Brian Redman (GB) Porsche 935 JLP-2 (000 00025) (IMSA GTX/GTP) John Paul Sr 235 laps

Nürburgring 1000km, 25 May, Germany
Started 74, finished 34
1st Stommelen (D)/Barth (D)/Porsche 908/4
2nd Fitzpatrick (GB)/Plankenhorn (D)/ Barbour (USA) Porsche 935 K3-80
3rd Stuck (D)/Piquet (BR) BMW M1 IMSA

Le Mans 24 Hours, 15 June, France
Started 55, finished 25
1st Rondeau (F)/Jaussaud (F)/Rondeau Ford-Cosworth M379
2nd Ickx (B)/Joest (D) Porsche 908/80 Gordon Spice (GB) J-M Martin (B) Martin (B) Rondeau M379 Ford-Cosworth DFV

Watkins Glen 6 Hours, 5 July, USA
Started 28, finished 23, classified 19 (Stopped for 63 minutes due to heavy rain)
1st Heyer (D)/Patrese (I) Lancia Beta Montecarlo
2nd Alboreto (I)/Cheever (USA) Lancia Beta Montecarlo
3rd Fitzpatrick (GB)/Redman (GB) Porsche 935 K3 (Kremer)

Mosport 6 Hours, 17 August, Canada
Started 32, finished 18
1st Fitzpatrick (GB)/Redman (GB) Porsche 935 K3 (Kremer)
2nd Paul Jr (USA)/Paul Sr Porsche 935 JLP-2 (Kremer)
3rd Field (USA)/Ongais (USA) Porsche 935-77A (Gp5)

Vallelunga 6 Hours, 7 September, Italy
Started 33, finished 15
1st Francia (I)/Marazzi (1) Osella-BMW PA48
2nd Brunn (D)/Bell (D) Porsche 908/3
3rd Patrese (I)/Cheever (USA) Lancia Beta Montecarlo

Dijon 1000km, 28 September, France
Started 26, finished 15
1st Pescaro (F)/Barth (D) Porsche 935 K3 (Kremer)
2nd Haldi (CH)/Beguin (F) Porsche 935-77A
3rd Justice (F)/Chelli (F) Chevron ROC-Chrysler-Simca B36

MUCH MORE
STUFF GOING ON

The sports/prototypes and the assorted category of GT cars et al. was progressing into something more cohesive but still lacking major manufacturer entries, in Europe at least.

There were 15 World Championship races for manufacturers/drivers of which two (the Daytona 6 Hours and the Spa 24 Hours) were for touring cars that are not relevant in this instance. The remaining 13 were broken down into the Manufacturers' Championship, at Daytona (24 Hours), Monza, Silverstone, Nürburgring, Le Mans, and Watkins Glen that also included the Drivers' Championship points at Sebring, Mugello, Riverside, Enna, Mosport, Elkhart Lake and Brands Hatch.

Once again an abundance of Porsche product was in evidence that included a one-off appearance of two modernised 936/81s at Le Mans, one of which won the race. Additionally, Joest raced his 936 clone again whilst the 935s won seven championship races, four in America, one in Canada, one in Great Britain and one in Italy. Also, to Porsche's dissatisfaction the brothers Kremer produced an updated 917 which raced at Le Mans where it was obviously not competitive and later at Brands Hatch where it was far more race-worthy and might have won but instead retired with suspension damage.

Their German rivals BMW had several privately entered M1s on the championship trail, a consequence of the dissolution of the Procar Championship of 1979/80. However, they were already beyond their best despite the efforts of Peter Sauber who produced three Group-5 space-frame BMW M1s with Heini Mader 500bhp motors.

Nevertheless, in a tragic race that saw veteran sports car racer Herbert Müller fatally burned, Hans-Joachim Stuck and Nelson Piquet won the truncated Nürburgring 1000km in the GS Tuning BMW M1 whilst the leading Porsche of Mass/Joest was in the pits having stopped for refuelling whilst the BMW had not. Also of note was Steve O'Rourke's M1 which finished 2nd at Silverstone with Derek Bell and David Hobbs, a consequence of others' problems.

Lancia were 1st and 2nd at Watkins Glen but otherwise had a frustrating season whilst their fellow Italian team, Jolly Club, finished 5th at the Daytona 24 Hours. In the under-2-litre sports-car category, the BMW-powered Osella PA9s were to the fore finishing 1st overall at Mugello, 2nd and 3rd at Monza, 4th at Silverstone, 2nd and 3rd at Enna-Pergusa and 5th at Brands Hatch. Another Italian exercise in what could/should have been a race winner was Carlo Facetti's much modified Ferrari 308 GTB Turbo which he raced with Martino Finotti. However, it was terminally unreliable and broke down at every race.

Other victors were the Lola T600 Ford Cosworth DFL running under Grid Team Lola at Pergusa and later Banco Occidental/Ultramar sponsorship, winning the final round at Brands Hatch. It was driven by Guy Edwards and Emilio de Villota but was not quite quick enough on the faster circuits.

Now 1982 was fast approaching and with it the return of Porsche that would dominate sports/prototype racing for several years, as we shall see.

Sebring 12 Hours, 21 March 1981 There were 78 starters for the Sebring 12 Hours including the Stratagraph Chevrolet Camaro (Frings) of Billy Hagan (on right) and Terry Labonte (at the rear). They were 20th on the grid, 10th fastest in the IMSA GTX class and 2nd fastest of the American GTX entrants but retired after 144 laps. Stratagraph was established by Billy Joe Hagan (22 March 1932 – 16 November 2007) in 1961 as an independent logging company that went on to become one of the largest of its kind in the industry. Terrance Lee 'Terry' Labonte (born 16 November 1956) is a former stock-car racer, two-time Winston Cup winner and 1989 IROC champion. He appeared on *The Dukes of Hazzard* (CBS) in 1984 and co-owned a Chevrolet dealership in North Carolina with Rick Hendrick. *GPL*

Daytona 24 Hours, 31 January/1 February 1981 The Firestone Tire & Rubber-entered experimental Ford Mustang of John Morton (at right by the pumps) and Tom Klausler was entered in the All American Grand Touring (AAGT) class. It was built by McLaren North America and featured a 2.3-litre turbo engine and Firestone road tyres, finishing a delayed 21st after failing to set a practice time. The talented Morton had been a Shelby mechanic with an SCCA licence at the Sebring 12 Hours in 1964 when he was paired with an injured Ken Miles (see *Sports Car Racing in Camera 1960–69, Volume 2* upper caption, page 103). He went on to become a very successful racer in many categories, taking a 2nd place at Sebring, 3rd at Le Mans in 1986 and 1st at Sebring in 1994. Born 14 July 1945, St Paul, Minnesota, Tom Klausler (sitting in the car) worked at McLaren Northern America and raced in a variety of categories including Formula Ford, Formula Atlantic, Can-Am, CART, the Indy 500 in 1981, IMSA et al., but his professional career seems to have ended in 1983. *GPL*

Daytona 24 Hours, 31 January/1 February 1981 In a race of attrition one team were really ecstatic, the Kegel Enterprises Porsche 911 SC of Bill Koll/Jeff Kline/Rob McFarlin finished 3rd overall and winner of the GTU class (Grand Touring cars, the letter 'U' indicating under 2.5 litres). Just behind is the Dave Kent Racing Mazda RX-7 of Lee Mueller (USA)/Kathy Rude (USA)/Philippe Martin (B), the last named the winner of two Spa 24 Hours (1979/80). Also in the GTU category, the Mazda was only 0.143 sec behind the Porsche, finishing 7th overall and 3rd in class after transmission problems. Mueller was the IMSA GTU Champion for 1981, Kathy Rude was very highly rated by Brian Redman, but sadly she suffered a serious career-ending crash at Brainerd, Minnesota in July 1983. Later on she became a corporate safe-driving instructor and speaker for Audi America and the Boeing Employees Automobile Club. *GPL*

Daytona 24 Hours, 31 January/1 February 1981 Bob Garretson began his racing career in the 1950s on the Southern California drag strips, but he later decided that it was a waste of time – "All that work and in 20 seconds you are done." Later he became part of the developing computer technology in the Bay Area of San Francisco. This funded his garage and racing career and in 1980 two young men arrived at his shop looking to have their Porsche serviced. They were Steve Jobs and Steve Wozniak, the founders of Apple Computers Inc., which became a major sponsor for Garretson's team. 1981 was a special year and he won the Daytona and Sebring rounds and the 1981 World Endurance Championship title. At Daytona the assorted Porsche 935s were running slightly downgraded 3.0- and 2.8-litre motors, but Garretson opted for the uprated 3.2-litre sprint engine. He shared the car with Brian Redman and Bobby Rahal, and they won the race after turning up the boost whilst their rivals suffered various problems. LAT

Daytona 24 Hours, 31 January/1 February 1981
In period, Daytona and Sebring were liberally blessed by road cars from Ford, Chevrolet, Pontiac et al. Some were re-engineered, re-bodied and lowered beyond all recognition; others were still recognisable, albeit with much-modified plastic bodywork as seen here. Tracy Wolf was the entrant via Howey Farms and she shared the Camaro with Clark Howey and Dale Koch. The car was engineered by Wolf, presumably either Tracy or a relative/father perhaps, and started 37th out of 69 on the grid. They were posted as a DNF in 37th place having completed 208 laps. Following is Swiss racer Angelo Pallavicini's Porsche 934 (930 670 0178), which he shared with John Sheldon (GB) and Neil Crang (AUS). They were another
DNF after 290 laps. *GPL*

Daytona 24 Hours, 31 January/1 February 1981 By contrast here are the de facto prototype Chris Cord-entered Chevrolet Monza Turbo (DeKon 1012) driven by Cord and Jim Adams showing some front wheel arch damage and Canadian Maurice Carter's (25 May 1921 – 28 March 2002) Chevrolet Camaro (Descon), which he shared with Eppie Wietzes (CDN) and Richard Valentine (USA). They were 14th and 13th fastest respectively, separated by just 0.572 sec, and both retired within three laps of each other, the former on lap 191 and the latter on lap 188 in an accident. Cord was the grandson of Errett Lobban Cord, the founder of the Cord Corporation, which also ran Cord Automobile. *LAT*

↑ **Sebring 12 Hours, 21 March 1981** Bob Tullius and his Group 44 team successfully raced and won a variety of championships with their Triumphs, Jaguars and finally Audis over 25 years before shutting down in 1990. At Sebring they entered two of the Triumph TR8 models powered by the re-engineered Buick V8 used in the Rovers of this period. Bob Tullius and Canadian journalist Bill Adam drove no.44, the signature number of the team, whilst no.4 seen here was raced by Americans Jim Kelly and Patrick Bedard. They were 41st and 42nd in the line-up and finished 10th and 20th respectively, the latter leading the class until it was slowed by gearbox problems. Just visible behind is the Momo/Penthouse no.30 Porsche 935 J of Gianpiero Moretti, Charles Mendez and Mauricio DeNarvaez that finished 6th but not running due to electrical problems. *GPL*

→ **Sebring 12 Hours, 21 March 1981** The GTO class was won by the Chuck Kendall Porsche 911 Carrera RSR (911 560 9121) after the faster BMW M1s began to fail. It was driven by Kendall, Pete Smith and Dennis Aase and finished 5th overall. Note the laid-back spot lights on the front bonnet which were raised up during the night-time hours. *GPL*

Sebring 12 Hours, 21 March 1981 Just as at Daytona there was a plethora of Porsche 935s in various guises and this is the winning car, Bruce Leven's Bayside Disposal 935-80 (000 00024) driven by Hurley Haywood/Al Holbert/Bruce Leven that was 3rd fastest in practice. Leven bought the modest waste-and-scrap Bayside Disposal in Seattle in 1964 and turned it into a thriving business, which he eventually sold in 1987. He later bought other similar operations which he ran up to his death in 2017. He had many successes including three wins at Sebring (1981/87/88) and finally ended his racing career in the 1990s. His portfolio encompassed car franchises, building hot rods and a commercial float-plane business amongst other interests. Bruce Leven, 27 September 1938 – 15 September 2017. *GPL*

Sebring 12 Hours, 21 March 1981 Amongst the opposition was Ted Field's Interscope Racing Porsche 935 K3/80 (000 00010) driven by Field and Danny Ongais. They briefly led the race whilst the other 935s suffered various problems, but then Ongais had to retire the car due to electrical problems or a blown engine, take your pick. Sebring's savage, lumpy concrete circuit was a car wrecker *par excellence*. Note the shredded front of the Porsche as Ted Field races on. His full name is Frederick Woodruff 'Ted' Field (born 1 June 1953), an American media mogul, entrepreneur and film producer and no.236 on the *Forbes* list of the 400 richest people according to sources. *GPL*

⬆ **Mugello 6 Hours, 12 April 1981** Only 21 cars started at Mugello and 14 finished. For nearly two hours Michele Alboreto and Piercarlo Ghinzani with the lone factory Lancia Beta Montecarlo Turbo (1009) were battling with the Lombardi/Francia Osella PA9 BMW. Soon after the Lancia's gearbox began to fail and the car was pitted to see if it could be repaired (seen here) which it duly was. This took less time than it should have and eventually race officials found the wrecked gearbox in the paddock so the Lancia was disqualified from its 3rd-place finish for fitting a new 'box. *LAT*

➡ **Mugello 6 Hours, 12 April 1981** Small, neat and very fast, the works Osella PA9 BMW (107) driven by Lella Lombardi and Giorgio Francia won the Mugello 6 Hours after the demise of the Alboreto/Ghinzani Martini Lancia. The Osella was nine laps ahead of the Charles Ivey Racing Porsche 935 K3 which finished in 2nd place. *LAT*

Monza 1000km, 26 April 1981 Monza had 32 starters of which nine were Porsches – five 935s, three 924s and Siegfried Brunn's 908. However, the fastest car by a comfortable margin was Carlo Facetti's Jolly Club Ferrari 308 GTB turbo, but it was terminally unreliable and this time its distributor failed during the warm-up. It was a wet race and half the grid retired with assorted problems including one of the Martini Racing Lancia Beta Montecarlo Turbos whilst the second one (Ghinzani/de Cesaris) finished 13th. Amidst all this the Weralit Racing Porsche 935 K3 (009 0003) of Edgar Dören, Jürgen Lässig and Gerhard Holup, which qualified 13th, had an incident-free race and ultimately won. Weralit were and still are a German manufacturer of screwdrivers and other tools, hence the large screwdriver decal over the rear wheel. Here is the 935 on the starting grid and how many of us have suffered the sudden and infuriating intrusion of an unseen person running across our lens, grr. *LAT*

Monza 1000km, 26 April 1981 Eric Broadley had not designed any open-top or sports coupé cars since the 1970s until the T600 (with Andrew Thorby), which was successful across the Atlantic but its European record was not so reliable. Entered by Ian Dawson (Grid Team Lola) it had a 3.3-litre Ford Cosworth DFL motor (the American market T600s used Chevrolet V8s). The drivers were Guy Edwards and Emilio de Villota, who were 5th fastest on the grid but retired on lap 61 due to a broken driveshaft. It was very long at 15ft 6in (4,737mm) and 6ft 6.5in (1,994mm) wide. The Banco Occidental sponsorship was courtesy of de Villota but note the Ultramar, RIZLA and other decals which were the domain of Edwards who was an expert on brokering sponsorship deals. *GPL*

→ Silverstone 6 Hours, 10 May 1981
Silverstone provided some interesting contrasts and an even more unexpected victory in a race dominated by rain. One welcome addition was the Jolly Club Ferrari 308 GTB Turbo (18935) for Martino Finotto/Carlo Facetti, which had briefly run at Daytona before retiring. They placed 6th on the grid here but once again the car failed, this time due to gearbox problems. Facetti squats down to speak to Finotto (11 November 1933 – 13 August 2014) who was team owner, during practice and could that be the famous Geoff Goddard in yellow and blue striped anorak photographing a team member at the back of the Ferrari? *LAT*

↓ Silverstone 6 Hours, 10 May 1981 Lancia entered two Beta Montecarlos at Silverstone but both retired. The Patrese/Cheever car was 3rd on the grid but retired when a back wheel came off on lap 156 whilst this car, driven by Andrea de Cesaris (I), collided with Mercer's Vogue after the latter spun on lap 3, leaving Piercarlo Ghinzani (I) without a drive. This image is from the dry practice as the Lancia passes the Canon-sponsored GTi Engineering Porsche 924 Carrera GT Turbo of Richard Lloyd/Tony Dron that finished 11th overall and 2nd in the GT class. *LAT*

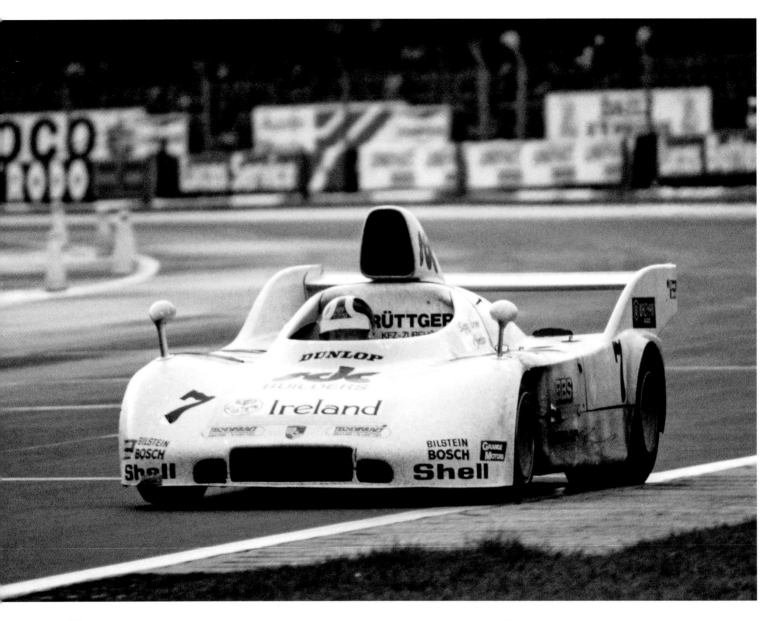

Silverstone 6 Hours, 10 May 1981 In later life the driver here was an F1 team owner and later TV pundit, but back then it was sometime F3 racer Eddie Jordan driving Siegfried Brunn's Porsche 908/03 Turbo. He set fastest race lap and they finished 3rd and 1st in the over-2,000cc sports cars. This was the last race that the Porsche finished as it crashed during the Nürburgring 1000km and collided with the abandoned Porsche 935 of Bobby Rahal, which had not been removed from the circuit despite Rahal's pleading to do so, killing well-known Swiss racer Herbert Müller. *LAT*

Silverstone 6 Hours, 10 May 1981 The direct consequence of the weather was the unlikely result of a Porsche 935 winning the race and this BMW M1 (WBS59910004301028), driven by Derek Bell, Steve O'Rourke and David Hobbs, finishing 2nd. It was entered by EMKA Productions aka Steve O'Rourke who was the manager of Pink Floyd for many years. This car was later painted blue and entered in the Group 5 class from Le Mans onwards. *LAT*

Silverstone 6 Hours, 10 May 1981 The precipitation certainly upset the status quo at Silverstone as the pole-position Joest Porsche 908/80, aka 936 clone, driven by Jochen Mass and Reinhold Joest crashed on lap 1 when Mass aquaplaned off at the Woodcote chicane. Nevertheless, a Porsche still won, in this instance Walter Röhrl accompanied by Harald Grohs and Dieter Schornstein in the Vegla Racing Team 935 J (000 00016) two laps ahead of the 2nd- and 3rd-placed cars. The lofty Röhrl rather dwarfs his co-drivers whilst Eddie Jordan in red with cap and glasses can be seen at far right talking to Siegfried Brunn. *LAT*

Nürburgring 1000km, 24 May 1981 Founded by Erich Zakowski in 1968, Zakspeed became an official Ford team during the 1970s and later produced the Group 5 Capri with a 1.4-litre engine and twin turbos for the German DTM series, which by 1981 had ground effects and 495bhp according to sources. It was driven by Manfred Winkelhock/ Klaus Niedzwiedz and the former was fastest in practice, 8.53 seconds quicker than Mass in Joest's pseudo Porsche 936/908/80, but alas the Ford's turbocharged engine detonated on race morning and did not start. Tragically Winkelhock (6 October 1951 – 12 August 1985) was fatally injured at Mosport, Canada during the Budweiser 1000km, driving a Porsche 962C for Kremer Racing. Niedzwiedz was a journalist and later TV presenter in Germany. *LAT*

→ Nürburgring 1000km, 24 May 1981 Jochen Mass sits in Reinhold Joest's Porsche 908/80 and should have won the race but for the delay caused by Herbert Müller's fatal crash that ended the race on lap 17. Bobby Rahal driving Bob Akin's Porsche 935 K3 crashed on the first lap after contacting Guy Edwards' Grid Team Lola T600 at Kesselchen below the Karusell. The 935 was left in the barrier on the narrow grass strip alongside the road, full of fuel where it remained, despite Rahal's pleading to have it removed. On lap 13 Müller arrived at the site with a local rain shower in progress and collided with a spinning Porsche, which caused his 908/03 to hit Rahal's car. The 935's full tank erupted and the 908 also caught fire, leaving the hapless Müller trapped in the inferno. At that point the Stuck/Piquet BMW M1 had not pitted for its second stop whereas the Porsche had. The identity of the Immo Klein transfer seen on the car was/still is a real-estate agency in Freiburg im Breisgau, Germany. *LAT*

→ Le Mans 24 Hours, 13/14 June 1981 This year's Le Mans turned out to be one of tragedy and a return to Porsche hegemony, albeit for this one race of the season for them. Amongst the entries was an ersatz Porsche 917 with backing by BP created by the Kremer brothers, Manfred and Erwin, a consequence of the return of larger-capacity engines in sports prototype racing. Alas it was not fully developed, slightly heavier to make it more robust and suffered aerodynamic problems which created overheating and slowed it down during practice due to the modified flat rear end. Having changed its initial 4.5-litre motor for the bigger 4.9-litre unit, it was slightly faster and started 18th in the echelon. Note also the reshaped nose and flat side panels. The drivers were Bob Wollek, Xavier Lapeyre and Guy Chasseuil, but it lasted only 82 laps after Lapeyre was forced off track, apparently by another car which split an oil pipe, and it retired due to loss of lubricant. Porsche were not amused. *LAT*

Le Mans 24 Hours, 13/14 June 1981 After a late decision Porsche came to Le Mans with a brace of improved 936/81 cars for Jacky Ickx/Derek Bell and Jochen Mass/Vern Schuppan. The cars were running a low-boost 2.65-litre motor which gave 620bhp and they were 1st and 2nd in practice and several seconds clear of the rest headed by the faux Joest 936, aka 908/80, driven by Joest/Niedzwiedz/Dale Whittington. Ickx, who had come out of retirement, and Bell led for most of the 24 hours and won by 14 laps over the 2nd-placed Rondeau but Mass/Schuppan in the 936/81 (001) (seen here with Mass) suffered myriad problems that began from lap 1 onwards. These culminated in an on-course breakdown late on Sunday morning due to a faulty fuel pump, but Schuppan managed to get it back to the pits for repair and the car finished 12th. *LAT*

Le Mans 24 Hours, 13/14 June 1981 Once again the WM (Welter/Meunier) team graced Le Mans, with four cars and two converted to Group-C specifications designated P81 with faired-in rear wheels. These were driven by Thierry Boutsen/Michel Pignard/Serge Saulnier and Max Mamers/Jean-Daniel Raulet/Michel Pignard. It was a tragic weekend for the team with only the Morin/Mendez/Mathiot WM79/80 finishing, in 13th place. This is Boutsen in the P81 which suffered a broken suspension on Mulsanne at maximum velocity (215mph/345kph) on lap 15. It slid along the guard rail and hit a marshal's post. One person died while another lost an arm and suffered a broken leg and collarbone and other minor head injuries. Later, on lap 46, the Dorchy/Frequelin WMP79/80 caught fire at Mulsanne corner and was extinguished but then Max Mamers hit Gabbiani's Lancia at the same spot on lap 50. *GPL*

Le Mans 24 Hours, 13/14 June 1981 Two other factory Porsches appeared at the Sarthe. This is the turbocharged, 16-valve, 4-cylinder 2.5-litre 944, which would be racing in a new Group B category for 1982. It was detuned to 370bhp for reliability and, driven by Walter Röhrl and Jürgen Barth, finished 7th and 1st in the over-3,000 GTP class, an impressive debut. The other car was a current 2-litre 924, which finished 11th overall and 1st in the IMSA GTO category. Interestingly the 944 was only 3 seconds quicker than the 924 in practice, but presumably it could have gone faster. *LAT*

↑ **Le Mans 24 Hours 13/14 June 1981** Jean Rondeau entered five cars (three in Group 6 and two in GTP) at Le Mans, but their 1980 victory was not to be repeated, the Porsche 936/81s were too fast. However, the two M379 C GTP cars finished 2nd (Haran/Schlesser/Streiff) and 3rd (Migault/Spice) despite Spice's rib injuries from a road crash. Far worse was the fatal accident that befell Jean-Louis Lafosse. He was partnered by rally and racing driver Jean Ragnotti and started the race from 10th position. On lap 28, nearing the end of his first stint, he touched a guardrail but was unaware of the extent of the damage. He carried on for another lap and the damaged front end opened up on the Mulsanne Straight. The car veered off to the right, hit the barrier and then ricocheted back across the road into a marshal's post. Lafosse died instantly although other sources suggest he passed away en route to hospital, whilst two marshals suffered broken legs. Jean-Louis Lafosse, 15 March 1941, Dakar, Senegal – 13 June 1981. *GPL*

↖ **Le Mans 24 Hours 13/14 June 1981** The familiar Charles Ivey Porsche 935 K3 (930 890 0022) driven by John Cooper, Dudley Wood and Claude Bourgoignie, was turned down by the ACO at Le Mans and only by nominating Bourgoignie, who was in need of a sponsor, as team entrant could they get an entry. Happily, the team had a successful race, finishing 4th overall and winning the G5 class despite some electrical problems, which apparently embarrassed the organisers. This is John Cooper on Sunday with the travel-worn 935 and note the original bodywork/bumper hiding beneath the plastic cladding at the rear and elsewhere. *LAT*

← **Le Mans 24 Hours 13/14 June 1981** The weird-looking Masao Ono-designed Dome Zero, which was over 16ft long, had first appeared in 1979 and was back at Le Mans for the third time in a row, still powered by a Cosworth DFV. It was now designated as RL81 and featured bigger front wheels and brakes driven again by Chris Craft and Bob Evans, the former knocking 3 seconds off his 1980 practice times and starting from 20th place on the echelon. Craft (seen here) reached 8th place but thereafter assorted problems culminating in a broken valve spring ended their race after 154 laps. *LAT*

←Le Mans 24 Hours, 13/14 June 1981 In 1981 there were five Ferrari 512 BB/LMs for Scuderia Supercar Bellancauto, Rennod Racing, Charles Pozzi, Simon Phillips and N.A.R.T. (North American Racing Team). The Pozzi car finished 5th overall and 1st in the IMSA GTX category, the Rennod Racing 512 9th overall and 3rd in class whilst the remaining trio all retired. Fabrizio Violati's Rome-based Bellancauto SA company hired the elderly Armand Palanca who created the rather odd-looking Bellancauto 512 BB/LM (35529) for Violati/Duilio Truffo/Maurizio Flammini, seen here at the Mulsanne corner. It was the second quickest of the 512s but retired during Saturday night due to electrical problems, a common problem at Le Mans for many years. *GPL*

↓Watkins Glen 6 Hours, 12 July 1981 Two weeks after Le Mans the Enna Coppa Florio, Sicily had just nine starters and seven finishers, the winner being de Villota/Edwards in the Lola T600 run by Grid Team Lola. The next round was the Watkins Glen 6 Hours, which had 32 starters with Ted Field's Interscope Porsche 935 K3/80 fastest in practice just shading the John Pauls senior and junior. However, both these cars retired and the no.1 Lancia Beta Montecarlo (1007) of Patrese/Alboreto finished 1st with teammates de Cesaris/Pescarolo 2nd and Bob Garretson's Porsche 935 K3/80 3rd. This is the winning car en route to the grid alongside Fitzpatrick's 935 K3/80, which finished 4th after problems with the wastegate and later a cracked fan pulley. *LAT*

Brands Hatch 1000km, 27 September 1981 The last race of the season saw the debut of Ford's C100, designed by Len Bailey and prepared by Eric Zakowski of Zakspeed fame. Manfred Winkelhock and Klaus Ludwig were the drivers and this was the first of the new Group-C cars for 1982. They put it on pole but it was a work in progress; increasing the Ford Cosworth DFV engine to its maximum 3.9 litres exacerbated the unit's known propensity for vibration, and then Bailey departed due to political infighting. Further complications arose from the appearance of a second chassis, a honeycomb version designed by John Thompson for Alain de Cadenet, the first being a sheet aluminium monocoque built by Hesketh Engineering. Meanwhile the C100 led the race but on lap 40 its transmission failed because there had been no time to fit a gearbox oil cooler. It pulled off at what was then the Surtees left-hander whilst in the background is the winning Edwards/de Villota Lola T600. *LAT*

Brands Hatch 1000km, 27 September 1981 After its less-than-impressive Le Mans debut the Kremer brothers' ersatz Porsche 917 designated K/81 made its final outing here driven by Bob Wollek and Henri Pescarolo. It was third fastest in practice and occupied 2nd and then 1st place after the Ford C100 failure, in front of the Edwards/de Villota Lola T600, but retired on lap 52 with front-suspension failure, denying co-driver Pescarolo a turn. Figures for the car claim that it produced 600bhp @ 8,400rpm and torque of 443lb ft @ 6,500rpm. It was later sold to private interests and more recently appeared at the 2017 Retromobile in Paris. *LAT*

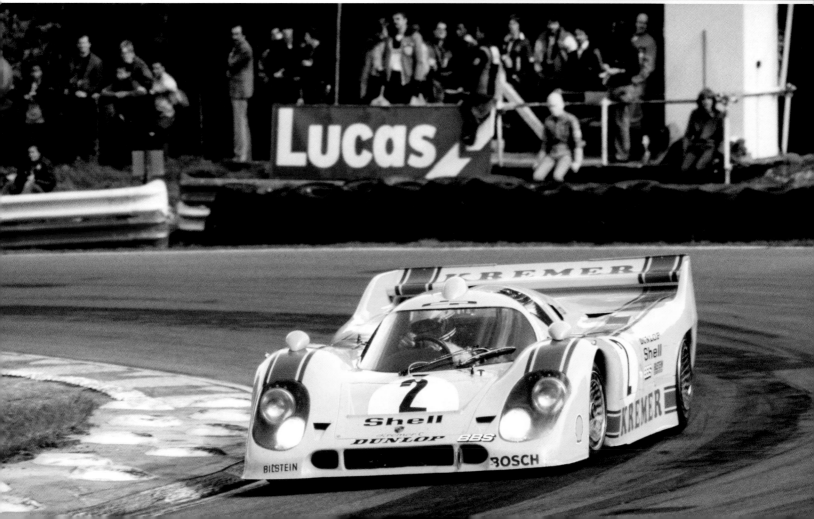

Brands Hatch 1000km, 27 September 1981 This was the second victory for the Spanish-sponsored Lola T600 Ford Cosworth DFL (HU3) of de Villota/Edwards in 1981 and one that was inevitable after the demise of the Ford C100 and the Kremer-built Porsche 917. They were second fastest in practice and won by an impressive eight laps. Note the 'MEN'S CLUB' decal on the front apron that presumably would not be acceptable now. *LAT*

Brands Hatch 1000km, 27 September 1981 There were seven Porsche 935s of various specifications at Brands Hatch including the bright yellow Bob Garretson K3 car (009 00030) which he shared with Bobby Rahal. They were the quickest of the 935s, starting 6th. Despite some very cautious driving in the wet period they finished 2nd overall and the Californian Garretson, seen here just about to mount his steed, became the first winner of the FIA World Endurance Championship. The 'FLYING TIGERS' motif was a reference to the official race, which was named the Flying Tigers 1000. *LAT*

Brands Hatch 1000km, 27 September 1981 Dorset Racing entered two cars at Brands Hatch: a Lola T297 (T290-HU22) for Martin Birrane/Roy Baker/Richard Jones and this car, no.5, the ex-Alain de Cadenet De Cadenet-Lola T380 (HU1) for South African racer Leon Walger and Richard Jones who was driving both cars. However, Walger, who raced in the 1980 Aurora AFX British F1 series, crashed on lap 15 whilst the other car finished 7th and 2nd in the Sports 2-litre class, which was won by the Lombardi/Francia Osella PA9 BMW. LAT

ENTRANTS

AC 1927 Mayen – TOJ SC302
Norbert Pryzbilla (D) NUR*
Peter Hoffman (D) NUR*

Bob Akin Motor Racing
– Porsche 935 K3/80
Bob Akin (USA) DAY, SEB, SIL, NUR* (DND),
LM, WG, MOS, ELK
Craig Siebert (USA) DAY, SEB, LM, WG
Derek Bell (GB) DAY, SEB
Bobby Rahal (USA) SIL, NUR*
Pete Lovett (GB) SIL
Paul Miller (USA) LM
Vivian Candy (IRL) WG Skeeter McKitterick
(USA) MOS, ELK

Alderman Datsun – Datsun 240Z
George Alderman (USA) SEB
John McComb (USA) SEB

Alex Porsche Haus
– Porsche 911 Carrera RSR
Bob Copeman (USA) RIV
Lawrence Farmer (USA) RIV (DND)
Ken Moore (USA) RIV (DND)

Alps Restoration
– Porsche 914/6
Peter Aschenbrenner (CDN) SEB, WG, MOS
Peter Moennick (CDN) SEB (DND) WG
Herman Lausberg (CDN) SEB (DND)
Peter Tescher (CDN) MOS

American Revolution
– Mazda RX-2
Bruce Nesbitt (USA) ELK
Glen Johnson (USA) ELK

Andial Racing/Meister Homes
– Porsche 935 M16
Rolf Stommelen (D) DAY, SEB, RIV,
MOS, ELK
Howard Meister (USA) DAY, SEB, RIV
Harald Grohs (D) DAY, SEB, MOS, ELK

Luigi de Angelis
– Osella PA6 Ford Cosworth
Luigi de Angelis (I) MZA
Adriano Gozzi (I) MZA

Arrow Heating Co.
– Chevrolet Corvette
John Chamberlain (USA) RIV
Joe Chamberlain (USA) RIV

Anatoly Arutunoff – Lancia Stratos HF
Anatoly Arutunoff (USA) ELK
José Marina (USA) ELK

Auto Kümpel – KMW SP30, Landar R8
Karl-Adolf Kneip (D) NUR*
Peter Hardt (D) NUR*
Heinz Hardt (D) NUR* (DND)

Autosport Technology – Porsche 914/6
M.L. Speer (USA) DAY
Dwight Mitchell (USA) DAY, SEB, RIV
Ray Ratcliff (USA) DAY, SEB, RIV
Bill Cooper (USA) SEB, RIV

BASF Team GS Sport/BASF
CassettenTeam GS Sport
– BMW M1, BMW M1 Sauber Gp5
Hans-Joachim Stuck (D) SIL, LM, BH
Hans Heyer (D) SIL, BH
Jean-Pierre Jarier (F) LM
Helmut Henzler (D) LM

BMW Challenge Team – BMW M1
Alf Gebarht (USA) SEB
Marc Surer (CH) SEB

BMW Italia-France – BMW M1
Bernard Darniche (F) LM
Johnny Cecotto (YV) LM
Philippe Alliot (F) LM

BMW Italia – BMW M1
Umberto Grano (I) ENN-PER
Christian Danner (D) ENN-PER (DND)
Marco Vanoli (CH) ENN-PER (DND)

BMW Motorsport – BMW M1
Dieter Quester (A) DAY
David Hobbs (GB) DAY
Marc Surer (CH) DAY

BMW Motorsports GmbH/BMW
North America/BMW Motorsport USA
– BMW M1 Gp5
David Hobbs (GB) WG, MOS
Marc Surer (CH) WG, MOS

BMW North America
– March 81P/BMW M1C
David Hobbs (GB) RIV, ELK
Marc Surer (CH) RIV
John Morton (USA) RIV
Vern Schuppan (AUS) ELK

BMW Zol Auto – BMW M1
Pierre-François Rousselot (F) MZA, LM
François Servanin (F) MZA, LM
Laurent Ferrier (F) MZA, LM

Banco Occidental/Ultramar/Team Lola
– Lola T600 Ford Cosworth DFV
Guy Edwards (GB) SIL, BH
Emilio de Villota (ES) SIL, BH

Pasquale Barberio – Osella PA8 BMW
Pasquale Barberio (I) MZA
Marcello Galli (I) MZA

Bavarian Motors International
– BMW M1, BMW 3.5 CSL
Hans-Joachim Stuck (D) DAY
Alf Gebhardt (USA) DAY, RIV
Walter Brun (CH) DAY
Bruno Beilcke (D) DAY, RIV
Kurt König (D) DAY
Rudi Walch (D) DAY
Mike Freberg (USA) RIV

Bayside Disposal Racing
– Porsche 935/80
Hurley Haywood (USA) DAY, SEB, RIV, WG
Jürgen Barth (D) DAY, SEB
Bruce Leven (USA) DAY, SEB, RIV, WG

Beach Ball Racing – Porsche 911
Tom Cripe (USA) DAY
Dick Gauthier (USA) DAY
Jack Swanson (USA) DAY

Bob Beasley – Porsche 911 Carrera RSR
George Stone (USA) DAY
Bob Beasley (USA) DAY (DND)
Werner Frank (USA) (DND)

Mario Benusiglio – Osell PA6 Armaroli
Mario Benusiglio (I) MZA
Mario Catanese (I) MZA

Bergisch-Gladbach Renngemein
– BMW 320i, BMW 2002
Richard Bremmekamp (D) NUR*
Werner Felder (D) NUR*
Hans Weißgerber (D) (DNS) NUR*
Jürgen Möhle (D) NUR*
Michael Martini (D) (DNS) NUR*

Berkenkamp Ford – Ford Escort
Dieter Selzer (D) NUR*
Andreas Schall (D) NUR*
Günther Braumüller (D)(DNS) NUR*

Klaus Bitterauf – Porsche 911
Klaus Bitterauf (USA) SEB
James Moxley (USA) SEB
Jim Leo (USA) SEB

Logan Blackburn Columbus Racing
– Datsun 280ZX
Logan Blackburn (USA) MOS, ELK
David Frellsen (USA) MOS, ELK

Blink & Nod Racing
– Chevrolet Corvette
Roger Blink (USA) ELK
Dan Schott (USA) ELK

Bob's Speed Products
– AMC AMX
Vicki Smith (USA) DAY, SEB
Sam Miller (USA) DAY
Bob Lee (USA) DAY, SEB
Tom Alan Marx (USA) SEB

Rick Borlase
– Porsche 911 Carrera RSR
Rick Borlase (USA) SEB, RIV
Michael Hammond (USA) SEB (DND), RIV
Don Kravig (USA) SEB (DND)

Claude Bourgoignie
– Porsche 935 K3
John Cooper (GB) LM
Dudley Wood (GB) LM
Claude Bourgoignie (B) LM

Ian Bracey – Ibec P6 (Hesketh)
Ford Cosworth DFV
Tiff Needell (GB) SIL, LM
Vivian Candy (IRL) SIL (DND)
Tony Trimmer (GB) (DND), LM

Brauneiser Renntechnik
– Ford Escort RS 2000
Jochen Felder (D) NUR*
Willi Wipperfürht (D) NUR*
Volker Imhof (D) NUR* (DNS)
Axel Felder (D) NUR*
Michael Bitschnau (D) NUR*
Franz-Josef Brohling (D) NUR* (DND)

Karl-Ernst Brune – Alfa Romeo GTV
Karl-Ernst Brune (D) NUR*
Winfried van Osten (D) NUR*
Gerhard Hennemann (D)(DNS) NUR*

Siegfried Brunn
– Porsche 908/3 TC
Siegfried Brunn (D) MZA, SIL, NUR*
Eddie Jordan (IRL) MZA, SIL
Herbert Müller (CH) NUR* (Fatal accident)

Jack Buchinger – Datsun 280ZX
Jack Buchinger (USA) ELK
Michael Guffy (USA) ELK (DND)

Peter Bulkowski – Triumph TR8
Peter Bulkowski (CDN) MOS
Luc Berhar (CDN) MOS

Christian Bussi – Porsche 935
Jürgen Barth (D) MZA
Christian Bussi (F) MZA (DND), BH
Jacques Guérin (F) MZA (DND), BH

Alain de Cadenet – De Cadenet
Lola LM -4 Ford Cosworth DFV
Alain de Cadenet (GB) LM
Jean-Michel Martin (F) LM
Philippe Martin (F) LM

Canon Cameras Racing/GTi Engineering
– Porsche 924 Carrera GTR
Richard Lloyd (GB) MZA, SIL, NUR*, BH
Tony Dron (GB) MZA, SIL, NUR*
Andy Rouse (GB) BH

Maurice Carter Racing
– Chevrolet Camaro
Maurice Carter (CDN) DAY, MOS
Eppie Wietzes (CDN) DAY
Richard Valentine (USA) DAY
Bill Adam (CDN) MOS

Casa Blanco Fan
– Porsche 911 Carrera RSR
Robert Kirby (USA) RIV
John Hotchkis (USA) RIV

Case Racing – Porsche 911
Ron Case (USA) DAY, SEB
Dave Panaccione (USA) DAY
Ren Tilton (USA) DAY
Ray Mummery (USA) SEB (DND)
Jack Rynerson (USA) SEB (DND)

Tommaso Casiglia – Alfa Romeo GTV
Tommaso Casiglia (I) ENN-PER
Claudio Cordo (I) ENN-PER

André Chevalley Racing – ACR 80B
(Lola) Ford Cosworth DFV
Patrick Gaillard (F) LM
André Chevalley (CH) LM
Bruno Sotty (F) LM

Gabriele Ciuti – Osell PA7 BMW
Gabriele Ciuti (I) ENN-PER
Enrico Unsini (I) ENN-PER

Richard Cleare Racing
– Porsche 934
Richard Cleare (GB) SIL, NUR*, BH
Andy Rouse (GB) SIL
David Kennedy (IRL) NUR*, BH

Luigi Colzani – Osella PA7 BMW
Luigi Colzani (I) MZA
Gabriele Ciuti (I) MZA

Compagnie Primagaz
– Lola T298 BMW
Pierre Yver (F) LM
Jacques Heuclin (F) LM
Michel Dubois (F) LM

Cooke Woods Racing/Garretson
Enterprises – Porsche 935 K3,
Lola T600 Chevrolet
Roy Woods (USA) SEB, RIV
Ralph Kent-Cooke (USA) SEB, RIV, LM
Skeeter McKitterick (USA) SEB
Bob Garretson (USA) SEB, RIV, LM, WG
Bobby Rahal (USA) SEB, RIV
Brian Redman (GB) SEB, RIV, MOS, ELK
Anny-Charlotte Verney (F) LM
Rick Mears (USA) WG
Johnny Rutherford (USA) WG
Eppie Wietzes (CDN) MOS
Sam Posey (USA) ELK

Chris Cord Racing – Chevrolet Monza
Turbo, Lola T600 Chevrolet
Chris Cord (USA) DAY, SEB, RIV, MOS, ELK
Jim Adams (USA) DAY, SEB, RIV, MOS, ELK

Corp Racing Ltd
– Mazda RX-7
Jim Burt (USA) DAY, SEB, ELK
Douglas Grunnet (USA) DAY, SEB, ELK
Steve Paquette (CDN) DAY, SEB

Corvettes Unlimited
– Chevrolet Corvette
Rusty Schmidt (USA) ELK
Scott Schmidt (USA) ELK

Alfred Cosentino/Faza Squadron
– Mazda RX-7
Bob Speakman (USA) DAY, SEB
Al Cosentino (USA) DAY (DND), SEB

Cotrone Racing Enterprises
– Chevrolet Corvette
Joe Cotrone (USA), SEB
Kal Showket (USA), SEB
Phil Currin (USA) SEB (DND)
Emory Donaldson (USA) SEB (DND)

Crevier Imports
– Ferrari 365 GTB/4, BMW M1
Pete Halsmer (USA) DAY
Joe Crevier (USA) DAY (DND), RIV, ELK
Al Unser, Jr. (USA) DAY (DND), RIV, ELK

Crossroads Coachwork
Centre/Motorfair Earls Court
– Porsche 911 RSR
Barry Robinson (GB) BH
Paul Edwards (GB) BH

The Cummings Marque
– Chevrolet Monza
Don Cummings (USA) SEB
Tom Juckette (USA) SEB

D.L. Performance Engineering
– Porsche 911 Carrera RSR
Doug Lutz (USA) DAY, SEB
Robin Boone (USA) DAY
Dave White (USA) DAY (DND)
Dave Panaccione (USA) SEB

DB Motorsport
– March 81S Ford Pinto
Allan Kayes (GB) BH
Robert Gibbs (GB) BH

David Deacon Racing
– BMW M1
Rudy Bartling (CDN) DAY, SEB, RIV (DND)
Mike Freberg (CDN) DAY, SEB, RIV (DND),
MOS
David Deacon (CDN) DAY, SEB, RIV, MOS

Mauricio DeNarvaez/ DeNarvaez
Enterprises – Porsche 935J
Mauricio DeNarvaez (CO) RIV, ELK
Bob Akin (USA) RIV
Skeeter McKitterick (USA) RIV
Derek Bell (GB) ELK

Pedro DeNarvaez
– Porsche 911 Carrera RSR
Honorato Espinosa (CO) DAY
Pedro DeNarvaez (CO) DAY
Jorge Cortes (CO) DAY

De Narvaez – Porsche 935J
Mauricio DeNarvaez (CO) MOS
Bob Garretson (USA) MOS

Dome Co Ltd – Dome Zero
RL 81 Ford Cosworth DFV
Chris Craft (GB) LM
Bob Evans (GB) LM

Dorset Racing Associates
– Lola T297 Ford Cosworth BDG,
De Cadenet Lola LM T380 Ford
Cosworth DFV/Alan Smith
Peter Clark (GB) SIL
Nick Mason (GB) SIL, NUR* (DNS)
Nick Faure (GB) SIL, LM
Tony Birchenhough (GB) NUR*
Brian Joscelyne (GB) NUR*
Vivian Candy (IRL) LM
Martin Birrane (GB) LM, BH
Roy Baker (GB) BH
Richard Jones (GB) BH (DND)
Leon Walger (ZA) BH

Douglas Dowden
– Porsche 911
Jerry Demele (USA) RIV
Terry Herman (USA) RIV

Downing/Maffucci Racing/Downing Atlanta – Mazda RX-7
Scott Hoerr (USA) DAY, SEB
Irv Hoerr (USA) DAY, SEB, RIV, ELK
Jim Downing (USA) DAY, SEB, RIV, ELK

Chris Doyle Racing – Mazda RX-7
Chris Doyle (USA) DAY, SEB
Hubert Phipps (USA) DAY, SEB (*DND*)
Robert Overby (USA) DAY

Drolsom Racing – Porsche 911 Carrera, Porsche 924 Carrera GTR
George Drolsom (USA) DAY, SEB
Rob Hoskins (USA) DAY, SEB
Bill Johnson (USA) DAY
Buzz Marcus (USA) SEB

Druckindustrie – TOJ SC205
Helmut Bross (D) NUR*
'Umberto Calvo' (Friedrich Glatz) (A) NUR*
Harald Brutschin (D) NUR* (*DND*)

Richard J. Dunham / Dunham Trucking – Mazda RX-7
Jack Dunham (USA) DAY, SEB, RIV
John Maffucci (USA) DAY
Stanton Barrett (USA) DAY (*DND*)
Tom Sheehy (USA) SEB
Luis Sereix (USA) SEB
Mike Meyer (USA) RIV (*DND*)

Dynasales – Chevrolet Corvette
John Carruso (USA) RIV, ELK
Phil Currin (USA) RIV, ELK

EMKA Productions – BMW M1, BMW M1 Gp5
(The team's name is a combination of O'Rourke's two daughters' Christian names, **EM**ma and **KA**theryne)
Derek Bell (GB) MZA, SIL, WG, BH
Steve O'Rourke (GB) MZA, SIL, LM, WG (*DND*)
Eddie Jordan (IRL) LM
David Hobbs (USA) LM
Chris Carft (GB) BH

Electramotive Inc. – Datsun 280ZX Turbo
Don Devendorf (USA) ELK   (IMAGE OF CAR/DRIVER)
Tony Adamowicz (USA) ELK

Electrodyne Inc. – Porsche 934
Chester Vincentz (USA) WG, MOS
Lance Van Every (USA) WG
John Wood (USA) WG
Derek Bell (GB) MOS

Eminence Racing Team – Porsche 924 Carrera GTR
Jacques Alméras (F) (LM)
Jean-Marie Alméras (F) (LM)

Scuderia Escalotte – Osella PA9 BMW
'Gimax' (Carlo Franchi) (I) MZA
Luigi Moreschi (I) MZA

Fantasy Racing – De Tomaso Pantera
Vic Manuelli (USA) RIV
Bruce Mallery (USA) RIV
Ron Woods (USA) RIV

Geoff Farmer – Lola T590 Ford Pinto
Jeremy Rossiter (GB) BH
Geoff Farmer (GB) BH

Fatcola – Porsche 911
Greg LaCava (USA) RIV
Claudia LaCava (USA) RIV (*DND*)

Bill Ferran – Porsche 911 Carrera RSR
Nort Northam (USA) SEB
Chiqui Soldevilla (USA) SEB

Firestone Tire & Rubber – Ford Mustang
John Morton (USA) DAY, SEB
Tom Klausler (USA) DAY, SEB

John Fitzpatrick Racing – Porsche 935 K3/80
John Fitzpatrick (GB) SEB, RIV, WG, MOS, ELK
Jim Busby (USA) SEB, RIV, WG, MOS, ELK

George Follmer – Toyota Celica, Toyota Celica
Mike Follmer (USA) ELK (*2nd car DND*)
Rameau Johnson (USA) ELK (*2nd car DND*)
George Follmer (USA) ELK (*drove 2nd car*)

Ford (GB) – Ford C100
Manfred Winkelhock (D) BH
Klaus Ludwig (D) BH

The Foreign Exchange – Porsche 911
John Higgins (USA) SEB
Chip Mead (USA) SEB
Bill Johnson (USA) SEB

Formel Rennsport Club, Zurich – Porsche 924 Carrera GTR, Lola T290 BMW
Peter Zbinden (CH) MZA, SIL, NUR*
Edi Kofel (CH) MZA, SIL, NUR*
Marco Vanoli (CH) SIL
Max Sigrist (CH)
Urs Neukomm (CH) NUR (DNS)*

Tom Frank – Chevrolet Camaro
Tom Frank (USA) WG
Dave Heinz (USA) WG

Werner Frank (see also Toyota Village) – Porsche 934
Rudy Bartling (CDN) ELK
Werner Frank (USA) ELK

Silvano Frisori – Osella PA8 Ford Cosworth
Silvano Frisori (I) MZA
Ruggero Parpinelli (I) MZA

GS Tuning – BMW M1 Sauber, Lancia Beta Montecarlo
Hans-Joachim Stuck (D) NUR*
Nelson Piquet (BR) NUR*
Piercarlo Ghinzani (I) NUR*
Hans Heyer (D) NUR*

G.T.P. International Racing – Chevron B31 Ford Cosworth, Chevron BT36 Ford Cosworth
Richard Jones (GB) SIL
Barrie Williams (GB) SIL
Axel Felder (D) NUR*
Michael Bitschnau (D) NUR* (*DND*)
Franz-Josef Bröhling (D) NUR* (*DND*)

Garcia Racing – Chevrolet Corvette
John Lino (USA) SEB
George Garcia (USA) SEB (*DND*)
Fernando Garcia (USA) SEB (*DND*)

Garretson Racing/Style Auto/Flying Tigers-Garretson Racing (see also Cooke Woods Racing/Garretson Enterprises) – Porsche 935 K3/80, Porsche 935 K3
Bob Garretson (USA) DAY, ELK, BH
Bobby Rahal (USA) DAY, BH
Brian Redman (GB) DAY
Tom Gloy (USA) ELK

Gassaway/Oftedahl – Chevrolet Camaro
Dave Heinz (USA) DAY
Chris Gleason (USA) DAY
Joe Cogbill (USA) DAY

Maurizio Gellini – Chevron B31 Ford Cosworth
Maurizio Gellini (I) MZA
Secondo Ridolfi (I) MZA (*DND*)

Gilden Koelsch – Opel Monza 3.0E
Herbert Herler (D) NUR*
Günter Filthaut (D) NUR*
Dieter Huenermann (D) NUR*

'Gimax' – Osella PA9 BMW
'Gimax' (Carlo Franchi) (I) ENN-PER
Luigi Moreschi (I) ENN-PER

Gabriele Gottifredi – Porsche 911 Carrera RSR
Gabriele Gottifredi (I) MZA
Giancarlo Galimberti (I) MZA
Giulio Rebai (I) MZA

Rolf Götz – Lola T296 BMW
Rolf Götz (D) SIL
Roland Binder (D) SIL

Jean-Philippe Grand – Lola T298 BMW
Jean-Philippe Grand (F) LM
Yves Courage (F) LM

Umberto Grano – BMW M1
Umberto Grano (I) MZA
Marco Vanoli (I) MZA

Bob Gregg Racing – Porsche 911 Carrera RSR
Bob Young (USA) DAY, SEB
Len Jones (USA) DAY, RIV
Bob Gregg (USA) DAY, SEB, RIV
Jo Varde (USA) SEB

Grid Team Lola/Banco Occidental/Ultramar/Team Lola (GB) – Lola T600 Ford Cosworth DFV
Guy Edwards (GB) MZA, NUR*, LM, PER
Emilio de Villota (ES) MZA, NUR*, LM, PER
Juan Fernandez (ES) LM

Group 44 – Triumph TR8
Bob Tullius (USA) SEB
Jim Adam (CDN) SEB
John Kelly (USA) SEB
Pat Bedard (USA) SEB

Jacques Guérin – Porsche 935
Jacques Guérin (F) SIL
Christian Bussi (F) SIL
Jean-Pierre Delaunay (F) SIL

HEP – Lola T492 Ford Pinto/Magnum
Hans Lundstrom (SWE) BH
Ulf Dahl (SWE) BH

H.S.M. Racing – Porsche 934
Mandy Gonzalez (PR) SEB
Bonky Fernandez (PR) SEB
Juan Cochesa (YV) SEB

Hacheney – Toyota Celica
Volker Strycek (D) NUR*
Bruno Schmitz-Moormann (D) NUR*
*Karl-Heinz Gürthler (D) (DNS) NUR**

Claude Haldi – Porsche 935/77A, Porsche 935 K3
Claude Haldi (CH) NUR*, LM, BH
Charles Mendez (USA) NUR*
Hervé Poulain (F) LM
Mark Thatcher (GB) LM
Rodrigo Téran (PA) BH

Hallet Motor Racing Circuit – Lancia Stratos HF
Anatoly Arutunoff (USA) SEB, WG
José Marina (USA) SEB, WG (*DND*)

Heidapel Racing – Ford Escort
Helmut Döring (D) NUR*
Bernhard Dransmann (D) NUR (DNS)*
Herbert Kummle (D) NUR* (DNS)
Bernhard Dransmann (D) NUR* (Drove second team car)
Dieter Gartmann (D) NUR*
Wilfried Vogt (D) NUR(DNS)*

Heimrath Racing – Porsche 935, Porsche 924 Carrera GTR
Ludwig Heimrath (CDN) DAY, SEB, WG, MOS
Ludwig Heimrath Jr (CDN) DAY, SEB, WG, MOS

Peter Herke – BMW 3.5 CSL
Peter Herke (USA) RIV
Dieter Schulz (D) RIV
Reinhard Riedel (USA) RIV

Herman & Miller Porsche-Audi – Porsche 924 Carrera GTR
Paul Miller (USA) DAY, WG
Kenper Miller (USA) WG (*DND*)
Pat Bedard (USA) DAY
Skeeter McKitterick (USA) DAY

Hi-Fi Express – Porsche 911
Rick Bye (CDN) MOS
Uli Bieri (CDN) MOS (*DND*)

Kurt Hild – TOJ SC306
Kurt Hild (D) NUR*
Ralf Walter (D) NUR* (*DND*)

Marty Hinze Racing – Porsche 935 K3
Marty Hinze (USA) SEB, WG
Milt Minter (USA) SEB
Bill Whittington (USA) SEB
Dale Whittington (USA) WG
Preston Henn (USA) WG

Fritz Hochreuter – Porsche 911 Carrera RSR
Fritz Hochreuter (CDN) SEB, MOS
Rainer Brezinka (CDN) SEB
Gary Hirsch (CDN) SEB
Rudy Bartling (CDN) MOS
Norm Ridgely (CDN) MOS

Holbert Racing – Porsche 924 GTR
Al Holbert (USA) DAY
Rick Mears (USA) DAY
Doc Bundy (USA) DAY

Dave Horchler Emerald Racing – Chevrolet Corvette
Dave Horchler (USA) ELK
Don Yenko (USA) ELK (*DND*)
Jerry Thompson (USA) ELK (*DND*)

Arthur Hough Pressings/Ark Racing – Lotus Elan
John Evans (GB) BH
Max Payne (GB) BH

Howey Farms – Chevrolet Camaro
Clark Howey (USA) DAY
Tracy Wolf (USA) DAY
Dale Koch (USA) DAY

George Hulse – Porsche 911
George Hulse (USA) WG
Bob Speakman (USA) WG (*DND*)

Italsponsor – Lola T286 Ford Cosworth DFV
Renzo Zorzi (I) MZA
Federico D'Amore (I) MZA (*DND*)

Interscope Racing – Porsche 935 K3/80
Ted Field (USA) DAY, SEB, RIV, WG, MOS, ELK
Danny Ongais (USA) DAY, SEB, RIV
Milt Minter (USA) DAY
Bill Whittington (USA) WG, MOS, ELK

Charles Ivey Racing – Porsche 935 K3
John Cooper (GB) MZA, SIL, NUR*, BH
Dudley Wood (GB) MZA, SIL, NUR*, BH

J.L.P. Racing – Porsche 935 JLP-2, Porsche 935 JLP-3
John Paul (USA) DAY, SEB, RIV, WG, MOS (*DND*), ELK
John Paul Jr (USA) DAY, SEB, RIV, WG, MOS, ELK
Gordon Smiley (USA) DAY (*DND*)
Carlos Moran (ES) RIV
Karen Erstad (USA) RIV

Jägermeister – BMW 320i
Walter Nussbaumer (CH) NUR*
Anton Fischhaber (D) NUR*
Mario Ketterer (D) NUR*
Jörg Denzel (D) NUR*
Eckhard Schimpf (D) NUR* (*DND*)

Janspeed/ADA Engineering – Triumph TR8
William Wykeham (GB) BH
Ian Harrower (GB) BH

Bruce R. Jennings – Porsche 911
Bruce Jennings (USA) SEB
Bill Bean (USA) SEB
Tom Ashby (USA) SEB

Joest Racing – Porsche 935 J, Porsche 908/80
Volkert Merl (D) DAY, SIL (*DND*), NUR*
Jochen Mass (D) DAY, SIL, NUR*
Reinhold Joest (D) DAY, SIL (*DND*), NUR*, LM
Jürgen Barth (D) NUR*
Mauricio DeNarvaez (CO) LM
Kenper Miller (USA) LM
Günter Steckkönig (D) LM
Klaus Niedzwiedz (D) LM
Dale Whittington (USA) LM

Jolly Club Italia – Lancia Beta Montecarlo Turbo, Ferrari 308 GTB Turbo
Martino Finotto (I) DAY (*Also shared the Ferrari 308 GTB Turbo with Facetti but this broke down before he could drive it*), SIL, LM, ENN-PER (*DND*)
Carlo Facetti (I) DAY (*Also drove the Ferrari 308 GTB Turbo*), SIL, ENN-PER
Emanuele Pirro (I) DAY
Giorgio Pianta (I) MZA, NUR*, LM
Giorgio Schön (I) MZA, NUR*, LM
Beppe Gabbiani (I) MZA
Siegfried Müller, Jr (D), NUR*

David A. Jones – Chevrolet Camaro
David Jones (USA) WG
Ted Sullivan (USA) WG (*DND*)

Zvonimir Jovanovic – Porsche 911
Zvonimir Jovanovic (USA) RIV
Carl Wong (USA) RIV

KMS Research – Porsche 935
Jamey Mazzotta (USA) RIV
Steve Earl (USA) RIV

KWS Motorsport – Ford Escort RS
Herbert Asselborn (D) NUR*
Hartmut Bauer (D) NUR* (*DND*)
Richard Jones (GB) NUR* (*DND*)

Jürgen Kannacher – Porsche 930
Helmut Gall (D) NUR*
Wolfgang Hansen (D) NUR*
Karl-Heinz Hauwarth (D) NUR*

Kannacher GT Racing – Porsche 930
Franz-Richard Friebel (D)
Karl-Josef Römer (D)
Matthias Lörper (D) NUR* (DNS)

Kegel Enterprises – Porsche 911 SC
Bill Koll (USA) DAY, SEB, RIV
Jeff Kline (USA) DAY, SEB, RIV
Rob McFarlin (USA) DAY

Philip Keirn – Chevrolet Corvette
Philip Keirn (USA) DAY
Gail Engle (USA) DAY
Bard Boand (USA) DAY

Kelly Girl Services Limited – Tiga SC80 Ford Pinto
Divina Galica (GB) BH
Tim Lee-Davy (GB) BH

Kemitex – Tiga SC80 Ford Pinto
Adrian Hall (GB) BH
Robert Parker (GB) BH
Mike Kimpton (GB) BH

Chuck Kendall/Kendall Racing – Porsche 911 Carrera RSR, BMW M1
Pete Smith (USA) DAY, SEB, RIV, ELK
Chuck Kendall (USA) DAY, SEB, ELK
Steve Earle (USA) DAY
Dennis Aase (USA) SEB, RIV, ELK
Alan Johnson (USA) RIV

Kent Racing – Mazda RX-7
Lee Mueller (USA) DAY, SEB, RIV, MOS, ELK
Kathy Rude (USA) DAY, SEB, RIV
Philippe Martin (B) DAY
Walt Bohren (USA) SEB, RIV, MOS, ELK
Divina Galica (GB) SEB, RIV

Kirby-Hitchcock Racing – Porsche 911 Carrera RSR
Siegfried Brunn (D) DAY
Robert Kirby (USA) DAY
John Hotchkis (USA) DAY

Kiron Camera Lenses – Tiga SC79 Ford Pinto
Chris Alford (GB) BH
John Walker (GB) BH
Roger Woodward (GB) BH

Robert Kivela – Chevrolet Corvette
Robert Kivela (USA) ELK
Ray Irwin (USA) ELK

Kurt König – BMW M1
Kurt König (D) NUR*
Peter Oberndorfer (D) NUR*

Dale Kreider Racing – Chevrolet Corvette
Dale Kreider (USA) ELK
Bill Nelson (USA) ELK

Kremer Racing (see also Porsche Kremer Racing) – Porsche 935 K3/80, Porsche 917 K/81,
John Fitzpatrick (GB) DAY
Jim Busby (USA) DAY
Bob Wollek (F) DAY, LM
Xavier Lapeyre (F) LM
Guy Chasseuil (F) LM

Kenneth LaGrow/Jack Holley – Chevrolet Camaro
Kenneth LaGrow (USA) SEB
Jack Turner (USA) SEB

Stephen Lax Racing – Porsche 911
Stephen Lax (CDN) WG, MOS
Herman Lausberg (CDN) WG (DND), MOS
Peter Moennick (CDN) MOS

Jean-Marie Lemerle – Lola T298 BMW
Max Cohen-Olivar (MA) LM
Jean-Marie Lemerle (F) LM
Alain Levié (F) LM

Jason Len – Chevrolet Corvette C3
Fred Markof (USA) RIV
Jason Len (USA) RIV (DND)

Levi's Team Highball – AMC Spirit AMX
Dennis Shaw (USA) DAY
Steve Whitman (USA) DAY
Les Blackburn (GB) DAY

Loud Car Racing – Mazda RX-7
Jim Mullen (USA) SEB, RIV, WG
Michael Zimicki (USA) SEB
Rick Knoop (USA) RIV
Walt Bohren (USA) WG

Lubrifilm Racing – Lancia Beta Montecarlo Turbo
Beppe Gabbiani (I) SIL
Giorgio Schön (I) SIL
Giorgio Pianta (I) SIL

MFG Valvoline Racing – Porsche 935
Peter Hähnlein (D)
Wolf-Dieter Feuerlein (D)

Mac's Bar Spec./Kend Co. – Chevrolet Camaro
Nort Northam (USA) DAY
Ed Kuhel (USA) DAY
Dick Neland (USA) DAY

Mandeville Racing Enterprises – Mazda RX-7
Roger Mandeville (USA) DAY, SEB, RIV, ELK
Amos Johnson (USA) DAY, SEB, RIV, ELK
Diego Febles (PR) DAY

Helmut Marko – BMW M1
Christian Danner (D) LM
Leopold von Bayern (D) LM
Peter Oberndorfer (D) LM

Martini Lancia Racing/Martini Racing – Lancia Beta Montecarlo Turbo
Riccardo Patrese (I) DAY, MZA, SIL, NUR*, LM, WG
Henri Pescarolo (F) DAY, NUR*, WG
Hans Heyer (D) DAY, LM
Michele Alboreto (I) DAY, LM, WG
Piercarlo Ghinzani (I) DAY, MZA, SIL (DND), LM, WG
Beppe Gabbiani (I) DAY
Andrea de Cesaris (I) MZA, SIL, NUR, WG
Eddie Cheever (USA) MZA (DND), SIL, NUR*, LM
Carlo Facetti (I) LM
Beppe Gabbiani (I) LM, WG
Emanuele Pirro (I) LM

Mayen Automobil Cub – Porsche 930
Armin Siefener (D) NUR*
Bernd Schiller (D) NUR*

Mazdaspeed – Mazda RX-7 253i (Mooncraft)
Youjirou Terada (J) SIL, LM
Win Percy (GB) SIL, LM (DND)
Tom Walkinsaw (GB) LM
Pete Lovett (GB) LM
Tetsu Ikuzawa (JPN) LM (DND)
Hiroshi Fushida (J) LM (DND)

McDonalds Houses – Datsun 240Z
Casey Mollett (USA) RIV
Frank Honsowetz (USA) RIV

Meldeau Tire Stores – Chevrolet Camaro
Bill Mcdill (USA) SEB
Robert Whitaker (USA) SEB

David Mercer – Vogue SP2 (Chevron) Ford Cosworth BDG
David Mercer (GB) SIL, NUR*, BH
Mike Chittenden (GB) SIL, NUR* (DND), BH

Mich Auto Tuning – Opel Ascona
Karl-Heinz Schäfer (D) NUR*
Lothar Mich (D) NUR*(DNS)

Modena Engineering – Ferrari 512 BB/LM
Richard Bond (GB) SIL
Bobby Bell (GB) SIL
Steve Griswold (USA) SIL

Momo/Penthouse/Momo Accessories – Porsche 935 J, Porsche 935/78-81
Gianpiero Moretti (I) DAY, SEB, RIV, WG, MOS, ELK
Charles Mendez (USA) DAY, SEB
Mauricio DeNarvaez (CO) DAY, SEB
Jochen Mass (D) RIV
Bobby Rahal (USA) WG, MOS, ELK

Montura Racing/Florida Crystals – Porsche 911 Carrera RSR, BMW M1
Tony Garcia (USA) DAY, SEB, RIV, MOS, ELK
Albert Naon (USA) DAY, SEB, RIV, MOS, ELK
Luis Sereix (USA) DAY
Hiram Cruz (USA) SEB, RIV, MOS, ELK

Miguel Morejon (see also T & R Racing) – Porsche 911 Carrera RSR
Fred Flaquer (USA) SEB
Joe Gonzalez (USA) SEB
Angelo Dominguez (USA) SEB

John Morgan – Datsun Z (No mention or record of this being a 240Z or 260Z)
John Morgan (USA) ELK
Charles Moseley (USA) ELK

Morgan Performance Group – Datsun 280ZX
Charles Morgan (USA) ELK
Jim Miller (USA) ELK

Jim Moyer – Chevrolet Corvette
Jim Moyer (USA) ELK
Phil Pate (USA) ELK

N.A.R.T. – Ferrari 512 BB/LM
Alain Cudini (F) LM
Philippe Gurdjian (F) LM
John Morton (USA) LM

NTS Racing – Datsun 280ZX Turbo
Sam Posey (USA) DAY, SEB, RIV
Fred Stiff (USA) DAY, SEB, RIV

Piero Nappi – Osella PA8 BMW
Piero Nappi (I) MZA
Pasquale Vecchione

Nardi Motors – Porsche 911 Carrera
Sergio Nardi (USA) RIV
Angel Nardi (USA) RIV
Steve Michaelson (USA) RIV

Germano Nataloni – Lancia Beta Montecarlo Turbo
Germano Nataloni (I) MZA
Gianfranco Ricci (I) MZA

ORECA(ORganisation Exploitation Compétition Automobile) – BMW M1 (Gp 5)
Dieter Quester (A) MZA
Teo Fabi (I) MZA

Osella Squadra Corse – Osella PA9 BMW
Lella Lombardi (I) MZA, SIL, PER, BH
Giorgio Francia (I) MZA, SIL, PER, BH

Ours & Hours Racing – Porsche 911
Jack Swanson (USA) SEB
Tom Cripe (USA) SEB
Van McDonald (USA) SEB

Robert Overby (see also Personalized Autohaus) – Chevrolet Corvette
Robert Overby (USA) ELK
Herb Forrest (USA) ELK

Angelo Pallavicini – Porsche 934
Angelo Pallavicini (CH) DAY, SEB, SIL, ENN-PER, BH
John Sheldon (GB) DAY
Neil Crang (AUS) DAY, SEB, SIL, BH
Dan Simpson (USA) SEB
Edgar Dören (D) ENN-PER

Pennzoil of Puerto Rico – Porsche 911
Mike Ramirez (PR) SEB
Luis Gordillo (PR) SEB
Manuel Villa (PR) SEB

Performance Marine Racing – Chevrolet Camaro
Jimmy Tumbleston (USA) SEB
Bobby Dumont (USA) SEB
Ford Smith (USA) SEB

"Perrier" – Osella PA6 Ford Cosworth
"Perrier" (I) MZA
Vito Veninata (I) MZA (DND)
Giuseppe Iacono (I) MZA (DND)

Thierry Perrier – Porsche 934
Valentin Bertapelle (F) LM
Thierry Perrier (F) LM
Bernard Salam (F) (LM)

Personalized Autohaus – Porsche 914/6, Porsche 914/4
Jeff Scott (USA) DAY, RIV, ELK
David Goodell (USA) DAY
Volker Bruckmann (USA) DAY
Wayne Baker (USA) DAY, SEB, RIV, MOS (drove both the 914/6 and the 914/4), ELK
Dan Gilliland (USA) DAY, SEB
Frank Harmstad (USA) DAY
Robert Overby (USA) SEB, RIV, MOS (drove both the 914/6 and the 914/4), ELK
David Finch (USA) ELK (DND)

Simon Phillips – Ferrari 512 BB/LM
Mike Salmon (GB) SIL, LM
Simon Phillips (GB) SIL, LM
Steve Earle (USA) SIL, LM

Giuseppe Piazzi – Fiat X1/9 (Dallara)
Giuseppe Piazzi (I) MZA
Leandro La Vecchia (I) MZA (DND)
Sandro Cinotti (I) MZA (DND)

Pioneer Racing – Opel Ascona, Opel Kadett
Wolfgang Offermann (D) NUR*
Wolf-Dieter Mantzel (D) NUR*
Jörg Helmig (D) NUR*
Michael Dagenhardt (D) NUR*
Wolfgang Offermann (D), NUR* (DNS)
Heinrich Haag (D), NUR* (DNS)
Christoph Esser (D) NUR*
Klaus Müller (D) NUR*
Christoph Bähr (D) NUR* (DND)

Porsche Kremer Racing (see also Kremer Racing) – Porsche 935 K3/81, Porsche 917 K/81
Ted Field (USA) LM
Bill Whittington (USA) LM
Don Whittington (USA) LM
Bob Wollek (F) BH
Henri Pescarolo (F) BH (DND)

Porsche System – Porsche 936/81, Porsche 944 LM, Porsche 924 Carrera GTR
Jacky Ickx (B) LM
Derek Bell (GB) LM
Jochen Mass (D) LM
Vern Schuppan (AUS) LM
Hurley Haywood (USA) LM
Jürgen Barth (D) LM
Walter Röhrl (D) LM
Manfred Schurti (FL) LM
Andy Rouse (GB) LM

Charles Pozzi S.A. – Ferrari 512 BB/LM
Jean-Claude Andruet (F) LM
Claude Ballot-Léna (F) LM

Prancing Horse Farms Racing – Ferrari 512 BB/LM
Tony Adamowicz (USA) DAY
Rick Knoop (USA) DAY

RG Racing – Lola T592 Ford Pinto
John Brindley (GB) BH
John L. Webb (GB) BH

RSR Associates – Porsche 911 Carrera RSR
Tom Alan Marx (USA) RIV
Dennis Lanfre (USA) RIV
Bill Follmer (USA) RIV

Rallye Gemeinschaft Ulm – Lola T297 BMW, TOJ SC206
Eugen Grupp (D) NUR*
Hans Forster (D) NUR* (DNS)
Ralf Walter (D) NUR* (DNS)
Hans Forster (D) NUR*
Eugen Grupp (D) NUR* (DND)

Raytown Datsun/Raytown Don Preston – Datsun 280ZX
Dick Davenport (USA) DAY, RIV, MOS, ELK
Frank Carney (USA) DAY, RIV, MOS, ELK
Rameau Johnson (USA) DAY

Red Lobster Racing – BMW M1
Kenper Miller (USA) DAY, SEB, RIV, MOS, ELK
Dave Cowart (USA) DAY, SEB, RIV, MOS, ELK
Ricardo Londono (CO) DAY

Jack Refenning – Porsche 934
Jack Refenning (USA) SEB
Ren Tilton (USA) SEB
Peter Welter (USA) SEB

Renault USA – Renault Le Car Turbo
Patrick Jacquemart (USA) RIV
James Brolin (USA) RIV (DND)

Ecurie Renard-Delmas – Renard-Delmas D1 Simca
Louis Descartes (F) LM
Hervé Bayard (F) LM
Bernard Preschey (F) LM (DNS)

Rennod Racing – Ferrari 512 BB/LM
Jean-Paul Libert (B) LM
Jean Xhenceval (B) LM
Pierre Dieudonné (B) LM

Rheydter Club – BMW 320i
Walter Preusser (D) NUR*
Peter Sieben (D) NUR* (DND)
Friedhelm Coenen (D) NUR* (DND)

**Roe/Selby Racing
– Porsche 911 Carrera RSR**
Tim Selby (USA) SEB, WG, ELK
Earl Roe (USA) SEB, WG, ELK

Pepe Romero – Porsche 935 M16
Pepe Romero (USA) DAY, MOS, ELK
Mandy Gonzalez (PR) DAY
Luis Mendez (DR) DAY
Diego Febles (PR) MOS
Jo Varde (USA) ELK

**Jean Rondeau – Rondeau M379 C
Ford Cosworth/Mader DFV, Rondeau
M379 C Ford Cosworth DFL/Dick
Samuel, Rondeau M379 C Ford
Cosworth DFL/Heidi Mader**
Jacky Haran (F) LM
Jean-Louis Schlesser (F) LM
Philippe Streiff (F) LM
François Migault (F) LM
Gordon Spice (GB) LM
Jean Rondeau (F) LM
Jean-Pierre Jaussaud (F) LM
Henri Pescarolo (F) LM
Patrick Tambay (F) LM
Jean Ragnotti (F) LM
Jean-Louis Lafosse (F) LM (fatal accident
lap 25)

Russell Porsche – Porsche 911 Carrera
Jean Kjoller (USA) MOS
Jay Kjoller (USA) MOS

Rynone Industries – Chevrolet Corvette
David Kicak (USA) WG
Thomas Rynone (USA) WG (DND)

John Samson – Alfa Romeo GTV
John Samson (USA) RIV
Bill Kohl (USA) RIV

Sanyo/Russ Boy – Chevrolet Corvette
John Carusso (USA) SEB
Russ Boy (USA) SEB
Rex Ramsey (USA) SEB

Sauber AG – BMW M1 Sauber
Marc Surer (CH) NUR*
Dieter Quester (A) NUR*

Donna Schons – Pontiac Firebird
Ron Esau (USA) RIV
S.B. Fritz (USA) RIV
Vince Giamformaggio (USA) RIV (DND)

Scorpio Racing – Porsche 935 M16
'Jamsal' (Enrique Molins) (ES), DAY,
SEB, RIV, MOS
Eduardo Barrientos (ES), DAY, SEB, RIV
Carlos Gonzalez (ES), DAY
Guillermo Valiente (ES) SEB
Eduardo Galdamez (ES) MOS

George R. Shafer – Chevrolet Camaro
George Shafer (USA) SEB
Craig Shafer (USA) SEB
Al Crookston (USA) SEB

**Sharkskin Racing
– Chevrolet Corvette**
C.C. Canada (USA) SEB
Earle Moffitt (USA) SEB (DND)
Harry Cochran (USA) (DND)

**Bob Sharp Racing
– Datsun 280ZX Turbo**
Paul Newman (USA) RIV
Masahiro Hasemi (JPN) RIV (DND)

**Southard Motor Racing
– Porsche 911 Carrera**
Steve Southard (USA) DAY, WG
Jay Kjoller (USA) DAY
Jean Kjoller (USA) DAY
Mark Altman (USA) WG
Gary Altman (USA) WG

**Morris Stapleton Motors
– Morgan Plus 8**
Bruce Stapleton (GB) SIL
Richard Down (GB) SIL
William Wykeham (GB) SIL

**Stratagraph
– Chevrolet Camaro**
Terry Labonte (USA) DAY, SEB
David Pearson (USA) DAY
Billy Hagan (USA) DAY (DND), SEB, LM
(DND), WG, ELK
Cale Yarborough (USA) LM
Bill Cooper (USA) LM (DND), WG
Bob Mitchell (USA) ELK

**Werner Struck
– Ford Escort RS 2000**
Werner Struck (D)
Kennerth Persson (S) NUR* (DND)
Olaf Manthey (D) NUR* (DND)

**Sunrise Auto Parts
– Chevrolet Camaro**
Jeff Loving (USA) SEB
Ralph Noseda (USA) SEB (DND)
Richard Small (USA) SEB (DND)

**Scuderia Supercar Bellancauto
– Ferrari 512 BB/LM**
Maurizio Flammini (I) MZA, LM
Spartaco Dini (I) MZA
Fabrizio Violati (I) MZA, LM, ENN-PER
Duilio Truffo (I) LM, ENN-PER

**T & R Racing
– Porsche 911 Carrera RSR**
Tico Almeida (USA) DAY, SEB, RIV
Rene Rodriguez (USA) DAY, SEB, RIV, ELK
Miguel Morejon (C) DAY, SEB
Ernesto Soto (YV) ELK

**Ian Taylor Racing Limited
– Tiga SC81 Ford Pinto/Nelson**
Mike Taylor (GB) BH
Richard Eyre (GB) BH
Ian Taylor (GB) BH
John Sheldon (GB) BH

**Janis Taylor
– Chevron GTP Buick**
Del Russo Taylor (USA) MOS, ELK
Janis Taylor (USA) MOS (DND), ELK (DND)

**Team Castrol Juergen Rassmussen
– BMW 320i**
Lars-Viggo Jensen (DK) SIL
Jens Winther (DK) SIL

**Vince Thompson
– Chevron GTP Alfa Romeo,
Alfa Romeo GTV**
Del Russo Taylor (USA) SEB
Rex Ramsey (USA) SEB
Janis Taylor (USA) SEB
Pat Godard (USA) SEB (DND)
Carol Cone (USA) SEB (DND)

**Thunderbird Swap Shop/ Preston
Henn – Porsche 935 K3/80,
Porsche 935 K3/80**
(NB Sometimes entrant is listed as
a team or owner name, also drivers
shared other cars in team and in some
instances did not drive their second car
due to early retirements: this applies

to various other American entrants
in period)
Preston Henn (USA) DAY, SEB, RIV, SIL,
NUR* (DNS), LM, MOS
Bob Bondurant (USA) DAY
Dale Whittington (USA) DAY (DND)
John Gunn (USA) SEB
Gary Belcher (USA) SEB, RIV (DND)
Marty Hinze (USA) RIV
Adrian Yates-Smith (GB) SIL, NUR* (DNS)
Bob Wollek (F) NUR*
Michael Chandler (USA) LM
Marcel Mignot (F) LM
Edgar Dören (D) MOS, ELK, BH
Danny Sullivan (USA) ELK
Desiré Wilson (ZA) BH

Toyota Village – Porsche 934
Werner Frank (USA) WG
Rudy Bartling (CDN) WG (DND)

Trinity Racing – Mazda RX-7
Bob Bergstrom (USA) DAY, SEB
John Casey (USA) DAY, SEB, RIV, ELK
Jim Cook (USA) DAY, SEB, RIV, ELK
Tom Winters (USA) DAY, SEB, RIV
Steve Dietrich (USA) DAY, SEB, RIV
Carter Alsop (USA) DAY
Hugh McDonough (USA) SEB

**Tuffe-Kote Dinol Racing
– Porsche 935 L1**
Mike Wilds (GB) SIL, NUR*, LM, BH
Jan Lundgardh (SWE) SIL, NUR*, LM, BH
Axel Plankenhorn (D) NUR* (DNS), LM
'Umberto Calvo' (Friedrich Glatz) (A) BH

**URD-Rennwagenbau-Grafenau
– URD 679 BMW**
Robin Smith (GB) BH
Joachim Winkelhock (D) BH (DND)

**USA Racing
– Chevrolet Corvette**
Richard Valentine (USA) SEB
Maurice Carter (CDN) SEB

**Valvoline Deutschland
– Audi 80, Porsche 935/77A**
Wolf-Dieter Feuerlein (D) NUR*
Heinz Schaaf (D) NUR*
Hagen Arlt (D) NUR* (DNS)
Franz Gschwender (D) NUR*
Wolf-Dieter Feuerlein (D) NUR* (DND)

**Van Every Racing
– Porsche 911 Carrera RSR**
Lance Van Every (USA) DAY, SEB
Ash Tisdelle (USA) DAY, SEB (DND)
Rusty Bond (USA) DAY
Richard Bond (GB) SEB (DND)

**Vegla Racing Team/Vegla Racing Team
- Aachen – Porsche 935 J**
Dieter Schornstein (D) MZA, SIL, NUR*,
LM, BH
Harald Grohs (D) MZA, SIL, NUR*, LM, BH
Walter Röhrl (D) SIL, NUR*
Götz von Tschirnhaus (D) LM

Veltmann Opel – Opel Ascona
Werner Prinz (D) NUR*
Wolfgang Walter (D) NUR*

**Vette Brakes
– Chevrolet Corvette**
Al Levenson (USA) SEB
Elizabeth Kleinschmidt (USA) SEB (DND)
Charles Kleinschmidt (USA) SEB (DND)

**Weigel Renntechnik
– Lola T296 BMW**
Roland Binder (D) NUR*
Rolf Götz (D) NUR*

**Welter/Meunier A.R.E.M. – WM-Peugeot
P79/80, WM Peugeot P81**
Denis Morin (F) LM
Charles Mendez (USA) LM
Xavier Mathiot (F) LM
Guy Fréquelin (F) LM
Roger Dorchy (F) LM
Max Mamers (F) LM
Jean-Daniel Raulet (F) LM
Michel Pignard (F) LM
Thierry Boutsen (B) LM
Michel Pignard (F) LM (DND)
Serge Saulnier (F) LM (DND)

**Wera Meissberg Team
– Porsche 935 K3, BMW M1**
Edgar Dören (D) SIL
Jürgen Lässig (D) SIL, NUR* (DND),
Herrman-Peter Duge (D) NUR*

**Weralit Racing Team
– Porsche 935 K3**
Edgar Dören (D) MZA, NUR*, LM
Jürgen Lässig (D) MZA, NUR*, LM (DND)
Gerhard Holup (D) MZA, LM

**Whitehall Capital Promotions Ltd
– Porsche 924 Carrera GTR**
Tom Winters (USA) WG, MOS, ELK
Bob Bergstrom (USA) WG, MOS, ELK

**Whittington Brothers Racing
– Porsche 935 K3**
Don Whittington (USA) DAY, SEB
Bill Whittington (USA) DAY, SEB
Dale Whittington (USA) DAY, SEB

Tracy Wolf – Chevrolet Camaro
Clark Howey (USA) ELK
Dave Koch (USA) ELK

Richard Woodbury – Porsche 911
Richard Woodbury (USA) RIV
Bruce Campbell (USA) RIV

**Wuerth-Lubrifilm Team Sauber
– BMW M1 Gp5**
Dieter Quester (A) LM
Marc Surer (CH) LM
David Deacon (CDN) LM

Yale Stapler – BMW 2002
Michael Middelhaufe (D) NUR*
Heiner Müller (D), NUR* (DNS)
Rainer Zweibäumer (D) NUR* (DNS)
Kurt Hens (D) NUR*
Peter Biewald (D) NUR* (DND)

Z&W Enterprises – Mazda RX-7
Dirk Vermeersch (B) DAY, SEB
Eddy Joosen (B) DAY, SEB
Jean-Paul Libert (B) DAY, SEB, MZA
M.L. Speer (USA) SEB, MZA, SIL
Pierre Honegger (USA) SEB, MZA, NUR*
(DNS), MOS (DND)
Pierre Dieudonné (B) SEB
Ray Radcliff (USA) SIL, NUR*
Fred Stiff (USA) SIL, NUR*, MOS
Sam Posey (USA) MOS (DND)

Zotz Garage – Porsche 914/6
Harro Zitza (USA) DAY
Doug Zitza (USA) DAY
Ara Dube (USA) DAY

RESULTS

**Daytona 24 Hours, 1 February, USA
Started 69, finished 27**
1st Garretson/Rahal/Redman Porsche
935 K3/80
2nd Akin/Siebert/Bell Porsche 935 K3
3rd Koll/Kline/McFarlin Porsche 911 SC

**Sebring 12 Hours, 21 March, USA
Started 78 , finished 33**
1st Hayward/Holbert/Leven
Porsche 935 K3/80
2nd Woods/Kent Cooke/McKitterick
Porsche 935 K3
3rd Hinze/Minter/Whittington
Porsche 935 K3

**Mugello 6 Hours, 12 April, Italy
Started 21, finished 14**
1st Francia/Lombardi Osella PA9 BMW
2nd Cooper/Wood Porsche 935 K3
3rd Fischhaber/Ketterer BMW 320i

**Monza 1000km, 26 April, Italy
Started 32, finished 14**
1st Dören/Lässig/Holup Porsche 935 K3
2nd Lombardi/Francia Osella PA9 BMW
3rd "Gimax"/Moreschi Osella PA9 BMW

**Riverside 6 Hours, 26 April, USA
Started 58, finished 32**
1st Fitzpatrick/Busby Porsche 935 K3/80
2nd Paul Jr./Paul Sr Porsche 935 JLP-3
3rd Rahal/Redman Porsche 935 K3/80

**Silverstone 6 Hours, 10 May, GB
Started 32, finished 17**
1st Röhrl/Grohs/Schornstein Porsche 935 J
2nd Bell/O'Rourke BMW M1
3rd Brunn/Jordan Porsche 908/3 TC

**Nürburgring 1000km, 24 May, Germany
Started 67, finished 47
(Race stopped at 17 laps after a fatal
accident, fire and circuit damage)***
1st Stuck/Piquet BMW M1 Sauber
2nd Mass/Jöst Porsche 908/80 Turbo
3rd Wollek/Henn*/Yates-Smith* Porsche
935 K3 *DND

**Le Mans 24 Hours, 14 June, France
Started 55, finished 20**
1st Ickx/Bell Porsche 936/81
2nd Haran/Schlesser/Streiff Rondeau M379
C Ford Cosworth DFV
3rd Migault/Spice Rondeau M379 C Ford
Cosworth DFV

**Pergusa 6 Hours, 28 June, Italy
Started 9, finished 7**
1st de Villota/Edwards Lola T600 Ford
Cosworth DFV
2nd Francia/Lombardi Osella PA9 BMW
3rd 'Gimax' (Franchi)/Moreschi Osella
PA9 BMW

**Watkins Glen 6 Hours, 12 July, USA
Started 30, finished 10**
1st Patrese/Alboreto Lancia Beta Montecarlo
2nd de Cesaris/Pescarolo Lancia Beta
Montecarlo
3rd Mears/Garretson/Rutherford Porsche
935 K3

**Mosport 6 Hours, 16 August, Canada
Started 33, finished 20**
1st Stommelen/Grohs Porsche 935 M16
2nd Redman/Wietzes Lola T600 Chevrolet
3rd Field/Whittington Porsche 935 K3/80

**Road America 500 Miles, 23 August,
USA. Started 50, finished 27**
1st Stommelen/Grohs Porsche 935 M16
2nd Redman/Posey Lola T600 Chevrolet
3rd Cord/Adams Lola T600 Chevrolet

**Brands Hatch 1000km 27 September,
GB. Started 32, finished 21**
1st Edwards/de Villota Lola T600 Ford
Cosworth DFV
2nd Rahal/Garretson Porsche 935 K3
3rd Bell/Craft BMW M1

1982

MORE CHANGE AS
IF IT WERE NEEDED

The relative complication of the previous regulatory diktats was continued albeit in a slightly more cohesive fashion.

There were two championships running side by side, the World Endurance Championship for Makes (Group C) and the World Endurance Championship for Drivers, which included all categories including Group 4, 5 and 6.

This last was only for the drivers, not the cars. There was also Group A, B and N, which were for production cars, A being for modified vehicles, B for more radical and N for warmed-up showroom models. The B class did not thrive and would be abandoned.

Additionally, the International Motor Sports Association (IMSA), the creation of John Bishop in the USA, had a different set of rules and regulations that remained separate from FISA, but these were in evidence at some European venues.

The result was a plethora of new cars from Porsche, Ford, Lola, Rondeau, WM Peugeot, Sauber, March, Lancia, March, Nimrod Aston Martin and others. In Porsche's case it was a return to more than just Le Mans as they had done in the late 1970s, beginning at the May Silverstone 1000km with their new 956. They finished 2nd here, but the new fuel regulations proved to be very restrictive and they had to cruise home, allowing Lancia to win.

They then missed the Nürburgring 1000km and reappeared at Le Mans to finish 1st, 2nd and 3rd, followed by a 1/2 at Spa (missing out Mugello) and also victory at Fuji and Brands Hatch. Thus Porsche won the Endurance series from Rondeau and the Drivers' Championship (Jacky Ickx) from Lancia (Riccardo Patrese).

Of the others Rondeau won at Monza (their last outright victory in the FIA series) and Lancia at Silverstone, Nürburgring and Mugello. As noted elsewhere, Lancia had taken advantage of a rule which allowed them to enter the Drivers' Championship rather than the Makes Championship to race a Group-6 car (now banned otherwise) with a minimum weight of 640kg (see fourth Monza caption). The two American IMSA venues at Daytona and Sebring were won by the John Paul Porsche 935.

The remaining competitors were really fillers. The Saubers were not quite fast enough or reliable enough, the March 82G looked good in the USA but in Europe it was mediocre, the Lola T610 was unreliable and the Nimrod Astons very large and unlucky.

Sadly, the Ford C100s, which had been re-engineered following Len Bailey's departure at the end of 1981, turned out to be duds. They were very fast but the Ford Cosworth DFL engines were prone to excessive vibration and the cars literally shook themselves to pieces. The project was abandoned in March 1983.

Meanwhile the occupants of FISA decided to impose a punitive fuel-consumption formula that would too often result in cars/drivers losing a race. This was a bureaucratic masterpiece of classic proportions, which the Americans wanted nothing to do with. Instead they based their regulatory diktats on the GTP equivalence of power and weight. Thus Daytona and Sebring, long-time members of the FIA endurance races passed to IMSA.

NB I have included the IMSA (International Motor Sport Association) Daytona 24 Hours and Sebring 12 Hours for each year of the decade, even though they were not part of the FIA Championship from 1982 onwards, because they are, along with Le Mans, an intrinsic part of the history of sports racing/prototype and GT racing.

Brands Hatch 1000km, 17 October 1982 Wherever it rained Hans-Joachim Stuck was usually supreme and he certainly was at Brands Hatch. However, when the rain stopped and the track started to dry he was inevitably caught and passed by both Ickx and Fabi, ultimately retiring on lap 79 with engine failure. The Sauber BMW C6 scrapes the tarmac at the bottom of Paddock Hill bend as Stuck in his star-spangled helmet gives it his all. Walter Brun had bought the car from Sauber, who had used a Schnitzer BMW 1.7-litre turbo motor (allegedly giving 590bhp) rather than the shake, rattle and roll Cosworth DFL. *LAT*

◀ **Daytona 24 Hours, 30/31 January 1982** Despite the presence of the new March Chevrolet 82G and a BMW-powered version, Daytona was a Porsche 935 fest with John Paul Sr/Rolf Stommelen and son John Paul winning the race in their 935 JPL-3 from Bob Akin's 935 K3/80 driven by Akin, Craig Siebert (19 July 1950 – 30 November 1999) and Derek Bell (GB) seen here at right. Akin had spun into a barrier and after replacing a wheel and patching up the bodywork they dropped 11 laps but still finished 2nd. Both were using the 3-litre endurance engine. Serious opposition included the Fitzpatrick, Interscope, Leven, Henn and Garretson 935s, the last named coming 3rd. *LAT*

◀ **Daytona 24 Hours, 30/31 January 1982** Bob Garretson's new March Chevrolet 82G for Bobby Rahal/Bruce Canepa/Jim Trueman was fastest in qualifying at Daytona. A second but BMW-powered 82G for Cowart/Miller/Mendez started 11th. The 82G was a remade version of the BMW M1C that March had raced in 1981 and this new evocation was created by a young Adrian Newey. It was 5in lower with its distinctive lobster-claw nose and engineered to accommodate differing engines. In the race the Porsche flotilla were unbeatable and both 82Gs retired, the Chevy version with gearbox failure very late on after 514 laps whilst the Red Lobster-sponsored BMW-powered car lasted only 68 laps before the engine broke. At Sebring the Garretson car finished 2nd. *Getty*

Sebring 12 Hours, 20 March 1982 Following Daytona, Bob Garretson's March Chevrolet 82G driven by Bobby Rahal, Mauricio DeNarvaez and Jim Trueman was comfortably fastest in qualifying ahead of the Fitzpatrick/Hobbs Porsche 935 K3/80. However, after only six laps, with Fitzpatrick pulling away in the lead, the car turned over due to a broken rear suspension. Unfortunately, the March had clutch and later gearbox problems caused by fluid loss and spent much of the race with just third gear. Despite this they finished 2nd behind the John Paul Sr and Jr Porsche 935 JLP3, which had lost a cylinder so they blanked off the offending part and won the race with only five cylinders on the same lap as the hobbled March. *Getty*

Monza 1000km, 18 April 1982 Richard Cleare's Porsche 934 (930 670 0155) was now in its *third* season and at Monza Cleare with Tony Dron finished a meritorious 9th place and 2nd in the IMSA category, despite a faulty fuel pump and a puncture. *Autosport* reported that it had been equipped with a new mechanical injection engine that produced 625bhp according to Porsche. Behind is the works Sauber SHS C6 Ford Cosworth DFL of Stuck/Heyer which qualified 3rd but retired after 21 laps with a broken fuel pump, depriving Heyer of a drive. Up till this point the Sauber was considered to be a front runner, but with the advent of the Porsche 956 at Silverstone in May it was soon relegated to second-class travel. *LAT*

Monza 1000km, 18 April 1982 The Grid C8 S1 (AKA GA01) was designed by Geoff Aldridge, formerly of Lotus, at the behest of Giuseppe Rise and Ian Dawson, their two names creating the GRID title. David Hobbs and Emilio de Villota started 10th at Monza but retired with a broken fuel pump, perhaps due to the vibrational cycles of its Cosworth DFL 3.3-litre engine. Amazingly the Grid weighed 907kg (1,995 lbs, 17.82 cwt) apparently due to its very thick GRP shell. In 1982 it had a busy season in Europe, and American racer Fred Stiff who had driven S1 at Brands Hatch persuaded Dawson to take it to the USA where it contested five races. Into 1983 it continued its US odyssey and also the Brands Hatch 1000km. In 1984 S1 and its lighter Porsche-powered successor S2 (GA-02) raced at Miami and the latter at Silverstone after which Ian Dawson departed to Gianpiero Moretti's MOMO IMSA outfit as team manager. *LAT*

Monza 1000km, 18 April 1982 The new Group-C category provided a win for Jean Rondeau's latest Rondeau, the M382 (004) Ford Cosworth DFL 3.9 driven by Pescarolo/Francia, much to the joy of FIA President Jean-Marie Balestre. The M382, which still looked like its predecessor, was occupying 3rd place until the Lancia LC1s retired (see next caption). Second place fell to Ted Field's Porsche 935 K3-81, which he shared with Rolf Stommelen, one lap behind and 3rd was occupied by the old Osella PA7 of Ciuti/Benusiglio/Piazzi. *GPL*

→ Monza 1000km, 18 April 1982 Lancia had seriously upset Jean-Marie Balestre by creating the new ground-effects LC1. It was built to the obsolete Group-6 formula, which counted only in the World Endurance Championship for Drivers and not in the World Endurance Championship for Makes. The Lancias qualified 1st (Patrese/Alboreto) and 2nd (Ghinzani/Fabi) just fractions apart and well clear of the rest of the grid. The Lancias weighed 640kg whilst the Group-C cars were punished by having an 800kg minimum weight limit and a fuel restriction of 100 litres. They dominated the race until fuel-injection problems gradually dropped them back, but ultimately both broke down with faulty distributors on lap 93 and lap 104 respectively, much to the joy of Balestre. Here is Piercarlo Ghinzani during practice in chassis no.001002 which looks very boat-like and curvy, a stark contrast to its Beta Montecarlo predecessor. *GPL*

→ Monza 1000km, 18 April 1982 The Ford C100 (02 Hesketh) made its 1982 championship debut here but little was left of Len Bailey's original car. It had new Group-C bodywork, a new chassis and was managed by Lothar Pinske of Ford Koln. However, it had handling issues and also a faulty fuel pump. *Autosport* noted that work on the car continued from pre-race testing to official practice and the race morning warm-up. It lasted 18 laps before retiring with engine problems driven by Klaus Ludwig, leaving Manfred Winkelhock and Marc Surer, who was recovering from a Kyalami crash, without a drive. On lap 1 Ludwig is followed by the new Lola T610 Ford Cosworth DFL (HU1) entered by Ultramar Team Lola for Guy Edwards/Rupert Keegan which was instantly disqualified. Space precludes any further detail but suffice to say that it was prejudicial and unnecessary. *GPL*

Silverstone 6 Hours, 16 May 1982 This was the debut for the flat-6 turbocharged 2.6-litre (the same power unit as used in the 936) Porsche 956 (001) with 620bhp during practice and 580bhp in race trim. Jacky Ickx was easily quickest in practice on Dunlop qualifying tyres, 1.07 seconds faster than Ghinzani's Lancia LC1 that had the Pirelli equivalent. It was the Belgian's first race of 1982 and he believed that he could have improved by another second given an empty track. However, come the race the Porsche had to let the Lancias go as only five fuelling stops were allowed in a 6-hour or 1000km race (another regulatory diktat). By half distance Ickx/Bell were forced to cruise round at 10 seconds off the pace and finished 2nd, three laps behind the Patrese/Alboreto Lancia LC1. Here is Jacky Ickx during qualifying, the car flat and stable. *LAT*

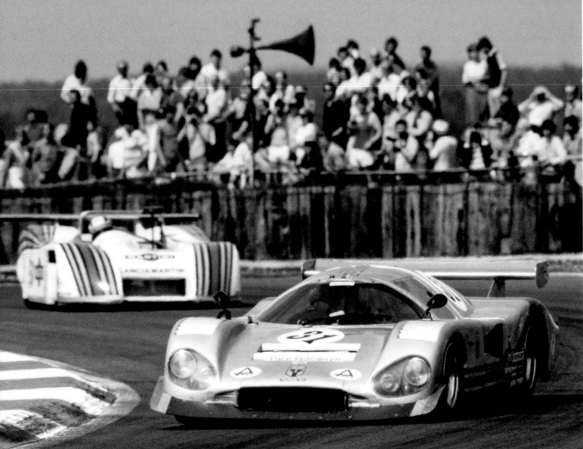

Silverstone 6 Hours, 16 May 1982 There were two Eric Broadley-designed Nimrod-Aston Martin NRA/C2s at Silverstone, but they were very large and weighed 1,050kg with Tickford-modified 5,340cc V8 engines giving 520bhp @ 7,000rpm, (later 570 and 580bhp are mentioned, the latter in the *Autosport* Le Mans report of 24 June 1982): the Viscount Downe chassis 004 for Ray Mallock/Mike Salmon and Victor Gauntlett's 'works' Nimrod (aka Aston Martin enthusiast and car dealer Robin Hamilton) chassis 003 for Geoff Lees/Bob Evans. They started 11th and 14th respectively. The Gauntlett entry seen here retired on lap 148 with a broken distributor, whilst the Downe entry finished 6th. The 'works' Nimrod only attended Silverstone, Le Mans and Spa but retired each time. *LAT*

▶ **Silverstone 6 Hours, 16 May 1982** Despite the Monza triumph Jean Rondeau could not afford to run at all the Drivers' Championship rounds so Pescarolo went to Joest. However, Jean had the M482, his new Group-C contender with a Don Foster aluminium monocoque designed to make the most of the ground-effect regulations. Max Sardou designed an unusual-looking body with a dramatically swooping nose and swept-down rear with side-mounted radiators and a huge venturi. Alas it was a dud, the aerodynamics were poor and it overheated because the Cosworth DFL exhaust was too close to the radiators so heat shields were quickly provided with large vents to expel the hot air. Jean Rondeau and François Migault drove the car at Silverstone, but it retired after 60 laps with broken suspension and bodywork and was not seen again until Le Mans 1983. *LAT*

▶ **Silverstone 6 Hours, 16 May 1982** The WM (Gerard Weltier/ Michel Meunier) Peugeot P82-01 was one of only two surviving WM monocoques after losing two cars at Le Mans 1981. They committed to a full season in Group C and raced at Monza finishing 6th, but at Silverstone the car started dead last after its twin turbos blew up due to a jammed wastegate. It was driven by the French trio of Roger Dorchy, Jean-Daniel Raulet and Michel Pignard (seen here) and reached 20th place after five laps. However, the punitive fuel diktats handicapped the turbo cars and the rapid WM was forced to back off and eventually finished 11th. They tried again at the Nürburgring 1000km with the same drivers, but only Pignard drove as the car retired on the first lap with ignition failure. *LAT*

↑ **Nürburgring 1000km, 30 May 1982** Team Castrol Denmark entered this Porsche 935 K3 for Jörgen Poulsen (DK) and Peter Hansen (DK) whilst alongside is Jens Winther's BMW M1 (WBS59910004301026) for Winther and Lars-Viggo Jensen, which had backing from Castrol Denmark. At far left is the no.56 Osella Mirabella Osella PA9/82 BMW of Giorgio Francia/Duilio Truffo. They qualified 25th, 28th and 10th respectively, and finished 16th, 7th and retired on lap 1 with a fuel leak. *LAT*

← **Nürburgring 1000km, 30 May 1982** Enzo Calderari's Sauber BMW Italia BMW M1(81.MIR.1) that he shared with Umberto Grano and Helmut Kelleners finished 3rd here having started 14th and 4th in the Group-5 class. They had passed the leading Group-5 Haldi Porsche 935 on lap 9 and were 4th after 20 laps and 3rd at the finish three laps behind the winning Lancia LC1. *LAT*

→ Nürburgring 1000km, 30 May 1982 Richard Lloyd's very smart GTi Engineering Porsche Carrera GTR (BS70006) should have finished 4th but had to make do with 5th place due to a deflating tyre. Lloyd shared the car with Tony Dron and Dutchman Hans Volker and this looks like Lloyd at the famous Karussel. *LAT*

↓ Nürburgring 1000km, 30 May 1982 Fresh from his Monaco GP win the previous weekend, Riccardo Patrese had a huge high-speed shunt at the Pflanzgarten during practice for the Nürburgring 1000km. The Lancia turned over with Patrese still inside and marshals and onlookers quickly tipped the car back onto its wheels. They laid an apparently comatose Riccardo on the grass bank, but suddenly he came to and stood up, a victim of shock but nothing more. Meanwhile, the latest iteration of the Ford C100 for Ludwig/Winkelhock was quickest in practice and in the race but retired after 32 laps with gearbox failure. However, it probably would not have lasted anyway because the massive vibrations of the DFL 3.95 motor had shaken out all but one of the engine-mounting bolts. Thus Patrese/Alboreto won by over a lap from the Pescarolo/Stommelen Rondeau whilst the second Lancia LC1 exited early on, also with a gearbox failure. *LAT*

Le Mans 24 Hours, 20 June 1982 Harley Cluxton (Grand Touring Cars) owned and entered the John Horsmann-designed Mirage M12 Ford Cosworth DFL 3.95 at Le Mans. Howden Ganley's Tiga Racing Car concern made the honeycomb chassis in England whilst the bodywork was manufactured by Lockheed Aerospace and perfectly fitted the Tiga chassis. Two were built but only one attended Le Mans, for Mario Andretti and son Michael. They qualified 9th but at 2.40pm on race day an official noticed that the oil coolers were beyond the rear axle, which was strictly *verboten*. They were disqualified despite the car having been passed by the scrutineers on the previous Tuesday and running in the 4-hour qualifying session. Allegedly the President of the ACO Alain Bertault claimed that the car was unsafe. Cluxton departed Le Mans permanently whilst the car raced briefly in the IMSA series in America. The Andrettis took action later. In Gordon Kirby's biography *A Driving Passion* Mario stated that, "Jabby Crombac wrote an exposé in *Sport Auto* with before and after photos that documented how we got screwed." *LAT*

Le Mans 24 Hours, 20 June 1982 By the end of 1981 John Fitzpatrick faced having to go back to racing for another team. A call from investment fund manager Jerry Dominelli, who was a Porsche fan, persuaded John to visit him in his office at La Jolla, San Diego. They discussed the cost of running two cars, a transporter and premises and John suggested $2 million, the response to which was "OK John, let's do it." When Fitzpatrick told him he could not attend the Daytona 24 Hours due to an engine rebuild and other outgoings, he was asked how much this would cost. The answer was $50,000, so Dominelli wrote out a cheque for the full amount, which would be in the bank the following Monday morning. Fitzpatrick recalled that, "I walked out of his office on a cloud." This is the Joest-built Porsche 935/78-81 JR-002 Moby Dick that Fitzpatrick and David Hobbs drove to 4th place and 1st in the IMSA GTX class. Following is the Cooke Racing Porsche 935 K3 005 0009 of SnobeckServanin/Metge that finished 5th and 2nd in the same class. *LAT*

Le Mans 24 Hours, 20 June 1982 For Le Mans March entered a March 82G Chevrolet, chassis no.4 (no.3 had gone to Gianpiero Moretti), with an upgraded motor for Jeff Wood/Eje Elgh/Patrick Neve, but it retired after 78 laps with electrical problems, having already suffered clutch trouble whilst the Garretson entry for Bobby Rahal/Jim Trueman/*Skeeter McKitterick (USA) – DND* only lasted 28 laps due to a split fuel tank. This is the works car exiting the chicane at the end of another lap. *LAT*

Le Mans 24 Hours, 20 June 1982 Both Reinhold Joest and the Kremer Brothers produced stop-gap Group-C Porsche-based cars in 1982 whilst awaiting their 'customer' 956s for 1983. This is the Joest 936C (JR005), a hybrid 908/936 suitably adapted to the Group-C regulations with a 2.5-litre flat-6 and a 4-speed Can-Am 917-30 gearbox, the car weighing 878kg. The Belgian brothers Jean-Michel and Philippe Martin (in picture) brought cigarette sponsorship from Belga, and Bob Wollek was also employed. They reached 3rd place but a misfire on Sunday morning ended with piston failure on lap 314, less than 2 hours from the finish. Following the Spa 1000km the Martin brothers departed and were replaced by Hans Heyer and Henri Pescarolo. *GPL*

Le Mans 24 Hours, 20 June 1982 One wonders just how safe your feet and legs were with such truncated noses in the event of an accident as per the no.30 URD C81 BMW (which Harald Grohs had crashed at the Nürburgring) driven by Michel Lateste, Hubert Striebig and Jacques Heuclin (10 July 1946 – 31 October 2007, lung infection). It had a sheet-aluminium-clad space frame with a 475bhp BMW M1 engine and started 25th, a worthy effort on par with the two Nimrod Aston Martins. It was the creation of Ernst Ungar, hence URD (Ungar Racing Developments). Unfortunately, the URD's BMW motor failed on lap 45. *LAT*

Le Mans 24 Hours, 20 June 1982 The Nimrod Aston Martins were another victim of the ACO scrutineers; this time it was the inadequate windscreen height, which was no problem at Silverstone of course. So the Viscount Downe no.32 car of Mallock/Salmon/Philipps had an enlarged windscreen with a really grotty looking extra piece tacked on above it whilst the works car of Lees/Needell/Evans no.31 was more subtle plus increased ride height. Needell survived a burst rear tyre on Mulsanne but hit the barrier on lap 55 which ended its race. However, the Downe car ultimately finished 7th albeit with only five cylinders due to burnt-out exhaust valves caused by falling fuel pressure. It is hard to believe that Eric Broadley designed this overweight behemoth. *GPL*

↑ **Le Mans 24 Hours, 20 June 1982** At Le Mans Rondeau's three M382s all retired with engine problems, albeit after Migault led the race in the no.11 car he shared with Spice/Lapeyre. This is Jean Rondeau giving the thumbs up in the no.24 M382 (005), perhaps during practice, that he apparently shared with Jaussaud as painted on the car. However, the first M382 to retire was the no.24 car of Pescarolo/Jaussaud, after which Pesca was moved to the no.12 car that according to stats was driven by Rondeau and Ragnotti. However, Rondeau still topped the World Championship Group-C category due to the 5th place in class of the Primagaz 382C driven by Pierre Yver/Bruno Sotty/Lucien Guitteny. *GPL*

← **Le Mans 24 Hours, 20 June 1982** It was not just Rondeau who failed at Le Mans; the 215mph Secateva WM Peugeots of Pignard/JRaulet/Theys (no.9) and Dorchy/Fréquelin/Couderc (no.10) both retired: no.9 on lap 127 (gearbox failure) and no.10 on lap 112 (crashed by Couderc but already delayed by a collision and a loose door). This is Roger Dorchy followed by the Migault/Spice/Lapeyre Rondeau M382 that led early in the race but suffered the dreaded DFL vibrational problem and retired with ignition failure at 150 laps. As already noted, the Secateva team had committed to a full season, but after this debacle they withdrew from all other races and concentrated only on Le Mans thereafter. *GPL*

➡️ **Le Mans 24 Hours, 20 June 1982** Porsche did not attend the Nürburgring 1000km, preferring to continue their development of the 956, and arrived at La Sarthe with three new cars, chassis no.2 (Ickx/Bell), chassis no.3 (Mass/Schuppan) and chassis no.4 (Holbert, Haywood, Barth). They were 1st, 2nd and 14th on the grid and finished 1st, 2nd and 3rd, but it was not without drama. The American/German car led the race from about 8pm to just after midnight before the driver's door decided to abandon ship. Later on they suffered a misfire, a contaminated fuel filter and finally a rear hub failure during the early morning. This dropped them way back, but they ultimately finished 3rd, 19 laps behind Ickx/Bell after the retirement of the Joest 936C. The winning car also had some minor problems but it was three laps ahead of the Mass/Schupann car at the end. Here they approach the finish in chassis and race-number order, what you would expect of course. *LAT*

⬇️ **Le Mans 24 Hours, 20 June 1982** This was the last hurrah for production-based/much-modified American muscle cars at Le Mans. Two Chevrolet Camaros with tube frames built by Dennis Frings and entered by Billy Jo Hagan (Stratagraph) managed to finish the race albeit far adrift. No.81 was the newer car driven by Hagan, Gene Felton and Tom Williams and was 33rd fastest in qualifying whilst the older no.80 of Hershel McGriff and Richard Brooks started 46th. The former was slowed by electrical problems and later having to repair the gearbox whilst the latter also had gearbox problems, ending in replacement, plus a blown exhaust system. They finished 17th and unclassified respectively. *Getty*

◀ **Spa 1000km, 5 September 1982** A grid of 37 at Spa (now half the lap distance of the post-war track) of which 17 were Group-C entries proved the popularity of the new class. Two 956s for Ickx/Mass (003) and Bell/Schuppan (004) occupied the top positions in practice courtesy of full boost and finished 1st and 2nd. Behind them are the two Lancia LC1s: Ghinzani on the left and Patrese on the right, who finished 3rd. They are followed by the two Ford C100s and to their left is the Kremer C-K5 of Stommelen/Bellof followed by a trio of Rondeaus and the no.20 Sauber SHS C6 (Stuck/Heyer) ahead of the Edwards/Keegan Ultramar Lola T610. Behind, the rest of the spread-out grid disappears around the curve. *LAT*

◀ **Spa 1000km, 5 September 1982** With an eye on the fuel-consumption problem, Porsche backed off and let the two Lancias past at Spa, but the Italians had a variety of problems and toward the final 30 laps it was Porsche 1st (Ickx/Mass) and 3rd (Bell/Schuppan) with Lancia 2nd (Ghinzani/Alboreto) and 4th (Patrese/Fabi). On the final lap Alboreto's car stopped after Eau Rouge and he was unable to restart it because the reserve fuel-tank switch was jammed. However, giving it one more desperate push did the trick and he was able to drive the LC1 back to the finish for his 2nd place. Alas an hour later the organisers decided that Alboreto had left the car when it was stationary so it could not be classified. Here is Ghinzani in the LC1 (001004) in the middle of the La Source hairpin, looking ever more like a boat. *LAT*

➡ **Spa 1000km, 5 September 1982** Shame about the slightly truncated image but it is otherwise a great shot of Gianpiero Moretti's Group-5 Momo Porsche 935/78-81 (JR 001) that he shared with Mauro Baldi. They won the class and finished 7th overall. Hidden behind the red devil is Christian Bussi's 13th-placed Rondeau M382 Ford Cosworth DFV (0030), which he shared with Bernard de Dryver and Pascal Witmeur. *LAT*

➡ **Spa 1000km, 5 September 1982** Whilst Ford had received the latest Cosworth DFL 3.9 with a larger crankshaft damper to try and alleviate its ferocious vibrational problems, Sauber team manager Domingos Piedade decided to use the smaller 3.3-litre DFL, rather than the shake-it-all-about bigger engine, for the Stuck/Heyer SHS C6. For a while they led the normally aspirated cars in 5th place ahead of the Jaussaud/Pescarolo Rondeau M382. This is Stuck doing his best, but a misfire later in the race, possibly caused by a malfunctioning metering unit, demoted them to 9th place having qualified 10th. *LAT*

◄ **Spa 1000km, 5 September 1982**
Two new Ford Mk3 C100s came to
Spa for Marc Surer/Klaus Ludwig
and Manfred Winkelhock/Klaus
Niedzwiedz, but despite all attempts
to stop the DFL vibrations both
cars had their exhausts shaken
apart. This is Ludwig in chassis
05 (note its hanging offside door
mirror, perhaps another victim of
'the shakes') overtaking the Joest
Porsche 936C (JR005) of Jean-Michel
Martin/Philippe Martin. According
to *Autosport*, the Ford stopped two
laps from the finish with fuel-pump
problems (apparently the new
crankshaft dampers created a fuel
pick-up problem). Ludwig was sent
back out but the car failed to return.
The Winkelhock/Niedzwiedz car (03)
spent 25 minutes in the pits having
its exhaust replaced and dropped
down the order, eventually finishing
18th. In contrast, the Martin brothers
finished 4th in their final race for the
Joest team. *LAT*

◄ **Fuji 6 Hours, Mount Fuji,
3 October 1982** There were no works
Porsche 956s at the Mugello 1000km
and of the leading European private
entrants only Walter Brun and Joest
appeared in a 19-car field. Lancia
finished 1/2, further increasing their
chances of winning the drivers'
championship whilst Ickx sat at
home without a ride. Two weeks
later Porsche, Lancia and Rondeau
works teams graced the Fuji 6 Hours
plus five American entrants, the best
of which was Ralph Kent-Cooke's
Porsche 935 K3. The rest were all
Japanese teams/drivers. Ickx/Mass
won by two laps ahead of the Patrese/
Fabi Lancia LC1 with Nakamura/
Misak in the Nakamura March-Toyota
3rd but 17 laps adrift. The second
works 956 of Bell/Schuppan retired
after a burst tyre sent the Australian
into the barriers. This is Bell in the 956
(04) followed by Ghinzani's Lancia
LC1 (001004), which also crashed,
eight laps after Schuppan's shunt,
passing the Masahiro Akiyama/
Ken'ichi Matsunami Datsun Fairlady,
which finished 12th. *LAT*

Fuji 6 Hours, Mount Fuji, 3 October 1982 Lest we forget. Michele Alboreto (23 December 1956 – 25 April 2001) was a versatile racer whose career was not given the kudos it deserved. It began in 1976 and by 1979 he was an established F3 driver, winning the Italian F3 series in 1980. From 1981 to 1994 he raced in F1 for Tyrrell (1981/82/83 and 89), Ferrari (1984/85/86/87/88), Larrousse (1989), Footwork Arrows (1990/91/92), and finally Scuderia Italia, which melded into Minardi (1993/94). He won five Grands Prix, three of them for Ferrari. Subsequently he also tried the Deutsche Tourenwagen Meisterschaft and the Indy Racing League, won at Le Mans in 1997 and at the Sebring 12 Hours in 2001. Less than a month later he died testing an Audi R8 at the Lausitzring in Germany when a tyre burst. At Fuji he and Piercarlo Ghinzani were fastest in qualifying, but suspension failure caused Alboreto to crash out of the race. *GPL*

Brands Hatch 1000km, 17 October 1982 Brands Hatch hosted the final race of the season, and Ford arrived with C100s for Surer/Ludwig (03), Winkelhock/Niedzwiedz (05) and Palmer/Wilson (04). They qualified 1st, 2nd and 8th respectively. On a cold, wet day Surer in no.1 and Winkelhock in no.2 led the race driving side by side for eight laps, allegedly so that they could see where they were going. In the background Stuck is exiting Druids in the Sauber SHS C6. He caught the Fords at Pilgrims Drop where Surer touched Winkelhock's car, which ended up in the barriers and the race stopped on lap 9 for repairs to the Armco. Surer/Ludwig finally finished 5th whilst Palmer/Wilson finished 4th. Decades later Gordon Spice recalled in Octane magazine that he had suggested to Karl Ludvigsen that he (Spice) take over the project which was agreed. However, in March 1983 Stuart Turner took over from Ludvigsen as Ford Europe's Director of Motorsports and immediately cancelled the C100 project. Nevertheless Ford paid Gordon off with premises and equipment which was de facto the start of Spice Engineering. *LAT*

Brands Hatch 1000km, 17 October 1982 Here is the line-up for the restart with Stuck's Sauber C6 BMW at the head of the queue with the Surer Ford C100 on the right and the two Lancia LC1s either side further back. Also visible is the third Ford C100 (Palmer/Wilson) and in the distance Dave Preece's abandoned yellow Aston Martin DBS-based DPLM (DP812H), which crashed on the first lap. Stuck had passed Surer's Ford C100 during the incident with Winkelhock and gained 6 seconds on the Swiss. Ickx was 3rd 4.4 seconds back whilst the Fabi Lancia LC1 was 8th and more pertinently 6.4 seconds behind the 956, which was to prove disastrous for Lancia and Patrese at the finish. *GPL*

Brands Hatch 1000km, 17 October 1982 The 11th Viscount Downe, John Christian George Dawnay (18 January 1935 – 15 March 2002), was President of the Aston Martin Owners Club from 1980 onwards. He owned the Aston Martin DP212 that Graham Hill and Richie Ginther had raced at Le Mans in 1962 for Aston Martin boss David Brown. This was later raced by Mike Salmon on behalf of Downe in British club events during the 1970s, so it was appropriate that Salmon should drive for him again in the Nimrod Aston Martin. This is co-driver Ray Mallock, son of the famous Major Arthur Mallock of U2 fame, at Paddock Hill bend. Note the front wing, and the wide rear spoiler. They finished 9th having at one time been as high as 6th, but the team finished 3rd in the 1982 Endurance Championship despite only contesting four races (Silverstone, Le Mans, Spa and Brands Hatch). *LAT*

**→ Brands Hatch 1000km,
17 October 1982** John Fitzpatrick
in the 3.2-litre Porsche 935 K4
(K4 01) is followed by the no.5
URD C81 BMW of Helmut
Gall and Harald Grohs with
the no.21 Joest Porsche 936C
(JR005) driven by Bob Wollek/
Henri Pescarolo/Hans Heyer just
visible at right. Fitzpatrick and
David Hobbs finished 3rd, Gall
and Grohs finished 13th and
9th in Group C whilst the Joest
Porsche 936C was 8th and 6th
in Group C. Note Fitzpatrick's
Bell XF twin window helmet
and the JDAVID logo on the 935,
an abbreviation of Jerry David
Dominelli, his sponsor. *LAT*

**↘ Brands Hatch 1000km,
17 October 1982** As part two of
the race progressed the Patrese/
Fabi Lancia LC1 (001002) looked
in good shape and had a solid
lead over the Ickx/Bell Porsche
956. The LC1 had an advantage
in the gradually drying
conditions as Bell was on wet
tyres and struggled to keep in
touch. At one point he was a lap
down on the Italian car. When
Fabi took over again the race was
shortened and in the darkening
conditions with no lights and
an unleashed Ickx at full tilt he
managed to cross the line 1st
on track but only 1.7 seconds
ahead of Ickx. Apparently
nobody in the Lancia pits had
told Fabi that he had to finish
more than 6.4 seconds ahead of
Ickx! So Porsche won the World
Endurance Championship
for Makes (Group C) anyway
but Ickx also won the World
Endurance Championship
for Drivers, leaving Patrese in
second place. In the darkness
Teo Fabi looks suitably worn
out and Patrese no doubt
completely pissed off whilst in
the background Jacky Ickx is
telling a journalist how it was
presumably. *LAT*

ENTRANTS

901 Shop – Porsche 934
Jack Refenning (USA) DAY
Ren Tilton (USA) DAY
Rusty Bond (USA) DAY

**Herb Adams
– Pontiac Firebird,
Chevrolet Camaro (Riggins)**
Roger Mears (USA) DAY
Leonard Emanuelson (USA) DAY
Herb Adams (USA) DAY
Gary English (USA) DAY
Jerry Thompson (USA) DAY
David Price (USA) DAY (*DND*)

**Bob Akin Motor Racing
– Porsche 935 K3/80,
Porsche 935 L**
Bob Akin (USA) DAY, SEB, LM
Craig Siebert (USA) DAY, SEB
Derek Bell (GB) DAY, SEB
Dave Cowart (USA) LM (*DND*)
Kenper Miller (USA) LM (*DND*)

**Alpha Cubic Racing
– Mazda RX-7**
Chiyomi Totani (J) FUJ
Keiichi Suzuki (J) FUJ
Kaoru Iida (J) FUJ

**Amada Dome/Dome Co. Ltd
– Dome RC82 Ford
Cosworth DFL**
Chris Craft (GB) SIL, LM
Raul Boesel (BR) SIL
Eliseo Salazar (RCH) SIL (*DND*), LM

**Herbert Asselborn
(no entrant listed)
– Ford Escort RS 2000**
Herbert Asselborn (D) NUR
Wolfgang Boller (D) NUR
Wolfgang Braun (D) NUR

**Auriga Racing
– Chevrolet Camaro (Riggins)**
Tom Nehl (USA) DAY
Tommy Riggins (USA) DAY
Nelson Silcox (USA) DAY

**Auto Beaurex Motor Sports
– BMW M1 Gp 5**
Fumiyasu Satou (J) FUJ
Naoki Nagasaka (J) FUJ

**Automobiles Jean Rondeau
– Rondeau M382 Ford
Cosworth DFV**
Henri Pescarolo (F) MZA
Giorgio Francia (I) MZA

**Autowest
– Mercury Capri**
Ron Hunter (USA) DAY
Richard Turner (USA) DAY
Duane Eitel (USA) DAY

**B.F. Goodrich
– Porsche 924 Carrera GTR**
Paul Miller (USA) LM
Pat Bedard (USA) LM
Manfred Schurti (FL) LM

**BASF Cassetten Team GS Sport
(see below) – Sauber SHS
C6 (Seger & Hoffman)
– Ford Cosworth DFL**
Siegfried Müller, Jr (D) SIL, LM
Walter Brun (CH) SIL, LM
Hans-Joachim Stuck (D) SIL, LM, SPA
Hans Heyer (D) SIL, SPA
Jean-Louis Schlesser (F) LM
Dieter Quester (A) LM

**Sauber Racing (Switzerland)/GS
RacingWalter Brun (*Brun bought
the GS Racing team from owner
Gerhard Schneider*) – Sauber
SHS C6 (Seger & Hoffman)
Ford Cosworth DFL**
Siegfried Müller, Jr (D) MZA,
MUG, BH
Walter Brun (CH) MZA (*DND*),
MUG, BH

BMW Italia – BMW M1 Gp5
Umberto Grano (I) MZA, NUR, SPA
Enzo Calderari (CH) MZ, NUR, SPA
Helmut Kelleners (D) NUR
Marco Vanoli (CH) SPA (*DND*)

**Bayside Disposal Racing
– Porsche 935/80**
Hurley Haywood (USA) DAY, SEB
Bruce Leven (USA) DAY, SEB
Al Holbert (USA) DAY, SEB

**Bob Beasley – Porsche 911
Carrera RSR**
Bob Beasley (USA) DAY
George Stone (USA) DAY
Jack Lewis (USA)

**Belcher Racing – Rondeau M382
Ford Cosworth DFV**
Danny Sullivan (USA) DAY
Garry Belcher (USA) DAY
Hubert Phipps (USA) DAY

**Belga Team Joest Racing/Joest
Racing – Porsche 936C**
Bob Wollek (F) MZA, SIL, NUR, LM,
MUG
Jean-Michel Martin (B) MZA, SIL,
NUR (*DND*), LM, SPA
Philippe Martin (B) MZA, SIL, NUR,
LM, SPA
Henri Pescarolo (F) MUG
Hans Heyer (D) MUG

**Scuderia Bellancauto
– Ferrari 512 LM/BB**
Giovanni Del Buono (I) MZA
Odoardo Govoni (I) MZA
Fabrizio Violati (I) MUG
Duilio Truffo (I) MUG

**Mario Benusiglio (no entrant
listed) – Lucchini BMW**
Mario Benusiglio (I) MUG
Giovanni Siliprandi (I) MUG
Fabio Siliprandi (I) MUG

Uli Bieri – Porsche 911
Uli Bieri (CDN) SEB
Jean-Pierre Zingg (CH) SEB
Herman Lausberg (CDN) SEB

Roland Binder – Lola T296 BMW
Roland Binder (D) NUR, BH
Rolf Götz (D) NUR (*DND*), BH

Bard Board – Chevrolet Corvette
Bard Board (USA) SEB
Richard Anderson (USA) SEB
Brian Utt (USA) SEB

Bob's Speed Products – AMC AMX
Guy Church (USA) DAY
Tom Alan Marx (USA) DAY
Bob Lee (USA) DAY (*DND*), SEB
Brian Erikson (USA) SEB
Guy Church (USA) SEB (*DND*)

Bon Temps Racing – Datsun 240Z
Ron Reed (USA) SEB
Mark Langlinais (USA) SEB

**Brauneiser Renntechnik
– Ford Escort RS 2000**
Axel Felder (D) NUR
Franz-Josef Bröhling (D) NUR
Joachim Scheefeldt (D) NUR
Olaf Manthey (D) NUR
Joachim Utsch (D) NUR
Peter Faubel (D) NUR
Jochen Felder (D) NUR
Heinz Gilges (D) NUR

**Brumos Racing
– Porsche 924 Carrera GTR**
Doc Bundy (USA) DAY, SEB
Jim Busby (USA) DAY, SEB
Manfred Schurti (FL) DAY
James Brolin (USA) SEB

**Christian Bussi/Auto Sport
Ch. Bussi – Rondeau M382
Ford Cosworth DFL**
Christian Bussi (F) MZA, LM, SPA
François Servanin (F) MZA
Jacques Guérin (F) MZA (*DND*)
Bernard de Dryver (B) LM, SPA
Pascal Witmeur (B) LM, SPA

**Canon Cameras - GTi Engineering
– Porsche 924 Carrera GTR**
Jonathan Palmer (GB) MZA, SIL, SPA
Richard Lloyd (GB) MZA, SIL, NUR,
LM, SPA, MUG, BH
Tony Dron (GB) NUR
Hans Volker (NL) NUR
Andy Rouse (GB) LM
Jeff Allam (GB) MUG, BH

**Carrera Motorsports
– Porsche 911 Carrera RSR**
Jean Kjoller (USA) DAY
Bob Nikel (USA) DAY
Grady Clay (USA) DAY

Case Racing – Porsche 911
Russ Long (USA) DAY
Craig Case (USA) DAY
Ron Case (USA) DAY, SEB
Michael Harry (USA) SEB
Angelo Pizzagelli (I) SEB

**Team Castrol Denmark
– Porsche 935 K3**
Jörgen Poulsen (DK) NUR, SPA, BH
Peter Hansen (DK) NUR, SPA, BH

**Central 20 Racing Team – March
75SC BMW, Nissan Silvia**
Haruhito Yanagida (J) FUJ
Shinji Uchida (J) FUJ
Kouji Tomioka (J) FUJ
Toshio Motohashi (J) FUJ
Yoshiaki Asaka (J) FUJ

Pierre Chauvet – TOJ SC205
Edgar Dören (D) SPA
'Pierre Chauvet' (Friedrich Glaz) (A)
SPA, BH
Helmut Gall (D) SPA (*DND*)
Jo Gartner (A) BH (*DND*)

**Chevron Racing Cars with Frox
Clothing Ltd/Chevron Racing
Cars/Martin Birrane/Frox
Clothing – Chevron B36B
Ford Cosworth BDX**
Martin Birrane (IRL) SIL, LM, SPA, BH
Robin Smith (GB) SIL
Neil Crang (AUS) SIL, LM
John Sheldon (GB) LM
Pascal Foix (F) SPA
Gerry Amato (GB) BH
David Kennedy (IRL) BH

**Richard Cleare Racing/R.H. Cleare
Ltd – Porsche 934**
Richard Cleare (GB) MZA, SIL, LM,
SPA, MUG, BH
Tony Dron (GB) MZA, SIL, LM, SPA,
MUG, BH
Richard Jones (GB) LM

**Antonio Codognelli (no entrant
listed) Lancia Stratos HF**
Antonio Codognelli (I) MUG
Giovanni Alberti (I) MUG

**Constructa Racing Team
– Ford Escort RS 2000**
Herbert Kummle (D) NUR
Karl Mauer (D) NUR

**Cooke Racing, Cooke Racing-BP ,
Cooke Racing- Malardeau– Lola
T600 Chevrolet, Porsche 935 K3,
Lola T610 Ford Cosworth DFL**
Ralph Kent-Cooke (USA) DAY, SEB,
LM, FUJ
Eppie Wietzes (CDN) DAY
Jim Adams (USA) DAY, SEB, LM
(*DND*), FUJ
David Hobbs (GB) SEB
Dany Snobeck (F) LM
François Servanin (F) LM
René Metge (F) LM
Brian Redman (GB) LM

**Copeman Racing
– Porsche 911 Carrera RSR**
Jerry Jolly (USA) DAY
Bob Copeman (USA) DAY
Tom Alan Marx (USA) DAY

**Yves Courage – Cougar C01
Ford Cosworth DFL**
Yves Courage (F) LM
Michel Dubois (F) LM
Jean-Philippe Grand (F) LM
Nick Faure (GB) SPA
Hervé Regout (B) SPA

Cox Speed – VW Golf Etilux
Syuuroku Sasaki (J) FUJ
Osamu Nakako (J) FUJ
Osamu Hatagawa (J) FUJ

**Crevier & Associates
– BMW M1**
Joe Crevier (USA) DAY, SEB
Fred Stiff (USA) DAY
Dennis Wilson (USA) DAY
Paul Fassler (USA) SEB
Bob Zeigel (USA) SEB

**The Cummings Marque
– Chevrolet Monza**
Don Cummings (USA) SEB
Irwin Ayes (USA) SEB

**D & L Performance
– Porsche 911 Carrera RSR**
Dave Panaccione (USA) DAY, SEB
Chip Mead (USA) DAY
John Graham (CDN) DAY
Doug Lutz (USA) SEB

Dudley Davis – Porsche 911
Dudley Davis (USA) SEB
Henry Godfredson (USA) SEB
Charlie Lloyd (USA) SEB

Der Klaus Haus – Porsche 911
Scott Flanders (USA) DAY, SEB
Klaus Bitterauf (USA) DAY, SEB
Vicki Smith (USA) DAY, SEB

**Edgar Dören
– Porsche 935 K3/81**
Edgar Dören (D) LM
Antonio Contreras (MEX) LM
Billy Sprowls (USA) LM (*DND*)

**Dorset Racing Associates/
Dorset Racing Associates-
Olympus Cameras – Lola
T298 Ford Cosworth BDG,
Lola T298 Ford Cosworth
BDX, De Cadenet Lola
– Ford Cosworth DFV**
Roy Baker (GB) SIL, NUR, BH
Eddie Arundel (GB) SIL, BH
Nick Faure (GB) SIL, NUR, BH
Bernard de Dryver (B) SIL
Mike Wilds (GB) SIL, LM
François Duret (GB) NUR, LM
Ian Harrower (GB) LM

**Rudolf Dötsch (no entrant name
listed) – Ford Escort RS 2000**
Rudolf Dötsch (D) NUR
Bodo Jähn (D) NUR
Hans Ruch (D) NUR

**Viscount Downe with Pace
Petroleum – Nimrod NRA/C2
Aston Martin**
Mike Salmon (GB) SIL, LM, SPA, BH
Ray Mallock (GB) SIL, LM, SPA, BH
Simon Phillips (GB) LM

**Downing/Atlanta/Jim Downing
– Mazda RX-7**
Tom Waugh (USA) DAY, SEB
Jim Downing (USA) DAY, SEB
John Maffucci (USA) DAY, SEB

Drolsom Racing
– Porsche 924 Carrera GTR
George Drolsom (USA) DAY, SEB
Bill Johnson (USA) DAY
Werner Frank (USA) DAY
Tom Davey (USA) SEB

Dunham Trucking
– Mazda RX-7
Jack Dunham (USA) DAY, SEB
Scott Smith, Jr (USA) DAY
Scott Smith (USA) DAY
Luis Sereix (USA) SEB

ERC Racing
– Mazda RX-3
Shin'ichi Katsuki (J) FUJ
Yoshio Ishikawa (J) FUJ
Mitsuo Sekiguchi (J) FUJ

Eichberg Racing
– Ford Escort RS 2000
Peter Feldin (D) NUR
Günther Bochem (D) NUR
Wilfried Oetelshoven (D) NUR
Hartmut Bauer (D) NUR
Hanno Schumacher (D) NUR
Frank Ossenberg (D) NUR (*DND*)

Electramotive Racing
– Datsun 280ZX Turbo
Don Devendorf (USA) FUJ
Tony Adamowicz (USA) FUJ

Elkoubi
– Lola T298 BMW
'Jean Hex' (Jean Eggericx) (B) SPA
Dirk Vermeersch (B) SPA
François-Xavier Boucher (B) SPA

EMKA Productions Ltd
– BMW M1, BMW M1 Gp 5
Steve O'Rourke (GB) SIL, LM
Nick Mason (GB) SIL, LM
Jeff Allam (GB) SIL
Richard Down (GB) LM

Scuderia Escolette
– Osella PA7 BMW
Gabriele Ciuti (I) MZA
Mario Benusiglio (I) MZA
Giuseppe Piazzi (I) MZA

Essen Werdener Automobil
Club e.V. im ADAC
– BMW320i
Friedrich Burgmann (D) NUR
Harald ten Eicken (D) NUR
Artur Deutgen (D) NUR

Esso
– WM Peugeot PRV
Michel Pignard (F) LM
Jean-Daniel Raulet (F) LM
Didier Theys (B) LM
Guy Fréquelin (F) LM
Roger Dorchy (F) LM
Alain Couderc (F)LM

Diego Febles Racing
– Porsche 911 Carrera RSR
Diego Febles (PR) DAY, SEB
Tato Ferrer (PR) DAY, SEB
Chiqui Soldevilla (PR) DAY, SEB

John Fitzpatrick Racing
– Porsche 935 K3/80, Porsche
935 78/81, Porsche 935 K4
John Fitzpatrick (GB) DAY, SEB,
LM, BH
David Hobbs (GB) DAY (*DND*), SEB
(*DND*), LM, BH
Wayne Baker (USA) DAY (*DND*)
Bob Wollek (F) BH

Ford GB – Ford C100 Ford
Cosworth DFL
Jonathan Palmer (GB) BH
Desiré Wilson (ZA) BH
Marc Surer (CH) BH
Klaus Ludwig (D) BH
Manfred Winkelhock (D) BH
Klaus Niedzwiedz (D) BH (*DND*)

Ford Werke AG – Ford C100
Ford Cosworth DFL
Klaus Ludwig (D) MZA, SIL, SPA
Manfred Winkelhock (D) MZA
(*DND*), SIL
Marc Surer (CH) MZA (*DND*), SPA

Fomfor Racing El Salvador
– BMW 3.0 CSL
'Fomfor' (Francisco Miguel) (ES) SEB
Guillermo Valiente (ES) SEB
Benjamin Gonzalez (ES) SEB (*DND*)

Ford Team Zakspeed
– Ford C100 Ford Cosworth DFL
Manfred Winkelhock (D) NUR
Klaus Ludwig (D) NUR

Ford Werke AG
– Ford C100 Ford Cosworth DFL
Klaus Ludwig (D) MZA, SIL, LM
Manfred Winkelhock (D) MZA (*DND*),
SIL, LM, SPA
Marc Surer (CH) MZA (*DND*), LM
Klaus Niedzwiedz (D) LM, SPA

Formel Rennsport Club
der Schweiz – FRC
– Porsche 924 Carrera GTR
Edi Kofel (CH) NUR, SPA, BH
Peter Zbinden (CH) NUR, SPA, BH
(*DND*)
Marco Vanoli (CH) NUR

Formel Rennsport Club Zurich
– Porsche 924 Carrera GTR
Peter Zbinden (CH) MZA, SIL, MUG
Edi Kofel (CH) MZA, SIL, MUG
Marco Vanoli (CH) MUG

Fuchs-Whitaker
– Chevrolet Camaro
Bruce Jernigan (USA) SEB
William Boyer (USA) SEB

Grid Racing
– Grid Plaza S1 Ford
Cosworth DFL
David Hobbs (GB) MZA, SIL
Emilio de Villota (ES) MZA, SIL,
LM, BH
Alain De Cadenet (GB) LM (*DND*)
Desiré Wilson (ZA) LM (*DND*)
Derek Daly (IRL) BH
Fred Stiff (USA) BH

GS Tuning (Gerhard Schneider)
– Sauber SHS C6 (Seger &
Hoffman) Ford Cosworth DFL
Hans-Joachim Stuck (D) MZA
Hans Heyer (D) MZA (*DND*)

Tony Garcia Racing
– BMW M1
Tony Garcia (USA) SIL, LM
Albert Naon (USA) SIL, LM
Fred Stiff (USA) LM

Garretson Ent./Garretson
Development – Porsche 935
K3/80, March 82G Chevrolet,
Porsche 935 K3
Mauricio DeNarvaez (CO) DAY, SEB
Bob Garretson (USA) DAY, LM
Jeff Wood (USA) DAY
Bobby Rahal (USA) DAY, SEB, LM
Bruce Canepa (USA) DAY
Jim Trueman (USA) DAY, SEB, LM
Ray Ratcliff (USA) SEB, LM
Grady Clay (USA) SEB
Skeeter McKitterick (USA) SEB, LM
(*DND*)
Anny-Charlotte Verney (F) LM

Genesis Racing
– Chevron GTP Mazda Rotary
Larry Chmura (USA) DAY
Jim Schofield (USA) DAY
Brent Regan (USA) DAY

Paolo Giangrossi (no entrant
listed) – Osella PA9 BMW
Paolo Giangrossi (I) MUG
Gerardo Vatielli (I) MUG
Pasquale Barberio (I) MUG

Golden Eagle Racing
– Rondeau M382 Ford
Cosworth DFV
Bill Koll (USA) DAY
Irv Hoerr (USA) DAY
Skeeter McKitterick (USA) DAY

Gontazaka Enterprise
– Nissan Fairlady 280Z
Yoshio Nagata (J) FUJ
Seiichirou Tsujimoto (J) FUJ
Takamichi Shinohara (J) FUJ

Paul Goral – Porsche 911
Paul Goral (USA) SEB
Nort Northam (USA) SEB
Jim Burt (USA) SEB

Bob Gregg Racing
– Porsche 911 Carrera RSR
Bob Young (USA) DAY
Bob Gregg (USA) DAY
Ray McIntyre (USA) DAY

Group 44 – Jaguar XJS
Bob Tullius (USA) DAY
Bill Adam (CDN) DAY
Gordon Smiley (USA) DAY

Jacques Guérin
– Rondeau M382
Jean-Pierre Delaunay (F) SIL
Christian Bussi (F) SIL
Jacques Guérin (F) SIL

H.W.R.T. Auto Tuning GmbH
– Ford Escort RS 2000
Manfred Burkhard (D) NUR
Norbert Brenner (D) NUR
Wilhelm Kern (D) NUR
Günther Braumüller (D) NUR
Andreas Schall (D) NUR
Dieter Selzer (D) NUR

Claude Haldi – Porsche 935 K3
Claude Haldi (CH) NUR, LM
Bernard Béguin (F) NUR
Harald Grohs (D) NUR (*DND*)
Rodrigo Téran (PA) LM
François Hesnault (F) LM

Hallet Motor Racing Circuit
– Lancia Stratos HF
Anatoly Arutunoff (USA) DAY
José Marina (USA) DAY

Jacky Haran – Rondeau M379 C
Ford Cosworth DFV
Jacky Haran (F) LM
Vivian Candy (IRL) LM
Hervé Poulain (F) LM

Heimrath Racing
– Porsche 924 GTR
Ludwig Heimrath, Jr (CDN) DAY
Ludwig Heimrath (CDN) DAY

Herman-Miller P.A.
– Porsche 924 Carrera GTR
Paul Miller (USA) DAY, SEB
Pat Bedard (USA) DAY, SEB (*DND*)
Jürgen Barth (D) DAY, SEB (*DND*)

Arthur Hough Racing/Castrol/Ark
Racing – Lotus Elan
Max Payne (GB) SIL, SPA, BH
Chris Ashmore (GB) SIL, SPA, BH

Italya Sport – Rondeau M382
Ford Cosworth DFL
Henri Pescarolo (F) FUJ
Thierry Boutsen (B) FUJ

Interscope Racing
– Porsche 935 K3/80
Ted Field (USA) DAY, SEB
Danny Ongais (USA) DAY (*DND*), SEB
Bill Whittington (USA) DAY (*DND*)

Charles Ivey Racing
– Porsche 935 K3
John Cooper (GB) MZA, SIL, NUR,
LM, BH
Paul Smith (GB) MZA, SIL, NUR
(*DND*), LM, BH
Claude Bourgoignie (B) LM
Eddie Jordan (IRL) BH
Glenn Loxton (ZA) BH
Dudley Wood (GB) BH

Jägermeister
Racing Team
– BMW 320i
Mario Ketterer (D) NUR
Anton Fischhaber (D) NUR
Eckhard Schimpf (D) NUR
Rick Köhler (D) NUR
Klaus Böhm (D) NUR
Jörg Denzel (D) NUR

JLP Racing
– Porsche 935 JLP-3,
Porsche 935 JLP-2
John Paul Jr (USA) DAY, SEB
John Paul (USA) DAY, SEB
Rolf Stommelen (D) DAY
M.L. Speer (USA) SEB
Terry Wolters (USA) SEB
Charles Mendez (USA) SEB

Jolly Club – Osella PA9/82
Carlo Facetti (I) SIL
Martino Finitto (I) SIL
'Gimax' (Carlo Franchi) (I) MUG
Sandro Cinotti (I) MUG
Giuseppe Piazzi (I) MUG

Kannacher GT Racing
– Porsche 930, URD C81 BMW
Klaus Drees (D) NUR
Horst Hoier (D) NUR
Matthias Lörper (D) NUR
Franz-Richard Friebel (D) NUR
Karl-Josef Römer (D) NUR
Jürgen Hamelmann (D) NUR (*DND*)
Harald Grohs (D) NUR, SPA
Helmut Gall (D) NUR (*DND*)
Willi Siller (D) SPA
Pierre Dieudonné (B) SPA

Kend Co. Ent.
– Chevrolet Camaro
Dick Neland (USA) DAY
Ed Kuhel (USA) DAY
Nort Northam (USA) DAY

Kendall Racing
– BMW M1
Dennis Aase (USA) DAY, SEB
Chuck Kendall (USA) DAY (*DND*), SEB
(*DND*), FUJ (*DND*)
John Hotchkis (USA) DAY (*DND*),
SEB (*DND*)
Jim Cook (USA) FUJ

Kent Racing
– MazdaRX-7
Kathy Rude (USA) DAY
Lee Mueller (USA) DAY
Allan Moffat (AUS) DAY
Jim Mullen (USA) DAY
Walt Bohren (USA) DAY
Ron Grable (USA) DAY

KennethLaGrow
– Chevrolet Monza
Kenneth LaGrow (USA) SEB
William Boyer (USA) SEB
Jack Turner (USA) SEB

Kremer Racing
– Porsche CK5
John Paul, Jr (USA) BH
Frank Jelinski (D) BH

Lässig Obermaier Team
– Porsche 935 K3, BMW M1
Edgar Dören (D) SIL, NUR
Jürgen Lässig (D) SIL, NUR (*DND*),
SPA
Hermann-Peter Duge (D) NUR
Kurt König (D) NUR
Teddy Pilette (B) SPA
Jean-Paul Libert (B) SPA

Michel Lateste – LMA 02 BMW, URD C81 BMW
Michel Lateste (F) MZA, LM
Jean Deret (F) MZA (DND)
Jean-Marie Lemerle (F) MZA (DND)
Hubert Striebig (F) LM
Jacques Heuclin (F) LM

Daniel Latour – Chevron B36 BMW
Adrian Fu (HK) FUJ
Sakae Obata (J) FUJ

Tim Lee – MercuryCapri
Timothy Lee (USA) SEB
Al White (USA) SEB
Craig Pearce (USA) SEB

Kenneth Leim – BMW 320i
Kenneth Leim (SWE) SIL
Kurt Simonsen (SWE) SIL (DND)

Jean-Marie Lemerle – Lancia Beta Montecarlo Turbo
Joe Castellano (USA) LM
Max Cohen-Olivar (MA) LM
Jean-Marie Lemerle (F) LM

Levi's Team Highball – AMC Spirit AMX
Les Delano (USA) DAY
Andy Petery (USA) DAY
Jeremy Nightingale (GB) DAY

Mandeville Racing – Mazda RX-7
Roger Mandeville (USA) DAY, SEB
Amos Johnson (USA) DAY, SEB
Jeff Kline (USA) DAY, SEB

Manns Garage – Mazda RX-7
Les Blackburn (GB) BH
David Palmer (GB) BH

Mantzel & Kissling Tuning – Opel Ascona 400
Wolfgang Offermann (D) NUR
Christoph Esser (D) NUR

March Racing – March 82G Chevrolet
Jeff Wood (USA) LM
Eje Elgh (S) LM
Patrick Neve (B) LM

Maribu Motorsport Club – Mazda RX-7
Takayuki Imadu (J) FUJ
Yoshiyuki Ogura (J) FUJ

Marketing Corporation of America – Ford Mustang
John Morton (USA) DAY, SEB
Tom Klausler (USA) DAY, SEB, FUJ
John Bauer (USA) DAY, SEB
Gary Pratt (USA) DAY
Milt Minter (USA) DAY, SEB, FUJ

Martini Racing/Italya Martini Racing – Lancia LC1 Spyder
Piercarlo Ghinzani (I) MZA, SIL, NUR, LM, SPA, MUG, FUJ, BH (DND)
Teo Fabi (I) MZA, SIL, NUR, LM, SPA, MUG, FUJ, BH

Michele Alboreto (I) MZA, SIL, NUR, LM, SPA, MUG, FUJ, BH
Riccardo Patrese (I) MZA, SIL, NUR, LM, SPA, MUG, FUJ, BH
Hans Heyer (D) LM
Rolf Stommelen (D) LM
Alessandro Nannini (I) MUG
Corrado Fabi (I) MUG

Mazda of North America – Mazda RX-7
Yoshimi Katayama (J) DAY
Takashi Yorino (J) DAY
Youjirou Terada (J) DAY

Mazda Rotary Racing - Autohaus Becker – Mazda RX-7
Armin Hahne (D) NUR
Heinz Becker (D) NUR

Mazda Sports Car Club – Mazda RX-7, Mazda RX-7 253
Kenji Seino (J) FUJ
Mutsuo Kazama (J) FUJ
Toyoshi Sugiyama (J) FUJ
Yoshikazu Koiso (J) FUJ (DND)
Kanjun Arai (J) FUJ (DND)

Mazdaspeed – Mazda RX-7 254i
Youjirou Terada (J) SIL, LM
Tom Walkinshaw (GB) SIL (DND), LM, FUJ
Pete Lovett (GB) SIL (DND), LM
Takashi Yorino (J) LM, FUJ
Allan Moffat (AUS) LM
Chuck Nicholson (GB) LM
Masanori Sekiya (J) FUJ

Meldeau Tire World – Chevrolet Camaro
Tom Juckette (USA) DAY, SEB
Mike Meldeau (USA) DAY, SEB
Bill McDill (USA) DAY, SEB

Mendener Automobil Sport Club e.V. – Opel Monza, BMW 320i
Walter Löffler (D) NUR
Herbert Hechler (D) NUR
Günter Filthaut (D) NUR (DND)
Peter Schumacher (D) (NUR)
Karl Helmich (D) (NUR)

David Mercer – Vogue SP2 Ford Cosworth BDG
David Mercer (GB) SIL, NUR, SPA
Mike Chittenden (GB) SIL, NUR, SPA
Barrie Williams (GB) SIL

Mich Opel Tuning – Opel Ascona 400, Opel Kadett
Karl-Heinz Schäfer (D) NUR
Karl-Heinz Gürthler (D) NUR
Friedrich Schütte (D) NUR
Altfrid Heger (D) NUR

Mishama Auto Hanbai – Mazda RX-7
Minoru Sawada (J) FUJ
Kaneyuki Okamoto (J) FUJ

Manfred Mohr – Alfa Romeo Alfetta
Jürgen Zehra (D) NUR
Frank Meyer (D) NUR

Momo Racing/Gianpiero Moretti – Porsche 935 78/81
Gianpiero Moretti (I) SIL, SPA, MUG
Mauro Baldi (I) SIL, SPA, MUG

Montura Racing – BMW M1
Tony Garcia (USA) DAY, SEB
Albert Naon (USA) DAY, SEB
Rob McFarlin (USA) DAY
Fred Smith (USA) SEB

Müllerbräu Team – Porsche 930
Fritz Müller (D) NUR, SPA, MUG
Georg Memminger (D) NUR, SPA, MUG

N.A.R.T. – Ferrari 512 BB/LM
Bob Wollek (F) DAY
Edgar Dören (D) DAY
Randy Lanier (USA) DAY
Desiré Wilson (ZA) SEB
Janet Guthrie (USA) SEB
Bonnie Henn (USA) SEB
Alain Cudini (F) LM
John Morton (USA) LM
John Paul (USA) LM

Nihon Sports Car Club – Mazda RX-7
Yoshimasa Matsumoto (J) FUJ
Yukio Moriya (J) FUJ
Masatoshi Oohashi (J) FUJ

Nimrod Racing Automobiles Ltd – Nimrod NRA/C2 Aston Martin
Geoff Lees (GB) SIL, LM, SPA
Bob Evans (GB) SIL, LM (DND)
Tiff Needell (GB) LM, SPA

Oberdorfer Research – Chevrolet Monza, Oldsmobile Starfire
Dave Heinz (USA) DAY
Peter Kirill (USA) DAY, SEB (DND)
Hoyt Overbagh (USA) DAY, SEB
Scott Smith Jr. (USA) (DND)

Oftedahl Racing – Pontiac Firebird, Chevrolet Camaro
Bob Raub (USA) DAY, SEB
Bob Leitzinger (USA) DAY
Art Pasmas (USA) DAY
Carl Shafer (USA) DAY, SEB
Joe Mooney (USA) DAY
Tony Brassfield (USA) DAY, SEB
Darin Brassfield (USA) SEB
Jerry Brassfield (USA) SEB
Bill Cooper (USA) SEB

Osella Mirabella Racing – Osella PA9 BMW
Duilio Truffo (I) MZA, SIL, NUR (DND)
Luigi Moreschi (I) MZA, SPA, MUG
Giorgio Francia (I) SIL, NUR, SPA, MUG

Ours & Hours Racing – Porsche 911
Jack Swanson (USA) DAY
Fred Snow (USA) DAY (DND)
Tom Cripe (USA) DAY (DND)

Angelo Pallavicini – Porsche 935
Angelo Pallavicini (CH) SEB
Neil Crang (AUS) SEB
John Sheldon (GB) SEB

Performance Plus Products – Chevrolet Corvette C3
Dale Kreider (USA) DAY
Keith Swope (USA) DAY
Peter Knab (USA) DAY

Thierry Perrier – Lancia Beta Montecarlo Turbo
Gianni Giudici (I) LM
Bernard Salam (F) LM
Thierry Perrier (F) LM

Peugeot-Talbot SA – WM P82 Peugeot
Michel Pignard (F) NUR
Jean-Daniel Raulet (F) NUR (DND)
Roger Dorchy (F) NUR (DND)

Simon Phillips – Ferrari 512 BB/LM, Martin BM8 Ford Cosworth FVC
Simon Phillips (GB) SIL, BH
Steve Earl (USA) SIL
Richard Jones (GB) SIL
Barrie Williams (GB) BH

Porsche Kremer Racing – Porsche 935 K3/81, Porsche CK5
Rolf Stommelen (D) MZA, SPA
Ted Field (USA) MZA, LM
Danny Ongais (USA) LM (DND)
Bill Whittington (USA) LM (DND)
Stefan Bellof (D) SPA

Porsche System/Rothmans Porsche – Porsche 956
Jacky Ickx (B) SIL, LM, SPA, FUJ, BH
Derek Bell (GB) SIL, LM, SPA, FUJ, BH
Jochen Mass (D) LM, SPA, FUJ
Vern Schuppan (AUS) LM, SPA, FUJ
Al Herbert (USA) LM
Hurley Haywood (USA) LM
Jürgen Barth (D) LM

Portia Parlor – Porsche 911 SC
Alan Howes (USA) DAY
Paul Nacthwey (USA) DAY
Oliver Jones (USA) DAY

Charles Pozzi-Ferrari France – Ferrari 512 LM/BB
Claude Ballot-Léna (F) LM
Jean-Claude Andruet (F) LM
Hervé Regout (B) LM

Prancing Horse Farm Racing – Ferrari 512 LM/BB
Rick Knoop (USA) DAY
Carson Baird (USA) DAY, SEB, LM
Tom Pumpelly (USA) DAY, SEB
Chip Mead (USA) SEB
Jean-Paul Libert (B) LM
Pierre Dieudonné (B) LM

Dave Preece – Aston Martin DPLM
Dave Preece (GB) BH (crashed on first lap)
Reg Woodcock (GB) BH (DND)

Primagaz – Rondeau M379C Ford Cosworth DFV
Pierre Yver (F) LM
Bruno Sotty (F) LM
Lucien Guitteny (F) LM

Promo. Ltd/Whitehall Cap. – Porsche 924 Carrera GTR
Bob Bergstrom (USA) DAY, SEB
Tom Winters (USA) DAY (DND), SEB
Robert Overby (USA) DAY (DND), SEB

R & H Racing – Porsche 911 Carrera RSR
Rainer Brezinka (CDN) SEB
Rudy Bartling (CDN) SEB
Fritz Hochreuter (CDN) SEB

Racing Mate Project Team – March 75SC BMW
Keiji Matsumoto (J) FUJ
Naohiro Fujita (J) FUJ

Rays Racing Division – Toyota Corolla G5
Norimasa Sakamoto (J) FUJ
Taidou Hashimoto (J) FUJ
Tadashi Iwawaki (J) FUJ

Raytown Datsun/D. Preston – Datsun 280ZX
Dick Davenport (USA) DAY
Frank Carney (USA) DAY
John McComb (USA) DAY

RE Amemiya Racing – Mazda RX-7
Isami Amemiya (J) FUJ
Haruo Inoue (J) FUJ
Satoshi Egura (J) FUJ

Red Lobster Racing – March 82G BMW
Dave Cowart (USA) DAY, SEB
Kenper Miller (USA) DAY, SEB
Charles Mendez (USA) DAY (DND)

Red Roof Inn – Mazda RX-7
Doug Carmean (USA) DAY, SEB
John O'Steen (USA) DAY
Ed Pimm (USA) DAY, SEB
Walt Bohren (USA) SEB

Rennax Racing – Porsche 935 L1
Jan Lundgardh (SWE) SIL
Per Stureson (SWE) SIL

Renngemeinschaft Bergisch-Gladbach e.V. im ADAC – BMW 535i, BMW 320i
Michael Martini (D) NUR
Hans Weißgerber (D) NUR
Jürgen Möhle (D) NUR
Jürgen Möhle (D) NUR (accident on lap 1)
Hans Weißgerber (D) NUR (DND)

Renngemeinschaft Sieglar e.V. im ADAC – Audi 80
Norbert Hoffman (D) NUR
Hermann-Josef Nett (D) NUR

**Road Runner Racing
– Porsche 914/6**
Tom Buckley (USA) SEB
Peter Aschenbrenner (CDN) SEB
Gene Rutherford (USA) SEB

**Roe-Selby Racing
– Porsche 911 Carrera RSR**
Earl Roe (USA) SEB
Tim Selby (USA) SEB

**Jean Rondeau/Jean Rondeau
– R. Malardeau/Otis Rondeau
– Rondeau M382 Ford
Cosworth DFL, Rondeau
M482 Ford Cosworth DFL**
Henri Pescarolo (F) SIL, NUR, LM, SPA
Gordon Spice (GB) SIL, LM, SPA
Jean Rondeau (F) SIL, LM, SPA
François Migault (F) SIL, LM, SPA
Rolf Stommelen (D) NU
Xavier Lapeyre (F) LM
Jean Ragnotti (F) LM
Jean-Pierre Jassaud (F) LM, SPA
Thierry Boutsen (B) SPA

**Scuderia Rosso
– Mazda RX-7**
Jim Fowells (USA) DAY, SEB
Ray Mummery (USA) DAY, SEB
John Carusso (USA) DAY, SEB

**John Rynerson
– Porsche 911**
Jack Rynerson (USA) SEB
Van McDonald (USA) SEB
Harvey McDonald (USA) SEB

R. Sanchez Racing – Mazda RX-7
Armando Ramirez (USA) DAY
Steve Cook (USA) DAY
Bill Cooper (USA) DAY
Luis Mendez (DR) SEB
Ralph Sanchez (USA) SEB
Armando Ramirez (USA) SEB (DND)

**Sanyo (John Carusso)
– Chevrolet Corvette**
Phil Currin (USA) SEB
John Carusso (USA) SEB

**Scorpio Racing
– Porsche 934**
'Jamsal' (Enrique Molins) (ES) DAY, SEB
Eduardo Barrientos (ES) DAY, SEB
Eduardo Galdamez (ES) DAY

**Matsunami Sekiyu
– Nissan Fairlady 280Z**
Masahiro Akiyama (J) FUJ
Ken'ichi Matsunami (J) FUJ

**Shafer Concrete
– Chevrolet Camaro**
George Shafer (USA) SEB
Craig Shafer (USA) SEB
Al Crookston (USA) SEB

**Shizumatsu Racing Team
– Mazda RX-7**
Tetsuji Shiratori (J) FUJ
Seisaku Suzuki (J) FUJ
Osamu Ihara (J) FUJ

**Shop Fujiwara
– Mazda RX-7**
Katsuhiko Ishii (J) FUJ
Hideki Okada (J) FUJ

Ned Skiff – Renault 12
Ned Skiff (USA) SEB
Jim leo (USA) SEB

**Societe Team – Cougar C01
Ford Cosworth DFL**
Patrick Gaillard (F) NUR
Yves Courage (F) NUR (DND)
Jean-Philippe Grand (F) NUR (DND)

**Speed House Alfa Auto Sports
– Mazda RX-7**
Tetsuji Tabata (J) FUJ
Yasuhiro Isozaki (J) FUJ
Seiji Kusano (J) FUJ

**Starved Rock Lodge – Chevrolet
Corvette**
Rusty Schmidt (USA) DAY
Scott Schmidt (USA) DAY
Kerry Hitt (USA) DAY

Stratagraph – Chevrolet Camaro
Billy Hagan (USA) DAY, SEB, LM
Terry Labonte (USA) DAY
Gene Felton (USA) DAY, SEB, LM
Hershel McGriff (USA) SEB, LM
Richard Brooks (USA) SEB (DND), LM
Tom Williams (USA) LM

**Sunrise Auto Parts – Chevrolet
Camaro**
Jeff Loving (USA) SEB
Edward Belin (USA) SEB (DND)

**Superior Racing – Chevrolet
Camaro**
Raul Garcia (USA) SEB
Armando Fernandez (USA) SEB

**T & R Racing – Porsche 911
Carrera RSR**
Ernesto Soto (YV) DAY, SEB
Rene Rodriguez (USA) DAY, SEB
Tico Almeida (USA) DAY, SEB

**Three Tech – Nissan
Fairlady 240ZG**
Haruji Tsuchiya (J) FUJ
Hiroyuki Miyagawa (J) FUJ

**Thunderbird Swap Shop
– Porsche 935 K3/80, Porsche
935 K3, Ferrari 512 LM/BB**
Preston Henn (USA) DAY, SEB, LM, FUJ
Bonnie Henn (USA) FUJ (DND)
Desiré Wilson (ZA) DAY
Marty Hinze (USA) DAY, SEB
Bill Whittington (USA) SEB
Don Whittington (USA) SEB
Dale Whittington (USA) SEB
Randy Lanier (USA) SEB, LM
Denis Morin (F) LM

**Tide Racing
– Ferrari 512 LM/BB**
Bernard de Dryver (B) DAY
Tom Davis (USA) DAY (DND)

**Tom's – March 75SC Toyota,
Toyota Celica C**
Masakazu Nakamura (J) FUJ
Kiyoshi Misaki (J) FUJ
Nobuhide Tachi (J) FUJ
Kaoru Hoshino (J) FUJ
Aguri Suzuki (J) FUJ

Total – BMW M1 Gp. 5
Franco Gasparetti (I) LM
Roland Ennequin (F) LM
Michel Gabriel (F) LM

Trinity Racing – Mazda RX-7
Jim Cook (USA) SEB
Jim Mullen (USA) SEB

Team Trust – Toyota Celica
Ryuusaku Hitomi (J) FUJ
Eiji Shibuya (J) FUJ
Mitsutake Koma (J) FUJ

**Ultramar Team Lola – Lola T610
Ford Cosworth DFL**
Guy Edwards (GB) MZA, SIL, NUR, LM, SPA, BH
Rupert Keegan (GB) MZA (DND), SIL, NUR, LM, SPA, BH
Nick Faure (GB) LM (DND)

**URD-Rennwagenbau GmbH
– URD C81 BMW**
Helmut Gall (D) BH
Harald Grohs (D) BH

**Van Every Racing
– Porsche 911 Carrera RSR**
Ash Tisdelle (USA) SEB
Lance Van Every (USA) SEB

**Vegla Racing Team-Joest/Vegla
Racing – Porsche 935J,
Porsche 936C**
Volkert Merl (D) MZA, MUG
Dieter Schornstein (D) MZA, SIL, MUG
Harald Grohs (D) SIL
Bob Wollek (F) MUG, BH
Henri Pescarolo (F) BH
Hans Heyer (D) BH

**Scuderia Vesuvio/Sivama
Vesuvio – Lancia Beta
Montecarlo Turbo**
Mario Casoni (I) MZA
Joe Castellano (USA) MZA, SIL, NUR, SPA, BH
Mark Thatcher (GB) MZA, SIL
Guido Daccò (I) MZA, SPA, MUG, BH
Gianni Giudici (I) MZA, SIL, NUR, SPA, MUG, BH
Jim Crawford (GB) SIL
Aldo Bertuzzi (I) SPA, MUG, BH
Bernard Salam (F) MUG

'Victor' – Porsche 935
'Victor' (Victor Coggiola) (I) MZA
Ivano Giuliani (I) MZA (DND)
Angelo Pallavicini (CH) (DND)

**Manuel Villa – Porsche 911
Carrera RSR**
Luis Gordillo (PR) SEB
Manuel Villa (PR) SEB
Mandy Gonzalez (PR) SEB

**W-S Ent. – Porsche 911
Carrera RSR**
M.L. Speer (USA) DAY
Ray Ratcliff (USA) DAY
Terry Wolters (USA) DAY

**Mark Wagoner
– Chevron GTP Buick**
Del Russo Taylor (USA) SEB
Wayne Dassinger (USA) SEB

**Welter/Meunier/S.E.C.A.T.E.V.A.
– WM P82 Peugeot PRV**
Guy Fréquelin (F) MZA
Roger Dorchy (F) MZA, SIL, SPA
Jean-Daniel Raulet (F) MZA, SIL, SPA
Michel Pignard (F) SIL, SPA

**Weralit Racing
– Porsche 935 K3**
Edgar Dören (D) MZA
Jürgen Lässig (D) MZA

**Jens Winther (Team Castrol,
Denmark) – BMW M1**
Jens Winther (DK) MZA, SIL, NUR, SPA, BH
Lars-Viggo Jensen (DK) MZA, SIL, NUR, SPA
Wolfgang Braun (D) BH

**Wolf Engine
– Chevrolet Camaro**
Clark Howey (USA) DAY
Dale Koch (USA) DAY
Tracy Wolf (USA) DAY

Gary Wonzer – Porsche 911
Gary Wonzer (USA) DAY, SEB
Bill Bean (USA) DAY, SEB
Chuck Grantham (USA) DAY

Team Yamato – Honda Civic SB1
Tsuguo Ooba (J) FUJ
Katsuaki Satou (J) FUJ
Ken Mizokawa (J) FUJ

Yours Sport – Mazda RX-7
Chikage Oguchi (J) FUJ
Toshio Fujimura (J) FUJ
Jin Ishikawa (J) FUJ
Kouichi Iwaki (J) FUJ

Zotz Garage – Porsche 914/6
Harro Zitza (USA)
John Belperche (USA)
Doug Zitza (USA)

RESULTS

**Daytona 24 Hours, 31 January,
USA. Started 69, finished 32**
1st Paul, Jr (USA)/Stommelen (D)/
Paul (USA) Porsche 935 JLP-3
2nd Akin (USA)/Siebert (USA)Bell (GB)
Porsche 935 K3/80
3rd DeNarvaez (CO)/Garretson (USA)/
Jeff Wood (USA) Porsche 935 K3

**Sebring 12 Hours, 20 March, USA
Started 67, finished 28**
1st Paul, Jr (USA)/Paul (USA) Porsche
935 JLP-3

2nd Rahal (USA)/DeNarvaez (CO)/
Trueman (USA) March 82G Chevrolet
3rd Speer (USA)/Wolters (USA)/
Mendez (USA) Porsche 935 JLP-2

**Monza 1000km, 18 April, Italy
Started 27, finished 12**
1st Pescarolo (F)/Francia (I) Rondeau
M382 Ford Cosworth DFL
2nd Stommelen (D)/Field (USA)
Porsche 935 K3/81
3rd Ciuti (I)/Benusiglio (I)/Piazzi (I)
Osella PA7 BMW

**Silverstone 6 Hours, 16 May,
Great Britain
Started 39, finished 26**
1st Alboreto (I)/Patrese (I) Lancia LC1
2nd Ickx (B)/Bell (GB) Porsche 956
3rd Wollek (F)/J-M Martin (B)/Martin
(B) Porsche 936C

**Nürburgring 1000km, 30 May,
Germany
Started 51, finished 24**
1st Alboreto (I)/Fabi (I)/Patrese (I)
Lancia LC1
2nd Pescarolo (F)/Stommelen (D)
Rondeau M382 Ford Cosworth DFL
3rd Kelleners (D)/Calderari (CH)/Grano
(I) BMW M1 Gp 5

**Le Mans 24 Hours, 20 June,
France. Started 55, finished 19**
1st Ickx (B)/Bell (GB) Porsche 956
2nd Mass (D)/Schuppan (AUS)
Porsche 956
3rd Holbert (USA)/Haywood (USA)/
Barth (D) Porsche 956

**Spa 1000km, 5 September,
Belgium. Started 36, finished 21**
1st Ickx (B)/Mass (D) Porsche 956
2nd Bell (GB)/Schuppan (AUS)
Porsche 956
3rd Patrese (I)/Fabi (I) Lancia LC1

**Mugello 1000Km, 19 September,
Italy. Started 19, finished 12**
1st Ghinzani (I)/Alboreto (I) Lancia LC1
2nd Nannini (I)/Fabi (I) Lancia LC1
3rd Wollek (F)/Heyer (D)/Pescarolo (F)
Porsche 936C

**Fuji 6 Hours, 3 October, Japan
Started 38, finished 18**
1st Ickx (B)/Mass (D) Porsche 956
2nd Patrese (I)/Fabi (I) Lancia LC1
3rd Nakamura (J)/Misaki (J) March
75SC Toyota

**Brands Hatch 1000km
17 October, Great Britain
Started 33, finished 21
(Race stopped after 9 laps
because of track damage,
restarted as a two-heat event.
One full-course caution for 2 laps.
Stopped because of darkness,
scheduled for 238 laps)**
1st Ickx (B)/Bell (GB) Porsche 956
2nd Fabi (I)/Patrese (I) Lancia LC1
3rd Fitzpatrick (GB)/Hobbs (GB)/Wollek
(F) Porsche 935 K4

WEISSACH IST WUNDERBAR

Porsche to a point saved the Group-C category by producing 'customer' versions of their 956, which were avidly taken up by Reinhold Joest, the Kremer Brothers, Obermaier, John Fitzpatrick and Richard Lloyd's Canon Racing GTi Engineering team.

Additionally, Nova Engineering Japan and American entrant/racer Preston Henn (Henn's Swap Shop Racing) also bought 956s. Another aspect of this situation was that, with exception, all the best drivers were racing 956s in Group C.

The rest of the category was really a filler except Lancia who joined the C1 club, albeit without a win. The drivers were Michele Alboreto, Riccardo Patrese, Piercarlo Ghinzani, Alessandro Nannini, Jean-Claude Andruet, Paolo Barilla, Hans Heyer and Teo Fabi, whilst the doomed Ford C100 project courtesy of Stuart Turner found a niche with Zakspeed.

One of the fillers was Robin Hamilton's doomed Nimrod Aston Martin project, some of which ended up in the USA but this was not sustainable. However, Viscount Downe employed Ray Mallock to redesign and re-body his Nimrod, which was much more attractive and faster but still too heavy and not fast enough. There was another Aston Martin powered car, Steve O'Rourke's EMKA-Aston Martin C83/1, designed by Len Bailey, which bore some resemblance to his original Ford C100, but as with the Downe car it was neither quick enough nor reliable.

Amongst the other British originated machinery the Lola T600 series cars and the March 82/83G cars were both more successful under IMSA rules in the USA, their otherwise rare outings in Europe now dependent upon Le Mans, without much success. A significant newcomer was the Bob Tullius Group 44 Jaguar XJR-5, which had a promising season under IMSA and would later travel to Le Mans in 1984/85 with rather less to show for it, as we shall see.

Also failing at this time were Sauber and their customer Swiss racer Walter Brun who bought out Peter Sauber's SHS C6s and renamed them as Sehcars, but this was also doomed. Following a DNS at Le Mans, Walter bought a customer Porsche 956 after which things improved exponentially. French expectations were predicated upon Rondeau and to a much lesser degree the WM-Peugeots and Cougars, the former now bankrupt and the other two not consistent contenders.

Beyond the prototypes was a plethora of Porsche 935s which inhabited the Group-5 and IMSA GTX classes, plus the soon-to-be-abandoned Group-B 930s.

Meanwhile the C1 and C Junior machines were in evidence, but this category would soon become C1, the best of which at this time and in 1984 being the Alba Gianninis which won their class in 1983. Worthy of comment is Mazdaspeed whose new Group C Junior 717C with twin-rotor 13B motor finished 1st and 2nd in the Junior C class at Le Mans.

There were seven races within the FIA World Championship Endurance series and Porsche won them all whilst the two IMSA races covered here, at Daytona and Sebring, were also Porsche dominated.

Ditto the Drivers' Championship which was won by Jacky Ickx followed by Derek Bell, Jochen Mass and Stefan Bellof, all members of the works Rothmans Porsche Team.

Nürburgring 1000km, 29 May 1983 The very smart no.6 is the Scuderia Mirabella 'customer' Lancia LC2 (0004) of Giorgio Francia/Piercarlo Ghinzani/Paolo Barilla that had a very pedestrian practice time compared to the single works LC2 of Patrese/Alboreto. The left bank turbo had self-destructed, but instead of replacing it they set about an engine change, presumably because the existing motor was terminally damaged. Both cars retired, the no.6 on lap 29 with differential failure and the works car on lap 35 with a probable crown-wheel-and-pinion failure after running 2nd on the road in part two. Note the white, military-style headwear of the pits marshals. *LAT*

↑ **Daytona 24 Hours, 1/2 February 1983** Following a disastrous 1982 Robin Hamilton crossed the Atlantic in search of monied racers/sponsors with his two works Nimrods, 002 and 003. This is chassis 003 and its drivers, Lyn St James (born Carol Gene Cornwall), Drake Olson in the red sweater and presumably Canadian racer John Graham, born in Belfast, Northern Ireland in 1966, who raced in a multitude of American series plus the Paris–Dakar Rally, 24 Hours of Daytona, 12 Hours of Sebring, Le Mans and Petit Le Mans. They were a solid 12th fastest in practice but alas the engine broke after 208 laps. *Revs*

← **Daytona 24 Hours, 1/2 February 1983** The Jaguar XJR-5 was the child of Bob Tullius partnered by Brian Feurstenau, whose Group 44 team had raced British cars (Jaguar, MG and Triumph during the late 1960s and early '70s). Tullius approached Mike Dale, head honcho of Jaguar Cars Inc., New Jersey who financed the venture whilst former GM and Ford designer Lee Dykstra created the aluminium ground-effect honeycomb semi-monocoque car. In its first race the 5.3-litre V12 XJR-5 finished 3rd at Road America on 23 August 1982. By February 1983 it had evolved into a better, faster car and won four races in the IMSA Championship that year. At Daytona Tullius/Adam/Petard started from 7th position and briefly led the race, but a wheel-bearing failure led to broken front suspension on lap 130. *LAT*

⬆ **Daytona 24 Hours, 1/2 February 1983** Preston Henn's 'Moby Dick' Porsche 935L (Andial) (002) was driven by Bob Wollek, Claude Ballot-Léna and Henn at Sebring. It suffered two turbo failures, but with the retirements and the rapid Wollek the car regained the lead on the Sunday morning, but then came more trouble. A.J. Foyt had retired the Nimrod at 121 laps so Henn and the race organisers allowed Foyt to join the team. At first, Wollek refused to let the American take the wheel during a pit stop but later Henn made Wollek relinquish the car to Foyt. He soon returned because he was unfamiliar with the car's gear-change pattern and indeed the Porsche itself. This was overcome and thereafter the 935 stayed ahead, helped by a 50-minute delay due to heavy rain, eventually winning by six laps from the Walters/Lanier/Hinze March Chevrolet 82G. *Revs*

➡ **Daytona 24 Hours, 1/2 February 1983** Perhaps the best and most impressive drive came from the Racing Beat Mazda RX-7 of Super Vee champion Pete Halsmer, Bob Reed and Rick Knoop, which finished a magnificent 3rd after Billy Hagan's Stratagraph Camaros retired. The Mazda was driven more or less flat out for the entire race and finished only 20 laps behind the much faster Porsche 935L and March Chevrolet. *Revs*

◄ **Daytona 24 Hours, 1/2 February 1983** This March 83G Chevrolet was entered by Motorsport Marketing and driven by Terry Wolters, Randy Lanier and Marty Hinze (28 July 1946 – 17 August 2016). They led the race during the night hours, but when the rain came, spark-plug problems slowed them down and but for this they would have won the race although they still finished 2nd. The car had been redesigned and improved by Adrian Newey who had created its predecessor, the 82G. Both Lanier and Hinze were involved in drug trafficking along with the Whittington Brothers and Lanier spent many years in prison, finally being released in October 2014. The others were not so heavily punished, Hinze being released after three years. *Revs*

◄ **Sebring 12 Hours, 19 March 1983** This was an unusual race as the winning car was Wayne Baker's GTO-class Porsche 934 (009 0030), which had started life as a 935. Drivers were Baker, Jim Mullen and Canadian Kees Nierop who crossed the line 1st after a race of multiple leaders and retirements. Ken Breslauer's book *SEBRING* informs us that there were 84 starters, 8 different leaders and 23 changes of the lead. Wayne Baker founded and managed Personalized Autohaus in 1974 and is a certified Porsche factory trained expert whilst Jim Mullen was a sometime biophysicist, charter-boat captain, offshore sail-boat racer and the CEO of Mullen Advertising until he sold it in 1999. Canadian domiciled Kees Nierop was born in Holland and is a long-time Porsche racer and associate, and race-car instructor. *Revs*

Sebring 12 Hours, 19 March 1983 Two Oftedahl Racing Pontiac Firebirds ran at Sebring: one for Carl Shafer, Carlos Ramirez and Mike Meldeau, which finished 26th, and this one, driven by Paul Fassler, Steve Pope and again Carl Shafer, which retired due to engine failure on lap 132. Shafer was a corn and soya-bean farmer, a successful and talented but perhaps underestimated racer in the 1970s/80s who suffered a very nasty crash at Road America in 2005 and died in his sleep of a heart attack some time later. *Revs*

Monza 1000km, 10 April 1983 There were intruders at the Monza 1000km. The AC di Milano allowed eight 2-litre Group-6 cars, which were competing in a national championship, to join the race at the back of the grid. This was supposed to be for 15 laps, but two of them stayed out and one, the Jolly Club Osella PA9/82 Carma Turbo of Facetti, Finotto and 'Gimax' (Carlo Franchi) finished 14th. This is Adriano Gozzi in the Lucchini-BMW S280 who finished 6th in the Group-6 race and went on to win the 1984 Italian Prototype Championship (Division 1). Lucchini Corse was both manufacturer of racing cars and a racing team started by Giorgio Lucchini in Porto Mantovano in 1980 and raced across Europe into the next century. Lucchini sold out in 2010 and the new owner died not long afterward, marking the end of the company and its team. *LAT*

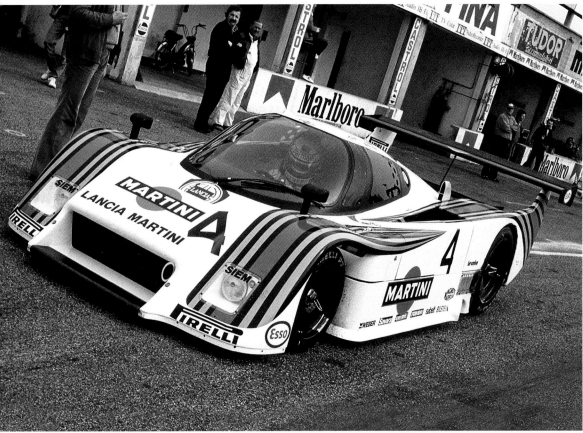

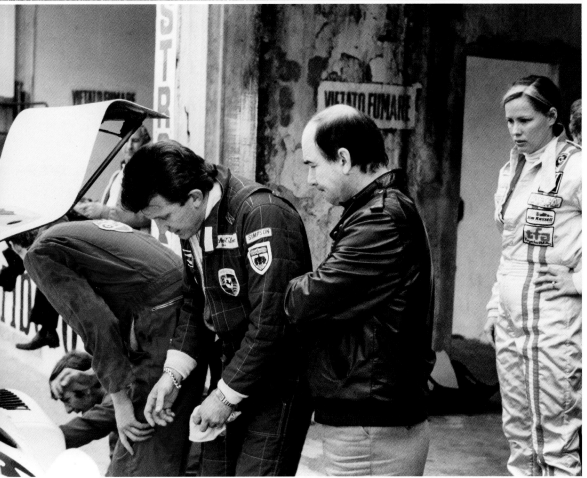

Monza 1000km, 10 April 1983 Lancia's new LC2-83 had a Ferrari 308-based engine and two were entered at Monza. The Ghinzani/Fabi (0003) was fastest in practice on Pirelli qualifying tyres and led the race until lap 8 when the left rear tyre exploded. Ghinzani pitted having lost time and had the mangled bodywork removed before rejoining the fray, but a water radiator had been damaged and the car retired on lap 24. Patrese shared chassis 002 with Alboreto and they finished 9th after some electrical glitches and a rear left tyre that had exploded three times, resulting in the Lancia stopping every 15 laps for a new tyre. After yet another blow-out Alboreto pitted and whilst the team repaired the rear-end damage a new turbo was installed, costing them some 30 minutes. *GPL*

Monza 1000km, 10 April 1983 After years of racing his Porsche 934 Richard Cleare arrived at Monza with the original Kremer Porsche C82-K5 (01). Cleare is looking at Tony Dron in the cockpit with Erwin Kremer (26 June 1937 – 27 September 2006) alongside and Margie Smith-Haas (who brought sponsorship from her company 'Toys for Adults') is in the background. Kneeling down is chief mechanic Don Holland with mechanic Geoff O'Connor bending forward. Dron qualified the car 10th and passed Plankenhorn's much faster Obermaier Porsche 956 in the race, handing over to Smith-Haas in 6th place. Margie was unfamiliar with the car and ran wide in the chicane to allow the faster 956s by, and in doing so collected the shrapnel from Ghinzani's Lancia tyre explosion. This penetrated the oil cooler, the rear tyres were liberally covered in lubricant and it spun round, but she kept the engine running and reversed the Porsche into a safe spot and walked away. *LAT*

Monza 1000km, 10 April 1983 The Joest Porsche 956 (104) Marlboro customer car for Bob Wollek (seen behind the car) and Thierry Boutsen using Dunlop qualifying tyres was second fastest at Monza behind the Ghinzani/Fabi Lancia LC2, just 0.07 seconds quicker than Ickx in the factory Rothmans 956. Despite all Porsche's efforts, the Joest car remained just out of reach in the race, being equally fast on track but able to go a lap or two further on their fuel allocation. Ickx/Mass finished in 2nd place 72.9 seconds behind the Franco/Belgian duo. The other Joest 956 of Stommelen/Heyer/Schickentanz finished 3rd. *LAT*

Monza 1000km, 10 April 1983 Al Holbert, son of legendary Porsche and Cobra racer Bob Holbert, shared the second Rothmans Porsche 956 with Derek Bell and they finished 7th due to a seized wheel bearing, having run in the first three earlier on. Holbert won at Daytona in 1986 and 1987, Sebring in 1976 and 1981, Le Mans in 1983, 1986 and 1987, finished 4th in the 1984 Indianapolis 500 and won five IMSA championships. Tragically he died in a light-aircraft accident, apparently due to an open baggage door that had not been shut properly at take-off from the Don Scott Field in Columbus, Ohio, after diverting his twin-engine Piper away from a group of houses. Alvah Robert 'Al' Holbert (11 November 1946 – 30 September 1988). *LAT*

 **Silverstone 1000km, 8 May 1983** Two new Group-C Aston Martins were announced before the Silverstone 1000km. One was Viscount Downe's Ray Mallock-redesigned Nimrod Aston Martin C2B, which was more aerodynamic, much lighter (allegedly 940kg) and prettier than its bulky predecessor. Its Tickford engine was also substantially improved and shortened, which allowed more space in the otherwise rather crowded engine bay. As before the drivers were Mallock and veteran 1960s Jaguar and Aston Martin racer Mike Salmon, seen here in typical laid-over fashion. They finished 7th at Silverstone, but this was to be their best result of the season and amazingly the four points it won was good enough for 4th place in the 1983 Marques' Championship. *GPL*

 **Silverstone 1000km, 8 May 1983** The other Aston Martin-powered car was Steve O'Rourke's EMKA-Aston Martin C83/1, designed by Len Bailey (hence its similarity to the Ford C100). As usual for O'Rourke's cars, it was built up in Michael Cane's Godalming, Surrey workshop. The budget for this was a measly £150,000, not even pocket money for the likes of Porsche and indeed many professional customer teams. Its 5,340cc Aston Martin engine was claiming 570bhp and the car weighed about 900kg, but it was 11 seconds off the pole-position Porsche (the Downe Nimrod was 9 seconds adrift). Drivers at Silverstone were O'Rourke, Tiff Needell and touring-car ace Jeff Allam. They started from 17th place and reached 13th before retiring within sight of the flag due to wheel-bearing failure. This is O'Rourke driving and after finishing a problematical 17th at Le Mans there was no more funding available so the car was mothballed for two years, reappearing in 1985. *LAT*

→ **Silverstone 1000km, 8 May 1983** Stefan Bellof in the factory Porsche 956-83 (007) shared with Derek Bell were 2 seconds faster than the Joest Marlboro Porsche 956 (104) of Wollek/Johansson in qualifying with Ickx/Mass 956-83 (006) 3rd fastest. All three used Dunlop tyres whilst the Pirelli-shod Lancia LC2s occupied 4th and 5th. Porsche had reset the Bosch settings, fuel tank calibration, mixture and compression after Monza and Bell/Bellof won the race from the Joest car with Lammers/Boutsen 3rd in Richard Lloyd's Canon Racing 956. Jochen Mass had another Silverstone crash in the second works 956 at Club. Bellof on slicks is pursued by Alan Jones in the Kremer 956 (101) who had started on grooved Goodyear slicks, with the track still wet but drying. Alan caught the works Porsches and Lancias to lead the race until the track dried out, eventually finishing 5th with Vern Schuppan. *LAT*

→ **Silverstone 1000km, 8 May 1983** Porsche 956s came in all colours and sponsors. This is the Boss-Obermaier Racing 956 (109) driven by Axel Plankenhorn, Jürgen Lässig and Harald Grohs. They qualified 8th and finished 4th. Plankenhorn's racing career began in Formula V and he raced for the Kremer team at Le Mans in 1979. In 1982 he joined the Obermaier Racing Team and retired from racing after the 1984 Monza 1000km. Jürgen Lässig drove for Obermaier Racing, Primagaz, Team Salamin and Porsche Kremer from 1981 to 1997 whilst Harald Grohs was an endurance-racing aficionado who said of his time with BMW in 1976: "Only Stuck and Peterson were a little faster, but partnered with Peterson, we could never finish a race." *LAT*

↑ Silverstone 1000km, 8 May 1983 After the disappointment of Monza, Tony Dron and Richard Cleare finished an impressive 6th at Silverstone in the Kremer CK5-82 (01). Note the rear fin that looks similar to latter-day F1 cars and prototypes. Later the team dispensed with the fin, improved the aerodynamics and fitted a Hewland gearbox. Here we see again the truncated nose syndrome, *à la* the Ford C100 and the EMKA-Aston Martin amongst others. *LAT*

↗ Nürburgring 1000km, 29 May 1983 Three weeks later at the Nürburgring, the start/finish area and paddock was being reformed, the Sud Kerve dug up and later the Nordschleife replaced by the new F1 circuit. Some were sorry but others were not. The Nordschleife was now 12.944 miles (20.832km) in length as against its previous 14.189 miles (22.835km). Porsche had further refined their 956 and Stefan Belloff set a time of 6 min 11.13 seconds (the fastest ever) to take pole position 5.73 seconds quicker than Mass in the other Rothmans 956. It was damp in places but most of the circuit was dry, which suited the slick-shod works 956s whilst others were on wets. At the second pit stop Bellof had a 16-second lead over Mass, but three laps later at the Pflanzgarten the car became airborne over the infamous jump. He was quoted in *Autosport* saying: "Suddenly I was looking at the sky. I just don't know what happened." The 956 (007) stayed right side up but hit the barriers and the cockpit was the only part of the car still relatively intact. Later when asked by somebody what it had been like he replied, "Apollo 16". In the background the Ickx/Mass 956 (005) passes by en route to victory. *LAT*

→ Nürburgring 1000km, 29 May 1983 Wealthy Swiss slot-machine boss Walter Brun had bought the two Sauber C6s from Peter Sauber and this is Brun's new Sehcar still wearing the Sauber C6 body. They raced one with the Cosworth DFL at Silverstone, but at the Nürburgring they had the second car (82-C6-01) with a 3.2-litre Schnitzer turbocharged short-stroke BMW engine, allegedly giving 650bhp. It was driven by Brun and Hans-Joachim Stuck who were 7th fastest in qualifying. However, they were delayed by a broken distributor drive in the race and after Brun rejoined the fray he crashed near to Kesselchen on lap 19, wrecking the car and damaging his arm. During the pit stop Brun can just be seen in the background to the right of the 'bitburger ADAC 1000km' banner. Note the *Bitte ein Bit!* ('Please, a Bit,' or 'A Bit, please') logo on the rear number square, a marketing slogan of the Bitburger brewery in Bitburg, Rhineland-Palatinate. *LAT*

← **Nürburgring 1000km, 29 May 1983** Brun Motorsport also entered this BMW M1 (WBS59910004301076) for Harald Grohs and Leopold von Bayern. They qualified 11th fastest ahead of the Jens Winther M1 but retired on lap 14 due to a broken gearbox, thus denying von Bayern a drive. He is Prince Leopold (Poldi) of Bavaria, (full name, Leopold Rupprecht Ludwig Ferdinand Adalbert Friedrich Maria et omnes sancti Prinz von Bayern), member of the Bavarian royal house of Wittelsbach, descended from King Ludwig I of Bavaria. His racing career began in 1969 and in 1984 he finished 4th at Le Mans with Walter Brun and Bob Akin in Brun's Porsche 956B, and seems to have retired in 1987. *LAT*

← **Nürburgring 1000km, 29 May 1983** The Canon Racing Porsche 956 was driven by World Champion Keke Rosberg, Jan Lammers and Jonathan Palmer. During part one the 956 (106) was understeering at every corner and it gradually dropped back. Following the restart it was behaving itself after a rear-wing adjustment and led the race on the road in part two with Palmer crossing the line 1st in the second half, which worked out as 3rd overall including part one. During this pit stop Palmer can be seen at far left with hands in pockets and wearing a dark red top. *LAT*

Le Mans 24 Hours, 18/19 June 1983 Realistically, by now only Porsche could be guaranteed to win; the opposition was either too slow, too unreliable, or just not good enough full stop. At Le Mans the first eight finishers were all 956s: 1st and 2nd for the works cars followed by the customer teams led by the Kremer Porsche 956 (101) of Michael Andretti with Philippe Alliot, which finished 3rd. This is the winning car, driven by Hurley Haywood (seen here), Vern Schuppan and Al Holbert. They were lucky, however, because teammates Ickx and Bell were miles faster than the rest and should and would have won but for various niggles including a collision on lap 2 with Lammers' Canon Racing 956 and later electrical problems. They were 3rd at 4 and 8 hours, 2nd at 12 hours, 3rd at 16 hours and 2nd at the finish whilst the American/Australian trio nearly succumbed to serious overheating in the last moments of the race. *LAT*

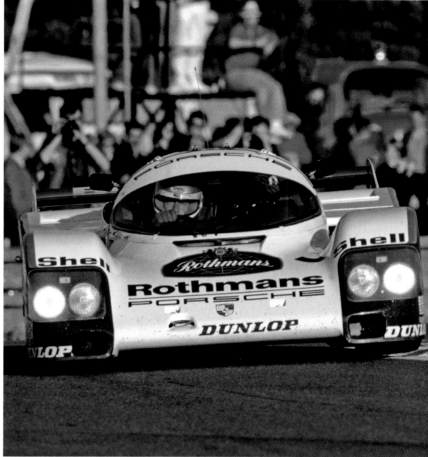

Le Mans 24 Hours, 18/19 June 1983 The new Sauber C7 used the ubiquitous BMW M88 that had powered the BMW M1, its Heini Mader engine giving 460bhp according to the period *Autosport*. It was Peter Sauber's relief from the unlamented C6 with its hostile Cosworth DFL engine and the control of Seger & Hoffmann. Three freelance Mercedes-Benz engineers drew the body and created the aluminium honeycomb monocoque whilst the drivers were IMSA regulars Diego Montoya, Albert Naon and Tony Garcia. Funding was supplied by Air Jamaica and a Colombian bank, in $20 notes allegedly. They qualified 33rd out of 54 in practice and finished 9th although at one point they were 7th until a leaking exhaust and later a gear linkage delayed them. *LAT*

⬆ **Le Mans 24 Hours, 18/19 June 1983** Ralph Kent-Cooke (29 April 1937 – 11 September 1995, liver failure) entered his Cosworth DFL 3.95-powered Lola T610 (HU2) for himself, Jim Adams and François Servanin at Le Mans. They were 27th in practice and despite an electrical problem were in 10th place at 10 hours, but the car was retired at around the 13th hour with head-gasket failure. The troublesome Cosworth DFL programme had already been abandoned and this car was later sold on to John Bartlett who raced it with the smaller 3.3-litre DFL motor in 1984. It was one of only two T610s; the other, HU1, was raced by Ultramar Team Lola for Edwards/Keegan in 1982 and later went to Terry Hook in Australia right at the end of December 1983 where it raced with a Chevrolet 366 motor. *LAT*

↗ **Le Mans 24 Hours, 18/19 June 1983** Jean Rondeau's improved M482 reappeared at Le Mans where three were entered with Cosworth DFL 3.95 motors and sponsored by Ford France. Drivers were Pescarolo/Boutsen, Streiff/Jaussaud and Rondeau/Alain Ferté/Michel Ferté. Sadly, they all retired, with engine failure on lap 174, an oil leak on lap 12 and another engine failure on lap 90 respectively. However, Jean Rondeau also ran two older M379Cs, this one, chassis no.002, driven by Joël Gouhier, Anny-Charlotte Verney (F) and Vic Elford, then 48 and returning nine years after he had apparently retired. Alas the car dropped a valve late at night after reaching 10th place two hours earlier, with Elford on board. His was a fascinating story of successfully racing in all manner of cars – in F1, championship sports/prototype and rallying – for many years. *LAT*

→ **Le Mans 24 Hours, 18/19 June 1983** Two new WM-Peugeot P83s attended Le Mans with a larger-capacity 3,053cc V6 engine developing a claimed 580bhp and new underpinnings and bodywork. They were driven by Roger Dorchy (in the car), Alain Couderc and Pascal Fabre in no.10, and Jean-Daniel Raulet, Michel Pignard and Didier Theys in the second car. They qualified 18th and 17th respectively, just 0.180 seconds apart. No.10 started from the pit lane after a cylinder-head oil leak which required a new gasket but later also suffered electrical problems involving batteries and alternators. Ultimately no.10 finished a delayed 16th whilst the other P83 retired due to overheating after 102 laps. *LAT*

Le Mans 24 Hours, 18/19 June 1983 The Kremer Brothers entered their now obsolete CK5 83(03) for Le Mans debutant Derek Warwick with German racer Frank Jelinski and Frenchman Partrick Gaillard. Warwick was an impressive 14th fastest on the grid but the car was out after 76 laps with head-gasket failure and exhaust problems. Note the now long-gone *Grand Prix International* magazine decal on the car's nose. Meanwhile, Richard Cleare's other, older CK5 82 lasted but eight laps before retiring due to gearbox failure, whilst the other pre-956 Porsche car, the Joest Belga Team 936C of Jean-Michel Martin, Philippe Martin and Marc Duez retired after a paltry nine laps with fuel-injection issues. *LAT*

Le Mans 24 Hours, 18/19 June 1983 Following their successful season in 1982 with an RX-7 254 IMSA car, Mazda produced a Group-C Junior 717C with the familiar twin-rotor 13B motor. It weighed in at a heavy 780kg (1,720lb, 15.35cwt). Despite this and a modest power output it was good for 190mph allegedly. Two were entered, one with a Japanese crew (Yoshimi Katayama, Yojiro Terada and Takashi Yorino) which finished 12th overall (303 laps) and 1st in the Junior-C class, and the other for Jeff Allam, Steve Soper and James Weaver which finished 18th overall (268 laps) and 2nd in class. This is the faster British car, 717C (001), which had a tyre burst on Mulsanne during the first hour. Later it developed a misfire, perhaps due to dirt ingestion from the tyre failure, that eventually disappeared, leaving the now healthy car to play catch-up. *LAT*

Spa 1000km, 4 September 1983 After the meagre 51 starters at Le Mans, the turnout at Spa was equally lacking with only 27 cars occupying the grid. Mass in the works 956 (005) leads the way on the formation lap with teammate Belloff 956 (004) next followed by the Kremer 956 (101) of Derek Warwick, now sporting Boss colours, Patrese Lancia LC2 (0002), Fitzpatrick 956 (102), the no.43 Zakspeed Ford C1/4 turbo for Klaus Ludwig and the rest. The Bell/Bellof car did occupy 1st place in the race but Mass went one more (slow) lap before refuelling which allowed Ickx to go faster later on without running dry. However, 004 developed a brake fault and the resultant pit stop allowed Ickx/Mass back into the lead where they stayed to the end despite Belloff's new lap record whilst Fitzpatrick with David Hobbs finished 3rd in the Fitzpatrick 956. *LAT*

Spa 1000km, 4 September 1983 The Cheetah G603 was the creation of Swiss engineer Charles 'Chuck' Graemiger and after a long transition it finally appeared at Spa in 1983. It had a 3.3-litre Cosworth DFL engine and was sponsored by Gatoil. The drivers were Jean-Pierre Jaussaud and Swiss racer Loris Kessel (1 April 1950 – 15 May 2010, leukaemia). It started 17th on the grid but retired on lap 26 with a blown engine. However, at the Imola 1000km on 16 October Kessel, Laurent Ferrier and Rolf Biland finished 9th and a week later at Mugello Kessel/Ferrier finished 8th. Loris Kessel had provided some finance for the team and during the winter of 1984 he began litigation against Graemiger on the basis of legal rights to the project. The outcome was that Graemiger rebuilt the car using an Aston Martin V8 engine from Tickford with the blessing of Gatoil and it appeared at Spa again in 1984. *LAT*

Spa 1000km, 4 September 1983 The Harrier RX83C was designed and built by Lester Ray in Epsom, Surrey for period racer Roy Baker. It was maintained and further developed by JQF Engineering (Jon Fisher). The 1.3-litre Mazda 13B rotary engine produced a modest 290bhp and it also had a tendency to run too hot. However, at Spa Baker, with Mazda's UK public relations chief David Palmer, finished 14th overall and 1st in the Junior Group-C class. Roy Baker was a motorcycle racer who had moved to cars and entered more Group-C races than anybody throughout the 1980s, especially Tigas, together with 16 appearances at Le Mans in period. He died just before Christmas 2002 after complications following an operation. Alongside is the Ghinzani/Fabi/Alboreto Lancia LC2 (0003) that finished 11th following electrical problems and Lancia switching around their drivers. *LAT*

➜ Spa 1000km, 4 September 1983 (Euro TV) Mirabella Racing beat the two works Martini Lancia LC2s at Spa, which suffered various problems as already noted. Driven by Paolo Barilla (I) and Giorgio Francia (I), they finished 6th overall and 6th in the Group-C category in the LC2 (0004). Barilla, born 20 April 1961, is one of the heirs of the Barilla pasta group, which had a net worth of US$1.39 billion in 2017. He was a successful karting racer who drove in many categories including F3, F2 and briefly F1 before retiring in 1990. This is the beginning of the now long departed 'Bus Stop' section at Spa. *LAT*

➜ Spa 1000km, 4 September 1983 A better view of the Bus Stop, this time with Eric Zakowski's honeycomb-chassis Ford C100 that he had managed to retain after Stuart Turner shut down the project in early 1983. It was renamed the C1/4 in deference to its Zakspeed 4-cylinder turbocharged 1.7-litre engine. Zakowski had two cars which were successfully raced in the German Sports Car Championship during 1983, one sponsored by GWB Service and this one by Jägermeister. Klaus Ludwig and Klaus Niedzwiedz qualified 6th but retired on lap 30 due to gearbox troubles, having reached 4th place. In 1984 chassis C1/8 was raced at the Nürburgring 1000km with a 3.3-litre Cosworth DFL, again by the two Klauses, but retired, this time with a broken driveshaft, and that was Zakowski's last race with this doomed project. *LAT*

Spa 1000km, 4 September 1983 No mistaking this shot, one of many over the decades, full tilt through the opening curve of Eau Rouge. The driver is former Zakspeed ace, German sports and saloon car racer Hans Heyer who amongst many victories won the 1984 Sebring 12 Hours and three Spa 24 Hours in succession, 1982/83/84. At Spa the Newman car was run by Joest (although Dieter Schornstein was the owner) but entered by Sorg S.A. The other driver was Volkert Merl, but a wastegate problem dropped the car to 12th so Joest inserted Wollek into the 956 (105) and after climbing back to 9th it retired on lap 90 with broken front suspension. Following is one of the Martini Lancia LC2s. *LAT*

Brands Hatch 1000km, 18 September 1983 This race was for the European Endurance Championship as were the Imola and Mugello rounds, rather than the WEC (World Endurance Championship). It was another murky day in Kent but good news for John Fitzpatrick who shared his JDAVID Porsche 956 (110) with Derek Warwick. They beat the works Porsches of Mass/Ickx and Bell/Bellof due to their superior Goodyear 'wets' and meteoric pace. Derek Warwick passed Bell on lap 2 and Ickx on lap 3 and by lap 20 was 44 seconds ahead of Bob Wollek in the Joest 956 who had passed Bell whilst Ickx was 15 seconds further down after an off on lap 7. During the dry period both works 956s unlapped themselves but their fuel stops were too long compared to the Fitzpatrick car. Although Bellof began to catch Warwick, a flat-spotted tyre slowed the German and Warwick/ Fitzpatrick won despite Warwick having a minor collision with another car. *LAT*

Brands Hatch 1000km, 18 September 1983 A delighted Derek Warwick lifts his cap whilst 'Fitz' is about to remove his after their stunning drive in beating the works Porsche 956s. Behind Warwick with hands in his race suit is Italian Martino Finotto (11 November 1933 – 13 August 2014) who with Carlo Facetti won the Group-C Junior class in the Jolly Club-entered Alba Carma-Giannini AR2. *LAT*

Fuji 1000km, 2 October 1983 This was another works Porsche 956 walkover with Bell/Bellof beating Ickx/Mass after the latter were delayed by a punctured tyre. Bellof was five-tenths quicker in qualifying than his teammates and 1.3 seconds quicker than the third-fastest car, the Boutsen/Pescarolo 956 (112) entered by Yoshiho Matsuda, which finished 4th in the race behind the Trust Engineering 956 (108) of Schuppan/Fujita. A jubilant Bellof celebrates as teammate Derek Bell crosses the line in the 956 (009) and note his protruding 'Adam's apple', usually a sign of high testosterone levels. *LAT*

Fuji 1000km, 2 October 1983 As ever, others plagiarise/copy or base their cars upon what works best and during this era quite a few had similar shapes to the 956 as seen here with the Nissan LM03 Fairlady Z of Central Racing Team, driven by Haruhito Yanagida/Takao Wada. They qualified an impressive 11th, 4 seconds slower than pole position given that the car's 2,083cc, 4-cylinder, 16-valve twin Garret turbo engine was no match for the 620bhp or more of Porsche's flat-6. The two Domes, one with a Cosworth DFL motor, and a March Nissan 83G were marginally quicker. Alas Wada spun off causing some minor damage, and later the car was disqualified on lap 90 for taking on oil too soon, according to stats. *LAT*

Kyalami 1000km, 10 December 1983 Two weeks after Fuji, the Imola 1000km was won by Teo Fabi/Hans Heyer in the works Lancia LC2-83 with Fitzpatrick/Hobbs 2nd in the Porsche 956 (110) and Wollek/Johansson 3rd in the Joest 956 (104). Porsche meanwhile had decided to miss the last two European races (Imola as above and Mugello won by the Joest 956 of Wollek/Johansson) but they did attend Kyalami. This featured some heavy rain storms which knocked out at least ten cars including three customer 956s, but the Bell/Bellof 956 (009), seen here passing the remnants of the rain storm, won the race four laps ahead of the Martini Racing Lancia LC2 of Patrese/Nannini with Ickx/Mass 3rd in their 956 (005). There was a third works 956 (003) for Holbert/Schuppan, but this retired on lap 143 with ignition problems. *LAT*

ENTRANTS

901 Shop – Porsche 911 SC
Mike Schaefer (USA) DAY, SEB
Jack Refenning (USA) DAY, SEB
John Belperche (USA) DAY
Doug Zitza (USA) DAY, SEB

Air Florida – BMW MI
'Fomfor' (Francisco Miguel) (ES) SEB
Arnoldo Kreysa (ES) SEB
Albert Naon (USA) SEB (*DND*)

**Bob Akin Motor Racing
– Porsche 935 K3/80**
Bob Akin (USA) DAY, SEB
John O'Steen (USA) DAY, SEB
Dale Whittington (USA) DAY (*DND*),
SEB

**Alfa Romeo SA
– Alfa Romeo Alfetta GTV6**
Arnold Chatz (ZA) KYA
Eric Saunders (ZA) KYA
Dick Pickering (ZA) KYA
Maurizio Bianco (I) KYA

**All American Racers
– Toyota Celica**
Wally Dallenbach, Jr (USA) DAY
Willy T. Ribbs (USA) DAY
Whitney Ganz (USA) DAY
Dennis Aase (USA) DAY
Al Unser, Jr (USA) DAY
Michael Chandler (USA) DAY
Gene Hackman (USA) DAY Masanori
Sekiya (J) DAY
Kaoru Hoshino (J) DAY

**Equipe Alméras Frères
– Porsche 930**
Jean-Marie Alméras (F) MZA, SIL, LM
Roland Biancone (F) MZA, SIL
Jacques Guillot (F) MZA, SIL, LM
Jacques Alméras (F) LM

**Alpha Cubic Racing Team
– MCS Guppy Renoma 83C**
Chiyomi Totani (J) FUJ
Taku Akaike (J) FUJ

Alpha Racing – Porsche 956
Preston Henn (USA) FUJ
Kunimitsu Takahashi (J) FUJ
John Paul, Jr (USA) FUJ (*DND*)

Giuseppe Arlotti – Porsche 930
Luigi Colzani (I) MZA
Bruno Rebai (I) MZA

Auriga Racing – Chevrolet Camaro
Tom Nehl (USA) DAY
Nelson Silcox (USA) DAY
Richard Valentine (USA) DAY

**Autax Motor
– Porsche 924 Carrera GTS**
Klaus Utz (D) NUR
Claude Haldi (CH) NUR

**Autobacs Dome Motorsport –
Dome RC83 Ford Cosworth DFL**
Eje Elgh (S) FUJ
Tiff Needell (GB) FUJ

**Auto Beaurex Motorsport
– Lotec M1C BMW**
Kurt Lotterschmid (D) FUJ
Naoki Nagasaka (J) FUJ (*DND*)
Keiichi Suzuki (J) (*DND*)

Avanti – Avanti II
Herb Adams (USA) DAY
John Martin (USA) DAY
Joe Ruttman (USA) DAY
Leonard Emanuelson (USA) DAY

**B de T Racing
– BMW M1**
Diego Montoya (CO) DAY
Terry Herman (USA) DAY
Tony Garcia (USA) DAY

**Bayside Disposal Racing
– Porsche 935/80**
Hurley Haywood (USA) DAY, SEB
Bruce Leven (USA) DAY
Al Holbert (USA) DAY, SEB

**Bob Beasley
– Porsche 911 Carrera RSR**
Bob Beasley (USA) DAY
John Ashford (USA) DAY
Jack Lewis (USA) DAY (*DND*)

**Valentin Bertapelle
– URD C81 BMW**
Bruno Sotty (F) LM
Gérard Cuynet (F) LM

**Bieri Racing
– BMW M1**
Uli Bieri (CDN) DAY, SEB
Matt Gysler (CDN) DAY, SEB (*DND*)
Duff Hubbard (CDN) DAY, SEB (*DND*)

**Bard Board
– Chevrolet Corvette**
Bard Board (USA) DAY
Richard Anderson (USA) DAY
Mike Stephens (USA) DAY

**Bob's Speed Products
– Ford Maverick**
Bob Lee (USA) SEB
Timothy S. Lee (USA) SEB
Gary Myers (USA) SEB

**Raymond Boutinnaud
– Porsche 928S**
Patrick Gonin (F) LM
Raymond Boutinaud (F) LM
Alain Le Page (F) LM

**BP BMW Dealer Team
– BMW 535i**
Tony Viana (ZA) KYA
John Moni (ZA) KYA

**BP/Nissan/Autoquip
– Nissan Skyline**
Hennie van der Linde (ZA) KYA
George Santana (ZA) KYA

**Brumos Racing
– Porsche 924 Carrera GTR**
Kathy Rude (USA) DAY, SEB
Deborah Gregg (USA) DAY, SEB
Bonnie Henn (USA) DAY, SEB

**Brun Motorsport (CH) BMW M1,
Porsche 956**
Harald Grohs (D) NUR, KYA (*DND*)
Leopold von Bayern (D) NUR (*DND*)
Umberto Grano (I) KYA (*DND*)
Hans-Joachim Stuck (D) KYA
Massimo Sigala (I) KYA

**Brun Motorsport GmbH
– Sehcar SH C6 Ford
Cosworth DFL, Porsche 956**
Hans-Joachim Stuck (D) SIL,
NUR, SPA
Walter Brun (CH) SIL, NUR, SPA
Ludwig Heimrath, Jr (CDN) LM
David Deacon (CDN) LM
Jacques Villeneuve, Sr (CDN) LM
Harald Grohs (D) SPA

**Brun Speedbox Motorsport (CH)
– Porsche 956**
Kenji Takahashi (J) FUJ
Clemens Schickentanz (D) FUJ

**Bryant & Graham Racing
– Ford Pinto, BMW 2002**
Cameron Worth (USA) SEB
Alan Crouch (USA) SEB
Janis Taylor (USA) SEB
Charles W. Bryant (USA) SEB
Alex Priest (USA) SEB
Mike Guido (USA) SEB

**Burdsall-Welter Racing
– Mazda RX-7**
Tom Burdsall (USA) DAY, SEB
Peter Welter (USA) DAY, SEB
Al Bacon (USA) DAY
Nort Northam (USA) SEB

**Christian Bussi – Rondeau M382
Ford Cosworth DFL**
Pascal Witmeur (B) LM
Daniël Herregods (B) LM
Jean-Paul Libert (B) LM

**Paul Canary Racing
– Pontiac Firebird**
Paul Canary (USA) DAY, SEB
Jean-Paul Libert (B) DAY
Pascal Witmeur (B) DAY
Roger Carmillet (F) DAY (*DND*)
Jim Sanborn (USA) SEB

**Canon Racing
– Porsche 956**
Jan Lammers (NL) MZA, SIL, NUR,
LM, SPA
Tiff Needell (GB) MZA
Richard Lloyd (GB) MZA, LM
Thierry Boutsen (B) SIL, SPA
Keke Rosberg (SF) NUR
Jonathan Palmer (GB) NUR, LM

Case Racing – Porsche 911
Jack Rynerson (USA) DAY
Ron Case (USA) DAY, SEB
Craig Case (USA) SEB
Dave Pannacione (USA) SEB

**Central 20 Racing Team
– LM03C Nissan**
Haruhito Yanagida (J) FUJ
Takao Wada (J) FUJ

**Centurion Leasing
– Chevrolet Camaro**
Tom Nehl (USA) SEB
Nelson Silcox (USA) SEB
Patty Moise (USA) SEB

**Cheetah Car
– Cheetah G603
Ford Cosworth DFL**
Jean-Pierre Jaussaud (F) SPA
Loris Kessel (CH) SPA
Laurent Ferrier (F) SPA (*DND*)

**Scuderia Chico D'Oro
– Porsche 930**
Olindo Del-Thé (CH) KYA
Mario Regusci (CH) KYA

**Thomas T. Ciccone
– Chevrolet Camaro**
Mike Gassaway (USA) DAY
Scott Smith, Sr (USA) DAY
Joe Cogbill, Sr (USA) DAY
Joe Cogbill (USA) DAY

**Richard Cleare Racing
– Porsche CK5**
Tony Dron (GB) MZA, SIL,
LM (*DND*)
Margie Smith-Haas (USA) MZA
Richard Cleare (GB) MZA, SIL, LM
Richard Jones (GB) LM (*DND*)

**Richard Cline
– Mazda RX-7**
Rick Cline (USA) DAY
Paul Romano (USA) DAY
Mike Powell (USA) DAY

**Pat Coles Racing with JVC
– Mazda RX-7**
Clarrie Taylor (ZA) KYA
Chris Swanepoel (ZA) KYA

**Cooke Racing
– Lola T600 Chevrolet,
Lola T610 Ford Cosworth DFL**
Ralph Kent-Cooke (USA) DAY,
SEB, LM
Jim Adams (USA) DAY,
SEB, LM
John Bright (GB) DAY
Josele Garza (USA) SEB
François Servanin (F) LM

**Hiram Cruz Racing
– Porsche 934**
Mandy Gonzalez (PR) SEB
Hiram Cruz (USA) SEB

**The Cummings Marque
– Chevrolet Monza**
Don Cummings (USA) SEB
Craig Rubright (USA) SEB
Charles Gano (USA) SEB

**D L Performance
Engineering
– Porsche 911 Carrera RSR**
Doug Lutz (USA) DAY, SEB
Dave Panaccione (USA) DAY
Larry Connor (USA) DAY, SEB
Fern Prego (USA) DAY
Mike Brummer (USA) SEB

**Bobby Diehl /Diehl Hi Pro
Enterprises – Mazda RX-7,
Chevrolet Camaro**
Bobby Diehl (USA) DAY, SEB
Roy Newsome (USA) DAY, SEB
Carmen Lista (USA) SEB
David Marks (USA) SEB

**Di Lella Racing
– Porsche 911**
Vince DiLella (USA) SEB
Manuel Cueto (USA) SEB

**Dingman Bros. Racing
– Chevrolet Corvette**
Billy Dingman (USA) SEB
Roger Bighouse (USA) SEB (*DND*)

**Dome Racing – Colin Bennet –
Dome RC82 Ford Cosworth DFL**
Chris Craft (GB) LM
Eliseo Salazar (RCH) LM
Nick Mason (GB) LM

Edgar Dören – Porsche 930
Edgar Dören (D) NUR
Helmut Gall (D) NUR
Jürgen Hamelmann (D) NUR, SPA
Jean-Marie Lemerle (F) LM
Alexandre Yvon (F) LM, (*DND*), SPA
Michael Krankenberg (D) LM (*DND*)
Axel Felder (D) KYA
Peter Hähnlein (D) KYA
Michel Lateste (D) KYA

**Viscount Downe with Pace
Petroleum – Nimrod NRA/C2 B
Aston Martin**
Ray Mallock (GB) SIL, LM, SPA
Mike Salmon (GB) SIL, LM, SPA
Steve Earle (USA) LM

**Drolsom Racing
– Porsche 924 Carrera GTR**
George Drolsom (USA) SEB
Steve Cohen (USA) SEB
William Gelles (USA) SEB

**François Duret
– De Cadenet Lola Ford
Cosworth DFV**
Mike Wilds (GB) SIL
François Duret (GB) SIL, LM
Ian Harrower (GB) SIL, LM
John Sheldon (GB) LM

**E.B.R.T. (Peter Reuter)
– Porsche 930**
Peter Reuter (D) SPA
Anton Hüweller (B) SPA
Bruno Beilcke (D) SPA

**Emka Productions
– EMKA C83/1 Aston Martin**
Tiff Needell (GB) SIL, LM
Jeff Allam (GB) SIL
Steve O'Rourke (GB) SIL, LM
Nick Faure (GB) LM

**A.S. Ecole Superieure
de Tourisme – Lancia LC1**
François Hesnault (F) LM
Thierry Perrier (F) LM
Bernard Salam (F) LM

ERC Racing – Mazda RX-7
Masaatsu Ooya (J) FUJ
Shin'ichi Katsuki (J) FUJ
Yoshio Ishikawa (J) FUJ

**Essen-Werdener Automobil Club
– BMW 320i**
Friedrich Burgmann (D) NUR
Harald ten Eicken (D) NUR

**John Fitzpatrick Racing/
Fitzpatrick-Carwill/Fitzpatrick-
Kreepy Krauly – Porsche 956**
John Fitzpatrick (GB) MZA, SIL, NUR,
LM, SPA
David Hobbs (GB) MZA, SIL, NUR, LM,
SPA, KYA
Dieter Quester (A) LM
Guy Edwards (GB) LM
Rupert Keegan (GB) LM
Preston Henn (USA) LM
Jean-Louis Schlesser (F) LM
Claude Ballot-Léna (F) LM
Thierry Boutsen (B) KYA
Desiré Wilson (ZA) KYA (*DND*)
Sarel van der Merwe (ZA) KYA
Tony Martin (ZA) KYA
Graham Duxbury (ZA) KYA

Don Flores – Porsche 911
Robert Gottfried (USA) SEB
Tom Turner (USA) SEB
Donald Flores (USA) SEB

**Ford France – Rondeau M482
Ford Cosworth DFL**
Henri Pescarolo (F) LM
Thierry Boutsen (B) LM
Philippe Streiff (F) LM
Jean-Pierre Jaussaud (F) LM (*DND*)
Jean Rondeau (F) LM
Alain Ferté (F) LM

Foreign Exchange – Porsche 911
John Higgins (USA) SEB
James King (USA) SEB
Chip Mead (USA) SEB

FU Jeans – BMW 535i
Cliff Coetzee (ZA) KYA
Paul Cox (ZA) KYA

**Mark Gassaway
– Chevrolet Camaro**
Tom Ciccone (USA) DAY
Vic Shinn (USA) DAY (*DND*)
Joe Cogbill, Sr (USA) (*DND*)

'Gimax' – Osella PA9/82 BMW
'Gimax' (Carlo Franchi) (1) MZA
(*Gp6 race within main race*)

**Glenwood Motors
– Alfa Romeo Alfetta GTV6**
Roffino Fontes (ZA) KYA
Abel D'Oliviera (ZA) KYA
Willie van Zyl (ZA) KYA
Mike Formato (ZA) KYA (*DND*)

Paul Goral – Porsche 911
Paul Goral (USA) DAY, SEB
Larry Figaro (USA) DAY, SEB
Nort Northam (USA) DAY, SEB
Peter Uria (USA) SEB

**Gontazaka Enterprise
– Nissan Fairlady 280Z**
Yoshio Nagata (J) FUJ
Hiroyuki Miyagawa (J) FUJ

**Rolf Götz – Rieger CJ 84 #
– Ford Cosworth DFV**
Rolf Götz (D) KYA
Siegfried Rieger (D) KYA

**Adriano Gozzi
– Lucchini S280 BMW**
Adriano Gozzi (I) MZA (*Gp6 race
within main race*)

**Bob Gregg Racing
– Chevrolet Camaro**
Bob Richardson (USA) DAY
Bob Young (USA) DAY
Bob Gregg (USA) DAY (*DND*)

**Grid Motor Racing
– Grid S1 Ford Cosworth DFL**
Skeeter McKitterick (USA) SEB
Milt Minter (USA) SEB
Dudley Wood (GB) LM
Fred Stiff (USA) LM
Ray Ratcliff (USA) LM

Group 44 – Jaguar XJR-5
Bob Tullius (USA) DAY, SEB
Bill Adam (CDN) DAY, SEB
Pat Bedard (USA) DAY

Team Gunston – Porsche 956
Jan Lammers (NL) KYA
Jonathan Palmer (GB) KYA

**HWRT Auto Tuning
– Ford Escort RS 2000**
Günther Braumüller (D) NUR
Dieter Selzer (D) NUR
Andreas Schall (D) NUR
Wilhelm Kern (D) NUR
Norbert Brenner (D) NUR
Jörg van Ommen (D) NUR (*DND*)

**Claude Haldi
– Porsche 930**
Claude Haldi (CH) LM
Günter Steckkönig (D) LM
Bernd Schiller (D) LM

**Harmonix Car Sound/Shellsport
– Rover 3500**
Mike O'Sullivan (ZA) KYA
Paddy O'Sullivan (ZA) KYA (*DND*)

**Hasemi Motorsport
– Nissan Skyline**
Masahiro Hasemi (J) FUJ
Kenji Tohira (J) FUJ

**Heimrath Racing
– Porsche 934**
Ludwig Heimrath (CDN) DAY
Ludwig Heimrath, Jr. (CDN) DAY

**Henn's Swap Shop Racing –
Porsche 935 L, Porsche 935
K3/80, Porsche 956**
Bob Wollek (F) DAY
Claude Ballot-Léna (F) DAY
Preston Henn (USA) DAY, SIL

**A.J. Foyt (USA) DAY (see also
Nimrod Racing)**
Derek Bell (GB) SEB
Michael Andretti (USA) SEB
John Paul, Jr (USA) SEB
Don Whittington (USA) SEB
Bill Whittington (USA) SEB
Guy Edwards (GB) SIL
Rupert Keegan (GB) SIL (*DND*)

**Herbst Tuning
– Ford Escort RS 2000**
Axel Felder (D) NUR
Udo Schneider (D) NUR
Franz-Josef Bröhling (D) NUR
Jochen Felder (D) NUR

**Herman & Miller P & A
– Porsche 924 Carrera GTR**
Paul Miller (USA) DAY, SEB
Jim Busby (USA) DAY, SEB
Ron Grable (USA) DAY, SEB

**Hi Fi Hospital
– Ford Capri**
Timothy Lee (USA) SEB
Al White (USA) SEB
Irwin Ayes (USA) SEB

**Hinze Fencing
– March 82G Chevrolet**
Marty Hinze (USA) SEB
Randy Lanier (USA) SEB
Terry Wolters (USA) SEB

**Holly Racing
– Phoenix JG1 GTP Chevrolet**
John Gunn (USA) SEB
Ricardo Londono (CO) SEB

**Hopf
– Ford Escort RS 2000**
Altfrid Heger (D) NUR
Hartmut Bauer (D) NUR

**Hoshino Racing
– March 83G Nissan**
Kazuyoshi Hoshino (J) FUJ
Akira Hagiwara (J) FUJ

**John Hulen
– Porsche 911 Carrera RSR**
John Hulen (USA) DAY
Ron Coupland (USA) DAY
Bob Speakman (USA) DAY

**Interscope Racing
– Lola T600 Chevrolet**
Ted Field (USA) DAY
Bill Whittington (USA) DAY
Danny Ongais (USA) DAY (*DND*)

**Charles Ivey Racing/Charles
Ivey-Black Widow-Metal Design
– Porsche 930**
John Cooper (GB) SIL, LM, SPA, KYA
Paul Smith (GB) SIL, LM, SPA, KYA
David Ovey (GB) SIL, LM, SPA, KYA
Giorgio Cavalieri (ZA) KYA

**Tomei Jidousha
– Nissan Sunny LZ14**
Yoshiaki Jitsukawa (J) FUJ
Motoji Sekine (J) FUJ

**JLP Racing – Porsche 935 JLP-3,
Porsche 935 JLP-4**
John Paul, Jr (USA) DAY
Rene Rodriguez (USA) DAY
Joe Castellano (USA) DAY
John Paul (USA) DAY
Phil Currin (USA) DAY (*DND*)

**Jägermeister Ford Zakspeed Team
– Zakspeed C1/4 Ford Capri**
Klaus Niedzwiedz (D) SPA
Klaus Ludwig (D) SPA

**Joest Racing/Joest Racing Belga
(see also Sorga SA)/Joest-
Lindsay Saker/Joest-Warsteiner
– Porsche 956, Porsche 936C**
Bob Wollek (F) MZA, NUR, FUJ, KYA
Thierry Boutsen (B) MZA
Rolf Stommelen (D) MZA
Hans Heyer (D) MZA, SIL, FUJ
Clemens Schickentanz (D) MZA, SIL
Volkert Merl (D) SIL, FUJ
Marc Duez (B) SIL, LM (*DND*)
Philippe Martin (B) SIL, LM (*DND*)
Jean-Michel Martin (B) SIL LM, SPA
Stefan Johansson (SWE) NUR, KYA
Dieter Schornstein (D) SPA, KYA
'John Winter' (Louis Krages) (D)
SPA, KYA
Chico Serra (BR) KYA
Leopold von Bayern (D) KYA
Siegfried Brunn (D) KYA
Klaus Grögor (ZA) KYA

**Scuderia Jolly Club – Osella
PA9/82 BMW, Alba AR2 Giannini**
Carlo Facetti (I) MZA, SIL, NUR,
LM, FUJ
Martino Finotto (I) MZA, SIL, NUR,
LM, FUJ
'Gimax' (Carlo Franchi) (I) MZA

**John Josey
– Chevrolet Corvette**
Gary Baker (USA) DAY
Sterling Marlin (USA) DAY

**Hans Christian Jürgensen
– BMW M1**
Edgar Dören (D) KYA
Helmut Gall (D) KYA (*DND*)

**Jürgen Kannacher/ Kannacher GT
Racing W.J. Schafer– URD C81
BMW, URD C83 Porsche**
Rolf Götz (D) NUR
Peter Kroeber (D) NUR
Bruno Sotty (F) SPA
Valentin Bertapelle (F) SPA
Gérard Cuynet (F) SPA
Walter Lechner (A) SPA
Jürgen Kannacher (D) SPA (*DND*)
Wolfgang Boller (D) SPA (*DND*)

**Kaye Eddie Estates/JSN Motors
– BMW 535i**
Paddy Driver (ZA) KYA
Robby Smith (ZA) KYA (*DND*)

**Kendco
– Chevrolet Camaro**
Dale Kreider (USA) DAY
Dick Neland (USA) DAY

**Karl Keck
– Chevrolet Corvette**
Karl Keck (USA) SEB
Bill McDill (USA) SEB
Robert Whitaker (USA) SEB

**Kent Racing
– Mazda RX-7**
Lee Mueller (USA) DAY, SEB
Hugh McDonough (USA) DAY
Terry Visger (USA) DAY, SEB

**Der Klaus Haus
– Porsche 911**
Klaus Bitterauf (USA) DAY, SEB
Vicki Smith (USA) DAY, SEB
Scott Flanders (USA) DAY, SEB

**Krautol Farben
– BMW 320i**
Martin Wagenstetter (D) NUR
Kurt Hild (D) NUR

**Peter Langenbach
– Audi 80 Coupé**
Herbert Schmitz (D) NUR
Peter Langenbach (D) NUR (*DND*)
Bernd Denter (D) NUR (*DND*)

**Lagenfeld Motor Sport Club
– Ford Escort II**
Wilfred Eichen (D) NUR
Walter Mertes (D) NUR
Olaf Manthey (D) NUR

**Michel Lateste
– Porsche 930**
Michel Lateste (F) LM, SPA
Michel Bienvault (F) LM, SPA
Raymond Touroul (F) LM

**Latino Racing
– Porsche 911 Carrera RSR**
Diego Febles (PR) DAY, SEB (*DND*)
Kikos Fonseca (CR) DAY, SEB
Roy Valverde (CR) DAY
Tato Ferrer (PR) SEB

**Richard Lloyd
– Porsche 924 Carrera GTR**
Richard Lloyd (GB) DAY
George Drolsom (USA) DAY
Jonathan Palmer (GB) DAY

**Londono Bridge Racing
– Porsche 911 Carrera RSR**
Gustavo Londono (CO) SEB
Carlos Munoz (USA) SEB
Hugo Gralia (USA) SEB

**Juan Lopez
– Porsche 911 Carrera RSR**
Juan Lopez (DR) SEB
Luis Mendez (DR) SEB
Fred Flaquer (USA) SEB
Gustavo Londono (CO) SEB
Ricardo Londono (CO) SEB (*DND*)
Rene Rodriguez (USA) SEB (*DND*)

**Mandeville Auto/Tech
– Mazda RX-7**
Roger Mandeville (USA) DAY, SEB
Amos Johnson (USA) DAY, SEB
Danny Smith (USA) DAY, SEB

**Manns Racing
– Harrier RX83C Mazda**
Les Blackburn (GB) MZA
Roy Baker (GB) MZA, SPA
David Palmer (GB) SPA

**Marketing Corporation of
America – Ford Mustang**
John Morton (USA) DAY, SEB
Tom Klausler (USA) DAY, SEB
Ronnie Bucknum (USA) DAY, SEB
Milt Minter (USA) DAY
John Bright (GB) SEB

Martini Racing – Lancia LC2/83
Michele Alboreto (I) MZA, SIL, NUR,
LM, SPA
Riccardo Patrese (I) MZA, SIL, NUR,
SPA, KYA
Piercarlo Ghinzani (I) MZA, SIL, SPA,
KYA
Teo Fabi (I) MZA (DND), SIL, LM, SPA
Alessandro Nannini (I) LM (DND), KYA
Piercarlo Ghinzani (I) LM
Hans Heyer (D) LM, KYA
Jean-Claude Andruet (F) LM
Paolo Barilla (I) LM

Matsuda Collection – Porsche 956
Thierry Boutsen (B) FUJ
Henri Pescarolo (F) FUJ

Mazdaspeed – Mazda 717C
Youjirou Terada (J) SIL, LM, FUJ
Pete Lovett (GB) SIL (DND)
Yoshimi Katayama (J) LM
Takashi Yorino (J) LM, FUJ
Jeff Allam (GB) LM
Steve Soper (GB) LM
James Weaver (GB) LM
Pierre Dieudonné (B) FUJ

**Mazda Sports Car Club – Mazda
RX-7 254i, Mazda RX-7**
Kenji Seino (J) FUJ
Masashi Kitagawa (J) FUJ
Kanjun Arai (J) FUJ
Yuuichi Hagiwara (J) FUJ (DND)

**Georg Memminger
– Porsche 930**
Heinz Kuhn-Weiss (D) MZA, SIL, NUR,
LM, SPA
Georg Memminger (D) MZA, SIL,
NUR, LM, SPA
Günter Steckkönig (D) NUR
Fritz Müller (D) LM

**Alfonso Merendino
– Osella PA9 BMW**
Alfonso Merendino (I) MZA
(Gp6 race within main race)

**Mike Meyer Racing
– Mazda RX-7**
Jack Dunham (USA) DAY, SEB
Jeff Kline (USA) DAY, SEB
Jon Compton (USA) DAY, SEB

**Mich Tuning – Opel Ascona 400,
Opel Ascona B, BMW 320i**
Karl-Heinz Schäfer (D) NUR
Karl-Heinz Gürthler (D) NUR
Wolfgang Holzem (D) NUR

Rainer Müller (D) NUR
Volker Strycek (D) NUR
Fred Michael Gubbin (D) NUR

**Andy Middendorf
– Ford Escort RS 2000**
Andy Middendorf (D) NUR
Erhard Hassel (D) NUR
Werner Lehnhoff (D) NUR

**Scuderia Mirabella/Euro TV
Mirabella Racing
– Lancia LC2/83**
Giorgio Francia (I) NUR, SPA
Piercarlo Ghinzani (I) NUR
Paolo Barilla (I) NUR, SPA

**Misaki Speed – MCS Guppy
Misaki Speed C (March) Toyota**
Kiyoshi Misaki (J) FUJ
Masakazu Nakamura (J) FUJ

**Mishima Auto Racing
– Mazda RX-7**
Minoru Sawada (J) FUJ
Kaneyuki Okamoto (J) FUJ
Toyoshi Sugiyama (J) FUJ

**Morgan Performance Group
– Datsun 280ZX**
Charles Morgan (USA) DAY
Bill Johnson (USA) DAY
Jim Miller (USA) DAY

Team Morrison – Mazda RX-7
Steve Dietrich (USA) DAY, SEB
Chris Ivey (USA) DAY
Jim Cook (USA) DAY, SEB
Al Bacon (USA) SEB

**Motorsports Marketing
– March 83G Chevrolet,
Chevrolet Camaro**
Terry Wolters (USA) DAY
Randy Lanier (USA) DAY
Marty Hinze (USA) DAY
Emory Donaldson (USA) DAY
Steve Pope (USA) DAY
Ken Murray (USA) DAY

**Bill Nelson
– Pontiac Firebird**
Bill Nelson (USA) SEB (engine failure
lap 1)
Dale Kreider (USA) SEB (DND)
Lojza Vosta (USA) SEB (DND)

**Nimrod Racing
– Nimrod NRA/C2**
Lyn St. James (USA) DAY
John Graham (CDN) DAY
Drake Olson (USA) DAY, SEB
A.J. Foyt (USA) DAY (see also
Henn's Swap Shop Racing)
Darrell Waltrip (USA) DAY
Guillermo Maldonado (RA) DAY
Victor Gonzalez (USA) SEB

Nissan ZA – Nissan Skyline
George Bezuidenhout (ZA) KYA
Andy Terlouw (ZA) KYA
Barry Flowers (ZA) KYA
(DQ illegal start)
Dick Sorensen (ZA) KYA (DND)

**Obermaier Racing/
Boss-Obermaier Racing
– Porsche 956**
Axel Plankenhorn (D) MZA, SIL,
NUR, LM, SPA
Jürgen Barth (D) MZA
Jürgen Lässig (D) MZA, SIL, NUR,
LM, SPA
Harald Grohs (D) SIL
Hans Heyer (D) NUR
Desiré Wilson (ZA) LM
Hervé Regout (B) SPA

**Gordon Oftedahl/Oftedahl Racing
– Pontiac Firebird**
Duane Eitel (USA) DAY
Mike Brummer (USA) DAY
Phil Pate (USA) DAY
Bob Raub (USA)
Sam Moses (USA) DAY
Carl Shafer (USA) DAY, SEB
Paul Fassler (USA) SEB
Steve Pope (USA) SEB
Carlos Ramirez (USA) SEB
Mike Meldeau (USA) SEB

OMR Engines – Chevrolet Monza
Hoyt Overbagh (USA) DAY, SEB
Peter Kirill (USA) DAY, SEB
David Price (USA) DAY
Paul Romano (USA) SEB

Marcus Opie – Chevrolet Corvette
Marcus Opie (USA) SEB
Tim Morgan (USA) SEB
Grant Bradley (USA) SEB

Overby's – Chevrolet Camaro
Robert Overby (USA) DAY, SEB
Chris Doyle (USA) DAY, SEB
Don Bell (USA) DAY, SEB

**Angelo Pallavicini
– Porsche 935, BMW M1**
Angelo Pallavicini (CH) DAY
Werner Frank (USA) DAY
Leopold von Bayern (D) LM
Angelo Pallavicini (CH) LM
Jens Winther (DK) LM

**Pametex-Victoria Brick
– Porsche CK5**
Franz Konrad (A) KYA
Kees Kroesemeijer (NL) KYA
George Fouché (ZA) KYA

**Panasport Japan – MCS Guppy
Panasport C BMW**
Toshio Motohashi (J) FUJ
Aguri Suzuki (J) FUJ

**Ruggero Parpinelli
– Osella PA8 BMW**
Ruggero Parpinelli (I) MZA
Silvano Frisori (I) MZA

**Pegasus Racing – Porsche 911
Carrera RSR, Porsche 914/4**
Paul Gilgan (USA) DAY
Al Leon (USA) DAY, SEB
Wayne Pickering (USA) DAY, SEB
Jack Griffin (USA) SEB
John Zouzelka (USA) SEB (DND)
Paul Gilgan (USA) SEB

**Pegasus III Racing
– Porsche 935 JLP-2**
M.L. Speer (USA) DAY, SEB
Ken Madren (USA) DAY, SEB
Ray Ratcliff (USA) DAY, SEB

**Peer Racing – Ford C100 Ford
Cosworth DFL**
François Migault (F) LM
David Kennedy (IRL) LM (DND)
Martin Birrane (IRL) LM (DND)

**Personalized Autohaus
– Porsche 934**
Wayne Baker (USA) DAY, SEB
Jim Mullen (USA) DAY, SEB
Bob Garretson (USA) DAY
Kees Nierop (CDN) SEB

**Arcadio Pezzali
– Osella PA8 BMW**
Arcadio Pezzali (I) MZA
(Gp6 race within main race)

**Porsche Kremer Racing
– Porsche 956, Porsche CK5-83**
Alan Jones (AUS) SIL
Vern Schuppan (AUS) SIL
Mario Andretti (USA) LM
Michael Andretti (USA) LM
Philippe Alliot (F) LM, FUJ
Derek Warwick (GB) LM, SPA
Frank Jelinski (D) LM
Patrick Gaillard (F) LM
Franz Konrad (A) SPA
Stefan Johansson (S) FUJ

**Primagaz – Cougar C01B Ford
Cosworth DFL, Rondeau M382
Ford Cosworth DFL**
Yves Courage (F) LM
Michel Dubois (F) LM
Alain De Cadenet (GB) LM,
Pierre Yver (F) LM
Lucien Guitteny (F) LM
Bernard de Dryver (B) LM

Probst & Mentel – Porsche 928S
Helge Probst (D) NUR
Norbert Haug (D) NUR
Wolfgang Walter (D) NUR

**R & H Racing – Porsche 911
Carrera RSR**
Rainer Brezinka (CDN) SEB
Rudy Bartling (CDN) SEB
Roger Schramm (USA) SEB

RGP 500 Racing – Mazda RX-7
Jim Downing (USA) DAY, SEB
John Maffucci (USA) DAY, SEB
Steve Potter (USA) DAY
Chuck Ulinski (USA) SEB

Racing Beat – Mazda RX-7
Pete Halsmer (USA) DAY, SEB
Bob Reed (USA) DAY
Rick Knoop (USA) DAY, SEB

**Racing Team Jürgensen GmbH
– BMW M1**
Edgar Dören (D) MZA, SIL, SPA
Hans Christian Jürgensen (D) MZA,
SIL, SPA (DND)

Antoniella Mandelli (I) SIL
Helmut Gall (D) SPA (DND)

**Red Lobster Racing
– March 82G Porsche**
Dave Cowart (USA) DAY, SEB
Kenper Miller (USA) DAY, SEB
Mauricio DeNarvaez (CO) DAY
(DND) SEB

Red Roof Inns – Mazda RX-7
Doug Carmean (USA) DAY, SEB
Don Herman (USA) DAY, SEB
John Finger (USA) DAY

Peter Reuter – Porsche 930
Peter Reuter (D) NUR
Franz-Richard Friebel (D) NUR
Hermann-Peter Duge (D) NUR

**Roe/Selby – Porsche 911
Carrera RSR**
Tim Selby (USA) SEB
Earl Roe (USA) SEB

**Pepe Romero
– March 83G Chevrolet**
Bill Whittington (USA) SEB
Pepe Romero (USA) SEB (DND)
Doc Bundy (USA) SEB (DND)

**Jean Rondeau – Rondeau M379
C Ford Cosworth DFV, Rondeau
M382 Ford Cosworth DFL**
Joël Gouhier (F) LM
Anny-Charlotte Verney (F) LM
Vic Elford (GB) LM
Xavier Lapeyre (F) LM
Dany Snobeck (F) LM
Alain Cudini (F) LM

Scuderia Rosso – Mazda RX-7
Jim Fowells (USA) DAY, SEB
Ray Mummery (USA) DAY, SEB
Tom Sheehy (USA) DAY
Steve Potter (USA) SEB

**Rothmans Porsche/Porsche
Racing International
– Porsche 956**
Jacky Ickx (B) MZA, SIL, NUR, LM,
SPA, FUJ, KYA
Jochen Mass (D) MZA, SIL, NUR, LM,
SPA, FUJ, KYA
Derek Bell (GB) MZA, SIL, NUR, LM,
SPA, FUJ, KYA
Al Holbert (USA) MZA, KYA
Stefan Bellof (D) SIL, NUR, LM, SPA,
FUJ, KYA
Vern Schuppan (AUS) LM, KYA
Al Holbert (USA) LM
Hurley Haywood (USA) LM

**Frank Rubino
– Porsche 935 M16**
Frank Rubino (USA) DAY
Pepe Romero (USA) DAY
Doc Bundy (USA) DAY
Dale Whittington (USA) DAY

Jack Rynerson – Porsche 911
Jack Rynerson (USA) SEB
Van McDonald (USA) SEB
Chris Wilder (USA) SEB

**Sansyou Kougyou Racing Team
– Mazda RX-7 825**
Tooru Shimegi (J) FUJ
Yoshiyuki Ogura (J) FUJ

**Sauber Racing Switzerland
– Sauber C7 BMW**
Diego Montoya (CO) LM
Albert Naon (USA) LM
Tony Garcia (USA) LM
Fulvio Ballabio (I) FUJ
Max Welti (CH) FUJ

Bernd Schiller – Porsche 930
Günter Steckkönig (D) MZA, SIL
Bernd Schiller (D) MZA, SIL
Wolfgang Braun (D) KYA
Charles Brittz (ZA) KYA

Secateva – WM P83 Peugeot
Jean-Daniel Raulet (F) LM
Michel Pignard (F) LM
Didier Theys (B) LM
Alain Couderc (F) LM
Pascal Fabre (F) LM
Roger Dorchy (F) LM

**Shafer Motor Racing
– Chevrolet Camaro**
Craig Shafer (USA) SEB
George Shafer (USA) SEB
Joe Maloy (USA) SEB

**Shelton Ferrari
– Ferrari 512 LM/BB**
Steve Shelton (USA) SEB
Tom Shelton (USA) SEB

Shizumaz Racing – Mazda RX-7
Tetsuji Shiratori (J) FUJ
Seisaku Suzuki (J) FUJ
Osamu Ihara (J) FUJ

**Sigma/Aloes Motors
– Mazda RX-7**
Ben Morgenrood (ZA) KYA
Willie Hepburn (ZA) KYA

**Scuderia Sivama/Grifone Sivama/
Sivama Motor – Lancia LC1**
Roberto Sigala (I) MZA
Duilio Truffo (I) MZA, SIL
Joe Castellano (USA) MZA, SIL
Luigi Moreschi (I) MZA
Massimo Sigala (I) SIL, NUR, LM
Oscar Larrauri (RA) SIL, NUR, LM
Max Cohen-Olivar (MA) LM
Pasquale Barberio (I) KYA
Mario Radicella (I) KYA
Maurizio Gellini (I) KYA
Nicolo Bianco (ZA) KYA
Fausto Carello (I) KYA

**Giovanni Siliprandi
– Lucchini BMW**
Giovanni Siliprandi (I) MZA

Ned Skiff – Renault 12
Ned Skiff (USA) SEB
Jim Leo (USA) SEB

**Sorga SA (see also Joest Racing)
– Porsche 956**
Bob Wollek (F) SIL, LM, SPA

Stefan Johansson (SWE) SIL, LM, SPA
Klaus Ludwig (D) LM
Volkert Merl (D) LM, SPA
Clemens Schickentanz (D) LM
Mauricio DeNarvaez (CO) LM
Hans Heyer (D) SPA

Ron Spangler – Ferrari 512 LM/BB
Carson Baird (USA) DAY
Chip Mead (USA) DAY
Tom Pumpelly (USA) DAY

**Starved Rock Lodge
– Chevrolet Corvette**
Rusty Schmidt (USA) DAY
Scott Schmidt (USA) DAY

**Stratagraph Inc.
– Chevrolet Camaro**
Billy Hagan (USA) DAY, SEB
Terry Labonte (USA) DAY
Lloyd Frink (USA) DAY, SEB
Gene Felton (USA) DAY, SEB
Tom Williams (USA) DAY, SEB
Sam Moses (USA) SEB

**Hubert Striebig
– Sthemo SM01 BMW**
Hubert Striebig (F) LM
Jacques Heuclin (F) LM
Noël del Bello (F) LM

**Superior Racing Team
– Chevrolet Camaro**
Raul Garcia (USA) DAY, SEB
Vince DiLella (USA) DAY
Armando Fernandez (USA) DAY
Eugenio Matienzo (USA) SEB

**T & R Racing – Porsche 911
Carrera RSR, Porsche 935 M16**
Tico Almeida (USA) DAY, SEB
Miguel Morejon (C) DAY
Ernesto Soto (YV) DAY, SEB

TFC Racing – Porsche 911
Tom Cripe (USA) DAY, SEB
Dick Gauthier (USA) DAY, SEB
David Duncan (USA) DAY
Jack Swanson (USA) DAY
Ron Collins (USA) SEB
Bill McVey (USA) SEB

**TRS Itabashi
– Mazda RX-7 253i**
Tsutomu Itabashi (J) FUJ
Tetsuji Tabata (J) FUJ

**Taca El Salvador
– Porsche 911 Carrera RSR**
'Jamsal' (Enrique Molins) (ES)
   DAY, SEB
Eduardo Galdamez (ES) DAY, SEB
Eduardo Barrientos (ES) DAY, SEB

**Team No.3 Racing
– Mazda RX-7 253i**
Seiji Kusano (J) FUJ
Yasuhiro Isozaki (J) FUJ
Tadao Furusawa (J) FUJ

**Tiga/DAW
– Tiga SC83Mazda**
Trevor van Rooyen (ZA) KYA
Peter Morrison (ZA) KYA

**Tom's
– Tom's 83C (Dome) Toyota**
Keiji Matsumoto (J) FUJ
Kaoru Hoshino (J) FUJ
Masanori Sekiya (J) FUJ

**Trans Am Specialties
– Pontiac Firebird**
Elliot Forbes-Robinson (USA) DAY
Gary Witzenburg (USA) DAY
Tony Swan (USA) DAY

**Trinity Racing
– Mazda RX-7**
Joe Varde (USA) DAY, SEB
John Casey (USA) DAY, SEB
Jack Baldwin (USA) DAY (*DND*), SEB

**Trust Racing Team
– Porsche 956, Toyota Celica**
Vern Schuppan (AUS) FUJ
Naohiro Fujita (J) FUJ
Ryuusaku Hitomi (J) FUJ
Mitsutake Koma (J) FUJ

**Van Every Racing
– Porsche 911 Carrera RSR**
Lance Van Every (USA) DAY (*first lap
   accident*), SEB
Ash Tisdelle (USA) DAY (*DND*), SEB

**Scuderia Vesuvio
– Osella PA9 BMW**
Pasquale Barberio (I) MZA
   (*Gp6 race within main race*)

**Vesuvio Racing SRL
(see also Jolly Club)
– Alba AR2 Giannini**
Carlo Facetti (I) SPA, KYA
Martino Finotto (I) SPA (*DND*), KYA
Guido Daccò (I)
Marco Vanoli (CH)
Massimo Faraci (I) KYA

**Daniel Vilarchao
– Chevrolet Camaro**
Reynaldo Fernandez (USA) SEB
Daniel Vilarchao (USA) SEB

**Manuel Villa
– Porsche 911 Carrera RSR**
Luis Gordillo (PR) SEB
Manuel Villa (PR) SEB
Chiqui Soldevilla (PR) SEB

**Vista Racing
– Chevrolet Monza**
Brent O'Neill (USA) DAY
Don Courtney (USA) DAY, SEB
Luis Sereix (USA) DAY, SEB
Brent O'Neill (USA) SEB

**Mark Wagoner
– Chevron GTP Buick**
Del Russo Taylor (USA) DAY, SEB
Mike Angus (USA) DAY
Wayne Dassinger (USA) DAY
Larry Figaro (USA) SEB (*DND*)

**Weld Fixturing
– Porsche 911 Carrera RSR**
Phil Byrd (USA) SEB
Freddy Baker (USA) SEB
Robert Kirby (USA) SEB

**Whitehall Promotions
– Porsche 924 Carrera GTR**
Tom Winters (USA) DAY, SEB
Bob Bergstrom (USA) DAY, SEB
Peter Dawe (USA) DAY, SEB

**Robert Whitaker
– Chevrolet Camaro**
Robert Whitaker (USA) DAY
Bill McDill (USA) DAY
Karl Keck (USA) DAY

**Jens Winther/Team Castrol
– BMW MI**
Jens Winther (DK) MZA, SIL, NUR,
   SPA, KYA
Wolfgang Braun (D) MZA, SIL, NUR
   (*DND*)
David Mercer (GB) SIL, SPA
Frank Jelinski (D) NUR, SPA
Lars-Viggo Jensen (DK) KYA

Gary Wonzer – Porsche 911
Bill Bean (USA) DAY, SEB
Buzz Cason (USA) DAY, SEB
Gary Wonzer (USA) DAY, SEB

**Wutterpal Motor Club
– Porsche 924 Carrera GTS**
Wolf-Georg von Staerh (D) NUR
Ulli Richter (D) NUR

**Yours Sport Racing Team
– Mazda RX-7 254**
Hideki Okada (J) FUJ
Akio Morimoto (J) FUJ
Seiichi Okada (J) FUJ
Chikage Oguchi (J) FUJ
Toshio Fujimura (J) FUJ

Z & W Enterprises – Mazda GTP
Walt Bohren (USA) DAY, SEB
Pierre Honegger (USA) DAY, SEB
David Palmer (GB) DAY

RESULTS

**Daytona 24 Hours, 6 February,
USA. Started 79, finished 31**
1st Bob Wollek (F)/Claude Ballot-Léna
(F)/Preston Henn (USA)/A.J. Foyt
(USA) Porsche 935 L
2nd Terry Wolters (USA)/Randy Lanier
(USA)/Marty Hinze (USA) March 83G
Chevrolet
3rd Pete Halsmer (USA)/Bob Reed
(USA)/Rick Knoop (USA) Mazda RX-7

**Sebring 12 Hours, 19 March, USA
Started 84, finished 43**
1st Wayne Baker (USA)/Jim Mullen
(USA)/Kees Nierop (CDN) Porsche 934
2nd Bob Akin (USA)/Dale Whittington
(USA)/John O'Steen (USA) Porsche
935 K3/80
3rd Hurley Haywood (USA)/Al Holbert
(USA) Porsche 935/80

**Monza 1000km, 10 April, Italy
Started 27, finished 14**
1st Bob Wollek (F)/Thierry Boutsen (B)
Porsche 956
2nd Jacky Ickx (B)/Jochen Mass (D)
Porsche 956
3rd Rolf Stommelen (D)/Hans Heyer
(D)/Clemens Schickentanz (D) Porsche
956

**Silverstone 6 Hours, 8 May,
Great Britain
Started 27, finished 15**
1st Bell (GB)/Bellof (D) Porsche 956
2nd Wollek (F)/Johansson (S) Porsche
956
3rd Jan Lammers (NL)/Thierry Boutsen
(B) Porsche 956

**Nürburgring 1000km, 29 May,
Germany. Started 35, finished 18**
1st Ickx (B)/Mass (D) Porsche 956
2nd Wollek (F)/Johansson (S) Porsche
956
3rd Rosberg (SF)/Lammers (NL)/
Palmer (GB) Porsche 956

**Le Mans 24 Hours, 19 June,
France. Started 51, finished 24**
1st Schuppan (AUS)/Holbert (USA)
Porsche 956
2nd Ickx (B)/Bell (GB) Porsche 956
3rd Mario Andretti (USA)/Michael
Andretti (USA)/Philippe Alliot (F)
Porsche 956

**Spa 1000km, 4 September
Belgium. Started 27, finished 16**
1st Ickx (B)/Mass (D) Porsche 956
2nd Bellof (D)/Bell (GB) Porsche 956
3rd Fitzpatrick (GB)/Hobbs (GB)
Porsche 956

**Fuji 1000km, 2 October, Japan
Started 33, finished 19**
1st Bellof (D)/Bell (GB) Porsche 956
2nd Mass (D)/Ickx (B) Porsche 956
3rd Schuppan (AUS)/Fujita (JPN)
Porsche 956

**Imola 1000km, 16 October, Italy
Started 23, finished 22**
1st Fabi (I)/Heyer (D) Lancia LC2/83
2nd Fitzpatrick (GB)/Hobbs (GB)
Porsche 956
3rd Wollek (F)/Johansson (SWE)
Porsche 956

**Mugello 1000km, 23 October, Italy
Started 24, finished 17**
1st Wollek (F)/Johansson (SWE)
Porsche 956
2nd Patrese (I)/Nannini (I) Lancia
LC2/83
3rd Palmer (GB)/Bell (GB)/Toivonen
(SF) Porsche 956

**Kyalami 1000km, 10 December,
South Africa
Started 40, finished 20**
1st Bellof (D)/Bell (GB) Porsche 956
2nd Patrese (I)/Nannini (I) Lancia
LC2/83
3rd Mass (D)/Ickx (B) Porsche 956

1984

YET MORE CHANGE WITHOUT CONSULTATION

There were no factory Porsches at Le Mans, the consequence of FISA president Jean-Marie Balestre's meddling with the rules.

He had been very impressed by his visit to the Daytona 24 Hours and summarily decided to allow IMSA-spec cars into European racing. Porsche had spent fortunes adapting their cars to the punitive Group-C fuel regulations in 1983 and now this.

Otherwise Weissach had the best of it, the Rothmans Porsches winning at Monza, Silverstone, the Nürburgring, Mosport, Spa, Fuji and Sandown Park. Apart from Le Mans they also missed Imola and Kyalami, the latter being won by Lancia. Thus Porsche won the World Endurance Championship of Makes by a country mile from Lancia, with Stefan Bellof the champion driver, followed by teammates Jochen Mass, Jacky Ickx and Derek Bell.

On the customer Porsche front John Fitzpatrick's backer J. David Dominelli's investment fund based upon foreign currency speculation turned out to be a gigantic Ponzi scheme. He had been successful early on but large currency fluctuations had eaten up investors' money and Dominelli was trying to hide the losses. Over three years many millions had been lost or spent by him. He suffered a stroke before being jailed in 1985 and was later paroled to Chicago in 1996 where he had relatives. He died on 2 August 2009.

Reinhold Joest's New Man Porsche 956 won at Le Mans (Pescarolo/Ludwig), Richard Lloyd's Canon GTi 956 (Palmer/Lammers) beat the Joest car at Brands Hatch and Stuck/Bellof raced the Brun Motorsport 956 to victory at Imola.

Despite a change of personnel that included employing Pierpaolo Messori, head of design at Abarth, Lancia had a disappointing season with only a 3rd place at Monza and an insignificant win at Kyalami to show for their efforts. As ever the cars were temperamental and inclined to fail, which would eventually result in Lancia withdrawing from racing. The drivers were Bob Wollek, Alessandro Nannini, Paolo Barilla, Mauro Baldi, Hans Heyer, Riccardo Patrese and Pierluigi Martini, so nothing wrong there.

It was a bad year for the British with Viscount Downe's Nimrod Aston Martin team literally written off at Le Mans, never to return. John Sheldon suffered severe burns, a marshal died and another was seriously injured in the fiery conflagration.

Bob Tullius's Group 44 Jaguar XJR-5s had been impressive in the American IMSA races but Le Mans was a disappointment with both cars retiring.

French interests were in decline, Rondeau was kaput even if its former proprietor (who finished 2nd with Preston Henn at Le Mans) and the cars were still in evidence, WM-Peugeot were Le Mans only, ditto Cougar's new Cosworth DFL-powered C02.

In C2 Alba Giannini were the winners (this was their last championship title in C2) ahead of the American Goodrich-entered Lola T616 Mazdas with the Gordon Spice Tiga Cosworth DFL 3rd. This category included the resurrection of the Ecurie Ecosse team, whilst Gebhardt, the odd-looking ADA, Ceekar, Mazda (the Japanese team), Lotec and others filled the gaps.

Le Mans 24 Hours, 16/17 June 1984 There were no factory Porsches at Le Mans, (see chapter opening) but all the other 956 teams came to the party including the ex-John Fitzpatrick Porsche 956 (110) owned by Paul Vestey. It was entered by Charles Ivey Racing for Alain de Cadenet, Chris Craft and Australian Allan Grice. He was twice winner of the Bathurst 1000 and his record in all categories in Australia and elsewhere from 1972 to 2005 would fill this page and beyond. This is the famous scrutineering area at the Place de Republique in Le Mans. Alas the 956 was down on power and was in 11th place at the 19-hour mark but retired on lap 272 with engine problems. *GPL*

↑ **Daytona 24 Hours, 5/6 February 1984** Deborah Gregg, widow of famous Porsche racer/dealer Peter Gregg, drove a Porsche 924 for El Salvador Racing with Jim Trueman and Alfredo Mena at Daytona but retired on lap 110. *Revs*

↗ **Daytona 24 Hours, 5/6 February 1984** Vicki Smith with Jack Miller and Carlos Ramirez drove the Nimrod NRA/C2 Aston Martin 002 for Performance Motorcar. They started 23rd but retired on lap 235. Do you remember those large 1980s sunglasses? Vicki was an IMSA regular during the early 1980s in the GTU and Camel GT championships. *Revs*

↗ **Daytona 24 Hours, 5/6 February 1984** Steve and Tom Shelton drove the Tide & Mosler Ferrari 512 BB/LM but it retired after 242 laps. Tom's sunglasses are even bigger than Vicki Smith's. *Revs*

→ **Daytona 24 Hours, 5/6 February 1984** Perhaps not the subtlest livery but it certainly catches your attention. Kenper Miller, Dave Cowart and Mauricio DeNarvaez drove the Red Lobster March Chevrolet 83G (3) but it retired after 60 laps (or 68 laps depending upon who you believe) when Miller overturned the car at the chicane. *LAT*

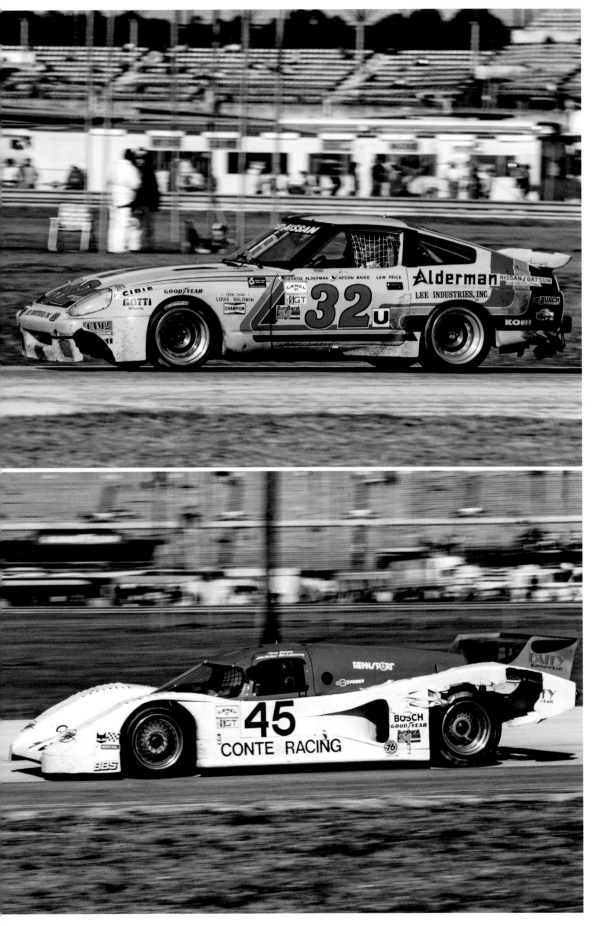

◀ **Daytona 24 Hours, 5/6 February 1984** Lew Price, George Alderman and Carson Baird drove the Lee Industries/Alderman Datsun 280ZX but crashed after 409 laps. Carson Baird (born 10 March 1938) started racing in the early 1960s with an MG Midget and in 1967 shared a Donald Healey Austin-Healey Sprite with Alec Poole and Roger Enever to finish 18th at Sebring. He finished 2nd overall there in 1976 with John Gunn in Dale Heyser's Porsche Carrera RSR and 3rd with Charlie Kemp in a Porsche Carrera RSR at the Daytona 24 Hours in 1975. His only appearance at Le Mans, in 1982, with Pierre Dieudonné and Jean-Paul Libert with the Prancing Horse Farm Racing Ferrari 512 BB produced a 6th place overall and 3rd in the IMSA GTX category. *LAT*

◀ **Daytona 24 Hours, 5/6 February 1984** Phil Conte's Conte Racing Lola T600 HU11 had a Chevrolet V8 rather than a Ford V8 motor and was driven by John Morton, Bob Lobenberg and Tony Garcia. According to the *Autosport* race report of 9 February 1984, it finished 11th after a series of incidents in Garcia's hands, one of which possibly resulted in the damage shown here. *LAT*

⇲ Daytona 24 Hours, 5/6 February 1984 The Kreepy Krauly March 84G with its Porsche 3.1-litre engine was *de facto* the March Engineering car. After the demise of the Andrettis' works Porsche 962 the March led most of the race and finished 1st with only a minor fuel issue that necessitated taking a 5-gallon fuel can out to the car on circuit when its reserve fuel pump gave up. The drivers (Sarel van der Merwe, Graham Duxbury and Tony Martin) were South African, but the Kreepy Krauly sponsor was/ is an Australian manufacturer and supplier of automatic pool cleaners. At Sebring they started 2nd but retired with an engine problem, the race being won by Mauricio DeNarvaez, Hans Heyer and Stefan Johansson in DeNarvaez's Porsche 935J. *Getty*

⇲ Daytona 24 Hours, 5/6 February 1984 The fastest car at Daytona was the new IMSA-specification Porsche 962 (001) with its 2,869cc turbocharged engine giving 680bhp @ 8,200rpm on 2.2-bar boost, for Mario and Michael Andretti. This had a nearly 5in-longer wheelbase than its 956 cousin as IMSA rules banned cars where the driver's feet extended over the centreline of the front wheels. It had a subtly different nose and used a single turbocharger, which was mandatory in IMSA races. The Andrettis led the field but with little testing behind it the car's gearbox was cooked by the heat from the turbocharger (although Gordon Kirby's report in *Autosport* mentioned the overheating he stated that it was a camshaft failure that stopped the car) and it was retired on lap 127, never to race again. *LAT*

← **Monza 1000km, 23 April 1984** Walter Brun and blonde companion at Monza. After the Sauber C6/Sehcar debacle in 1983 Walter had quickly purchased a Porsche 956 and at Monza he shared the driving duties with Brun regular Stuck and Harald Grohs. They qualified 6th and finished 4th in the Porsche 956 (101). Note the Warsteiner patch, *EINE KÖNIGIN UNTER DEN BIEREN*, which literally translates as A KING AMONG BEERS. In 1988 Walter Brun made a wrong decision by becoming an F1 entrant in partnership with Euro Racing to create EuroBrun. It was a disaster for Walter and driver Oscar Laurrari, and fizzled out in 1989. *LAT*

→ **Monza 1000km, 23 April 1984** The Rothmans Porsche 956s finished 1st Bell/Bellof and 2nd Ickx/Mass at Monza, but 956 engines were burning pistons including the Ickx/Mass car during practice. The result was seven trashed motors, four of which were using a new Bosch Motronic engine-management system. Some believed that this was a Bosch problem but others thought it might be the fuel provided by Monza (which it was apparently). The GTi Engineering team brought its own Mobil fuel supply and had no problems. In the race four of the privateer teams' 956s suffered engine failure plus a 935 and a 930. This is Dieter Schornstein's 956 (105) that he shared with Volkert Merl who qualified in a leisurely 13th place and finished 6th. Post race the winning 956 and the 3rd-placed Lancia were disqualified for being 2 and 3kg underweight respectively, but this was subsequently repealed a few weeks later. *GPL*

← **Monza 1000km, 23 April 1984** Italian Massimo Sigala (born 7 January 1951) was a fast and regular Walter Brun driver during this period but also in other teams and categories right up to 1995. At Brun he was usually partnered by Argentinian racer Oscar Laurrari and at Monza they raced the Porsche 956 (111), qualifying 7th but Laurrari crashed it on lap 19. *LAT*

→ **Monza 1000km, 23 April 1984** Alba Engineering was created in 1982 by Giorgio Stirano whose career included the Forti and Osella F2 and F1 projects and also work for Alfa Romeo later on. The handsome Alba AR1 and AR2 were built for Italian industrialist and racer Martino Finotto, whose composite chassis was almost unique at that time. The AR2 1.8- or 1.9-litre water fuel injection, turbocharged 4-valve, 4-cylinder 410/420bhp engine was designed and built by Facetti's Carma organisation, a combination of CARlo and MArtino. In 1983 Finotto with Carlo Facetti won the Group-C Junior Cup and in 1984 the Group-C Cup despite being sometimes unreliable. At Monza they entered under the Jolly Club banner, qualifying fastest in the C2 class, and finished 11th overall and 3rd in their class after a fuel-starvation problem. *GPL*

⬆ **Monza 1000km, 23 April 1984** Jim Busby entered his two BF Goodrich Lola T616 Mazdas at Monza, one for himself and Rick Knoop and this one, chassis HU2, for rapid Dutchman Johan 'Boy' Hayje and accomplished Austrian F2, Le Mans, sports/prototypes, GT/touring cars and brief F1 racer, Dieter Quester. The Busby/Knoop car finished 8th and 1st in C2 whilst the faster second car seen here was not classified after Hayje hit a chicane and lost over an hour having the front end and radiator repaired. Perhaps this is Hayje given the angle of attack shown here at one of the aforementioned chicanes. *LAT*

⬅ **Monza 1000km, 23 April 1984** Two Martini Lancia LC2-84s attended Monza: this one, chassis 0006 driven by Mauro Baldi and Paolo Barilla, qualified 2nd and finished 3rd in the race whilst the no.4 car for Riccardo Patrese and Bob Wollek qualified 4th and retired on lap 128 after catching fire approaching the pits. Lancia had commissioned new wheels and now used Dunlop Denloc tyres following the 1983 debacle. A practice incident when one of the new Speedline wheels split open resulted in the team having to revert back to the late 1983 tyre specification. Whenever and wherever I see this particular brand I can never forget the omnipresent ad campaign of the 1970s that dominated our screens. "Try a taste of Martini, the most beautiful drink in the world, it's the bright one, it's the right one, it's Martini." *GPL*

↑ **Silverstone 1000km, 13 May 1984** The Spice-Tiga Racing Tiga GC84 Ford-Cosworth (250) was created by former F1 racer Howden Ganley. Drivers were owner Neil Crang with Ray Bellm and Gordon Spice. It would appear that chassis 250 had started life in 1983 with a Chevrolet V8 motor, but Neil Crang decided to re-engineer it into the junior C class with a Cosworth engine. At Silverstone it qualified 21st but firstly a door sprang open, which caused it to be black-flagged, then the gear linkage went AWOL and was attended to but it was non-classified after the long pit stop. Spice, seen here, did break the class lap record, however, but it was a small consolation for all that effort. *LAT*

→ **Silverstone 1000km, 13 May 1984** It was probable that the works Porsches would dominate the Silverstone round but this nearly didn't happen. Firstly, the Patrese/Wollek Lancia LC2-84 was fastest in qualifying and led the race until a turbocharger problem, then Richard Lloyd's Canon Porsche 956 (Lammers/Palmer) took over but a split oil line dropped them back to 5th place whilst the Bell/Bellof works 956 finished 10th after various travails. So Ickx/Mass won the day despite excessive oversteer (according to the Historic Porsche website 010 was used as a crash test mule) with Joest's Newman Porsche 956 for Ludwig/Pescarolo 2nd and Keegan/Edwards 3rd in the Fitzpatrick Porsche 956. *LAT*

Silverstone 1000km, 13 May 1984 Viscount Downe came to Silverstone with the Ray Mallock-modified Nimrod Aston Martin (004) from 1983 plus the similarly re-engineered ex-John Cooper 005. However, 005's engine was now equipped with a turbocharger and proved to be hardly more powerful than the normally aspirated 004 and, worse still, was dropping oil. It was also substantially heavier than 004. This is 005 (Mallock/Olson) which started 19th whilst 004 was 20th with Richard Attwood, John Sheldon and Mike Salmon. Alas both cars retired, 004 dropped a valve at around the 103-lap mark, something unknown before, whilst 005 lasted 41 laps before the team withdrew the car due to its ferocious oil consumption. As disappointing as this was, far worse was just over the horizon. *GPL*

Le Mans 24 Hours, 16/17 June 1984 Viscount Downe entered two Nimrods, 005 sans its turbo engine for Mallock/Olson and 004 for Salmon/Attwood/Sheldon. Mallock out-qualified the Group 44 Jaguars much to his and the team's delight whilst the second car was driven more sedately. Around 9.15pm John Sheldon (seen here) passed the pits in 004 ahead of Olson in 005 who was about to be lapped by Palmer in the Canon Porsche 956. At the Mulsanne kink 004 burst a rear tyre and went out of control. Palmer slowed but the unsighted Olson shot past him and was hit by flying debris from the crash, ending in the Armco whilst 004 had set fire to the trees. Olson was unharmed but Sheldon had severe burns to his throat, chest and hands, and both wrists were broken, but he managed to escape the inferno. Tragically a marshal, Jacky Loiseau, died and another, André-Guy Lefebvre, was seriously injured. It was the end of 004 and the team, although a 'new' 004 was conjured up later using a spare tub and existing parts and was still owned by Viscount Downe in 1992. *LAT*

Le Mans 24 Hours, 16/17 June 1984 Despite being in receivership, Jean Rondeau was still entering at Le Mans, having picked up sponsorship and paying drivers during a visit to the Daytona 24 Hours in February. Thus the McCormack & Dodge financial consultancy sticker on the car whilst Americans Jim Mullen and Walt Bohren were the drivers with the rapid Alain Ferté to sweeten the deal. The M482 (001) was powered by a 3.3-litre Ford Cosworth DFL engine and other than minor problems they were doing very well, reaching 7th on early Sunday morning. Alas later that morning a piston broke and having blocked off the cylinder the car was driven carefully, later stopping for 40 minutes before rejoining for the last lap and finishing 13th. Here is the not-often-seen flamboyant back end of the M482 body created by Max Sardou. *LAT*

↑ **Le Mans 24 Hours, 16/17 June 1984** Bob Wollek's pole-position time in the Lancia LC2-84 just failed to beat Ickx's 1983 record, due to slower cars getting in the way. Wollek/Nannini in the no.4 car were 3.36 seconds quicker than their 2nd-placed teammates Paolo Barilla/Mauro Baldi/Hans Heyer. The Ferrari-based Abarth 268C supercharged 3,014cc V8 engines were claiming 680bhp in 1.3-bar race trim. Bob Wollek leads away at the start from the other Lancia, but an inherent weakness in the Abarth/Hewland gearbox caused them delay and they finished 8th when they could have won whilst Barilla/Baldi/Heyer had the same issues but ultimately retired due to a broken camshaft. *LAT*

↗ **Le Mans 24 Hours, 16/17 June 1984** The odd-looking ADA-01 was the result of Chris Crawford and Ian Harrower buying ADA (Anglo Dutch American) in 1977. It was built for French racer François Duret and was based upon a Group-6 Lola show car with a monocoque designed by Crawford and powered by a Ford Cosworth DFV. It had a Porsche 906 windscreen and debuted at the 1982 Silverstone 6 Hours (entered as a de Cadenet Lola). In 1983, Duret sold the car back to ADA who now had other priorities, but they entered it in 1984 at Silverstone (18th and 3rd in the C2). At Le Mans it had a 3.3-litre Ford Cosworth DFL for Harrower and Americans Bill Wolff and Glenn Smith and started from the pits due to the searing heat. After 41 laps they suffered a suspension failure which was repaired but the car was withdrawn on safety grounds. Underpowered during its brief C1 career and then overweight for the C2 class, a shame but there you are. *LAT*

→ **Le Mans 24 Hours, 16/17 June 1984** Following the success in America with their XJR-5 in 1982/83 and a favourable Silverstone test by Derek Bell, Bob Tullius's Group 44 team entered two 6-litre XJR-5s at Le Mans in 1984. Drivers were Tullius/Brian Redman/Doc Bundy (no.44) and Tony Adamowicz/John Watson/Claude Ballot-Léna (no.40). They started 14th and 19th respectively. No.44 briefly led the race during the first pit stops, but the team's radio communications ceased during the night when a Jaguar employee fell asleep at the microphone. Later a burst rear tyre on no.40 ripped off the oil cooler and filter, damaging the rear suspension and ending their race at 6.15am. Then at 7am Redman pitted no.44 with gearbox problems. Four hours later the car rejoined the race but soon returned and Jaguar withdrew the car at 12.03pm. Bob Tullius was asleep and unaware of this until someone woke him up: "There was nothing I could do about it, but those assholes withdrew my car without me knowing about it." *LAT*

Le Mans 24 Hours, 16/17 June 1984 In 1982 Hugh McCaig and author/journalist Graham Gauld brought the famous Ecurie Ecosse team back to life to contest the C2 category. McCaig acquired an ex-de Cadenet Group 6 Lola monocoque and had Ray Mallock build a car around it. The Ecosse C284, powered by the ubiquitous Ford Cosworth DFV, made its debut at the Monza 1000km driven by Ray Mallock, David Duffield and David Leslie, finishing 10th and 2nd in the C2 class. At Silverstone Wilds and Duffield retired after a door departed and the clutch failed. At Le Mans the car driven by Wilds, Leslie and Duffield firstly lost a side window and then the fuel pressure disappeared out on circuit on lap 38, ending their race. It has just passed the French Equipe Alméras Freres Porsche 930 driven by Jacques Alméras, Jean-Marie Alméras and American Tom Winters which finished 18th overall and 2nd in the GTO class. On 22 July 1984 at the British GP, Brands Hatch, David Leslie crashed the car in a Thundersports race (it was second fastest in practice) and it was written off. Allegedly the owner later cut it up into small pieces. *GPL*

Le Mans 24 Hours, 16/17 June 1984 Preston Henn entered his Porsche 956 (103) for Jean Rondeau and John Paul Jr and his new 962 (104) for himself, Edgar Dören and Michel Ferté. This latter car was running in the GTP category whilst the 956 was a pukka C1 car. The 962 retired in the 20th hour due to ignition failure but the 956 was driven brilliantly and but for losing a front wheel in the Porsche Curves on Sunday morning they might have won the race. Fortunately, Rondeau managed to coax the car back to the pits and they finished 2nd just two laps behind the winning New Man Joest Porsche 956B of Pescarolo/Ludwig. *LAT*

Le Mans 24 Hours, 16/17 June 1984 The BF Goodrich Lola T616 Mazdas of Jim Busby's team were having a good season and at Le Mans they finished 10th Yoshimi Katayama/John Morton/John O'Steen (1st in C2) and 12th Jim Busby/Boy Hayje/Rick Knoop (3rd in C2) separated by just 0.250sec in qualifying. The second car had a variety of problems (fuel pick-up troubles, bodywork damage, fractured exhaust pipe and gearbox issues) that cost it 25 laps compared to their teammates. The 2-rotor Mazda engine (rated at 1,308cc) produced 300bhp @ 8,000rpm whilst the car weighed 700kg (1,540lb), and top speed was 173mph according to Mazda. This is the second T616, the bodywork shape is similar to the Gebhardt cars and note the front wing. *GPL*

Le Mans 24 Hours, 16/17 June 1984 There were 14 Porsche 956s and two Porsche 962s at Le Mans and seven 956s occupied the first seven places at the finish whilst both 962s retired. The factory 956B specification introduced in 1984 was for chassis numbers 113–118. Henri Pescarolo had already won at Le Mans on three consecutive occasions with Matra (1972/73/74) and in 1984 he won again in the New Man Joest Porsche 956B (117) with Klaus Ludwig. Apart from a broken suspension, which was repaired, and some minor issues they won the race by two laps. There had been serious issues with the high-downforce noses on the 956s/962s, which were highly unstable and prone to porpoising on Mulsanne, while those who still had the old-type front end were far less affected. This in turn made for slower lap times compared to 1983. Apparently the 956s had never been tested in a rolling-road wind tunnel. *LAT*

← **Nürburgring 1000km, 15 July 1984** Porsches finished 1st, 2nd, 4th, 5th, 6th, 7th, 8th, 9th, 10th and 11th (962), with the Lancia LC2-84s of Barilla/Nannini 3rd and Wollek/Patrese a delayed 12th. Amongst this plethora of Weissach excess was the New Man Joest 956 (104), driven by Pescarolo/Johansson and Ayrton Senna, that lost eight laps due to a clutch problem and finished 8th. This is Senna driving in his familiar yellow and black striped helmet and note how immaculate the car is despite its hard life. Senna never drove in this category again, or indeed any others at championship level; he was already lost to F1. *LAT*

↙ **Nürburgring 1000km, 15 July 1984** After the magnificence of the Nordschleife, *Der Neue Nürburgring* was described by one period observer as having "absolutely no soul". Ten Porsche 956s, two of which were to the B specification, competed including the returning Rothmans Porsches for Ickx/Mass and Bell/Bellof. The Bell/Bellof car (seen here) won the race despite handling problems but might not have if the Fitzpatrick Porsche for Boutsen/Hobbs (after disappointing results with Yokohama tyres the team changed to Goodyear here) had not been nudged by a backmarker later in the race. (In his book *My Life at the Wheel* Fitzpatrick recalls that the car had to have an extra fuel stop because their rig was giving only 65 litres rather than 100). Hobbs finished 2nd with a damaged turbocharger 15 seconds behind the works car. *LAT*

↓ **Brands Hatch 1000km, 29 July 1984** A classic hot July day at Brands Hatch with some 25,000 spectators watching as the GTi Engineering/Canon Racing Porsche 956 (106) leads the way in the early stages. Note the proper mesh fencing and the relatively small numbers of spectators on the south bank fencing compared to the hordes opposite. At the back of the pack is the DS Porsche Racing Team Porsche 956 (105) entered by owner driver Dieter Schornstein but wearing the familiar Joest New-Man yellow, which he usually entered under his team's name. It finished 9th here with Volkert Merl and 'John Winter'. *LAT*

Brands Hatch 1000km, 29 July 1984 Down amongst the C2 racers was the Charles Ivey Racing C1 Grid 2 Porsche driven by Dudley Wood and Barry Robinson. They finished 11th and 10th in C1. It had a Porsche 935 twin-turbo engine, but the team thought it was a disaster. Olney Galleries were owned by Dudley Wood. Coincidentally the yellow no.94 is the Grid S1 Ford Cosworth entered by Gil Baird Techspeed Racing for Steve Thompson, Tony Lanfranchi and Divina Galica which qualified 12th but was pushed over the line and disqualified. Otherwise it would have finished 12th. Needless to say the Spice Racing Tiga GC84 driven by Tiga owner Neil Crang and Ray Bellm won the C2 class, finishing 10th overall. *LAT*

Brands Hatch 1000km, 29 July 1984 The immaculate Richard Lloyd GTi Engineering/ Canon Racing Porsche 956 (106) had a front wing and a high-downforce nose to ameliorate understeer. Jonathan Palmer and Jan Lammers drove it to victory eight laps ahead of the Joest Racing Porsche 956B (117) of Henri Pescarolo and Jochen Mass with Guy Edwards, Rupert Keegan and Thierry Boutsen in John Fitzpatrick's Skoal Bandit Porsche 962 (105) 3rd. Originally 38 entries were expected but 10 failed to show. *LAT*

→ **Mosport 1000km, 5 August 1984** Mosport attracted only eight C1 entries of which seven were Porsche 956s and the Grid S2 Porsche of Charles Ivey Racing. One of the two Fitzpatrick Skoal Bandit Porsches (Keegan/Konrad) was damaged during free practice when the centre of a rear Momo wheel departed and the car was withdrawn due to body stress damage. It is the no.55 956 (102) seen here with the Hobbs/Michael Roe no.35 956B (114). The team borrowed some BBS wheels for no.35 with Keegan and Konrad joining Hobbs whilst Roe departed to a Can-Am race at Lime Rock. In the race Konrad also suffered a wheel departure, this time the front left because the BBS rims needed to be tightened up more than the Momo originals. They finished 2nd, nearly eight laps adrift of the winning works 956 of Ickx/Mass. *LAT*

→ **Mosport 1000km, 5 August 1984** As was now the status quo, the Bell/Bellof duo were quickest in qualifying in this 956 (09), with Ickx/Mass six-tenths adrift. Bell recalled that in the race a nut holding the alternator pulley came loose and sheared the drive to the crankshaft and as a result they had no alternator. This required regular stops to fit another new battery and they eventually finished 4th, 32 laps behind Ickx/Mass in the winning car. Weissach had also entered a 'camera car' 956 for Vern Schuppan/Nick Mason which finished unclassified. Hobbs/Keegan/Konrad finished 2nd in a Fitzpatrick 956 whilst Finotto/Facetti/Sebastiani finished 3rd and winner of the C2 class in Finotto's Alba AR3. *LAT*

Spa 1000km, 2 September 1984
The parade lap led by the pole-position Fitzpatrick Skoal Bandit Porsche 956B (114) of Thierry Boutsen followed by Ickx in the works 956 (010), Jan Lammers in the Canon Racing GTi Engineering Porsche 956B (106B) then Bellof in the second works 956 (09), Hans-Joachim Stuck in the Gaggia Brun 956B (116), the Fitzpatrick Skoal Bandit 962 (105) *et al.* The factory Lancias did not attend. The new GTi Engineering car was arguably not a Porsche 956 at all. It had a honeycomb monocoque designed by Nigel Stroud that was both lighter and more structurally rigid than the standard car and it also had much revised front suspension. Jonathan Palmer recalled that: "Certainly it was stiffer and in many ways it handled stiffer; it wasn't always a clear-cut advantage, but it was certainly stronger." *LAT*

Spa 1000km, 2 September 1984
Following the appearance of a front wing on the Canon Porsche at Brands Hatch John Fitzpatrick followed suit at Spa with Thierry Boutsen taking pole, just 0.3 seconds quicker than Spa maestro Ickx. However, Boutsen was 2nd behind Ickx after the first lap, then 3rd on lap 2 after Bellof blasted by, but he re-passed the Belgian on lap 6. Two laps later his throttle stuck wide open approaching the Bus Stop section and the Porsche slid over the kerbing, damaging the front left side bodywork. A new nose was fitted but the underside damage was causing odd handling. Even so Boutsen/Hobbs were back to 2nd place by 100 laps but alas 20 laps later the car stopped on track with no oil pressure. The team's Skoal Bandit sponsorship was discontinued later on due to health issues associated with chewing tobacco and banned by the British government whilst the BBC in the person of Esther Rantzen also damned it. *LAT*

Spa 1000km, 2 September 1984 With Bell/Bellof and Ickx/Mass finishing 1/2 at Spa the rest were back where they expected to be. Nevertheless, the Fitzpatrick car had offered some resistance and the Walter Brun Porsche 956B (116) was spectacular in the hands of Hans-Joachim Stuck. He rather overshadowed his teammates, Brun and Harald Grohs, and they finished 3rd two laps behind the Weissach cars. Note that 116 also had a front wing device. *LAT*

Spa 1000km, 2 September 1984 Gebhardt was the creation of Günther and Fritz Gebhardt and every one of their cars was a version of the original 1983 monocoque JC83 produced by Günther and Bill Harris at their Silverstone base. Somehow they never quite achieved what should have been possible. Danish driver Jan Thoelke, Canadian George Schwarz and German Frank Jelinski drove the Gebhardt Motorsport Gebhardt JC842 BMW (01) to 14th place and 3rd in the C2 class. They were five laps down on the 2nd-placed C2 Rondeau (Jean-Philippe Grand/Jean-Paul Libert/Pascal Witmeur) and 12 laps behind the winning Tiga (Spice/Bellm/Crang). *LAT*

↑ **Fuji 1000km, 30 September 1984** The Imola 1000km was for the Drivers' Championship and with only one factory Porsche attending (Ickx/Watson, retired on lap 2) Bellof partnered Stuck in the Brun car and won. The Canon Racing GTi Engineering Porsche finished 2nd whilst Mass joined the Joest team with Pescarolo and Heyer to finish 3rd. (Bell was away chasing IMSA glory and did not attend.) Lancia reappeared but both works cars retired (accident and engine failure). So to Fuji two weeks later and another Rothmans Porsche 1/2 with Bellof/Watson 1st and Ickx/Mass 2nd followed by three more 956s. Here is the no.20 Central Racing Team LM 03C Nissan (Nissan Fairlady ZC) of Takao Wada/Haruhito Yanagida (DND) which qualified 13th in the C1 class but retired on lap 27 (engine failure). It has more than a whiff of Porsche 956 about it. *LAT*

← **Sandown Park, 2 December 1984** Following Fuji the Kyalami 1000km (3 November 1984) produced a Lancia 1/2 (Patrese/Nannini and Wollek/Barilla) with no works Porsches or any other European entries except Schornstein's 956 (105) shared with Pescarolo and 'John Winter'. This was due to a dispute over travel expenses. A month later and even further away the final race of the season took place at Sandown Park, a part horse-racing, part motor-racing track. Appropriately in this Australian venue, three times World Champion Jack Brabham, together with Johnny Dumfries, was driving a camera car 956 (007) for Porsche. He was a little surprised to begin with by the grip and huge tyres of such a modern machine but soon adapted and the duo covered about half race distance for their footage. *LAT*

Sandown Park, 2 December 1984 Something different is (nearly) always welcome and this is a Mercedes-Benz 450SLC but packing a small-block Chevrolet V8 engine, twin turbos and Holley carburettors. It was entered in the Australian Class (AC) by Peter Fowler and driven by Brad Jones and Bryan Thompson. The body is presumably part or all composite and the car was 26th fastest out of 30 but did not start due to overheating. Pity. Bryan Thompson was a renowned racer of many different cars whose career began in 1959 with an Austin-Healey 100-4. He competed in eight Bathurst 500/1000 races between 1964 and 1990 and was a Volvo dealer in period. Brad Jones was a multitalented entrant and racer of all types and makes. Starting in 1980, he was a long-time V8 Supercar Championship driver who retired in 2009. *GPL*

Sandown Park, 2 December 1984 Another Australian AC entry was the Re-Car Racing Pty Chevrolet Monza driven by Allan Grice, Dick Johnson and driver/engineer Ron Harrop, which qualified 18th out of 29. The car was originally owned by famous Australian racer Bob Jane who employed designer Pat Purcell to build his Chevrolet Monza, which allegedly had a 625bhp Chevy motor. Later the car was extensively rebuilt by Les Small and raced by Peter Brock for Bob Jane T-Marts in 1982–83. Re-Car driver Allan Grice won the 1984 Australian GT Championship in the Monza, but at Sandown the team was disqualified on lap 114 for receiving outside assistance. *LAT*

Sandown Park, 2 December 1984 There were five AC entries at Sandown: one did not start, one was disqualified, one retired, one was unclassified and one finished 14th and 1st in class (JPS Team BMW 320i of Jim Richards and Tony Longhurst). The unclassified car was Baptiste Romano's Romano WE84 Ford Cosworth 3.9 DFL, shared with Alfred Constanzo who qualified it a modest 13th with too much front understeer and finished unclassified after 106 laps due to gearbox and brake problems. Romano had a long career into the early 21st century (except for a period during the late 1980s) as driver and entrant whilst Italian-born Constanzo raced from 1967 to 1998 in a variety of categories and cars. Note the horse racing track in the background. *GPL*

Sandown Park, 2 December 1984 There were three Gebhardts: the BMW F2-powered JC842 (01) for the French, Australian and American trio of Cathy Muller, Sue Ransom and Margie Smith-Haas (seen here), which lasted 95 laps before retiring with suspension trouble; the ADA JC842 (02) Ford Cosworth DFV-powered car for Ian Harrower (GB), Neville Crichton (NZ) and Richard Davison (AUS) that retired on lap 64 due to an engine fire; and the works JC843 (03) Ford Cosworth DFV for the German trio of Frank Jelinski, Beate Nodes and Günter Gebhardt that finished 12th and 2nd in C2. The Alba Gianninis both retired but they had won the C2 championship already whilst the C2 winner here was the rapid Gordon Spice-entered Tiga GC84 250 Ford Cosworth DFV driven by Spice and Neil Crang that finished 10th. *GPL*

Sandown Park, 2 December 1984 Although the Porsche 956 (105) is liberally decorated with BOB JANE T-MARTS logos it is in fact the Fitzpatrick car usually raced by Rupert Keegan. It was driven by Colin Bond, famous Holden, Ford et al. multiple touring car champion and Andrew Miedecke, sometime Australian F2 and later touring car racer who ran his own team until 1989. He returned to racing in 2015/16 with Aston Martin Vantage GT3s and won the second round of the 2016 Australian Endurance Championship at Sydney Motorsport Park with his son George. Miedecke can be seen in the black helmet with name behind the open door and beyond is Colin Bond wearing the black cap. They finished 6th. Note the *AUSTRALIAN PLAYBOY* sponsorship – different times, different attitudes. Boutsen and Hobbs in the other Fitzpatrick car briefly led the race but retired on lap 171 with an electrical failure. *LAT*

Sandown Park, 2 December 1984 Derek Bell and Stefan Bellof celebrate their victory and Bellof's championship title. This was to be one of only two FIA World Sportscar Championship races held in Australia. It reappeared here in 1988 after which it was abandoned. This was supposed to have been the first of a three-year contract to race at Sandown, which failed to secure a major sponsor and was late in arranging a television deal so the race could be broadcast back to Europe. Eventually the ABC network televised the race (the rest of Australia's other major TV stations were screening sports/politics). The official attendance was 13,860, though many observers put the figure at less than 10,000. It was estimated that the LCCA lost between A$300,000 and A$500,000 on the race. *LAT*

ENTRANTS

901 Shop – Porsche 911 SC
Mike Schaefer (USA) DAY
Jeff Andretti (USA) DAY
Nick Nicholson (USA) DAY
Jack Refenning (USA) DAY

ADA Engineering – ADA 01 Ford Cosworth DFV, Ford Cosworth DFL
Ray Taft (GB) SIL
Tom Dodd-Noble (GB) SIL
Ian Harrower (GB) SIL, LM
Bill Wolff (USA) LM
Glenn Smith (USA) LM

Bob Akin Motor Racing – Porsche 935/84
Bob Akin (USA) DAY, SEB
John O'Steen (USA) DAY, SEB
Bobby Rahal (USA) DAY
Hans-Joachim Stuck (D) SEB

Alderman Datsun – Datsun 280ZX
George Alderman (USA) SEB
Carson Baird (USA) SEB
Lew Price (USA) SEB

Alfa Romeo S.A. – Alfa Romeo Alfetta GTV6
Mike Formato (ZA) KYA
Paul Moni (ZA) KYA
Arnold Chatz (ZA) KYA
Nicolo Bianco (ZA) KYA

Alfa Romeo S.A./VSA Motors – Alfa Romeo Alfetta GTV6
Dick Pickering (ZA) KYA
Luis Parsons (ZA) KYA

All American Racers – Toyota Celica
Chris Cord (USA) DAY
Jim Adams (USA) DAY
Wally Dallenbach, Jr (USA) DAY
Michael Chandler (USA) DAY
Dennis Aase (USA) DAY

Equipe Alméras Freres – Porsche 930
Jacques Alméras (F) LM
Tom Winters (USA) LM
Jean-Marie Alméras (F) LM

Roger Andreason Racing – Lola T610 Ford Cosworth DFL
Roger Andreason (GB) IMO
John Brindley (GB) IMO
Richard Jones (GB) IMO

Alpha Cubic Racing Team – Renoma 84C BMW (MCS Guppy)
Noritake Takahara (J) FUJ
Chiyomi Totani (J) FUJ

Alps Restoration – Audi 80 Coupé
Peter Aschenbrenner (CDN) MOS
Mike Freberg (CDN) MOS (*DND*)

Team Australia – Porsche 956
Larry Perkins (AUS) SIL, LM
Peter Brock (AUS) SIL, LM

Auto Bureaux Motorsport – Lotec M1C BMW
Naoki Nagasaka (J) FUJ
Keiichi Suzuki (J) FUJ

Auto-Line Motorsport/Dole Racing – Pontiac Fiero
Clay Young (USA) DAY, SEB
Doug Grunnet (USA) DAY (*DND*), SEB
Jim Burt (USA) DAY (*DND*), SEB

Autoquip-BP-Nissan – Nissan Skyline
Hennie van der Linde (ZA) KYA
George Santana (ZA) KYA
Errol Shearsby (ZA) KYA

Al Bacon Racing – Mazda RX-7
Al Bacon (USA) DAY, SEB
Dennis Krueger (USA) DAY
Charles Guest (USA) DAY, SEB

Gil Baird Techspeed Racing – Ford Cosworth DFL
Steve Thompson (GB) BH
Tony Lanfranchi (GB) BH
Divina Galica (GB) BH

Gianfranco Barberio – Alba AR3 Ford Cosworth DFL
Pasquale Barberio (I) NUR
Gerardo Vatielli (I) NUR
Maurizio Gellini (I) NUR

John Bartlett – Lola T610 Ford Cosworth DFL
John Brindley (GB) SIL
Steve Kempton (GB) SIL, BH
John Bartlett (GB) SIL, SAN
François Migault (F) LM
François Servanin (F) LM
Steve Kempton (GB) LM
Roger Andreason (GB) BH
Max Cohen-Olivar (MA) BH
Richard Jones (GB) SAN
David Burroughs (GB) SAN

Bayside Disposal Racing/Bayside-Löwenbräu – Porsche 935/80
Al Holbert (USA) DAY, SEB
Claude Ballot-Léna (F) DAY, SEB
Hurley Haywood (USA) DAY, SEB
Bruce Leven (USA) DAY

Scuderia Bellancauto – Ferrari 512 LM/BB
Maurizio Micangeli (I) LM, IMO
Roberto Marazzi (I) LM
Dominique Lacaud (F) LM
Marco Micangeli (I) IMO
"Gero" (Cristiano Del Balzo) (I) IMO

BF Goodrich – Lola T616 Mazda
Jim Busby (USA) DAY, MZA, LM, NUR, FUJ
Rick Knoop (USA) DAY, MZA, LM, NUR, FUJ
Boy Hayje (NL) DAY, MZA, LM
Pete Halsmer (USA) DAY, NUR, FUJ
Dieter Quester (A) DAY, MZA, NUR, FUJ
Ron Grable (USA) DAY
Yoshimi Katayama (J) LM
John Morton (USA) LM
John O'Steen (USA) LM

BP Motorsport– Mazda RX-7
Willie Hepburn (ZA) KYA
Robbie Smith (ZA) KYA (*DND*)

BP Motorsport/Randfontein Panel Beaters – Mazda RX-7
Ben Morgenrood (ZA) KYA
John Coetzee (ZA) KYA
Willie Hepburn (ZA) KYA

BP Nissan – Nissan Skyline
Charles Britzz (ZA) KYA
Colin Clay (ZA) KYA

BP Résidences Malardeau – Lancia LC2/84
Xavier Lapeyre (F) LM
Pierluigi Martini (I) LM
Beppe Gabbiani (I) LM

Bieri Racing – BMW M1
Uli Bieri (CDN) DAY, SEB, MOS
Angelo Pallavicini (CH) DAY, SEB
Matt Gysler (CDN) DAY, SEB, MOS

Blue Thunder Racing – March 83G Chevrolet
Marty Hinze (USA) SEB (see also Marty Hinze Racing)
Randy Lanier (USA) SEB
Bill Whittington (USA) SEB

Bob's Speed Products – Buick Skyhawk
Bob Lee (USA) SEB
Gary Myers (USA) SEB
Bill Julian (USA) SEB

Bonanza Shopfitters Z.A. – Rover 3500 SDS
Mike O'Sullivan (ZA) KYA
Paddy O'Sullivan (ZA) KYA

Philip Booysen – BMW 530i
Dick Claver (ZA) KYA
Philip Booysen (ZA) KYA (*DND*)
Geoff Goddard (ZA) KYA (*DND*)

François-Xavier Boucher – Porsche 930
Bernard Carlier (B) SPA
François-Xavier Boucher (B) SPA
Marc Vensterman (B) SPA

Raymond Boutinaud – Porsche 928S
Raymond Boutinaud (F) SIL, LM, BH
Philippe Renault (F) SIL
Gilles Guinand (F) SIL, LM
Edgar Dören (D) BH
Gerard Brucelle (F) BH (*DND*)

Brumos Racing – Porsche 928S
Richard Attwood (GB) DAY
Vic Elford (GB) DAY
Howard Meister (USA) DAY
Bob Hagestad (USA) DAY

Brun Motorsport (CH) – Porsche 956, Porsche 956 B
Oscar Larrauri (RA) MZA, LM, SPA, IMO
Massimo Sigala (I) MZA, LM, SPA, IMO
Walter Brun (CH) LM, NUR
Leopold von Bayern (D) LM, NUR
Bob Akin (USA) LM
Joël Gouhier (F) LM
Hans-Joachim Stuck (D) IMO
Stefan Bellof (D) IMO

Brun Motorsport (Kremer) (CH) – Porsche 956
Hans-Joachim Stuck (D) MZA, SPA
Harald Grohs (D) MZA, SPA
Walter Brun (CH) MZA, SIL, SPA
Vern Schuppan (AUS) SIL

Budweiser Racing – Porsche 924 Carrera GTR
John Jellinek (USA) SEB
Stefan Edlis (USA) SEB
Tom Brennan (USA) SEB

Christian Bussi – Rondeau M382 Ford Cosworth DFL
Christian Bussi (F) LM
Bruno Ilien (F) LM
Jack Griffin (USA) LM

CAM Motorsports – Nimrod NRA/C2
John Cooper (GB) DAY
Bob Evans (GB) DAY
Paul Smith (GB) DAY

C.A.M.S. – Grid S2 Porsche
Dudley Wood (GB) LM
John Cooper (GB) LM (*DND*)
Barry Robinson (GB) LM (*DND*)

Paul Canary Racing – Chevrolet Corvette, McLaren M12 GT Chevrolet
Paul Canary (USA) DAY, SEB
Jim Sanborn (USA) DAY
Victor Gonzalez (USA) SEB
Eppie Wietzes (CDN) SEB
Bob Barnett (USA) SEB (*DND*)

Case Racing – Porsche 911
Ron Case (USA) SEB
Dave Panaccione (USA) SEB

Central 20 Racing Team – LM 03C Nissan (Nissan Fairlady Z C)
Takao Wada (J) FUJ
Haruhito Yanagida (J) FUJ (*DND*)

Centurian Auto Transport – Chevrolet Camaro
Tommy Riggins (USA) DAY
Les Delano (USA) DAY
Andy Petery (USA) DAY

Cheetah Automobiles Switzerland – Cheetah G604 Aston Martin
Bernard de Dryver (B) SPA
Ray Mallock (GB) SPA

Tim Chitwood – Chevrolet Monte Carlo
Tim Chitwood (USA) SEB
Joe Llauget (USA) SEB (*DND*)
Jose Rios (USA) SEB (*DND*)

Classic Motor Car – Pontiac Firebird
Frank Jellinek (USA) SEB
Paul Fassler (USA) SEB
Jerry Molnar (USA) SEB

Richard Cleare – Porsche CK5
John Cooper (GB) BH
Richard Cleare (GB) BH
David Leslie (GB) BH (*DND*)

Coin Operated Racing – Porsche 934
Rick Borlase (USA) SEB
Michael Hammond (USA) SEB
Don Kravig (USA) SEB (*DND*)

Comp. Fibreglass (Bard Boand) – Chevrolet Corvette
Mitchell Bender (USA) DAY
Bard Boand (USA) DAY
Brian Utt (USA) DAY
Phil Currin (USA) DAY, SEB
Steve Gentile (USA) SEB
Jim Cook (USA) SEB
Tommy Morrison (USA) SEB

Conte Racing – Lola T600 Chevrolet
John Morton (USA) DAY, SEB
Bob Lobenberg (USA) DAY
Tony Garcia (USA) DAY, SEB
Tony Adamowicz (USA) SEB

Bob Copeman – Porsche 911 Carrera RSR
Bruce Redding (USA) DAY
H.J. Long (USA) DAY
Bob Copeman (USA) DAY
Jerry Jolly (USA) DAY

Cornight Motors – Toyota Corolla
Don Bruins (ZA) KYA
Brian Rowlings (ZA) VKYA

Team Dallas – Porsche 911 Carrera RSR
Margie Smith-Haas (USA) DAY
Paul Gilgan (USA) DAY
John Zouzelka (USA) DAY

Rick Davis – Mazda Capella
Rick Davis (ZA) KYA
Bruno Baleta (ZA) KYA
Andre Pretorius (ZA) KYA

DAW Supplies – Tiga SC83 Mazda
Trevor van Rooyen (ZA) KYA
Peter Morrison (ZA) KYA

Daytona Racing – Pontiac Firebird
Robert Overby (USA) DAY
Don Bell (USA) DAY
Charles Pelz (USA) DAY

Deco Sales Associates – Chevrolet Monza, Argo JM16 Ford Cosworth DFV
Brent O'Neill (USA) DAY, SEB
Don Courtney (USA) DAY, SEB
Luis Sereix (USA) DAY
Steve Shelton (USA) SEB (*DND*)

DiLella Racing – Porsche 911
Vince DiLella (USA) SEB
Manuel Cueto (USA) SEB

Dillon Enterprises – Chevrolet Camaro
Joe Ruttman (USA) DAY
Mike Laws (USA) DAY
Don Schoenfeld (USA) DAY
Tich Richmond (USA) DAY

Dingman Bros Racing – Chevrolet Corvette C3
Walt Bohren (USA) DAY, SEB
Billy Dingman (USA) DAY, SEB
Roger Bighouse (USA) DAY

Dole Racing – Pontiac Fiero
Clay Young (USA) SEB
Doug Grunnet (USA) SEB
Jim Burt (USA) SEB

Dome Motorsport – Dome 84C Toyota
Eje Elgh (SWE) FUJ
Masanori Sekiya (J) FUJ

Dorset Racing – Dome RC82 Ford Cosworth DFL
Richard Jones (GB) SIL, LM
Mark Galvin (GB) SIL, LM
John Williams (GB) SIL (*DND*)
Nick Faure (GB) LM

Viscount Downe with Aston Martin Lagonda – Nimrod NRA/C2B Aston Martin
Richard Attwood (GB) SIL, LM
John Sheldon (GB) SIL, LM
Mike Salmon (GB) SIL, LM
Ray Mallock (GB) SIL, LM
Drake Olson (USA) SIL, LM

Ecurie Ecosse – Ecosse C284 Ford Cosworth DFV
Ray Mallock (GB) MZA
Mike Wilds (GB) MZA, SIL, LM
David Duffield (GB) MZA, SIL, LM (*DND*)
David Leslie (GB) LM

English Motorsport Enterprizes
– Chevrolet Camaro
Gary English (USA) MOS
Mike Laws (USA) MOS

Alan Esterhuizen – Alfa Romeo Giulietta
Alan Esterhuizen (ZA) KYA
Koos Roos (ZA) KYA

Nick Faure – Porsche 930
Nick Faure (GB) SAN
Pete Clarke (AUS) SAN (*DND*)
Kenneth Leim (SWE) SAN (*DND*)

Diego Febles Racing
– Porsche 911 Carrera RSR
Diego Febles (PR) DAY
Tato Ferrer (PR) DAY

Firestone (Casey/Haggard)
– Mazda RX-7
Lee Mueller (USA) DAY
John Casey (USA) DAY
Terry Visger (USA) DAY

John Fitzpatrick Racing
– Porsche 935 K4, Porsche 956
Bob Wollek (F) SEB
John Graham (CDN) SEB
Hugo Gralia (USA) SEB
Preston Henn (USA) SEB
Al Holbert (USA) SEB
Renzo Zorzi (I) MZA
Giorgio Francia (I) MZA (*DND*)
Franz Konrad (A) NUR, SPA (*DND*)
David Hobbs (GB) NUR, BH
Thierry Boutsen (B) BH
Guy Edwards (GB) BH
Pierre Yver (F) SPA
Colin Bond (AUS) SAN
Andrew Miedecke (AUS) SAN

Fomfor Racing – Sauber C7 BMW
'Fomfor' (Francisco Miguel) (ES) DAY, SEB
Albert Naon (USA) DAY
Diego Montoya (CO) DAY
Max Welti (CH) SEB
Willy Valiente (ES) SEB

G & H Development
– Porsche 911 Carrera RSR
Worth Williams (USA) SEB
Jim Leeward (USA) SEB
Steve Zwiren (USA) SEB (*DND*)

Team Gaggia Porsche – Porsche 956
Oscar Larrauri (RA) SIL, NUR, MOS
Massimo Sigala (I) SIL, NUR
Walter Brun (CH) MOS

Helmut Gall – BMW M1
Helmut Gall (D) SIL, NUR, SPA, IMO, SAN
Max Cohen-Olivar (MA) SIL
Ulli Richter (D) SIL (*DND*)
Pierre de Thoisy (F) LM
Jean-François Yvon (F) LM
Philippe Dagoreau (F) LM
Kurt König (D) NUR, IMO
Altfrid Heger (D) NUR, SAN
Edgar Dören (D) SPA
Michel Maillien (B) SPA

Gebhardt Motorsport
– Gebhardt JC842 BMW, Gebhardt
JC843 Ford Cosworth DFV
Frank Jelinski (D) MZA, SIL (*DND*), NUR,
BH, SPA, IMO, SAN
Cliff Hansen (USA) MZA
Bob Evans (GB) SIL
Jan Thoelke (D) NUR, BH, SPA, IMO
Udo Wagenhäuser (D) NUR (*DND*)

Jürgen Weiler (D) NUR (*DND*), IMO
Mario Ketterer (D) NUR
Günter Gebhardt (D) NUR, SPA, IMO, SAN
Gerry Amato (GB) BH (*DND*)
George Schwarz (CDN) SPA
Ian Harrower (GB) SAN
Neville Crichton (NZ) SAN
Richard Davison (AUS) SAN
Beate Nodes (D) SAN
Cathy Muller (F) SAN
Sue Ransom (AUS) SAN
Margie Smith-Haas (USA) SAN

Maurizio Gellini
– Alba AR3 Ford Cosworth DFL
Maurizio Gellini (I) SIL, MOS, IMO
Pasquale Barberio (I) SIL, MOS, IMO
Gerardo Vatielli (I) SIL, MOS, IMO

Glenwood Motors ZA/Lepair-Glenwood
Motors-Pretoria Brick
– Alfa Romeo Alfetta GTV6
Giovanni Piazza-Musso (ZA) KYA
Willie van Zyl (ZA) KYA
Rofino Pontea (ZA) KYA
Abel D'Oliveira (ZA) KYA

Paul Goral – Porsche 935
Paul Goral (USA) SEB
John Hayes-Harlow (GB) SEB (*DND*)

Rolf Göring – BMW M1
Hans-Jörg Dürig (CH) SIL, NUR, IMO
Rolf Göring (D) SIL, NUR, IMO
Mario Ketterer (D) SIL
Fritz Müller (D) NUR
Claude Haldi (CH) IMO

Jean-Philippe Grand – Rondeau M379
C – Ford Cosworth DFV
Jean-Philippe Grand (F) MZA, LM, SPA
Jean-Paul Libert (B) MZA, LM, SPA
Pascal Witmeur (B) MZA (*DND*), LM, SPA

Bob Gregg Racing
– Chevrolet Camaro
Bob Young (USA) DAY
Joe Varde (USA) DAY
Bob Gregg (USA) DAY

Group 44 – Jaguar XJR-5
Bill Adam (CDN) DAY
Pat Bedard (USA) DAY, SEB
Brian Redman (GB) DAY, SEB, LM
Doc Bundy (USA) DAY, SEB, LM
David Hobbs (GB) DAY
Bob Tullius (USA) DAY, SEB, LM
Tony Adamowicz (USA) LM
John Watson (GB) LM
Claude Ballot-Léna (F) LM

Kenny Grover – Ford Escort Sport
Kenny Grover (ZA) KYA
Michael Kurz (ZA) KYA

GTi Engineering/Canon Racing GTi
Engineering – Porsche 956
Jonathan Palmer (GB) MZA, SIL, LM, NUR,
BH, SPA (*DND*), IMO, FUJ, SAN
Jan Lammers (NL) MZA, SIL, LM, NUR, BH,
SPA, IMO, FUJ, SAN
Richard Lloyd (GB) SIL, LM, SPA (*DND*)
Nick Mason (GB) SIL, LM
René Metge (F) LM
Christian Danner (D) NUR
Johnny Dumfries (GB) SPA

GWB Ford Zakspeed Team
– Zakspeed C1/8 Ford Cosworth DFL
Klaus Niedzwiedz (D) NUR
Klaus Ludwig (D) NUR

Richard Habersin
– Chevrolet Camaro
Rick Habersin (USA) SEB
Bob Murray (USA) SEB

Claude Haldi – Porsche 930
Claude Haldi (CH) LM
Altfrid Heger (D) LM
Jean Krucker (CH) LM

Jeff Harris – JWS C2 Mazda
Jeff Harris (AUS) SAN
Ray Hanger (AUS) SAN
Barry Jones (AUS) SAN

Hasemi Motorsport – LM 04C Nissan
(Nissan Skyline Turbo C)
Masahiro Hasemi (J) FUJ
Kenji Tohira (J) FUJ

Heimrath Racing – Porsche 930
Ludwig Heimrath (CDN) DAY
Ludwig Heimrath, Jr (CDN) DAY

Henn's Thunderbird Swap Shop
– Porsche 935 L, Porsche 956,
Porsche 962
A.J. Foyt (USA) DAY, SEB
Bob Wollek (F) DAY, SEB
Derek Bell (GB) DAY, SEB
Jean Rondeau (F) LM
John Paul, Jr (USA) LM
Preston Henn (USA) LM
Edgar Dören (D) LM
Michel Ferté (F) LM

Hi-Tech Racing – Porsche 935 M16
Miguel Morejon (C) DAY, SEB
Fernando Garcia (USA) DAY
Tico Almeida (USA) DAY, SEB

Hino Truck – Porsche 935 K3
Wayne Baker (USA) SEB
Jim Mullen (USA) SEB
Tom Blackaller (USA) SEB

Marty Hinze Racing – March 83G
Chevrolet, March 82G Chevrolet
Randy Lanier (USA) DAY, SEB
Marty Hinze (USA) DAY, SEB (*withdrawn*
second driver Dale Whittington DNA) Hinze
was also sharing the newer March 83G
at Sebring with Lanier and Bill Whittington
*(see **Blue Thunder Racing***)
Bill Whittington (USA) DAY

Hobby Rallye – Porsche 930
Mario Regusci (CH) MZA
Jean-Pierre Frey (CH) MZA
Olindo Del-Thé (CH) MZA

Hoshino Racing – March 83G Nissan
(Nissan Silvia Turbo C)
Kazuyoshi Hoshino (J) FUJ
Akira Hagiwara (J) FUJ (*DND*)

Arthur Hough Pressings/Ark Racing
– Ceekar 83J-1 Ford Cosworth BDX
Max Payne (GB) SIL, NUR, BH
Chris Ashmore (GB) SIL, NUR, BH

Howey Farms – Chevrolet Camaro
Clark Howey (USA) DAY
David Crabtree (USA) DAY
Tracy Wolf (USA) DAY

John Hulen
– Porsche 911 Carrera RSR
Ron Coupland (USA) SEB
John Hulen (USA) SEB
Dan Hartill (USA) SEB (*DND*)

Team Ikuzawa – Tom's 84C Toyota
Tiff Needell (GB) FUJ
James Weaver (GB) FUJ

Import Service Center
– Mazda OVS-1
Larry O'Brien (USA) SEB
Mike Van Steenburg (USA) SEB

Charles Ivey Racing – Grid S2 Porsche,
Porsche 930, Porsche 956
John Cooper (GB) MZA, SIL
Dudley Wood (GB) MZA, SIL, BH, MOS
Paul Haas (USA) MZA, SIL (*DND*)
Margie Smith-Haas (USA) MZA (*DND*), SIL
(*DND*), LM
Barry Robinson (GB) SIL, BH, MOS
Paul Smith (GB) SIL, LM, NUR
Alain De Cadenet (GB) LM
Allan Grice (AUS) LM
Chris Craft (GB) LM
David Ovey (GB) LM
Pete Lovett (GB) NUR
Roger Eccles (GB) NUR

Team Iwaki – Misakispeed 83C Toyota
(MCS Guppy)
Masakazu Nakamura (J) FUJ
Kouichi Iwaki (J) FUJ
Takashi Tosa (J) FUJ (*DND*)

J.Q.F Engineering/J.Q.F. Engineering
Esso Canada Petroleum
– Tiga GC284 Ford Cosworth BDT
Jeremy Rossiter (GB) SIL, BH, MOS,
SPA, IMO
Roy Baker (GB) SIL, BH, MOS, SPA, IMO
François Duret (GB) SIL (*DND*)
Peter Lockhart (CDN) MOS
Paul Smith (GB) SPA

Joest Racing/New Man Joest Racing
– Porsche 956, Porsche 956 B
Klaus Ludwig (D) MZA, SIL, LM, SAN
Stefan Johansson (SWE) MZA (*DND*), LM,
NUR, SPA, FUJ
Henri Pescarolo (F) MZA (*DND*), SIL, LM,
NUR, BH, SPA, IMO, FUJ, SAN
Jean-Louis Schlesser (F) LM
Mauricio DeNarvaez (CO) LM
Ayrton Senna (BR) NUR
Jochen Mass (D) BH, IMO
Hans Heyer (D) SPA, IMO

La Jolla Trading Group
– Porsche 935 K3
Wayne Baker (USA) DAY
Jim Mullen (USA) DAY
Tom Blackaller (USA) DAY

Jolly Club – Lancia LC2/83 Ferrari/
Abarth, Alba AR2 - Giannini
Beppe Gabbiani (I) MZA, SIL
Pierluigi Martini (I) MZA, SIL, IMO
Carlo Facetti (I) MZA, SIL, LM, NUR, BH,
MOS, SPA, IMO, FUJ, SAN
Martino Finotto (I) MZA SIL (*DND*), LM,
NUR, BH, MOS, SPA, IMO (*DND*), FUJ,
SAN
Almo Coppelli (I) MZA, SIL, LM, NUR, BH,
MOS, SPA, IMO, FUJ
Davide Pavia (I) MZA, SIL, LM, NUR, IMO
Marco Vanoli (CH) SIL, LM, SPA, FUJ
Guido Daccò (I) LM, NUR, MOS, SPA, IMO,
FUJ, SAN
Alfredo Sebastiani (I) NUR, MOS, SPA
(*DND*), IMO (*DND*), FUJ
Mauro Baldi (I) IMO
Pasquale Barberio (I) FUJ
Maurizio Gellini (I) FUJ
Lucio Cesario (AUS) SAN

Walter Johnson
– Pontiac Firebird
Del Russo Taylor (USA) DAY
Larry Figaro (USA) DAY, SEB
Enrique Novella (GUA) DAY (*DND*)
Fernando Sabino (BR) SEB

JPS Team BMW – BMW 320i
Jim Richards (AUS) SAN
Tony Longhurst (AUS) SAN

Racing Team Jürgensen
– BMW M1
Edgar Dören (D) MZA, SIL
Hans Christian Jürgensen (D) MZA
Walter Mertes (D) MZA, SIL

K & P Racing
– Chevrolet Corvette
Karl Keck (USA) DAY, SEB
William Wessel (USA) DAY, SEB
Allan Chastain (USA) DAY
Robert Whitaker (USA) SEB

Kalagian/Ardisana
– Lola T600 Chevrolet
John Kalagian (USA) DAY, SEB
John Lloyd (USA) DAY (*DND*), SEB
John Mills (USA) DAY (*DND*)

Kendall Racing – Lola T600 Chevrolet
Chuck Kendall (USA) FUJ, SAN
Jim Cook (USA) FUJ, SAN
Peter Fitzgerald (AUS) SAN

Der Klaus Haus – Porsche 911
Klaus Bitterauf (USA) SEB
Vicki Smith (USA) SEB
Arvid Albanese (USA) SEB (*DND*)

Kreepy Krauly Racing – March 83G
Porsche
Sarel van der Merwe (ZA) DAY, SEB
Graham Duxbury (ZA) DAY, SEB
Tony Martin (ZA) DAY, SEB

Kreider Racing – Chevrolet Camaro
Dale Kreider (USA) SEB
Roy Newsome (USA) SEB
Bobby Diehl (USA) SEB

Kremer Racing/Porsche Kremer
Racing/Kremer Brothers-Sperry
Turbo – Porsche 956,
Porsche 956 B, Porsche CK5
Franz Konrad (A) SIL
David Sutherland (GB) SIL, LM, BH
Vern Schuppan (AUS) LM
Alan Jones (AUS) LM
Jean-Pierre Jarier (F) LM
Tiff Needell (GB) LM
Rusty French (AUS) LM, SAN
Manfred Winkelhock (D) NUR, FUJ, SAN
Marc Surer (CH) NUR
George Fouché (ZA) NUR, BH, MOS, SPA,
IMO, SAN
Kees Kroesemeijer (NL) NUR, SPA, SAN
Desiré Wilson (ZA) BH
Bill Adam (CDN) MOS
Kees Nierop (CDN) MOS
Walter Brun (CH) IMO
Leopold von Bayern (D) IMO
Mike Thackwell (NZ) FUJ
Jésus Pareja (ESP) SAN
Peter Janson (AUS) SAN
Sarel van der Merwe (ZA) SAN

Michel Lateste – Porsche 930
Michel Lateste (F) MZA, LM
Michel Bienvault (F) MZA, LM
'Segolen' (André Gahinet) (F) LM

Latino Racing
– Porsche 911 Carrera RSR
Kikos Fonseca (CR) DAY, SEB
Carlos Fallas (CR) DAY
'Jamsal' (Enrique Molins) (ES) DAY, SEB
Diego Febles (PR) SEB

Lee Industries/Alderman Datsun
– Datsun 280ZX
Lew Price (USA) DAY
George Alderman (USA) DAY
Carson Baird (USA) DAY

Leon Brothers Racing
– March 84G Chevrolet
Al Leon (USA) DAY, SEB
Art Leon (USA) DAY, SEB
Terry Wolters (USA) DAY, SEB (*DND*)

Luger Reality
– Chevrolet Corvette
Roy Newsome (USA) DAY
Bobby Diehl (USA) DAY
Dale Kreider (USA) DAY
Luis Sereix (USA) DAY

Lyncar Motorsport
**– Lyncar MS83 Hart 420, Lyncar
MS83 Ford Cosworth DFV**
Les Blackburn (GB) MZA, SIL (DND)
Costas Los (GR) MZA, BH, MOS, IMO
Richard Down (GB) SIL, SIL (*DND*)
John Nicholson (NZ) BH, IMO
Allen Berg (CDN) MOS

Malibu Grand Prix – Mazda RX-7
Ira Young (USA) DAY, SEB
Bob Reed (USA) DAY, SEB
Jack Baldwin (USA) DAY, SEB
Jim Cook (USA) DAY

Ray Mallock Racing
– Nimrod NRA/C2 B Aston Martin
Ray Mallock (GB) DAY
Drake Olson (USA) DAY
John Sheldon (GB) DAY

Mandeville Auto/Tech – Mazda RX-7
Roger Mandeville (USA) DAY, SEB
Amos Johnson (USA) DAY, SEB
Danny Smith (USA) DAY, SEB

Martini Racing
– Lancia LC2/84 Ferrari/Abarth
Riccardo Patrese (I) MZA, SIL, NUR,
IMO, KYA
Bob Wollek (F) MZA, SIL, LM, NUR, BH,
IMO, KYA
Mauro Baldi (I) MZA, SIL, LM, BH
Paolo Barilla (I) MZA, SIL, LM, NUR, BH,
IMO, KYA
Alessandro Nannini (I) LM, NUR, IMO, KYA
Hans Heyer (D) LM
Pierluigi Martini (I) BH

Mason Racing
– Chevrolet Monza
Herb Adams (USA) DAY
Kim Mason (USA) DAY
Jerry Thompson (USA) DAY

Mazdaspeed
– Mazda 727C, March 84G Toyota
Yojiro Terada (J) SIL, LM, FUJ
Pierre Dieudonné (B) SIL, LM
Takashi Yorino (J) LM, FUJ
Jean-Michel Martin (B) LM
David Kennedy (IRL) LM, FUJ
Philippe Martin (B) LM
David Kennedy (IRL) FUJ
Yoshimi Katayama (J) FUJ

Mazda Sports Car Club
– Mazda RX-7 254i
Iwao Sugai (J) FUJ
Hiroshi Sugai (J) FUJ

John McComb (Group 44)
– Jaguar XJS
John McComb (USA) SEB
Paul Pettey (USA) SEB (*DND*)

McCormack and Dodge
– Rondeau M482 Ford Cosworth DFL
Jim Mullen (USA) LM
Walt Bohren (USA) LM
Alain Ferté (F) LM

Meiju Sport – Mazda RX-7 254i
Akio Morimoto (J) FUJ
Seiichi Okada (J) FUJ
Fuminori Shimogishi (J) FUJ

Luis Mendez Racing
– Porsche 911 Carrera RSR
Luis Mendez (DR) SEB
Chiqui Soldevilla (PR) SEB
Chris Marte (DR) SEB

Georg Memminger – Porsche 930
Georg Memminger (D) NUR
Heinz Kuhn-Weiss (D) NUR
Bruno Rebai (I) NUR

Walter Mertes – BMW M1
Olaf Manthey (D) NUR
Walter Mertes (D) NUR

Anton Meyer Racing/Volkswagen Z.A.
– Volkswagen Golf GTI
Geoff Mortimer (ZA) KYA
Peter Lanz (ZA) KYA

Mike Meyer Racing
– Mazda RX-7
Jack Dunham (USA) DAY, SEB
Paul Lewis (USA) DAY, SEB
Jeff Kline (USA) DAY, SEB (*DND*)

Mid-O Racing – Mazda RX-7
Kelly Marsh (USA) DAY, SEB
Don Marsh (USA) DAY, SEB
Ron Pawley (USA) DAY, SEB
Whitney Ganz (USA) SEB

**Mishima Auto Racing – Mishima Auto
84C BMW (MCS Guppy)**
Kaneyuki Okamoto (J) FUJ
Minoru Sawada (J) FUJ

Team Morrison – Mazda RX-7
Jim Cook (USA) DAY
Tommy Morrison (USA) DAY
Tony Swan (USA) DAY

Tim Morgan
– Chevrolet Corvette
Tim Morgan (USA) SEB
Peter Morgan (USA) SEB
Charles Bair (USA) SEB
Marcus Opie (USA) SEB

Motorsportclub Rosenheim e.V.
– TOJ C390 Ford Cosworth DFL
Martin Wagenstetter (D) NUR
Kurt Hild (D) NUR (*DND*)

Motorsports Marketing
– Chevrolet Camaro
Ken Murray (USA) DAY, SEB
Richard Valentine (USA) DAY, SEB
Bob Barnett (USA) DAY
Russ Boy (USA) SEB

DeNarvaez Enterprises
– Porsche 935 J
Mauricio DeNarvaez (CO) SEB
Stefan Johansson (SWE) SEB
Hans Heyer (D) SEB

Naylor Road & Motorsport
– 83TSGT Hart 420
Tim Lee-Davey (GB) BH
Adrian Hall (GB) BH
Mike Kimpton (GB) BH

New Raytown Datsun
– Datsun 200SX
Frank Carney (USA) DAY
Dick Davenport (USA) DAY (*DND*)
Bob Hindson (USA) DAY (*DND*)

Nova Engineering – Porsche 956
Jirou Yoneyama (J) FUJ
Chikage Oguchi (J) FUJ

Obermaier Racing – Porsche 956
Axel Plankenhorn (D) MZA
Jürgen Lässig (D) MZA, SIL, LM, NUR,
SPA, IMO
George Fouché (ZA) MZA, SIL, LM
Hervé Regout (F) SIL, SPA, IMO
John Graham (CDN) LM
David Sutherland (CDN) NUR
Mike Thackwell (NZ) NUR
Philippe Martin (B) SPA
Harald Gohs (D) IMO

Oftedahl Racing
– Pontiac Firebird
George Schwarz (CDN) DAY, SEB
Craig Allen (CDN) DAY, SEB
Richard Spenard (CDN) DAY
Mike Field (USA) DAY
Jack Newsum (USA) DAY
Rob McFarlin (USA) DAY
Andre Schwartz (CDN) SEB

OMR Engines – Chevrolet Camaro
William Gelles (USA) DAY
Mike Brummer (USA) DAY
Steve Cohen (USA) DAY
Hoyt Overbagh (USA) SEB
Robert Theall (USA) SEB (*DND*)
Peter Kirill (USA) SEB (*DND*)

**Panasport Japan – LM 04C Nissan
(Nissan Panasports Turbo C)**
Toshio Suzuki (J) FUJ
Osamu Nakako (J) FUJ

**Pegagus Racing – March 84G Buick,
Porsche 935 JLP-2**
Ken Madren (USA) DAY, SEB, LM
Wayne Pickering (USA) DAY, SEB (*DND*), LM
M.L. Speer (USA) DAY, SEB, LM
Bobby Hefner (USA) DAY
Jack Griffin (USA) DAY, SEB
Hugo Gralia (USA) DAY

Stuart Pegg – VW Golf GTI
Roelof Fekken (ZA) KYA
Jan Hettema (ZA) KYA
Michael Sapiro (ZA) KYA

Pennzoil de P. R.
– Porsche 911 Carrera RSR
Luis Gordillo (PR) SEB
Eduardo Salguero (PR) SEB
Manuel Villa (PR) SEB

Pepsi Challenger
– Gebhardt JC84 Ford Cosworth DFV
John Graham (CDN) MOS
George Schwarz (CDN) MOS

Performance Motorcar
– Nimrod NRA/C2 Aston Martin
Jack Miller (USA) DAY
Carlos Ramirez (USA) DAY
Vicki Smith (USA) DAY

Performance Motorsports
– Porsche 924 Carrera GTR
Elliot Forbes-Robinson (USA) DAY, SEB
John Schneider (USA) DAY, SEB (*DND*)
Ken Williams (USA) DAY

Porsche – Porsche 962
Mario Andretti (USA) DAY
Michael Andretti (USA) DAY

Preston & Son/Walt Preston
– Mazda RX-7
Richard Stevens (CDN) DAY
Mark Brainard (USA) DAY
Don Herman (USA) DAY
Whitney Ganz (USA) SEB
Gene Hackman (USA) SEB

Primagaz Team Cougar
**– Cougar C01B Ford Cosworth DFL,
Cougar C2 Ford Cosworth DFL**
Alain de Cadenet (GB) SIL
Yves Courage (F) SIL, LM
Michael Dubois (F) LM
John Jellinek (USA) LM
Pierre Yver (F) LM
Bernard de Dryver (B) LM
Pierre-François Rousselot (F) LM

Probst und Mentel
– Porsche 928 S
Helge Probst (D) NUR
Knuth Mentel (D) NUR
Karl-Heinz Gürthler (D) NUR

Procar Automobile AG
– Sehcar C830 – Porsche
Huub Rothengatter (NL) SIL
Clemens Schickentanz (D) SIL
Didier Theys (B) SPA, IMO
Boy Hayje (NL) SPA
Pierre Dieudonné (B) SPA, IMO

E.J. Pruitt & Sons
– Porsche 911
Blake Pridgen (USA) DAY, SEB
Rusty Bond (USA) DAY, SEB
Ren Tilton (USA) DAY, SEB

RB (Roy Baker) Promotion
– Tiga GC284 Ford Turbo
Philippe Colonna (F) FUJ
Altfrid Heger (D) FUJ
Jeremy Rossiter (GB) FUJ (*DND*) SAN
Gary Evans (GB) SAN
Roy Baker (GB) SAN

Re-Car Racing (Alan Browne)
– Chevrolet Monza
Alan Grice (AUS) SAN
Dick Johnson (AUS) SAN
Ron Harrop (US) SAN

Red Lobster Racing
**– March 83G Chevrolet ,
March 82G Porsche**
Dave Cowart (USA) DAY, SEB
Kenper Miller (USA) DAY, SEB
Mauricio DeNarvaez (CO) DAY

Rennsport Enterprise
– Porsche 911 Carrera RSR
Jack Lewis (USA) DAY
Bob Beasley (USA) DAY
John Ashford (USA) DAY

Peter Reuter – Porsche 930
Wolf-Dieter Feuerlein (D) NUR
Uwe Reich (D) NUR
Peter Reuter (D) NUR

RGP 500 Racing
– Argo JM16 Mazda
Jim Downing (USA) DAY, SEB (*DND*)
John Maffucci (USA) DAY, SEB
Whitney Ganz (USA) DAY

Siegfried Rieger
– Rieger CJ84 Ford Cosworth DFV
Rolf Götz (D) NUR
Carl Kirts (USA) NUR
Siegfried Rieger (D) NUR (*DND*)

Steve Roberts – Chevrolet Camaro
William Boyer (USA) SEB
Steve Roberts (USA) SEB

Roe/Selby – Racing – Porsche 914/6
Tim Selby (USA) SEB
Earl Roe (USA) SEB

**Bap Romano Racing – Romano WE84
Ford Cosworth DFL**
Alfredo Constanzo (AUS) SAN
Baptiste Romano (AUS) SAN

Roserace/Morrison – Mazda RX-7
Dennis Krueger (USA) SEB
Tom Henrickson (USA) SEB
Rick Kinner (USA) SEB

Scuderia Rosso – Mazda RX-7
Jim Fowells (USA) DAY, SEB
Steve Potter (USA) DAY, SEB
Ray Mummery (USA) DAY, SEB

Rothmans Porsche – Porsche 956
Jacky Ickx (B) MZA, SIL, NUR, MOS, SPA,
IMO, FUJ, SAN
Jochen Mass (D) MZA, SIL, NUR, MOS,
SPA, FUJ, SAN
Stefan Bellof (D) MZA, SIL, NUR, MOS, SPA,
FUJ, SAN
Derek Bell (GB) MZA, SIL, NUR, MOS,
SPA, SAN
Vern Schuppan (AUS) MOS, SPA, SAN
Nick Mason (GB) MOS
John Watson (IRL) SPA, IMO (*DND*), FUJ
Richard Lloyd (GB) FUJ
Alan Jones (AUS) SAN
Johnny Dumfries (GB) SAN (THIS
DUMFRIES/BRABHAM ENTRY WAS USED
AS A CAMERA CAR)
Jack Brabham (AUS) SAN

Rubino Racing – Mazda RX-7
Frank Rubino (USA) SAN
Jose Rodriguez (USA) DAY (*DND*), SEB
Dennis Vitolo (USA) DAY (*DND*)
David Leira (USA) SEB

El Salvador Racing
– Porsche 924 Carrera GTR
Jim Trueman (USA) DAY, SEB
Deborah Gregg (USA) DAY, SEB (*DND*)
Alfredo Mena (USA) DAY, SEB

Michael Sapiro Motors
– Mazda Capella
Harry Kibel (ZA) KYA
Paul Cox (ZA) KYA
Peter Greaves (ZA) KYA

Schiesser Porsche Brun (CH)
– Porsche 956 B
Hans-Joachim Stuck (D) NUR
Harald Grohs (D) NUR

Bernd Schiller – Porsche 930
Claude Haldi (CH) NUR
Roy Baker (GB) NUR
Wolfgang Braun (D) NUR

**Schornstein Racing/DS Porsche
Racing – Porsche 956**
Volkert Merl (D) MZA, SIL, LM, NUR, BH,
Dieter Schornstein (D) MZA, SIL, LM, NUR,
BH, SPA, IMO, KYA, SAN
'John Winter' (Louis Krages) (D) SIL, LM,
NUR, BH, SPA, IMO, KYA, SAN
Hans Heyer (D) SPA, IMO
Henri Pescarolo (F) KYA
Paul Belmondo (F) SAN

**Scorpion Racing Services – Arundel
C200 Ford Cosworth DFV**
Eddie Arundel (GB) SIL
James Weaver (GB) SIL (DND)
John Jellinek (USA) SIL (DND)

**Bobby Scott Motorcycles ZA
– Mazda Capella**
Bobby Scott (ZA) KYA
Neville Scott (ZA) KYA
Colin Burford (ZA) KYA

Secateva – WM P83 B Peugeot PRV
Alain Couderc (F) LM
Gérard Patté (F) LM
Roger Dorchy (F) LM
Michel Pignard (F) LM
Jean-Daniel Raulet (F) LM
Pascal Pessiot (F) LM

Setrab Racing By Yours – Mazda 727C
Hideki Okada (J) FUJ
Masatomo Shimizu (J) FUJ
Tomohiko Tsutsumi (J) FUJ

**Shafer Concrete/George R. Shafer
– Chevrolet Camaro, Porsche 911**
George Shafer (USA) SEB
Craig Shafer (USA) SEB
Joe Maloy (USA) SEB
John Hofstra (USA) SEB
Peter Uria (USA) SEB
Mick Robinson (USA) SEB

**Shell Sport ZA – VW Golf GTI,
Nissan Stanza, Ford Escort Sport**
John Stewart (ZA) KYA
Clive Wesson (ZA) KYA
Trevor Trautman (ZA) KYA
Dick Sorensen (ZA) KYA
Johan Coetzee (ZA) KYA
Peter Southwood (ZA) KYA
Tim Mackintosh (ZA) KYA

**Shimegi Racing Team
– Mazda 83C Mazda (MCS Guppy)**
Tooru Shimegi (J) FUJ
Kaoru Iida (J) FUJ
Norimasa Sakamoto (J) FUJ

**Silver Lake Plantation
– Rondeau M382 Chevrolet**
Gary Belcher (USA) SEB
Jean Rondeau (F) SEB
John Gunn (USA) SEB

**Skoal Bandit Porsche Team – Porsche
956, Porsche 956 B, Porsche 962**
Thierry Boutsen (B) MZA, SIL, NUR, BH, SPA,
IMO, SAN
David Hobbs (GB) MZA, SIL, LM, NUR, MOS,
SPA, IMO, SAN
Rupert Keegan (GB) MZA, SIL, NUR, BH,
MOS, SPA, IMO, SAN
Guy Edwards (GB) MZA, SIL, NUR, BH

Philippe Streiff (F) LM
Sarel van der Merwe (ZA) LM
Roberto Moreno (BR) LM
Franz Konrad (D) MOS, SPA, SAN
Franz Konrad (A) IMO

Smith's Wheels – Ford Escort RS
Brian Cook (ZA) KYA
Alan Brough (ZA) KYA

**Southern Racing Promotions
(John Josey) – Chevrolet Corvette**
Gary Baker (USA) DAY
Sterling Marlin (USA) DAY

Speedparts – Toyota Corolla
Johnny Knez (ZA) KYA
Dave repsold (ZA) KYA

**Spice Tiga Racing/Gordon Spice Racing
– Tiga GC84 Ford Cosworth DFL**
Neil Crang (AUS) SIL, LM, NUR, BH, SPA,
IMO, SAN
Ray Bellm (GB) SIL, LM, NUR, BH, SPA, IMO
Gordon Spice (GB) SIL, LM, NUR, SPA,
IMO, SAN

Starved Rock Lodge – Chevrolet Corvette
Rusty Schmidt (USA) DAY
Scott Schmidt (USA) DAY
Max Schmidt (USA) DAY

**Wolf-Georg von Staerh
– Porsche 924 Carrera GTS**
Wolf-Georg von Staerh (D) MZA, NUR
Ulli Richter (D) MZA, NUR

Strandell Racing – Porsche 930
Kenneth Leim (SWE) MZA, SIL, NUR
Tomas Wiren (SWE) MZA, SIL
Götz von Tschirnhaus (D) NUR

**Stratagraph/Piedmont /Stratagraph
– Chevrolet Camaro**
Billy Hagan (USA) DAY, SEB
Terry Labonte (USA) DAY, SEB
Gene Felton (USA) DAY, SEB

Hubert Striebig – Sthemo SMC2 BMW
Hubert Striebig (F) LM, NUR, SPA, IMO (DND)
Jacques Heuclin (F) LM
Noël del Bello (F) LM, NUR
Max Cohen-Olivar (MA), NUR, SPA (DND), IMO

Sunrise Auto Parts – Chevrolet Camaro
Jeff Loving (USA) SEB
Richard Small (USA) SEB

Super Exhaust/Shellsport – Nissan 160Z
Jimmy Williamson (ZA) KYA
Larry Wilford (ZA) KYA

Superite – Nissan Stanza
Jannie van Rooyen (ZA) KYA
Nico van Rensburg (ZA) KYA

Tangent Racing – Pontiac Firebird
Bill Gardner (USA) DAY, SEB
Ronnie Sanders (USA) SEB
James Durovy (USA) DAY, SEB

**THR Foreign Car – Porsche 911 Carrera
RSR, Porsche 911**
George Hulse (USA) DAY, SEB
Pat Lott (USA) DAY
Jerry Kennedy (USA) DAY, SEB
Michael DeFontes (USA) DAY
Mike Cheung (?) SEB
John Higgins (USA), SEB
James King (USA), SEB
Howard Cherry (USA), SEB

**Tide & Mosler Racing
– Ferrari 512 BB/LM**
Steve Shelton (USA) DAY, SEB
Tom Shelton (USA) DAY, SEB
Claude Ballot-Léna (F) SEB
John McComb (USA) SEB

**Tiga Cars South Africa
– Tiga SC83Mazda**
Lew Baker (ZA) KYA
Gordon Hatch (ZA) KYA

Tom's – Tom's 84C Toyota
Satoru Nakajima (J) FUJ
Keiji Matsumoto (J) FUJ

Top Fuel Racing – Mazda RX-7
Mutsuo Kazama (J) FUJ
Hironobu Tatsumi (J) FUJ
Yoshiyuki Ogura (J) FUJ

Raymond Touroul – Porsche 930
Valentin Bertapelle (F) MZA, LM
Raymound Tourol (F) MZA (DND), LM
Thierry Perrier (F) LM

Trepal Motors – Ford Escort Sport
Dorino Treccani (ZA) KYA
Graham Cooper (ZA) KYA

Trinity Racing – Mazda RX-7
Lee Mueller (USA) SEB
Terry Visger (USA) SEB
John Casey (USA) SEB

**Trust Racing Team
– Porsche 956 B, Toyota Celica**
Hans-Joachim Stuck (D) FUJ
Vern Schuppan (AUS) FUJ
Mitsutake Koma (J) FUJ
Ryuusaku Hitomi (J) FUJ

Tuff Kote Dinol Racing – Porsche 935 L1
Jan Lundgardh (SWE) NUR
Kurt Simonsen (SWE) NUR

Tycos Racing – Pontiac Firebird
Paul Fassler (USA) DAY
Frank Jellinek (USA) DAY
Jerry Molnar (USA)

**Van Every Racing
– Porsche 911 Carrera RSR**
Ash Tisdelle (USA) DAY, SEB
Lance Van Every (USA) DAY, SEB

**Gerardo Vatielli – Alba AR3
Ford Cosworth DFL**
Pasquale Barberio (I) SPA
Maurizio Gellini (I) SPA
Gerardo Vatielli (I) SPA

Vero Racing Enterprises – Mazda RX-7
Tom Burdsall (USA) DAY, SEB (DND)
Nort Northam (USA) DAY, SEB (DND)
Peter Welter (USA) DAY, SEB

'Victor' (Victor Coggiola) – Porsche 935
'Victor' (Victor Coggiola) (I) MZA, SIL, NUR,
SPA, IMO
'Gimax' (Carlo Franchi) (I) MZA
Giani Mussato (I) MZA, SIL
Gianni Giudici (I) SIL, NUR, BH, SPA
Angelo Pallavicini (I) NUR, BH, SPA, IMO
Bruno Rebai (I) IMO

Walker-Brown Racing – BMW M1
Paul Davey (GB) DAY
Diego Montoya (CO) DAY, SEB
Brian Goellnicht (USA) DAY, SEB
Michael Roe (IRL) SEB

**Team Warsteiner
– Porsche 956**
Walter Brun (CH) BH
Leopold von Bayern (D) BH
Stefan Bellof (D) BH
Harald Grohs (D) BH

**Dave White Racing
– Porsche 924 Carrera GTR**
Jerry Kendall (USA) DAY, SEB
Bill Johnson (USA) DAY
Dave White (USA) DAY, SEB
George Drolsom (USA) SEB

**Whitehall Promotions (Paul Gentilozzi)
– Porsche 924 Carrera GTR**
Bob Bergstrom (USA) DAY, SEB
Innes Ireland (GB) DAY
Tom Winters (USA) DAY, SEB
Bill Adam (CDN) SEB (DND)

Chris Wilder – Porsche 911
Chris Wilder (USA) DAY
Dennis DeFranceschi (USA) DAY, SEB
Buz McCall (USA) DAY
Van McDonald (USA) SEB

**Rodney Williams (no entrant listed)
– Ford Escort Sport**
Rodney Williams (ZA) KYA
Barry Botes (ZA) KYA
Tony Botes (ZA) KYA

**Jens Winther/Team Castrol
– BMW M1, URD C81 BMW**
Jens Winther (DK) MZA, SIL, LM, NUR,
BH, SPA, SAN
Lars-Viggo Jensen (DK) MZA, LM, NUR,
BH, SPA, SAN
David Mercer (GB) SIL (DND), LM, NUR,
BH, SPA

Gary Wonzer – Porsche 911
Buzz Cason (USA) SEB
Peter Uria (USA) SEB
Gary Wonzer (USA) SEB (DND)

**XEBEC Motorsport Division
– Tom's 83C Toyota**
Kaoru Hoshino (J) FUJ
Kiyoshi Misaki (J) FUJ
Kazuo Mogi (J) FUJ

**Pierre Yver – Rondeau M382 Ford
Cosworth DFL (DFV at Silverstone)**
Pierre Yver (F) MZA, SIL
Bernard de Dryver (B) MZA, SIL

**Z & W Motorsports
– Mazda GTP**
David Weitzenhof (USA) DAY
David Loring (USA) DAY
Pierre Honegger (USA) DAY

**Zabatt
– Chevrolet Corvette**
Tom Nehl (USA) DAY
Jerry Hansen (USA) DAY
Nelson Silcox (USA)

RESULTS

**Daytona 24 Hours, 5 February, USA
Started 82, finished 32**
1st van der Merwe (ZA)/Duxbury(ZA)/Martin
(ZA) March 83G Porsche
2nd A.J. Foyt (USA)/ Wollek (F)/Bell (GB)
Porsche 935 L
3rd Bundy (USA)/Hobbs (GB)/Tullius (USA)
Jaguar XJR-5

**Sebring 12 Hours, 24 March, USA
Started 81, finished 34**
1st DeNarvaez (COL)/Heyer (D)/Johansson
(SWE) Porsche 935J
2nd Lainier (USA)/Bill Whittington (USA)/Hinze
(USA) March 83G Chevrolet
3rd A.J. Foyt (USA)/Wollek (F)/Bell (GB)
Porsche 935 L

**Monza 1000km, 23 April, Italy
Started 32, finished 16**
1st Bellof (D)/Bell (GB) Porsche 956
2nd Ickx (B)/Mass (D) Porsche 956
3rd Baldi (I)/Barilla (I) Lancia LC2/84

**Silverstone 6 Hours, 13 May, GB
Started 44, finished 25**
1st Mass (D)/Ickx (B) Porsche 956
2nd Ludwig (D)/Pescarolo (F) Porsche 956
3rd Keegan (GB)/Edwards (GB) Porsche 956

**Le Mans 24 Hours, 16 June, France
Started 53, finished 22**
1st Pescarolo (F)/Ludwig (D) Porsche 956
2nd Jean Rondeau (F)/John Paul Jr (USA)
Porsche 956
3rd Hobbs (GB)/Streiff (F)/van der Merwe
(ZA) Porsche Porsche 956 B

**Nürburgring 1000km, 15 July, Germany
Started 42, finished 30**
1st Bellof (D)/Bell (GB) Porsche 956
2nd Boutsen (B)/Hobbs (GB) Porsche 956
3rd Nannini (I)/Barilla (I) Lancia LC2/84

**Brands Hatch 1000km, 29 July, Great
Britain. Started 26, finished 23**
1st Palmer (GB)/Lammers (NL) Porsche 956
2nd Mass (D)/Pescarolo (F) Porsche 956 B
3rd Edwards (GB)/Keegan (GB)/Boutsen (B)
Porsche 962

**Mosport 1000km, 5 August, Canada
Started 16, finished 9**
1st Ickx (B)/Mass (D) Porsche 956
2nd Hobbs (GB)/Keegan (GB)/Konrad (A)
Porsche 956B
3rd Daccò (I)/Coppelli (I) Alba RA2

**Spa 1000km, 2 September, Belgium
Started 26, finished 17**
1st Bellof (D)/Bell (GB) Porsche 956
2nd Ickx (B)/Mass (D) Porsche 956
3rd Stuck (D)/Grohs (D)/Brun (CH) Porsche
956 B

**Imola 1000km, 16 September, Italy
Started 28, finished 15**
1st Stuck (D)/Bellof (D) Porsche 956 B
2nd Palmer (GB)/Lammers (NL) Porsche 956
3rd Mass (D)/Heyer (D)/Pescarolo (F) Porsche
956 B

**Fuji 1000km, 30 September, Japan
Started 35, finished 24**
1st Bellof (D)/Watson (GB) Porsche 956
2nd Mass (D)/Ickx (B) Porsche 956
3rd Stuck (D)/Schuppan (AUS) Porsche 956B

**Kyalami 1000km, 3 November, South
Africa. Started 32, finished 18**
1st Patrese (I)/Nannini (I) Lancia LC2/84
2nd Wollek (F)/Barilla (I) Lancia LC2/84
3rd van der Linde (ZA)/Santana (ZA)/
Shearsby (ZA) Nissan Skyline

**Sandown Park 1000km, 2 December,
Australia. Started 29, finished 20**
1st Bellof (D)/Bell (GB) Porsche 956
2nd Mass (D)/Ickx (B) Porsche 956
3rd Palmer (GB)/Lammers (NL) Porsche 956

JAGUAR RETURNS BUT TRAGEDY INTRUDES

At long last Porsche had some serious competition with the advent of the Tom Walkinshaw Racing Jaguar XJR-6 designed by Tony Southgate that debuted at Mosport. The cars had an immediate impact but inevitably suffered from various teething problems and were not quite on par with their Weissach counterparts.

Nevertheless, they finished 3rd at Mosport, 5th at Spa, retired at Brands Hatch and Fuji and 2nd at Selangor. Drivers were Jean-Louis Schlesser, Martin Brundle, Jan Lammers, Mike Thackwell, Hans Heyer, Alan Jones, John Nielsen, Steve Soper and Gianfranco Brancatelli although the last two did not drive due to early retirements at Fuji and Selangor in Malaysia.

Selangor's Shah Alam circuit (originally named Batu Tiga) had been lengthened but it drew a modest entry and an even smaller crowd, probably due to high prices, its remote location and humid weather, so this was an expensive one-off never to be repeated.

Porsche by contrast won every race they entered bar Spa (Lancia) after the fatal Bellof crash and Fuji (withdrawn due to extreme weather). The works Rothmans cars finished 1st at Mugello, Silverstone, Hockenheim, Mosport and Brands Hatch. The Kremer Brothers took Monza whilst the Joest 956 won at Le Mans for the second successive time, all of which gave Rothmans Porsche the FIA Endurance Championship for C1 teams.

In C2 Spice Engineering were overwhelming winners from the Ecurie Ecosse team with Ark Racing and its unique Ceekar 83J 3rd. The Drivers' Championship in C1 went to Hans-Joachim Stuck (Rothmans Porsche) with Gordon Spice and Ray Bellm winning in C2 with the Spice Engineering car.

Of note was Richard Lloyd's much modified Porsche 956 GTi (106B) that had evolved into a honeycomb-chassis lookalike driven by Jonathan Palmer and Jan Lammers. They finished 5th after losing a front wheel at Monza having qualified 3rd, 5th at Silverstone after leading before another lost wheel, 2nd at Le Mans (Palmer/Weaver/Lloyd) and 5th at Hockenheim, but the car was destroyed at Spa during practice.

As for the rest, Lancia had a win and a 4th place at Spa but otherwise their best results were a 5th and a retirement at Mugello, a 3rd and a retirement at Monza, a 3rd and a 12th at Silverstone, a 6th and 7th at Le Mans, a 4th and a retirement at Hockenheim and a 3rd and 4th at Brands Hatch. They finished second in the Team Championship and 5th in the Drivers' Championship (Ludwig/Wollek).

Sadly, the excitement and derring-do of the teams/drivers and the advent of a British racing Jaguar team/cars were overshadowed by the deaths of Manfred Winkelhock at Mosport and Stefan Bellof at Spa. The first was an accident with no apparent cause whilst the latter was reckoned to be driver error by those on the ground.

At Daytona A.J. Foyt, Bob Wollek, Al Unser and Thierry Boutsen won the Daytona 24 Hours in Preston Henn's Porsche 962 clone from arch rival Al Holbert's similar car driven by Holbert, Al Unser Jr and Derek Bell.

Remarkably it was the same result at Sebring. This was an ongoing struggle between teams over the years that eventually fizzled out in favour of Holbert.

Spa 1000km, 1 September 1985 TWR arrived at Spa with various modifications for their Jaguars including a new nose, bigger front tyres and rear wheel covers. A determined Mike Thackwell in the XJR-6 (TWR-J12C-185) with Martin Brundle finished 5th, the first naturally aspirated car. However, the no.52 of Schlesser/Heyer retired on lap 14. It had developed severe oversteer on right-hand corners according to *Autosport* and despite attempts to ameliorate this it had to be withdrawn. *LAT*

Daytona 24 Hours, 3 February 1985 Once again one of Preston Henn's cars was aided by another driver from another team, in this case Thierry Boutsen who moved from the retired Leven Bayside Disposal Porsche 962 to join Bob Wollek in the Henn's Swap Shop Porsche 962 (104) with Indy racers A.J. Foyt and Al Unser. They benefited from the electrical problems of the Holbert Racing Porsche 962 driven by Al Holbert (USA), Al Unser Jr (USA) and Derek Bell (GB), who finished 2nd after leading the race, and the demise of the Group 44 Jaguar of Tullius/ Redman/Haywood, the March 85G Buick of John Paul Jr with Bill Adam and Whitney Ganz (fastest qualifier) and the Kreepy Krauly Racing March 84G Porsche of South Africans Sarel van der Merwe, Tony Martin and Ian Scheckter. *LAT*

Sebring 12 Hours, 23 March 1985 At a superficial level it seems astonishing that Sebring produced the same 1/2 for the same teams but so it was. In reality the Foyt/Wollek car was lucky to win, Wollek's 3.2-litre rocket engine expired during qualifying and started 13th, the Al Holbert 962 lost a wheel on lap 1, the Busby/Morton/Mass 962 led the race for over 6 hours, but a bizarre incident when the car ran over something very sharp that cut through the bottom of the car ended the 962's race. So Henn's 104, now wearing different colours, won again with the recuperated Holbert 962 finishing 2nd, four laps behind despite gearbox gremlins, and the second Busby Porsche 962 of Dieter Quester, Pete Halsmer and Rick Knoop 3rd, whilst the Group 44 Jaguar XJR-5 of Robinson/Tullius finished 4th. Look carefully and you can see AJ on Foyt's helmet. *LAT*

Mugello 1000km, 14 April 1985

Mugello opened the FIA season, which was now subject to the delayed 15% fuel reduction from 1984 (this was not applied to the C2 class) including special brews for the major teams. There were 17 starters (and less than 2,000 spectators apparently). Lancia entered two of their LC85s that looked very familiar. However, they had a new engineer, better Marelli electronics and a wider track amongst many other tweaks. The Ferrari-based V8 was giving 600bhp in race trim whilst Michelin was now the tyre supplier. Patrese/Nannini in no.4 were the fastest qualifiers with teammates Wollek/Baldi 5th fastest. Patrese in the no.4 car led at the start but ultimately retired with engine problems whilst Wollek/Baldi in no.5 finished 4th. This is Nannini who later drove for Benetton in F1, winning the 1989 Japanese GP. A helicopter accident in 1990 severed his right arm and despite microsurgery to reinstate it he had only partial right-hand movement and F1 was no longer possible. However, he did have a touring-car career with Alfa Romeo and later Mercedes-Benz in the 1990s before retiring in 1997. These days he looks after the family café and bakery in Siena, Tuscany. *GPL*

Mugello 1000km, 14 April 1985

Roy Baker entered the Tiga GC284 Ford Turbo (277) for Paul Smith, Dudley Wood and Jeremy Rossiter. It finished 13th and last but was not the slowest of the C2 class in qualifying. Smith awaits his ride whilst the car is fettled in the pits. He was a regular competitor in this category and also had raced a March 782 in the 1980 British F1 Championship, finishing 6th at Mallory Park and 7th at Thruxton. He later raced in F2 before moving to sports prototypes. His father Don Smith, who raced a Jaguar 3.8 in the 1960s, is chairman of BMTR (Birmingham Motor Tyre Repository) and Paul, who retired from racing during the mid 1980s (although later raced an F1 Ensign in 1992), is the MD. *LAT*

← Mugello 1000km, 14 April 1985 The farcical fuel restriction and the final lap that should be not more than 400% of the pole position time regulation caught out several front runners including the factory Bell/Stuck Porsche 962C (003). They were eking out their fuel consumption and Stuck stopped just short of the line to await the winning Ickx/Mass car to finish, but in doing so he passed the aforementioned 400% rule. Cue instant disqualification. Note the 17in front and 19in rear wheels/Dunlop tyres whose narrower, taller rear wheel/tyre assemblies allowed wider and deeper air tunnels compared to the 1984 cars. The 'customer' 962s were still using 16in wheels/tyres. *LAT*

→ Monza 1000km, 28 April 1985 Stefan Bellof was the epitome of the racing driver of legend: fearless, daring and faster than a speeding bullet, to paraphrase the Superman movies. His pristine driver's suit, balaclava, helmet, matching gloves and boots look new. His decision to leave Porsche and join the Brun team was because he could not commit to a full season with Weissach due to his escalating F1 career. He shared the Brun Motorsport Porsche 962C with Thierry Boutsen but they were disqualified for refuelling too quickly apparently. *LAT*

← Monza 1000km, 28 April 1985 Using a highly boosted engine (possibly over 800bhp) Riccardo Patrese was on pole at Monza, 1.2 seconds faster than teammate Bob Wollek. Here is one of the LC2-85s waiting to get out there and go for it in qualifying, but note the absence of a race number in sight. Patrese/Nannini finished 3rd when they could/should have won the race but then came the storm. Meanwhile, Baldi and Surer in the Kremer Porsche 962C punted each other off at the Parabolica, leaving Baldi stranded in the barriers. *GPL*

◁ Monza 1000km, 28 April 1985
Richard Lloyd's Goodyear-shod, re-engineered GTi Engineering Porsche 956B (106B) (Jonathan Palmer/Jan Lammers) had been further modified and was quicker than all the other Porsches, factory and privateer. They were 3rd fastest behind the Lancias and Palmer was challenging Wollek's LC2-85 for 2nd place on lap 27, but the left front wheel came off approaching the first corner. He trickled the three-wheeled car all the way back to the pits, losing 13 minutes, and restarted 18th. Ultimately the duo finished 5th (after the disqualification of the Boutsen/Bellof Brun 962) whilst fate and nature conspired to give him one more fright when an ever-worsening gale blew down a tree between the Campari chicane and the first Lesmo. Fortunately, Palmer, who was first on the scene, stopped in time. *LAT*

▷ Monza 1000km, 28 April 1985
Given his clash with Baldi and the later blown-down tree, Marc Surer with Manfred Winkelhock were lucky to win at Monza. The Kremer 962C (110) was sadly the car that Manfred Winkelhock, seen here, crashed fatally at Mosport Park on 11 August 1985. *LAT*

◁ Monza 1000km, 28 April 1985
Dane Jens Winther, sometime BMW M1 aficionado, and British dentist David Mercer finished 12th and 3rd in the C2 class in the URD C83 BMW. Winther bought the much-used car in late 1984 and raced it at Sandown at the end of the season. It was now better prepared and wearing the Castrol livery that Winther always used. The C2 victors were Spice and Bellm in the Spice Tiga GC85 which finished 7th overall ahead of the Ecurie Ecosse Ecosse C285 of Mallock/Wilds. Meanwhile, the new AR6 Alba driven as ever by Finotto/Martino was significantly faster but, perhaps inevitably, unreliable. *LAT*

▷ Monza 1000km, 28 April 1985
Here is the felled arboreal growth that stopped the race on lap 138 whilst a woman was killed in the nearby Parco di Monza by another falling tree. *LAT*

Silverstone 1000km, 12 May 1985 The start with the two Lancias, no.4 Patrese and no.5 Wollek ahead of the numerous Porsche 962 and 956 variants. Both Lancias and the no.14 Canon/GTi 956B of Palmer will lead the race. Once again note the period catch fencing and the far better (for viewing) grandstands. *GPL*

Silverstone 1000km, 12 May 1985 Weissach reinstated their supremacy at Silverstone. Ickx/Mass and Bell/Stuck were 7th and 3rd respectively in qualifying but finished 1/2 in the race. However, the RLR/Canon GTi Engineering 956B of Palmer/Lammers and the Lancia LC2-85 twins were the quickest cars in practice and the race. The fuel regs were not a problem and all the front runners were well inside the 100-litre limit. Unbelievably the Canon car lost yet another front wheel (this time the hub was to blame) on lap 103 whilst leading the Patrese Lancia. Boutsen's Brun Motorsport 962C lost two wheels (but still finished 10th) and two other Porsches also shed wheels. Palmer fought his way back to 5th place and a new lap record whilst Patrese caught and passed Winkelhock's Kremer 962C for 3rd place. Ultimately the factory Porsches won the race by avoiding trouble although the 2nd-placed Bell/Stuck car had a loose windscreen. Jochen Mass presses on to victory in the 962C (002). *LAT*

Silverstone 1000km, 12 May 1985 Spice Engineering entered the old Tiga GC284 (250) with a 3.9-litre Ford Cosworth DFL to join the C1 brigade at Silverstone. It was driven by Neil Crang and Tim Lee-Davey but was only marginally quicker than the 3.3-litre DFL-powered GC285 of Spice and Bellm who were beaten in the C2 class by the Ecurie Ecosse Ecosse C285 due to fuel pick-up problems. Worse still, 250 only managed 28 laps before the gearbox casing split open and terminally damaged the right rear suspension. *LAT*

⬆️ **Le Mans, 16 June 1985** Factory Porsches won at Le Mans in 1982/83 and now Reinhold Joest's private team, having finished 1st in 1984 without the factory cars, won again in 1985 with the same car. The New Man Joest 956B (117) was driven by Klaus Ludwig, Paolo Barilla and 'John Winter' aka Louis Krages. They led from the third hour onwards with the Canon GTi Engineering 956B finishing 2nd whilst the factory Porsche 962Cs all suffered assorted problems with Bell/Stuck their highest finisher in 3rd place. *LAT*

⬅️ **Le Mans, 16 June 1985** Weissach entered three *langheck* 962Cs for Ickx/Mass, Stuck/Bell and Holbert/Watson/Schuppan. They finished 10th, 3rd and retired. The first named had gearbox problems including a new oil cooler, an ignition fault and later a replacement gearbox. The second named had a puncture and then wheel-bearing failures whilst the third car retired late Sunday morning with a broken crankshaft. Beyond this they were victims of the fuel restrictions. Of note was Stuck's sensational qualifying record of 3m 14.800 with a high-boost 3-litre engine; ditto the Ickx/Mass car but for the race all three 962s used the smaller 2.6 motors. John Watson at left prepares to take over 962C (004). *LAT*

Le Mans, 16 June 1985 There were two similar Toyota-powered cars at Le Mans, one from the Dome Team and the other from Tom's Team. Both were powered by the production-based 2.1-litre 8-valve 4T-GT engine which produced circa 560bhp in race trim. They arrived with long-tail rear ends, which were insufficiently tested and unstable on Mulsanne and so were replaced with standard rear ends. Additionally, they were overweight, the Tom's car weighing 959kg and finishing 12th driven by Satoru Nakajima/Masanori Sekiya/Kaoro Hoshino seen here. Meanwhile the Dome 85C-L Toyota (Eje Elgh/Geoff Lees/Toshio Suzuki) had a gearbox problem and later a serious clutch issue, causing their retirement on lap 141. *LAT*

Le Mans, 16 June 1985 Both Lancia LC2-85s went the distance at Le Mans but they finished 6th and 7th led by the Wollek/Nannini/Lucio Cesario car, the last named being Lancia's reserve driver. Wollek led the race at the start, reaching 226mph on Mulsanne, but both cars were victims of the fuel restrictions. Nannini was in 4th position on early Sunday morning but lost 30 minutes with a turbo change. The other car was driven by Henri Pescarolo and Mauro Baldi and they finished 7th, two laps behind their teammates. This is possibly Cesario, born in Melbourne, Australia in 1951, whose career encompassed many different classes over 30-plus years mainly in Australia, in LC2-85 (0002). *LAT*

◀ **Le Mans, 16 June 1985** The three-car WM Peugeot P83B team used twin-turbo Peugeot 2,750cc V6 engines producing 650bhp @ 8,000rpm at Le Mans. Jean Rondeau joined Michel Pignard and Jean-Daniel Raulet and they finished 17th after delays caused by a sticking wheel nut, plus turbocharger and cooling-system problems. The Pascal Pessiot/Dominique Fornage and Patrick Gaillard car was using a ZF gearbox (the others had Hewland 'boxes) and suffered assorted troubles but was disqualified after the race for being slightly underweight. Team owner Roger Dorchy was partnered by Claude Haldi and Jean-Claude Andruet, the latter crashing on Mulsanne without injury, after overheating and brake difficulties although the *Autosport* report blamed it on a burst tyre. This is the Rondeau car and it was to be his final race because on 27 December 1985 outside Champagné whilst following a police car across some train tracks – while the boom gates were down – his car was hit by a train and he died. *LAT*

◀ **Le Mans, 16 June 1985** The C2 class at Le Mans included the Ecurie Ecosse Ecosse C285 (02) for Ray Mallock/David Leslie/Mike Wilds and the Spice-Tiga GC85, both Ford Cosworth DFL powered. Mallock qualified 3.9 seconds faster than the Spice car although both were outgunned by the new Alba AR6 Carma of Finotto/Dacco/Bertuzzi. In the race the Ecosse lasted just 45 laps before its oil pump failed whilst the Alba AR6 retired with electrical trouble after 228 laps. Meanwhile Gordon Spice/Ray Bellm/Mark Galvin in the Spice were fortunate as the leading Mazda (Kennedy/Martin), which had led the C2 class for 11 hours, retired with a broken gearbox. Also the Tiga's engine was failing and they spent the last four hours nursing it to the finish in 14th place overall and 1st in the C2 category. *GPL*

→ **Le Mans, 16 June 1985** Nearly two years after its last appearance at the 1983 Le Mans, Steve O'Rourke's EMKA Aston Martin returned as the EMKA C84/1 Aston Martin MC 02 84C, driven by the owner, Tiff Needell and Bob Evans at Silverstone. It had new suspension all round with strengthened components and Needell qualified it 15th. Alas the engine gave up after 70 laps. At Le Mans it was 9 seconds faster than it had been in 1983 and started in 13th place, courtesy of Tiff Needell again, with Nick Faure and O'Rourke, and was the fastest non-turbo car in the race. The team pitted Needell early for a top-up so that the car would be in 1st place when the leaders pitted for their planned fuel stops. Needell was soon caught and passed and he then pitted for a full tank. Apart from a faulty clutch slave cylinder and a fuel leak, the car was reliable and they finished 11th. *LAT*

→ **Le Mans, 16 June 1985** Richard Lloyd was the third man in his Canon GTi Engineering Porsche 956B (106B) at Le Mans with Jonathan Palmer and James Weaver. Lloyd drove one stint and their much modified car ultimately finished 2nd although they might have won but for an electronic glitch which dropped them to 7th place earlier on. Lloyd was an employee at Decca Records (1964–70) who started his own public-relations business, Motor Race Relations, in 1971. He won many Saloon Car Championship races, which led to his GTi Engineering concern in 1978, using Volkswagen Golf GTIs and Audi 80s. Into the 1980s he entered and occasionally raced his own variation of the Porsche 956s and 962s. Tragically on 30 March 2008 he died along with David Leslie, Christopher Allarton and the two pilots Mike Roberts and Michael Chapman when a private jet on which they were travelling crashed into a house, shortly after take-off from Biggin Hill Airport. *LAT*

Le Mans, 16 June 1985 Group 44 returned to Le Mans but were only marginally quicker than their 1984 outing. They brought two XJR-5Bs for Bob Tullius, Chip Robinson and Claude Ballot-Léna (008) and Brian Redman, Jim Adams and Hurley Haywood (006). During qualifying both cars suffered burnt-out pistons (not unknown at Le Mans), which required rebuilding and detuning the engines to prevent a recurrence. In the race 006 retired with a broken driveshaft whilst 008 suffered a broken valve or burnt-out piston depending upon who you believe. Afterwards a fuel sample from the official supply showed it to be a bad batch (according to Martin and Wells in their book *PROTOTYPES The history of the IMSA GTP series*). However, the now V11 008 survived and finished 13th and winner of the GTP class but it was their final time here. Bob Tullius is at far left in the picture as 008 is fed its liquids. *LAT*

Le Mans, 16 June 1985 Over the decades Le Mans was as much a private/amateur race as it was a professional one. One such amateur was the A. Bellanger-R. Bassaler entry of an old Sauber SHS C6 BMW (82-C6-02) for Dominique Lacaud, Roland Bassaler and Yvon Tapy. They finished 23rd and 5th in the C2 class. The Sauber's profile is typical of the period with a very short 'nose', overlong rear end and a large v-shaped rear wing. It started life in 1982 with GS Tuning/ Walter Brun and then went to Bassaler in 1985. He still had it in 1994 when it was entered as an Alpa LM at Le Mans for Nicolas Minassian, Patrick Bourdais and Olivier Couvrier where it retired. If you look at the bottom of the gullwing door you can see the drivers' blood groups that are displayed there. *LAT*

Hockenheim 1000km, 14 July 1985 At a very hot Hockenheim, 11 of the 36 starters were Porsche 962/956s. The Kremer and Brun customer cars were now equal to or marginally faster than the factory 962s. Manfred Winkelhock in the Kremer 962C (110) is alongside Stuck in the 962C (003) approaching the first corner after the start and he made it stick. Behind is Mass in the other Rothmans Porsche followed by Bellof in the Brun 956B (116) and the rest. By lap 3 Bellof was leading from Winkelhock but both would retire, the Kremer car a victim of one of the three pit-stop fires and the Brun car running out of fuel. Ickx/Mass retired with turbo problems and Stuck/Bell won from the second Brun 956 of Sigala/Larrauri with Ludwig/Barilla 3rd in the New Man Joest 956B. Amongst those injured in the conflagrations were four Porsche mechanics, engineer Helmut Schmidt and team manager Norbert Singer who had first- and second-degree burns. *LAT*

↑ **Hockenheim 1000km, 14 July 1985** This is Chuck Graemiger's Cheetah G604 Aston Martin (1) looking very sleek and fast but in reality not. In 1984 it had been raced at Spa by Mallock/de Dryver but retired, followed in 1985 by Mugello (de Dryver/Brancatelli) retired, Monza (de Dryver/ Brancatelli) retired, Silverstone (Cooper/Brindley) retired, Hockenheim (Needell/Cooper) retired, Spa (de Dryver/Dieudonne/Bourgoignie) 10th, Brands Hatch (Brindley/de Dryver/Regout) retired and Fuji (de Dryver/ Ferrier) withdrawn due to weather. The Tickford Aston Martin engine was too heavy, too fragile and probably not giving the claimed 570bhp so he moved to Heini Mader but without success. Long-time sponsor Gatoil departed and Graemiger was in court over unpaid invoices, outstanding salaries and a dispute about ownership of the car, presumably Loris Kessel again. *LAT*

← **Hockenheim 1000km, 14 July 1985** Manuel Reuter (born 6 December 1961) was racing here for Team Labatt in a Gebhardt JC 853 Ford with Frank Jelinski and John Graham. Unfortunately, the car retired very early on with fuel-pressure trouble, no doubt made worse by or because of the very high temperatures in the race. Reuter began by racing karts in the 1970s and later became a sports car regular and DTM champion for Opel together with two Le Mans victories, in 1989 for Sauber-Mercedes and in 1996 for Joest Racing. *LAT*

⬆ Hockenheim 1000km, 14 July 1985 Gordon Spice had a successful year with his Spice-Tiga GC85 and was on his way to the C2 championship. However, at Hockenheim he was beaten in class by the Ecurie Ecosse Ecosse C285 of Mallock/Leslie/Wilds. Here is the Spice team in the Hockenheim pits, the very tall Ray Bellm at far right with the stocky Gordon Spice to his right and their helmets on the rear wing. *LAT*

➡ Mosport 1000km, 11 August 1985 After much anticipation Tom Walkinshaw's TWR Jaguar XJR-6s arrived at Mosport with two cars for Brundle/Heyer and Thackwell/Schlesser. Here are race director Roger Silman (ex-March Engineering, Toleman and now TWR and much later MD of the Arrows F1 team in 1999) with Tony Southgate checking the small print. Walkinshaw wanted to race asap and as a result certain aspects of the XJR-6 were makeshift at launch. The first car was tested at Snetterton on 2 July 1985, just five weeks before Mosport. *LAT*

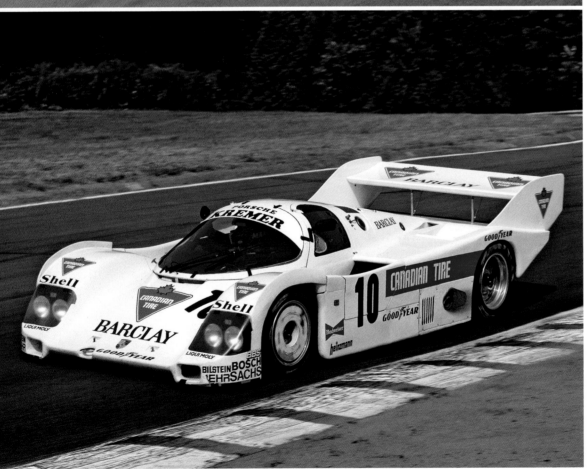

Mosport 1000km, 11 August 1985 Following the retirement of the Brundle/Thackwell no.51 XJR-6 (TWR-J12C-185) early in the race at Mosport, the two drivers were transferred to the no.52 Schlesser/Heyer car (TWR-J12C-285), yet here the no.51 car is being followed by Mike Thackwell in the no.52 car. Was this a practice shot perhaps? Either way Hans Heyer lost his drive and Brundle/Thackwell joined Jean-Louis Schlesser in the no.52 car to finish 3rd. *LAT*

Mosport 1000km, 11 August 1985 Mosport saw a return to Rothmans Porsche domination, albeit in very tragic circumstances. There were two Kremer Porsches, the 956 (105) for Canadian father and son Ludwig Heimrath and Ludwig Heimrath Jr and Dutch racer Kees Kroesemeijer, which finished 4th, and the Surer/Winkelhock 962C (110). This is Marc Surer who had a collision with a backmarker, which broke the right rear suspension on lap 5 and lost them nine laps. When Winkelhock took over he continued the car's progress up the field, but on lap 83 he went straight on at turn 2 and hit a concrete wall, having missed the fencing at high speed. Why is not known and Winkelhock died in hospital the next day from massive head and neck injuries. Stuck/Bell won ahead of Ickx/Mass, but I don't suppose they cared much about their victory. *LAT*

Spa 1000km, 1 September 1985 The Spa round started off badly when Jonathan Palmer had a very nasty accident in the Canon GTi 956B during practice when a front tyre deflated and the car hit a barrier and folded up. Palmer escaped with a couple of broken bones in one foot, a crack to his right fibula and a black eye. Following the Mosport tragedy this was unnerving but far worse was to follow. The shortened race was won by the Wollek (seen here)/ Baldi/Patrese Lancia LC2-85 (0003) with Bell/Stuck in the Rothmans Porsche 962C 2nd and Ludwig/Barilla 3rd in the New Man Joest 956B (117). The other Lancia LC2-85 (0002) of Riccardo Patrese/Alessandro Nannini/ Mauro Baldi (note the shared cars) finished 4th. *LAT*

Spa 1000km, 1 September 1985 The Schiesser-sponsored Brun Porsche 956B (116) driven by Thierry Boutsen and Stefan Bellof qualified 3rd fastest at Spa. On lap 72 Bellof had taken over from Boutsen for the second time, but the car had to have a pad change, while Ickx replaced Mass and took the lead. On lap 78, racing past the pits, Bellof caught up with Ickx and his front wheel was just ahead of Ickx's rear wheel as the 962 turned into the first part of Eau Rouge and made contact at 140mph plus. The Schiesser car spun right round and hit the barriers on the left, front first and burst into flames whilst Ickx went off backwards at the foot of the hill toward Raidillon with only a minor fire. Ickx was shocked but otherwise hardly hurt but Bellof was too weak to be taken to hospital according to *Autosport* and he died about an hour later at the circuit's medical facility. According to the press, eyewitnesses thought that this was a disastrous error of judgement by Bellof. Here he is pressing on as ever and let us remember him for this. *LAT*

Spa 1000km, 1 September 1985 The Ceekar 83J-1 Ford Cosworth BDX was created by Master Mariner Derek Matthews and Lotus racer Max Payne. Matthews designed the GRP body by eye and it was sponsored by Payne's company General Provisions and Arthur Hough Pressings, who also entered it. Matthews used a rigid full-length central box section and, as per IMSA rules, the driver's feet and pedals had to be behind the axis of the front wheels. He was concerned to keep the driver as far away from any accident as possible, hence the 17.5 inches that separated the pedals from the front axle and the very long nose. From its debut at Silverstone in 1984 to the last race of 1985 at Selangor the Ceekar made ten starts and finished in eight of them. Note the plastic sink waste pipe that is providing airflow into the cockpit. At Spa it finished 16th and 6th in the C2 class driven by Max Payne, David Andrews and Chris Ashmore. *LAT*

Brands Hatch 1000km, 22 September 1985 Lancia started from the front row led by the Patrese/Nannini LC2-85 and Wollek/de Cesaris/Baldi alongside. At the end of lap 1 Patrese has already gone by, leaving Wollek in no.5 leading the Stuck 962C ahead of teammate Mass and the two Jaguars of Alan Jones and Jan Lammers next. As was the norm the fuel limitation created a fast/slow seesaw whilst Ickx was penalised for 10 seconds because his refuelling rig was flowing too fast as distinct to the Bell/Stuck rig which had temporarily been too slow. Ultimately the Lancias finished 3rd and 4th with the no.5 car 3rd after de Cesaris and Patrese came together during an unnecessary duel. The former was unharmed but the Patrese car had to pit with a broken exhaust pipe and lost four laps. *GPL*

Brands Hatch 1000km, 22 September 1985 The TWR Jaguars were just off the pace of the works Porsches and Lancias in the race and both retired, Alan Jones in no.51 over-revved the V12 motor when the throttle slides seized up on lap 20 whilst the no.52 car of Lammers/Heyer retired on lap 77. Heyer is at far left with his overalls down on a warm sunny day. He had to stop due to a loose seat, which was repaired and he drove for 35 laps before handing over to Lammers, but the car then blew a head gasket and they were out which might be what is happening here. Note the nose front wing. *LAT*

◄ Brands Hatch 1000km, 22 September 1985
Richard Cleare only attended one race in 1984 (at Brands Hatch) due to funding problems and he repeated this in 1985. His Porsche Kremer CK-5 (01) now had a fully designed ground-effect chassis and a restyled nose with an adjustable wing, a more aerodynamic rear end and 19in wheels. The design and manufacture of the new parts was overseen by freelance designer Val Dare-Bryan. Cleare shared the car with David Leslie who qualified it 18th and it raced with the leading C2 cars, but the exhaust pipe 'twixt engine and turbo broke and it retired on lap 59. The car looks very new and sparkling but note the absence of any sponsorship decals. *LAT*

↓ Brands Hatch 1000km, 22 September 1985
Following its Le Mans appearance, Steve O'Rourke's EMKA C84/1 Aston Martin MC 02 84C retired at Spa after 19 laps with failing fuel pressure and at Brands Hatch Tiff Needell was 10th fastest qualifier. He was partnered by Irish driver Mark Galvin, F3 and sports-car racer in period, and O'Rourke. It lasted 74 laps before the belt that ran the oil, water and fuel pumps broke and that was it, *finis*. The Dow Corning sponsorship had gone, the costs were too high and O'Rourke withdrew from racing although he did grace Le Mans in the 1990s twice, finishing 4th in 1998 in a BMW F1 GTR. *LAT*

Brands Hatch 1000km, 22 September 1985
This is the ALD 01 BMW of Louis Descartes and Jacques Heuclin that finished 9th and 3rd in the C2 class at Brands Hatch. ALD (Automobiles Louis Descartes) was a small private concern in Levallois Perret that employed four persons plus a number of unpaid enthusiasts. His friend Heuclin was the Mayor of Seine-et-Marne and as noted elsewhere in this book died on 31 October 2007 of a lung disease. Tragically, three days before his 40th birthday on 27 December 1991, Louis Descartes died after crashing into a tree north of Paris. The driver here has a yellow helmet matching with the car so this might be Descartes. Someone will know, please tell me if you do. *LAT*

Fuji 1000km, 6 October 1985 The race was a victim of firstly a mild earthquake and later a typhoon, just what you need at a motor-racing venue. There were 13 entrants from Europe and Great Britain but all of these were withdrawn during the race because of the weather. This is the Trust Racing Team Porsche 956 (111) driven by Vern Schuppan (he finished 6th) with George Fouché and Keiichi Suzuki who did not drive as the race was halted after 62 laps. As you can see, the conditions were not conducive for racing 600bhp-plus cars. The winner was the Hoshino Racing March 85G Nissan driven by Kazuyoshi Hoshino. *LAT*

Fuji 1000km, 6 October 1985 Amongst the British contingent was the Canon GTi Engineering Porsche 956B (106B II) for Kenny Acheson and Johnny Dumfries (qualified 9th) who are talking to one of the team's members. They do not look too happy, unsurprisingly, and Acheson started the race but was withdrawn after nine laps. *LAT*

Selangor 800km, 1 December 1985 Rainbow's end was the Selangor 800km at Shah Alam, Malaysia which had replaced Kuala Lumpur as the capital city of the state of Selangor in 1978. It attracted only 17 cars of which 15 started. Three Rothmans Porsches attended – presumably they were looking for customers given that they already had two championships in their pocket. Drivers were Mass/Ickx, Stuck/Bell (in the 956 PDK car) and Schuppan/Weaver. TWR fielded Thackwell/Nielsen and Lammers/Brancatelli. Fitzpatrick Racing, Brun Motorsport and Joest (car withdrawn after practice accident) also attended but the rest of the field was just filling in the gaps. Jochen Mass in the 962C (002) leads one of the other Rothmans Porsches with the two TWR Jaguars in the background. Mass/Ickx won the race ahead of the Thackwell/Nielsen Jaguar XJR-6 (TWR-J12C-185) plus Jan Lammers whose car had blown a tyre on lap 19 and was trapped off circuit. Thackwell retired with heat exhaustion leaving Nielsen/Lammers to finish 2nd with the Schuppan/Weaver Porsche 3rd. *LAT*

ENTRANTS

49th Star Racing – Porsche 911
William Phalf (USA) DAY
Skip Winfree (USA) DAY
Wally Hopkins (USA) DAY

901 Shop – Porsche Carrera 911 RSR
Mike Schaefer (USA) DAY, SEB
Peter Uria (USA) DAY, SEB
Jack Refenning (USA) DAY, SEB
Larry Figaro (USA) DAY, SEB

**ADA Engineering – Gebhardt JC843
Ford Cosworth DFL**
Ian Harrower (GB) MZA, SIL, BH, LM,
BH, SEL
Richard Jones (GB) MZA
David Duffield (GB) MZA
Mark Galvin (IRL) SIL
Steve Earle (USA) SIL, LM
John Sheldon (GB) LM
Ian Taylor (GB) BH
Evan Clements (GB) SEL
Richard Piper (GB) SEL

Advan Sports Nova – Porsche 962 C
Kunimitsu Takahashi (J) FUJ
Kenji Takahashi (J) FUJ (DNS race
abandoned)

**Aerex Manufacturing
– Tiga GT284 Mazda**
Peter Welter (USA)
Nick Nicholson (USA)
Tom Burdsall (USA)

**Bob Akin Motor Racing
– Porsche 962, Porsche 935/84**
Hans-Joachim Stuck (D) DAY, SEB
Bob Akin (USA) DAY, SEB
Paul Miller (USA) DAY
Jim Mullen (USA) DAY, SEB
Kees Nierop (CDN) DAY
Ray McIntyre (USA) DAY

**All American Racers
– Toyota Celica**
Chris Cord (USA) DAY
Dennis Aase (USA) DAY

**Alpha Cubic Racing Team
– Porsche 956 B**
Noritake Takahara (J) FUJ (Withdrew due
to weather)
Chiyomi Totani (J) FUJ (DNS race abandoned
due to weather)

**Auto Beaurex Motorsport
– Lotec M1C BMW**
Kazuo Mogi (J) FUJ
Toshio Motohashi (J) FUJ (DNS race
abandoned due to weather)
Naoki Nagasaka (J) FUJ
Taku Akaike (J) FUJ (DNS race abandoned
due to weather)

**Automobiles Louis Descartes
– ALD 01 BMW**
Jacques Heuclin (F) LM, HCK, SPA, BH
Louis Descartes (F) LM, HCK, SPA, BH
Daniël Hubert (B) LM

Al Bacon Racing – Mazda RX-7
Al Bacon (USA) DAY, SEB
Charles Guest (USA) DAY, SEB
Steve Millen (NZ) DAY
Bobby Akin (USA) SEB

**Roy Baker Promotions
– Tiga GC84 Ford Cosworth BDT,
Tiga GC285 Ford Cosworth BDT**
Paul Smith (GB), MZA, LM, HCK, SPA, BH
Dudley Wood (GB) MUG, BH
Jeremy Rossiter (GB) MUG, SPA

Thorkild Thyrring (DK) SIL, HCK, SPA
Will Hoy (GB) MZA, SIL (DND), LM, HCK, BH
Nick Nicholson (USA) LM
François Duret (GB) LM
David Andrews (GB) LM, FUJ (DND)
Duncan Bain (GB) LM BH, SEL
Mike Kimpton (GB) HCK, SPA, BH
Roy Baker (GB) HCK, FUJ, SEL (DND)
Joe DeMarco (CDN) MOS
Chuck Grantham (USA) MOS
Mike Catlow (GB) BH
Andy Wallace (GB) SEL
Michael Hall (GB) SEL
David Palmer (GB) SEL

**John Bartlett Chevron Racing
– Chevron B62 Ford Cosworth DFL**
Max Cohen-Olivar (MA) LM, HCK, MOS
(DND), SPA, BH
Richard Jones (GB) LM, HCK, SPA (DND)
Robin Smith (GB) LM (DND), HCK, MOS,
FUJ (Withdrew due to weather), SEL
Stanley Dickens (S) MOS (DND), BH
Kenneth Leim (S) SPA, FUJ, FUJ (DNS due
to weather), SEL
John Sheldon (GB) BH (DND)
Martin Birrane (IRL) FUJ (DNS due to
weather)
Robin Donovan (GB) SEL

Roland Bassaler – Sauber SHS C6 BMW
Dominique Lacaud (F) LM, SPA, BH
Roland Bassaler (F) LM, BH
Yvon Tapy (F) LM
Gerard Brucelle (F) SPA
Gérard Tremblay (F) SPA

Bäuerle Farben Team – BMW M1
Rolf Göring (D) HCK
Claude Haldi (CH) HCK
Michael Krankenberg (D) HCK

Bayside Disposal Racing – Porsche 962
Thierry Boutsen (B) DAY
Bruce Leven (USA) DAY
Henri Pescarolo (F) DAY

Bob Beasley – Porsche 911 Carrera RSR
Bob Beasley (USA) DAY
Jack Lewis (USA) DAY
Chuck Grantham (USA) DAY

Bieri Racing – Sauber C7 Chevrolet
'Fomfor' (Francisco Miguel) (ES) MOS
Uli Bieri (CDN) MOS
Matt Gysler (CDN) MOS

**Ecurie Blanchet-Locatop – Rondeau
M379 C Ford Cosworth DFV**
Michel Dubois (F) LM, HCK
Hubert Striebig (F) LM, HCK
Noël del Bello (F) LM, HCK (DND)

**Blue Thunder Racing Team
– March 84G Chevrolet**
Bill Whittington (USA) SEB
Randy Lanier (USA) SEB

Bo-And Racing – Lola T600 Chevrolet
Richard Anderson (USA) DAY
Bard Boand (USA) DAY
Mike Brummer (USA) DAY

Bob's Speed Products – Buick Skyhawk
Bob Lee (USA) SEB
Bill Julian (USA) SEB
Jeff Hudlett (USA) SEB

**Brun Motorsport – Porsche 962 C,
Porsche 956 B, Porsche 956**
Stefan Bellof (D) MUG, MZA, HCK, SPA
(Fatal accident)
Thierry Boutsen (B) MUG, MZA, SIL,
HCK, SPA
Walter Brun (CH) MUG (DNS), SIL, LM, HCK
Leopold von Bayern (D) MUG (DNS)

Oscar Larrauri (RA) MUG, MZA, SIL, LM,
HCK, SPA, SEL
Massimo Sigala (I) MUG, MZA, SIL, LM,
HCK, SPA, SEL
Renzo Zorzi (I) MZA
Gabriele Tarquini (I) LM
Didier Theys (B) LM
Joël Gouhier (F) LM
Gerhard Berger (A) HCK
Frank Jelinski (D) SEL

Ken Bupp – Chevrolet Camaro
Ken Bupp (USA) SEB
Guy Church (USA) SEB
E.J. Generotti (USA) SEB

**Burdsall-Welter Racing
– Tiga GT284 Mazda**
Tom Burdsall (USA)
Peter Welter (USA)
Nick Nicholson (USA)

Busby Racing – Porsche 962
Pete Halsmer (USA) SEB
Dieter Quester (A) SEB
Rick Knoop (USA) SEB

**Bussi Racing – Rondeau M382
Ford Cosworth DFL, Rondeau M482
Ford Cosworth DFL**
Jean-Claude Justice (F) LM
Bruno Sotty (F) LM
Patrick Oudet (F) LM
Christian Bussi (F) LM
Jack Griffin (USA) LM
M.L. Speer (USA) LM

**Carma FF/Totip Carma
– Alba AR2 Carma, Alba AR6 Carma**
Carlo Facetti (I) MUG, MZA, SIL, HCK, MOS,
SPA, BH
Martino Finotto (I) MUG, MZA, SIL, LM,
HCK, MOS, SPA, BH
Guido Daccò (I) MUG, MZA, SIL, LM
Jean-Pierre Frey (CH) SIL, HCK, MOS
Loris Kessel (CH) SIL
Aldo Bertuzzi (I) LM
Lucio Cesario (I) HCK
Marco Vanoli (CH) HCK
Almo Coppelli (I) SPA, BH

Case Racing – Porsche 911
Ron Case (USA) SEB
Dave Panaccione (USA) SEB

**Central 20 Racing Team
– Lola T810 Nissan**
Aguri Suzuki (J) FUJ
Haruhito Yanagida (J) FUJ (DNS race
abandoned due to weather)

**Centurian Auto Trans
– Chevrolet Camaro**
Harold Shafer (USA) DAY
Tom Nehl (USA) DAY
Kent Painter (USA) DAY

**Championship Motorsports
– Mazda RX-7**
Don Wallace (USA) DAY
John Petrick (USA) DAY
Don Sikes (USA) DAY

**Cheetah Automobiles Switzerland
– Cheetah G604 Aston Martin**
Bernard de Dryver (B) MUG, MZA (DND),
LM (DND), SPA, BH, FUJ (Withdrew due
to weather)
Gianfranco Brancatelli (I) MUG (DND), MZA
John Cooper (GB) SIL, LM, HCK (DND)
John Brindley (GB) SIL, BH
Claude Bourgoignie (B) LM, SPA
Tiff Needell (GB) HCK
Pierre Dieudonné (B) SPA
Hervé Regout (B) BH
Laurent Ferrier (F) FUJ (DNS due to weather)

Richard Cleare Racing – Porsche CK5
David Leslie (GB) BH
Richard Cleare (GB) BH

Coin Operated Racing – Porsche 934
Jim Torres (USA) DAY, SEB
Don Kravig (USA) DAY
Michael Hammond (USA) DAY, SEB
Rick Borlase (USA) SEB

Conrad Racing – Porsche 911
Albert Naon, Jr (USA) DAY
Dennis Vitolo (USA) DAY
Fernando Garcia (USA) DAY
Carlos Munoz (USA) SEB
Louis Lopez (USA) SEB
Herman Galeano (USA) SEB

**Conte Racing
– March 85G Buick V6 Turbo**
John Paul, Jr (USA) DAY
Bill Adam (CDN) DAY
Whitney Ganz (USA) DAY

**Cosmik Racing Promotions (Costas
Los) – March 84G Porsche**
Mikael Nabrink (S) HCK, MOS
Christian Danner (D) HCK, MOS, SPA, SEL
Costas Los (GR) HCK, MOS, SPA, BH, SEL
Anders Olofsson (S) BH
Divina Galica (GB) BH

Team Dallas – Porsche 911 Carrera RSR
M.L. Speer (USA) DAY
Bobby Hefner (USA) DAY, SEB
Jack Griffin (USA) DAY, SEB
Skip Winfree (USA) SEB

**DeAtley Motorsports
– March 84G Chevrolet
(as listed at Daytona), March 85G
Chevrolet (as listed at Sebring)**
Michael Roe (IRL) DAY
Tommy Byrne (IRL) DAY
Darrin Brassfield (USA) DAY, SEB
Arie Luyendyk (NL) SEB
Jerry Brassfield (USA) SEB

**Dingman Brothers Racing
– Pontiac Firebird**
Walt Bohren (USA) DAY, SEB
Ron Bouchard (USA) DAY
Billy Dingman (USA) DAY (DND), SEB (DND)
Steve Millen (NZ) SEB

**Dome Team/Motorsport
– Dome 85C Toyota**
Eje Elgh (S) LM, FUJ
Geoff Lees (GB) LM, FUJ
Toshio Suzuki (J) LM

**Ecurie Ecosse – Ecosse C285 Ford
Cosworth DFV**
Ray Mallock (GB) MZA, SIL, LM, HCK, BH
Mike Wilds (GB) MZA, SIL, LM, HCK,
SPA, BH
David Leslie (GB) LM, HCK, SPA

**EMKA Productions
– Emka C84/1 Aston Martin**
Tiff Needell (GB) SIL, LM, SPA, BH
Steve O'Rourke (GB) SIL, LM, SPA (DND),
BH
Bob Evans (GB) SIL
Nick Faure (GB) LM
James Weaver (GB) SPA (DND)
Mark Galvin (IRL) BH

**English Enterprizes (Gary English)
– Chevrolet Camaro**
Jerry Thompson (USA) MOS
Gary English (USA) MOS

Jean-Claude Ferrarin – Isolia 001 BMW
Jean-Claude Ferrarin (F) SPA, BH
Lucien Rossiaud (F) SPA (DND), BH

**John Fitzpatrick Racing
– Porsche 956 B, Porsche 956**
Jo Gartner (A) MZA, SIL, LM,
FUJ (withdrew due to weather)
Kenny Acheson (GB) MZA
Dudley Wood (GB) MZA, SIL
Klaus Niedzwiedz (D) MZA
Manuel Lopez (PE) MZA, SIL
David Hobbs (GB) SIL, LM
Guy Edwards (GB) SIL (DND), LM
Michael Roe (IRL) FUJ (DNS due to weather)
Franz Konrad (A) SEL
Andrew Miedecke (AUS) SEL

From A Racing – Porsche 956
Jirou Yoneyama (J) FUJ (Withdrew due to
weather)
Hideki Okada (J) FUJ (Withdrew due to
weather)

**Helmut Gall/Sportwagen Center
Dieter Oster – BMW M1**
Helmut Gall (D) MUG HCK, BH
Axel Felder (D) MUG
Edgar Dören (D) LM, HCK, BH
Martin Birrane (IRL) LM
Jean-Paul Libert (B) LM
Uwe Reich (D) HCK
Jürgen Hamelmann (D) SPA
Jean-Paul Libert (B) SPA
Marco Micangeli (I) SPA

Raul Garcia – Pontiac Firebird
Raul Garcia (USA) DAY
Eugenio Matienzo (USA) DAY

**Gebhardt Motorsports/Gebhardt
Engineering – Gebhardt JC843 Ford
Cosworth DFV, Gebhardt JC842 BMW,
Gebhardt JC843 Ford Cosworth DFL**
George Schwarz (CDN) SEB
Frank Jelinski (D) SEB, MZA, SIL
Jan Thoelke (D) SEB (DND)
Walter Lechner (A) MZA, SEL
Günter Gebhardt (D) MZA
John Graham (CDN) SIL
Nick Adams (GB) SIL
Stanley Dickens (S) SEL

**B.F. Goodrich/Jim Busby
– Porsche 962**
Jim Busby (USA) DAY, SEB
Rick Knoop (USA) DAY
Jochen Mass (D) DAY, SEB
Pete Halsmer (USA) DAY
Dieter Quester (A) DAY, SEB
John Morton (USA) DAY, SEB

**Gopher Motion
– Ferrari 512 BB/LM**
Steve Cohen (USA) DAY, SEB
Don Walker (USA) DAY, SEB (DND)
William Gelles (USA) DAY, SEB

Paul Goral /Goral Racing– Porsche 935
Hugo Gralia (USA) DAY
Emory Donaldson (USA) DAY
Paul Goral (USA) DAY, SEB
Rick Wilson (USA) SEB

**Jean-Philippe Grand
– Rondeau M482 Ford Cosworth DFL**
Patrick Gonin (F) LM
Pascal Witmeur (B) LM
Pierre de Thoisy (F) LM

**Grifo Autoracing
– Alba AR3 Ford Cosworth DFL**
Paolo Giangrossi (I) SIL, LM, HCK (DND)
Pasquale Barberio (I) SIL, LM (DND), HCK,
MOS, SPA, BH, SEL
Maurizio Gellini (I) SIL (DND), HCK (DND),
MOS, SPA, BH
Mario Radicella (I) LM (DND)
Jean-Pierre Frey (CH) BH, SEL
John Nicholson (NZ) SEL

Group 44 – Jaguar XJR-5
Claude Ballot-Léna (F) DAY, LM
Jim Adams (USA) DAY, LM
Chip Robinson (USA) DAY, SEB, LM
Brian Redman (GB) DAY, SEB, LM
Bob Tullius (USA) DAY, SEB, LM
Hurley Haywood (USA) DAY, SEB, LM

Habersin Camera Shop – Chevrolet Camaro
Rick Habersin (USA) SEB
Art Habersin (USA) SEB

Hasemi Motorsport – March 85G Nissan
Masahiro Hasemi (J) FUJ
Takao Wada (J) FUJ (DNS race abandoned due to weather)

Dave Heinz Imports – Chevrolet Corvette
Dave Heinz (USA) DAY, SEB
Dave Barnett (USA) DAY
Jerry Thompson (USA) DAY, SEB
Jim Trueman (USA) SEB

Henn's Swap Shop Racing (See also Preston Henn below) – Porsche 962, Porsche 935 L
A.J. Foyt (USA)/Bob Wollek (F) DAY
Al Unser (USA) DAY
Thierry Boutsen (B) DAY
Harald Grohs (D) DAY
Jean-Louis Schlesser (F) DAY (DND)
Preston Henn (USA) DAY (DND), SEB
Walter Brun (CH) DAY (DND)
Bob Wollek (F), SEB
Don Whittington (USA), SEB

Preston Henn – Porsche 962
A.J. Foyt (USA) SEB
Bob Wollek (F) SEB

Team Highball – Mazda RX-7
Amos Johnson (USA) DAY, SEB
Jack Dunham (USA) DAY, SEB
Youjirou Terada (J) DAY
Dennis Shaw (USA) SEB (DND)

Marty Hinze Racing – Porsche 935 K3
Marty Hinze (USA) SEB
Milt Minter (USA) SEB
Art Yarosh (USA) SEB

Hobbit Racing – Mazda RX-7
Tony Swan (USA) DAY
Bob Ruth (USA) DAY
Steve Dietrich (USA) DAY

Holbert Racing – Porsche 962
Al Holbert (USA) DAY, SEB
Al Unser, Jr (USA) DAY, SEB
Derek Bell (GB) DAY, SEB

Fritz Hochreuter – Porsche 911 Carrera RSR
Rudy Bartling (CDN) MOS
Fritz Hochreuter (CDN) MOS

Hoshino Racing – March 85G Nissan
Kazuyoshi Hoshino (J) FUJ
Akira Hagiwara (J) FUJ (DNS race abandoned due to weather)
Keiji Matsumoto (J) FUJ (DNS race abandoned due to weather)

Arthur Hough/Ark Racing – Ceekar 83J-1 Ford Cosworth BDX
David Andrews (GB) MUG, MZA, SIL, HCK, MOS, SPA, BH, SEL
Chris Ashmore (GB) MUG, MZA, SIL, SPA, BH
Max Payne (GB) MUG, MZA, SIL, HCK, MOS, SPA, BH, SEL

Tom Hunt – Mazda RX-7
Tom Hunt (USA) SEB
James Shelton (USA) SEB
Dean Jameson (USA) SEB (DND)

Team Ikuzawa – Tom's 85C Toyota
Tiff Needell (GB) FUJ
James Weaver (GB) FUJ (DNS race abandoned due to weather)

Walter Johnson – Pontiac Firebird
Del Russo Taylor (USA) DAY, SEB
John Hayes-Harlow (GB) DAY, SEB
Bob Lee (USA) DAY
Arvid Albanese (USA) SEB

K & P Racing – Chevrolet Corvette
William Wessel (USA) DAY, SEB
Robert Whitaker (USA) DAY
Mark Kennedy (USA) DAY
Karl Keck (USA) DAY, SEB
Mark Montgomery (USA) SEB

KJJ Enterprises – Triumph TR8
John Bossom (CDN) DAY
Ken Hill (CDN) SEB (DND)
Reagan Riley (CDN) SEB (DND)

Kalagian Racing – March 84G Chevrolet
John Kalagian (USA) DAY, SEB
John Lloyd (USA) DAY, SEB
Tom Grunnah (USA) DAY, SEB

Tommy Kendall – Mazda RX-7
Tom Kendall (USA) SEB
Bart Kendall (USA) SEB
Max Jones (USA) SEB

Kendall Racing – Porsche 935 K3/80
Chuck Kendall (USA) DAY, SEB
Peter Fitzgerald (AUS) DAY
John Hotchkis (USA) DAY, SEB
Robert Kirby (USA) SEB

Kreepy Krauley Racing – March 84G Porsche
Sarel van der Merwe (ZA) DAY
Tony Martin (ZA) DAY
Ian Scheckter (ZA) DAY
Christian Danner (D) LM
Graham Duxbury (ZA) LM
Almo Coppelli (I) LM
Anders Olofsson (S) FUJ (Withdrew due to weather)
Costas Los (GR) FUJ (DNS due to weather)
Richard Cleare (GB) FUJ (DNS due to weather)

Kremer Porsche Racing – Porsche 956 B, Porsche 962 C
Klaus Ludwig (D) MUG
George Fouché (ZA) MUG, MZA, SIL, LM
Gianni Mussato (I) MUG
Marc Surer (CH) MUG, MZA, SIL, HCK, MOS, SPA
Manfred Winkelhock (D) MUG, MZA, SIL, HCK, MOS (FATAL ACCIDENT)
Bruno Giacomelli (I) MZA
Saral van der Merwe (ZA) MZA, SIL, LM
Almo Coppelli (I) SIL
Mario Hytten (CH) LM
Jean-Pierre Jarier (F) LM
Mike Thackwell (NZ) LM
Franz Konrad (A) LM
Klaus Niedzwiedz (D) HCK
Kees Kroesemeijer (NL) HCK, MOS, SPA
Ludwig Heimrath, Jr (CDN) MOS
Ludwig Heimrath (CDN) MOS

Kumsan Tiger Team (Jan Thoelke) – Zakspeed C1/8 Ford Cosworth DFL
Jan Thoelke (D) HCK
Harald Becker (D) HCK

Team Labatt – Gebhardt JC853 Ford Cosworth DFV, Gebhardt JC853 Ford Cosworth DFL
Frank Jelinski (D) LM, HCK, MOS, SPA, FUJ (Withdrew due to weather)
John Graham (CDN) LM, HCK (DND), MOS, SPA, FUJ (DNS due to weather)
Nick Adams (GB) LM
Manuel Reuter (D) HCK (DND)
Stanley Dickens (S) SPA, FUJ (DNS race due to weather)

Latino Racing (see also Scorpio Racing) – Porsche 934
'Jamsal' (Enrique Molins) (ES) SEB
Kikos Fonseca (CR) SEB
Alfredo Mena (USA) SEB

Lee Racing – Listed as Lola T711 Chevrolet at Daytona, listed as Chevrolet Corvette GTP (Lola T711) at Sebring
Lew Price (USA) DAY
Carson Baird (USA) DAY, SEB
Billy Hagan (USA) DAY, SEB (DND)
Terry Labonte (USA) DAY, SEB

Leon Brothers Racing – March 85G Porsche, March 84G Chevrolet
Bill Whittington (USA) DAY
Randy Lanier (USA) DAY
Al Leon (USA) DAY, SEB
Skeeter McKitterick (USA) DAY, SEB
Terry Wolters (USA) DAY
Art Leon (USA) DAY, SEB

Lindley Motor – Chevrolet Camaro
Neil Bonnet (USA) DAY
Jim Derhaag (USA) DAY
Les Lindley (USA) DAY

Richard Lloyd Racing with Porsche-Richard Lloyd Racing – Porsche 956
Jonathan Palmer (GB) MZA, SIL, LM, HCK
Jan Lammers (NL) MZA, SIL
Vern Schuppan (AUS) SIL
James Weaver (GB) SIL, LM
Richard Lloyd (GB) LM
David Hobbs (GB) HCK
Kenny Acheson (GB) FUJ (withdrew due to weather)
Johnny Dumfries (GB) FUJ (DNS due to weather)

LSJ (Lyn St James) Racing – Argo JM16 Ford Cosworth DFV
Lyn St James (USA) DAY
Tim Coconis (USA) DAY
Eric Lang (USA) DAY

Malibu Grand Prix (Ira Young) – Mazda RX-7
Jack Baldwin (USA) DAY, SEB
Ira Young (USA) DAY
Jeff Kline (USA) DAY, SEB

Mandeville Auto-Tech – Mazda RX-7
Takashi Yorino (J) DAY
Logan Blackburn (USA) DAY, SEB
Roger Mandeville (USA) DAY, SEB
Danny Smith (USA) DAY, SEB
Tom Waugh (USA) DAY, SEB
Diego Febles (PR) DAY

Martini Racing – Lancia LC2/85
Bob Wollek (F) MUG, MZA, SIL, LM, HCK, SPA, BH
Mauro Baldi (I) MUG, MZA, SIL, LM, HCK, SPA, BH
Riccardo Patrese (I) MUG, MZA, SIL, HCK, SPA, BH
Alessandro Nannini (I) MUG, MZA, SIL, LM, HCK, SPA, BH
Lucio Cesario (AUS) LM
Henri Pescarolo (F) LM
Andrea de Cesaris (I) BH

Mazdaspeed – Mazda 737C
Yoshimi Katayama (J) SIL, LM, FUJ (Withdrew due to weather)
Takashi Yorino (J) SIL, LM, FUJ (DNS due to weather)
David Kennedy (IRL) SIL
Youjirou Terada (J) SIL, LM, FUJ (Withdrew due to weather)
David Kennedy (IRL) LM, FUJ (DNS due to weather)
Jean-Michel Martin (B) LM
Philippe Martin (B) LM

Mazda Sports Car Club – Mazda RX-7 254
Iwao Sugai (J) FUJ
Hiroshi Sugai (J) FUJ

Mike Meyer/Daffy – Mazda RX-7
Scott Pruett (USA) DAY, SEB
Paul Lewis (USA) DAY, SEB
Joe Varde (USA) DAY, SEB

Mid-O-Rusty Jones – Argo JM16 Mazda
Kelly Marsh (USA) DAY, SEB
Ron Pawley (USA) DAY, SEB
Don Marsh (USA) DAY, SEB

Misaki Speed – Tom's 85C Toyota
Toshio Suzuki (J) FUJ
Kaoru Hoshino (J) FUJ (DNS race abandoned)
Kiyoshi Misaki (J) FUJ (DNS race abandoned)

Allan Moffat Racing – Mazda RX-7
Allan Moffat (AUS) DAY
Gregg Hansford (AUS) DAY
Kevin Bartlett (AUS) DAY
Peter McCloud (AUS) DAY

Momo Course – Alba AR5 Ford Cosworth DFL
Gianpiero Moretti (I) DAY
Jim Trueman (USA) DAY
Massimo Sigala (I) DAY

Morgan Performance – Royale RP40 JM16 - Buick V6
Charles Morgan (USA) DAY
Bill Alsup (USA) DAY
Jim Miller (USA) DAY

Mosler Racing – Ferrari 512 BB/LM, Ferrari 308 GTB
John McComb (USA) DAY, SEB
Rick Mancuso (USA) DAY, SEB
Fred Fiala (USA) DAY, SEB
Steve Alexander (USA) DAY
Joe Hill (USA) DAY
George Alderman (USA) DAY

Motorsportclub Wasserburg – Lotec C302 Ford Cosworth DFV
Martin Wagenstetter (D) HCK
Kurt Hild (D) HCK (DND)

Mr S Racing Product – MCS Guppy Mishima Auto 84C BMW
Syuuji Fujii (J) FUJ
Seiichi Sodeyama (J) FUJ (DND)
Tooru Sawada (J) FUJ (DND)

DeNarvaez Enterprises (see also Red Lobster Racing) – Porsche 935 J
Mauricio DeNarvaez (CO) SEB
Dave Cowart (USA) SEB
Kenper Miller (USA) SEB

New Man Joest Racing – Porsche 956, Porsche 956 B
Paolo Barilla (I) MZA, SIL, LM, HCK, SPA, FUJ (withdrew due to weather)
Hans Heyer (D) MZA
Klaus Ludwig (D) SIL, LM, HCK, SPA
Paul Belmondo (F) SIL, FUJ (DNS due to weather)

'John Winter' (Louis Krages) (D) LM, HCK, SPA, FUJ (withdrew due to weather)
Mauricio DeNarvaez (CO) LM, FUJ (withdrew due to weather)
Kenper Miller (USA) LM
Paul Belmondo (F) LM
Franz Konrad (A) HCK
Volker Weidler (D) HCK, SPA
Mark Duez (B) SPA, FUJ (DNS due to weather)

Don Nooe – Chevrolet Corvette
Don Nooe (USA) SEB
Jim Stricklin (USA) SEB
Tim Stringfellow (USA) SEB

Jens Nykjaer – Nykjaer BMW CSL
Jens Nykjaer (DK) HCK, SPA
Holger Knudsen (DK) HCK, SPA

Obermaier Racing Team – Porsche 956
Mike Thackwell (NZ) MUG
Hervé Regout (B) MUG, MZA, SIL, LM, HCK, SPA
Jürgen Lässig (D) MUG, MZA, SIL, LM, HCK, SPA
Jésus Pareja (E) MZA, SIL, LM, HCK, SPA

O'Brien-van Steenburg Racing – Mazda OVS-1
Larry O'Brien (USA) SEB
Mike Van Steenburg (USA) SEB

OMR Engines – Chevrolet Camaro
Chris Gennone (USA) DAY, SEB
Fern Prego (USA) DAY, SEB (DND)
Hoyt Overbagh (USA) DAY, SEB
Lewis Fuller (USA) DAY

Ormond Racing – Chevrolet Corvette
Don Cummings (USA) DAY, SEB
Craig Rubright (USA) DAY, SEB
Greg Walker (USA) DAY (DND), SEB (DND)

OZ Racing – Mazda RX-7 254
Kenji Seino (J) FUJ
Mutsuo Kazama (J) FUJ

Angelo Pallavicini – BMW M1
Angelo Pallavicini (CH) LM
Enzo Calderari (CH) LM
Marco Vanoli (CH) LM

Panasport Japan – LM 05C Nissan
Osamu Nakako (J) FUJ (DNS due to weather)
Emanuele Pirro (I) FUJ (DNS due to weather)
Akio Morimoto (J) FUJ (DNS due to weather)

Pegasus Racing – March 84G Buick V6
Bobby Allison (USA) DAY
Wayne Pickering (USA) DAY, SEB
Ken Madren (USA) DAY, SEB
John Paul, Jr (USA) SEB

Pennzoil de P. R. – Porsche 911 Carrera RSR
Luis Gordillo (PR) SEB
Rolando Falgueras (PR) SEB
Manuel Villa (PR) SEB

Performance Motorsports – Porsche 924 Carrera GTR
Elliot Forbes-Robinson (USA) DAY
John Schneider (USA) DAY
Don Istook (USA) DAY

Personalized Autohaus – Porsche 935 K3
Jack Newsum (USA) DAY
Wayne Baker (USA) DAY
Chip Mead (USA) DAY
Ren Tilton (USA) DAY

Pettit Wholesale – Mazda RX-3
Cameron Worth (USA) SEB
Foko Gritzalis (USA) SEB

Preston & Sons Enterprises
– Mazda RX-7
Robert Peters (CDN)
George Schwarz (CDN)
Andre Schwartz (CDN)

(Cougar) Primagaz/Sovico-Primagaz
– Rondeau M382 Ford Cosworth DFV,
Cougar C12 Porsche
Pierre-François Rousselot (F) SIL, LM
Pierre Yver (F) SIL (*DND*), LM
Jean Rondeau (F) SIL, LM
Yves Courage (F) LM, SPA
Alain De Cadenet (GB) LM
Jean-François Yvon (F) LM
François Servanin (F) SPA
Henri Pescarolo (F) SPA

R & H Racing
– Porsche 911 Carrera RSR
Rainer Brezinka (CDN) SEB, MOS
John Centano (CDN) SEB, MOS
Fritz Hochreuter (CDN) SEB
John Centano (CDN) MOS

Ray's Racing Division
– Tom's 84C Toyota
Hitoshi Ogawa (J) FUJ
Tsunehisa Asai (J) FUJ

Red Lobster Racing
– March 83G Chevrolet
Kenper Miller (USA) DAY
Dave Cowart (USA) DAY
Mauricio DeNarvaez (CO) DAY

RGP 500 Racing
(Jim Downing)
– Argo JM16 Mazda
Jim Downing (USA) DAY, SEB
John Maffucci (USA) DAY, SEB
Yoshimi Katayama (J) DAY

RNGC Racing
– Mazda RX-7
Roy Newsome (USA) SEB
Bill McVey (USA) SEB
Dale Kreider (USA) SEB

Road Circuit Tech
– Pontiac Firebird
Les Delano (USA) DAY, SEB
Andy Petery (USA) DAY, SEB
Tommy Riggins (USA) DAY
Patty Moise (USA) SEB

Steve Roberts
– Chevrolet Camaro
William Boyer (USA) SEB
Steve Roberts (USA) SEB
John Barben (USA) SEB

Paul Romano/Simms-Romano
– Mazda RX-7
Drake Olson (USA) DAY, SEB
Steve Potter (USA) DAY, SEB
Willard Howe (USA) DAY
Paul Romano (USA) SEB (*DND*)

Rothmans Porsche
– Porsche 962 C, Porsche 956
Jacky Ickx (B) MUG, MZA, SIL, LM, HCK,
  MOS, SPA, BH, FUJ (*withdrew due to
  weather*), SEL
Jochen Mass (D) MUG, MZA, SIL, LM, HCK,
  MOS, SPA, BH (*DNS due to weather*), SEL
Derek Bell (GB) MUG, MZA, SIL, LM, HCK,
  MOS, SPA, BH, FUJ (*withdrew due to
  weather*), SEL
Hans-Joachim Stuck (D) MUG, MZA, SIL,
  LM, HCK, MOS, SPA, BH, FUJ (*DNS due
  to weather*), SEL
Al Holbert (USA) LM, BH
John Watson (GB) LM
Vern Schuppan (AUS) LM, BH, SEL
James Weaver (GB) SEL

Team Roush Protofab
– Ford Mustang
John Bauer (USA) DAY
Jim Miller (USA) DAY
Willy T. Ribbs (USA) DAY
Wally Dallenbach, Jr (USA) DAY, SEB
John Jones (CDN) DAY, SEB
Doc Bundy (USA) DAY

Rubino Racing – Mazda RX-7
Frank Rubino (USA) DAY, SEB (*DND*)
Dennis Wagoner (USA) DAY, SEB
Ken Knott (USA) DAY, SEB

Sachs Sporting (Günter Gebhardt) –
Gebhardt JC 843 Ford Cosworth DFV
Walter Lechner (A) HCK
Miroslav Adámek (CS) HCK
Günter Gebhardt (D) HCK

Scorpio Racing (see also
Latino Racing) – Porsche 934
'*Jamsal*' (Enrique Molins) (ES) DAY
Eduardo Galdamez (ES) DAY
'*Anbagua*' (Andre Bauer) (GUA) DAY

Scyphers Ankor Racing
– Chevrolet Corvette
Billy Scyphers (USA) DAY
Allen Glick (USA) DAY
Bill Cooper (USA) DAY

Shafer Racing – Chevrolet Camaro
Craig Shafer (USA) SEB
George Shafer (USA) SEB
Joe Maloy (USA), SEB

Southern Racing Promo
– Chevrolet Corvette
Gary Baker (USA) DAY
Robin McCall (USA) DAY
Joe Ruttman (USA) DAY

SP Racing – Porsche 911 Carrera RSR
Gary Auberlen (USA) SEB
Peter Jauker (USA) SEB
Adrian Gang (USA) SEB
Cary Eisenlohr (USA) SEB

Spice Engineering – Tiga GC85 Ford
Cosworth DFL, Tiga GC84 Ford
Cosworth DFV
Ray Bellm (GB) MUG, MZA, SIL, LM, HCK,
  MOS, SPA, BH (*DND*)
Gordon Spice (GB) MUG, MZA, SIL, LM,
  HCK, MOS, SPA, BH
Tim Lee-Davey (GB) SIL
Neil Crang (AUS) SIL (*DND*), BH
Mark Galvin (IRL) LM
Neil Crang (AUS) LM
Tony Lanfranchi (GB) LM
Tim Lee-Davey (GB) LM, BH

Spirit of Cleveland – Porsche 935 JLP-2
Freddy Baker (USA)/Don Herman (USA)
  DAY, SEB
Rich Maher (USA) DAY
Richard Silver (USA) DAY (*DND*), SEB
Don Herman (USA) SEB

Starved Rock Lodge
– Chevrolet Corvette
Rusty Schmidt (USA) DAY
Scott Schmidt (USA) DAY
Max Schmidt (USA) DAY

Strandell Motors – Strandell 85 Porsche
Stanley Dickens (S) MZA, SIL
Martin Schanche (N) MZA (*DND*), SIL
Anders Olofsson (S) SPA
Tryggve Gronvall (S) SPA

Team USA-Deco Sales – Royale RP40
Ford Cosworth V8 (DFV or DFL?),
Chevrolet Monza
Steve Shelton (USA) DAY

Don Courtney (USA) DAY, SEB
Brent O'Neill (USA) DAY, SEB
Mike Hackney (USA) SEB

Tokima Zoom Lenses
– Porsche 911 Carrera RSR
John Higgins (USA) SEB
Chip Mead (USA) SEB
James King (USA) SEB

Tom's Team – Tom's 85C Toyota
Satoru Nakajima (J) LM, FUJ
Masanori Sekiya (J) LM, FUJ
Kaoru Hoshino (J) LM

Top Fuel Racing – Mazda RX-7 855
Norimasa Sakamoto (J) FUJ
Hironobu Tatsumi (J) FUJ (*DNS race
  abandoned*)

Raymond Touroul – Porsche 911 SC
Raymond Touroul (F) LM
Thierry Perrier (F) LM
Philippe Dermagne (F) LM

Toyota Village – Porsche 935/80
Werner Frank (USA) SEB
Dave White (USA) SEB
Jerry Kendall (USA) SEB

Monty Trainer's Restaurant
– Chevrolet Camaro
Buz McCall (USA) SEB
Pancho Carter (USA) SEB
Tom Sheehy (USA) SEB (*DND*)

Trust Racing Team
– Porsche 956, Toyota Celica
Mitsutake Koma (J) FUJ
Ryuusaku Hitomi (J) FUJ (*DNS race
  abandoned*)
Vern Schuppan (AUS) FUJ
George Fouché (ZA) FUJ (*DNS due to
  weather*)
Keiichi Suzuki (J) FUJ (*DNS due to weather*)

TWR Jaguar GB – Jaguar XJR-6
Martin Brundle (GB) MOS, SPA (*Also took
  over Schlesser/Heyer car*), SPA
Mike Thackwell (NZ) MOS (*DND*) (*Also took
  over Schlesser/Heyer car*), SPA, FUJ
  (*Withdrew due to weather*), SEL
Jean-Louis Schlesser (F) MOS, SPA, BH
  (*DND*)
Martin Brundle (GB) (*Aso took over
  Schlesser/Heyer car*)
Hans Heyer (D) MOS (*DND after Brundle/
  Thackwell took over Schlesser's car*), SPA,
  BH, FUJ (*withdrew due to weather*)
Alan Jones (AUS) BH
Jan Lammers (NL) BH, SEL
John Nielsen (DK) FUJ (*DNS due to
  weather*), SEL
Steve Soper (GB) FUJ (*DNS due to weather*)
John Nielsen (DK) SEL
Gianfranco Brancatelli (I) SEL

Unlimited Telephones
– Pontiac Firebird
Luis Sereix (USA) DAY
Ralph Noseda (USA) DAY

Van Every Racing – Porsche 935
Lance Van Every (USA) DAY, SEB
Ash Tisdelle (USA) DAY, SEB
Jack Refenning (USA) DAY, SEB (*DND*)

'Victor' – Porsche 935
'*Victor*' (Victor Coggiola) (I) MUG, MZA, HCK
  (*DND*), SPA
Livio Bertuzzi (I) MUG
Gianni Giudici (I) MUG, MZA
Aldo Bertuzzi (I) MZA
Angelo Pallavicini (CH) HCK
Luigi Taverna (I) HCK, SPA
Tony Palma (I) SPA

Vogelsang Automobile – BMW M1
Altfrid Heger (D) LM
Harald Grohs (D) LM, HCK
Kurt König (D) LM (*DND*), HCK

WM-Peugeot – WM P83 B Peugeot
Pascal Pessiot (F) LM
Patrick Gaillard (F) LM
Dominique Fornage (F) LM
Jean Rondeau (F) LM
Michel Pignard (F) LM
Jean-Daniel Raulet (F) LM
Jean-Claude Andruet (F) LM
Claude Haldi (CH) LM
Roger Dorchy (F) LM

Robert Whitaker – Chevrolet Camaro
Robert Whitaker (USA) SEB
Ed Crosby (USA) SEB
Richard McDill (USA) SEB

Whitehall Motorsports/Promotions
(see also Performance Motorsports)
– Porsche 924 Carrera GTR
Paul Gentilozzi (USA) DAY, SEB
Kent Hill (USA) DAY (*DND*), SEB
Austin Godsey (USA) DAY (*DND*), SEB
Bobby Akin (USA) DAY (*DND*)
Elliot Forbes-Robinson (USA) SEB
Tom Winters (USA) SEB
Bob Bergstrom (USA) SEB

Jens Winther (Castrol Denmark)
– URD C83 BMW
Jens Winther (DK) MUG, MZA, SIL, LM,
  HCK, SPA, BH
Lars-Viggo Jensen (DK) MUG
David Mercer (GB) MZA, SIL, LM, HCK,
  SPA, BH
Margie Smith-Haas (USA) LM
Martin Birrane (IRL) HCK

Wolf Engines – Chevrolet Camaro
Clark Howey (USA) DAY
Dale Koch (USA) DAY
Tracy Wolf (USA) DAY

Gary Wonzer/Wonzer Racing – Porsche
934, Porsche 911 Carrera RSR
Tom Cripe (USA) SEB
Gary Wonzer (USA) SEB (*DND*)
Bruce Dewey (USA) SEB (*DND*)
John Hofstra (USA) SEB
Charles Slater (USA) SEB
Mick Robinson (USA) SEB

Charles Young – Argo JM16 Buick V6
Don Bell (USA) SEB
Mike Brockman (USA) SEB
Tommy Riggins (USA) SEB

Clay Young – Pontiac Fiero
Clay Young (USA) DAY
Lake Speed (USA) DAY (*DND*)
Ron Grable (USA) DAY (*DND*)

Zwiren Racing – Mazda RX-7
Steve Zwiren (USA) DAY, SEB, MOS
Tony Pio Costa (USA) DAY
Mike Allison (USA) DAY
Wes Donnington (USA) DAY
Mike Tearney (USA) SEB
Robert Peters (CDN) SEB, MOS
Peter Dawe (USA) MOS

RESULTS

Daytona 24 Hours 2/3 February, USA
Started 76 , finished 29
1st Foyt USA)/Wollek (F)/Al Unser (USA)/
  Boutsen (B) Porsche 962
2nd Holbert (USA)/Al Unser, Jr (USA)/Bell
  (GB) Porsche 962
3rd Busby (USA)/Knoop (USA)/Mass (D)
  Porsche 962

Sebring 12 Hours, 23 March, USA
Started 74, finished 27
1st Foyt (USA)/Wollek (F) Porsche 962
2nd Holbert (USA)/Bell (GB)/Al Unser, Jr
  Porsche 962
3rd Halsmer (USA)/Knoop (USA)/Quester (A)
  Porsche 962

Mugello 1000km, 14 April, Italy
Started 17, finished 14
1st Ickx (B)/Mass (D) Porsche 962C
2nd Surer (CH)/Winkelhock (D) Porsche
  962C
3rd Bellof (D)/Boutsen (B) Porsche 962C

Monza 1000km, 28 April, Italy
Started 25, finished 17
1st Winkelhock (D)/Surer (CH) Porsche 962C
2nd Bell (GB)/Stuck (D) Porsche 956
3rd Patrese (I)/Nannini (I) Lancia LC2/85

Silverstone 1000km, 12 May,
Great Britain
Started 31, finished 18
1st Mass (D)/Ickx (B) Porsche 962C
2nd Bell (GB)/Stuck (D) Porsche 956
3rd Patrese (I)/Nannini (I) Lancia LC2/85

Le Mans 24 Hours, 15/16 June, France
Started 49, finished 29
1st Ludwig (D)/Barilla (I)/ '*John Winter*' (Louis
  Krages) (D) Porsche 956B
2nd Palmer (GB)/Weaver (GB)/Lloyd (GB)
  Porsche 956GTI
3rd Bell (GB)/Stuck (D)/Ickx (B) Porsche
  962C

Hockenheim 1000km, 14 July,
Germany
Started 36, finished 18
1st Stuck (D)/Bell (GB) Porsche 962C
2nd Larrauri (RA)/Sigala (I) Porsche 956
3rd Ludwig (D)/Barilla (I) Porsche 956B

Mosport 1000km, 11 August, Canada
Started 19, finished 14
1st Stuck (D)/Bell (GB) Porsche 962C
2nd Ickx (B)/Mass (D) Porsche 962C
3rd Schlesser (F)/Thackwell (NZ)/Brundle
  (GB) Jaguar XJR-6

Spa 1000km, 1 September, Belgium
Started 33, finished 22 (Race stopped
at 122 laps due to fatal accident to
Stefan Bellof)
1st Baldi (I)/Wollek (F)/Patrese (I) Lancia
  LC2/85
2nd Bell (GB)/Stuck (D) Porsche 962C
3rd Ludwig (D)/Barilla (I) Porsche 956B

Brands Hatch 1000km, 22 September,
Great Britain. Started 26, finished 12
1st Stuck (D)/Bell (GB) Porsche 962C
2nd Mass (D)/Ickx (B) Porsche 962C
3rd Wollek (F)/de Cesaris(I)/Baldi (I)
  Lancia LC2/85

Fuji 1000km, 6 October, Japan
Started 35, finished 16
(Race abandoned due to extreme
weather. Most European drivers
withdrew after safety car period
and most finishers were driven
by the first driver only)
1st Hashino (JPN) Nissan 85G
2nd Nakako (JPN) LM 05C Nissan
3rd Nakajima (JPN) /Sekiya (JPN) Tom's 85C
  Toyota

Selangor 800km, 1 December, Malaysia
Started 15, finished 11
1st Mass (D)/Ickx (B) Porsche 962C
2nd Thackwell (NZ)/Nielsen (DK)/Lammers
  (NL) Jaguar XJR-6
3rd Schuppan (AUS)/Weaver (GB)
  Porsche 956

1986

THE TIMES THEY ARE A CHANGIN' (WELL ALMOST)

Porsche at last faced a real foe in the TWR Jaguar team but for now Weissach and their customers still had the upper hand.

Of the nine venues in use, the Rothmans Porsches only won at Monza and Le Mans, Weissach having made a very poor decision in using the PDK double-clutch semi-automatic gearbox, which added extra weight and brought reliability problems.

Fortunately for them the Joest and Brun customer cars won four races, Norisring and Fuji for the former and Jerez and Spa for the latter. Additionally, Richard Lloyd's Liqui Moly-sponsored carbon-fibre mock 962 GTi won the Brands Hatch 1000km, which Weissach chose to miss as they were cutting back on their race programme. It was another bad year for Kremer who lost Jo Gartner in a horrific accident at Le Mans.

This left two races for the others, in this case TWR Jaguar who won at Silverstone on merit but otherwise suffered a frustrating season with various problems. Fuel vapour lock (ran out of fuel) and a broken driveshaft at Monza, a complete loss at Le Mans, the three cars had a fuel-pump failure, a driveshaft failure following a fuel-cell problem and a rear tyre burst late in the race that terminally damaged bodywork and suspension.

They did, however, finish 2nd and 3rd at the Norisring, 4th and 6th at Brands Hatch, and 3rd at Jerez but both cars retired at the Nürburgring and then came 2nd and 5th at Spa and 3rd and 17th at Fuji.

The other victor was the quixotic Kouros Sauber Mercedes C8 (usually driven by Mike Thackwell and Henri Pescarolo) which won at the Nürburgring. Otherwise they finished 9th (Monza), 8th (Silverstone), both cars retired at Le Mans (the only time there were two entries from them in the season) and a 6th at Spa.

These then were the only winning C1 cars, the rest were privateer entries that lacked speed, finance and reliability, with exception. Porsche of course were the victors, but Weissach was beaten into a shared 3rd place with TWR in the Team Championship, which was won by Brun Motorsport ahead of arch rival Reinhold Joest's team. Derek Bell won the Drivers' Championship, just pipping teammate Hans-Joachim Stuck with Derek Warwick 3rd.

However, the C2 category was rather more intensely contested with Ecurie Ecosse winning the World Sports Prototype Championship by just two points ahead of Spice Engineering with ADA Engineering 3rd. It was the other way round in the Drivers' Championship with Gordon Spice and teammate Ray Bellm winning and Ray Mallock finishing 3rd.

Back in IMSA land Al Holbert, Derek Bell and Al Unser Jr won the Daytona 24 Hours in Holbert's Porsche 962 GTP ahead of their former nemesis Henn's similar Swap Shop Porsche (Foyt/Sullivan/Luyendyk) with the BF Goodrich Porsche 962 (Warwick/Brassfield/Busby/Mass) 3rd.

At Sebring Bob Akin's Porsche 962 won driven by Akin, Hans-Joachim Stuck and Jo Gartner with Goodrich 962 2nd (Brassfield/Morton/Busby) and Holbert, Bell and Al Unser Jr 3rd in Holbert's similar car.

Spa 1000km, 15 September 1986 By 1986 John Fitzpatrick was living in Spain and had done a deal with Spanish racers Emilio de Villota and Fermin Velez to run his Porsche 956B (114). Sponsored by Spanish yogurt company Danone, he finished 4th at Le Mans with George Fouché. He also brokered a deal with Paco Romera with his older 956. At a wet Spa the Porsche 956B (114) was driven to 11th place by de Villota/Velez and this was the end of John Fitzpatrick Racing. Soon after he sold the entire team, cars, spares and transporter to Jochen Dauer having realised that the costs, lack of sponsorship and little or no television coverage were not worth the effort anymore. *LAT*

Daytona 24 Hours, 2 February 1986 BMW North America entered two new March 86G-BMWs, aka BMW GTPs, at Daytona for Davy Jones/Dieter Quester/John Andretti and John Watson/David Hobbs/Bobby Rahal, but one of them driven by Andretti was burnt out during testing at Road Atlanta. Nevertheless, the surviving car came to Daytona but having run there the team decided to withdraw because there were no indications as to why the first car had self-immolated. They wanted to rebuild it, check out the car(s) and enter the Miami 3 Hours in two weeks' time. Just to confuse matters, the stats have it that it was no.18 that was burnt out but it must have been the no.19 car because as we can see here no.18 was at Daytona, unless of course they swapped numbers. *LAT*

Daytona 24 Hours, 2 February 1986 There were two Group 44 XJR-7s at Daytona: no.44 carried Bob Tullius, Claude Ballot-Léna and Chip Robinson whilst no.04 had Brian Redman, Vern Schuppan and Hurley Haywood. They looked like the XJR-5, but apart from the windscreen they were wholly new and qualified 10th and 13th and finished 6th (after delays) and retired, apparently due to a con-rod failure. Both cars featured a new, stiffer chassis but were hampered by gearbox problems caused by transmission overload. More problems surrounded designer Lee Dykstra who was fired by Tullius pre-Sebring, having been hired by Jaguar. Group 44 crew chief Lanky Foushee had this to say: "As much as anything, it was different expectations… Bob expected it to go first time round." *LAT*

Daytona 24 Hours, 2 February 1986 Holbert Racing and Henn's Swap Shop teams continued their Daytona duels but this time it was Camel IMSA GT Champion Al Holbert's turn. He shared the Porsche 962 (103) with Derek Bell and Al Unser Jr, but they had to overcome a broken brake line, excessive pad wear and a split throttle cable which lost them 35 laps. It was a long, hard race and both cars and drivers suffered, but eventually Holbert in no.14 won by just under a lap ahead of the Swap Shop 962 (Foyt, Sullivan and Luyendyk) with Busby's Goodrich-entered 962 driven by Derek Warwick, Darin Brassfield and Jim Busby just one lap down. *Getty*

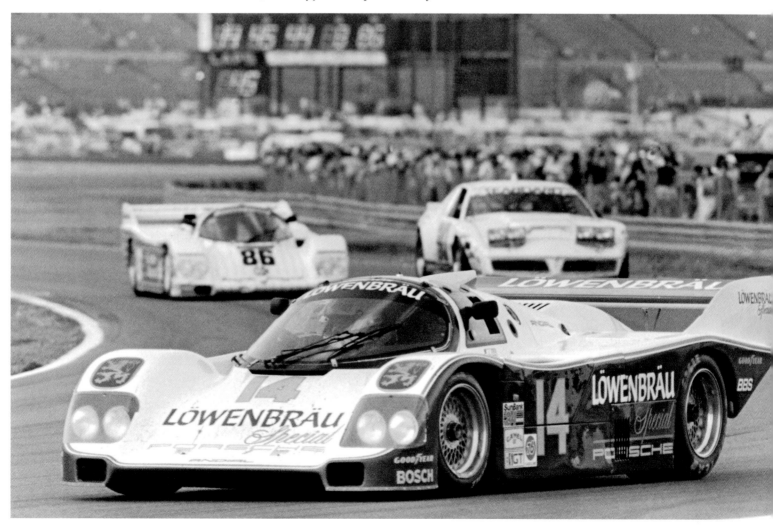

↑ Sebring 12 Hours, 22 March 1986
Neither of the Holbert or Henn teams won at Sebring this time; instead it was the Bob Akin Porsche 962 (113) that finished 1st with the same crew as at Daytona. Al Holbert's 962 finished 3rd after replacing a turbo whilst the Henn car (962 104) driven by Drake Olson and A.J. Foyt (seen here) retired at 184 laps, possibly due to one too many impacts with other cars, as per the three-tyre-ring damage evident here. *LAT*

← Monza Supersprint 360km, 20 April 1986 This was the last year for the Porsche 956 as the FIA imposed IMSA's pedal-box-behind-front-axle rule in 1987. Reinhold Joest entered two 956s for Ludwig/Barilla (956B 117) and 'John Winter' (Louis Krages)/Marc Duez. The famous twice Le Mans-winning Porsche 956B is pushed up the pits amongst a large crowd of mainly spectators/hangers on with the second Joest car just visible behind. Alas 117's clutch failed and they retired from a dominant 1st place on lap 50 whilst the second car also retired right at the end of the race by running out of fuel, another victim of the unnecessary fuel limits, in this case 190 litres for the entire race. *LAT*

➡ Monza Supersprint 360km, 20 April 1986 This was the first of the 'Sprint' races that qualified for the championships and it attracted 27 starters. One such was Peter Sauber's new Sauber C8 with its factory 5.6-litre Mercedes-Benz V8 developed by Heini Mader for the team. (The first C8 was the victim of a dramatic accident at Le Mans in 1985 when it became airborne on the Mulsanne straight during practice.) Dane John Nielsen and Henri Pescarolo started 12th and they finished 9th, the car lacking properly developed ground effects. They did, however, have some serious sponsorship as we can see but as yet it was a one-car team. *LAT*

➡ Monza Supersprint 360km, 20 April 1986 Gordon Spice became a constructor in 1986 when he was contracted by General Motors to build two Camel Lights honeycomb chassis with 3-litre straight-4 Pontiac engines. These were called Spice Pontiac Fieros. Meanwhile he built a C2 version with the same chassis using the Ford Cosworth 3.3-litre DFL, which made its debut at Monza. Spice and Ray Bellm qualified 17th and 2nd in the C2 class, which had become more competitive, and they finished 14th and 2nd in class to the Gebhardt Motorsport JC853 Ford of Frank Jelinski/Stanley Dickens. As with many others the Spice was a victim of the fuel limitation. *LAT*

Monza Supersprint 360km, 20 April 1986 TWR came to Monza with their 1986 Jaguar XJR-6s for Eddie Cheever/Derek Warwick (TWR J12C-286) and Jean-Louis Schlesser/Gianfranco Brancatelli (TWR J12C-186). The cars weighed just over 850kg (really?) with 17in front and 19in rear wheels, and came with Silk Cut sponsorship to qualify 6th and 9th respectively. Around lap 21 Cheever was running 2nd but lost the place to Stuck's Rothmans Porsche before pitting for fuel, which was hampered by a vacuum in the fuel system. Ultimately this car retired with a driveshaft failure whilst their teammates in no.52 ran out of petrol on lap 61 (of 63) due to a fuel vapour lock when it still had 8 litres in the tank – perhaps a victim of their fuel system as per the other car. *LAT*

Monza Supersprint 360km, 20 April 1986 Bell/Stuck were now in the no.1 car for Porsche and Jacky Ickx had retired from circuit racing to participate in Rally Raid events like the Paris–Dakar. The 1986 works 962s had a 3-litre engine and the PDK (Porsche *Doppelkupplungsgetriebe*, or Porsche 'dual-clutch transmission') transmissions, which added extra weight making the winning car 912kg. At Monza they were thrashed by the leading Joest 956B until it retired and then took 1st place whilst the Mass/Wollek car finished 6th after losing two laps in the early stages due to an air lock in a hydraulic hose that fed the PDK unit. Bell commented afterwards: "I drove the last 2½ laps with the fuel warning light on…I couldn't touch the throttle at the end. I was just idling." This is Stuck with his star-decorated helmet in the 962C (003). *LAT*

Monza Supersprint 360km, 20 April 1986 Riccardo Patrese had left the building after nine years with Lancia and returned to Brabham in the F1 arena. This left Andrea de Cesaris, sometime Alfa Romeo, McLaren and in 1986 Minardi F1 racer, as team leader. Wollek had crossed to Porsche, fed up with the inconsistencies and only one LC2-86 appeared for de Cesaris and Nannini. They used an updated 1985 LC2 for qualifying and the new 1986 LC2-86 (007) for the race. A faulty computer had given de Cesaris a negative fuel reading and it was Nannini who benefitted, going quicker and quicker but when he had the leading Porsche almost within reach he had to back off to finish 2nd, 49 seconds behind Bell/Stuck. Then, after starting from pole position at the following Silverstone 1000km and leading before retiring, they left motor racing to concentrate on their already successful and long-standing rally career. *LAT*

Silverstone 1000km, 4 May 1986 This was the long-awaited victory for Jaguar supporters; the older ones had at least seen the 1950s Le Mans victories and later the lesser GT and saloon car wins of the 1960s. Now the TWR cars could add to their successful touring-car victories here. Derek Warwick and Eddie Cheever won by two laps in the TWR J12C-286 car from the Bell/Stuck Porsche 962 C (the Mass/Wollek 962's PDK gearbox expired) whilst the second XJR-6 (Schlesser/Brancatelli) finished 7th following gear-linkage problems. However, the singleton Lancia of de Cesaris/Nannini gave them some real opposition and the two cars swapped 1st place on several occasions until the Italian car was withdrawn with falling fuel pressure. It was Lancia's final race – they had decided that the ongoing reliability problems were not worth the effort and withdrew from motor racing. The Jaguars had rear wheel 'spats' but as you can see 286 has lost its right rear one with no ill effects. *LAT*

Silverstone 1000km, 4 May 1986 Contrast the profile of the Sauber C8 Mercedes 86-C8-02 with the Jaguar XJR-6: it has a very short nose and proportionally a very long tail like its predecessors. Mike Thackwell, John Nielsen and Henri Pescarolo drove it to 8th place having qualified 12th. They were hampered by heavy fuel consumption and might well have been in the first six but for this. *LAT*

Silverstone 1000km, 4 May 1986 Jo Gartner and Tiff Needell drove the Kremer Porsche 962 to 3rd place at Silverstone whilst three places and two laps behind them was the Taka-Q Joest Racing Porsche 956 (104) driven by Paolo Barilla with Americans John Morton and 52-year-old George Follmer, the latter a deal done by US enthusiast Ted Gildred. Morton had never raced at Silverstone and found the old 956 rather different to his IMSA Goodrich racing 962. For the pedants amongst us (i.e. me) Taka-Q Co. Ltd sells men's and women's clothing and related clothing products through its 299 retail stores. It is based in Tokyo, was founded in 1947 and is a subsidiary of Aeon Co. Ltd. *LAT*

Le Mans 24 Hours, 31 May/1 June 1986 A pensive-looking Derek Bell spread over the Rothmans Porsche 962C (003) pre-race. No doubt the sheer velocity that Le Mans demanded was a worrying factor. Bell and Hans-Joachim Stuck were 2nd fastest in qualifying, Stuck's 3m 16.600 just shaded by Jochen Mass in the no.2 car who posted a 3m 15.990, both using the 3.0-litre engine. The third Rothmans car had the PDK gearbox for Schuppan/Drake Olson and Schuppan qualified 8th in 3m 25.340 using the 2.6-litre race engine. In a race of tragedy and attrition Bell/Stuck finished 1st but the other two cars retired. *LAT*

⬆ **Le Mans 24 Hours, 31 May/1 June 1986** Walter Brun entered three Porsche 962Cs for Le Mans, the no.17 Fortuna car (Oscar Larrauri/Jésus Pareja /Joël Gouhier), the no.18 TORNO car (Massimo Sigala/Walter Brun/Frank Jelinski) and the fastest of the trio, the no.19 car (Thierry Boutsen, Didier Theys, Alain Ferté). The last two retired, no.19 due to an accident when Alain Ferté crashed at the Virage Ford and the no.18 during the night with a busted gearbox. This left the no.17 car (C115), which went on to finish 2nd, a welcome result for the Brun team after the tragedy of 1985. *LAT*

⬅ **Le Mans 24 Hours, 31 May/1 June 1986** There were 16 starters in C2 amongst which was the works Gebhardt JC853 Ford Cosworth DFL (01) no.74 driven by Stanley Dickens, Pierre de Thoisy and Jean-François Yvon. They led the C2 category until early evening, but then de Thoisy had a collision with another car and had to pit after which Yvon took over but crashed it on lap 68. The C2 winner was another Gebhardt, the older JC843 Ford Cosworth entered by ADA Engineering, which also used a Cosworth DFL engine and the benefit of much development. Evan Clements, Tom Dodd-Noble and Ian Harrower finished an impressive 8th overall. The Spice SE86C (Spice/Bellm) finished a delayed 19th; the new Ecurie Ecosse C286 (Mallock/Wilds) was 1st in class for several hours but was later hit by Mass's 962 and was subsequently disqualified for outside assistance; and the older C285 driven by Americans Les Delano, Andy Petery and John Hotchkis finished 15th and 4th in C2. *LAT*

➡ Le Mans 24 Hours, 31 May/1 June 1986
The 4WD Porsche 961 had evolved from
their Raid version of the road-going 959
that was used successfully for desert rallies
in 1984–86. After this, Porsche wanted an
IMSA GTO production road-racing car and
this was it, the 961 (WPOZZZ93ZFS010016)
that weighed 1,159kg and was entered in
the IMSA GTX class for rally driver René
Metge and Claude Ballot-Léna. It finished
7th which seems good enough, but it was
slow, qualifying 26th and flattening out at
190mph on Mulsanne. *LAT*

**⬇ Le Mans 24 Hours, 31 May/1 June
1986** Yves Courage's Cougar C12 Porsche
(01) driven by Courage, Alain de Cadenet
and F3000 racer Pierre-Henri Raphanel
qualified a splendid 10th courtesy of de
Cadenet, only 3.5 seconds off the Brun
962C that finished 2nd in the race. The
Cougar had undergone some changes
which included a refined body, longer
tail and 19in wheels, but the driver's
door departed on the first lap and its
replacement did not last too long either. So
the team had to fabricate another door out
of sheet Duralumin which took 4 hours.
Thus they finished 18th when they would
have been in the top six. *LAT*

Le Mans 24 Hours, 31 May/1 June 1986 March sold six new 86Gs to Nissan and they entered a new March-based 86V at Le Mans for Hoshino/ Matsumoto/Suzuki together with an older 85V for Weaver, Hasemi and Wada. March hired Keith Greene to run the team. Nissan's motor-sport director Nanba did not tell Keith that the cars had a serious crankshaft problem and that most of the cars' downforce had been removed. The mechanics had severely limited the revs whilst Hoshino and Hasemi refused to let Weaver drive either car. Greene discovered the rev-limiters and Nanba admitted that the only intention was for the cars to finish. Meanwhile, the Japanese drivers told the mechanics to up the boost so Greene removed the controls but the mechanics then did this via the turbochargers. Both Nissans blew up in qualifying as a result. Greene delivered an ultimatum to the drivers: either do as they were told or they were on their own. Predictably the R86V's crankshaft broke in the race, but the R85V no.32 survived, finishing 16th having at one point suffered an ignition-system failure. *LAT*

Le Mans 24 Hours, 31 May/1 June 1986 The Kremer-entered Porsche 962C (118) was brand new and driven here by Jo Gartner, Sarel van der Merwe and Kunimitsu Takahashi. It had been in 7th place earlier on but a pit stop around midnight for a replacement suspension-damper mounting cost them approximately 30 minutes. At around 3.12am Gartner was accelerating up the Mulsanne straight when he selected 5th gear but the gear-selector rod had jammed 4th gear and now both gears and the rear wheels were locked solid. The resulting accident was catastrophic with the car hitting both sides of the road, a tree, a telegraph pole and landing on top of the Armco barrier. The Kremer Brothers, Erwin and Manfred, who were still suffering from the tragic Winkelhock accident in 1985, immediately withdrew their second car, the 956 (105) of Pierre Yver/Max Cohen-Olivar/Hubert Striebig. *LAT*

Le Mans 24 Hours, 31 May/1 June 1986 TWR came to Le Mans on a high from Silverstone, entering three cars for Warwick/Cheever/Schlesser no.51, Heyer/Haywood/Redman no.52 and Brancatelli/Percy/Hahne (DND) no.53. They qualified 5th, 7th and 14th and respectively were 4th, 5th and 6th after 3 hours. At 6 hours they were 4th, retired (fuel pump) and 5th, and at 12 hours only the no.51 seen here was still racing whilst the no.53 car had a driveshaft failure following a fuel-cell problem. After 239 laps whilst in 2nd place Schlesser was driving TWR-J12C-286 when a rear tyre burst on Mulsanne and caused a lot of bodywork and suspension damage. He got the stricken car back to the pits where it was retired. Cue much dismay for the Jaguar camp and its followers. *GPL*

Nuremberg Supersprint, 29 June 1986 The Norisring hosted the next round of the championship, having been otherwise a national German sports-car venue for many years. It boasted 24 starters, a lot for the bumpy, savage 1.43-mile (2.3km) circuit around the Nuernberg Steinetribune arena, (Stones Tribune) site of the Nazi rallies and Herr Hitler in the 1930s. Hans-Joachim Stuck in the first hairpin was the fastest in qualifying with the works Porsche 962C (005) half a second quicker than Ludwig. However, Ludwig led away but on lap 12 Stuck passed into the lead, which he held until the PDK electronic gear-lever control gave up. This took 8 minutes to mend and Stuck set off to break the lap record set by Bellof in 1985 and ended up 15th and eight laps down. *LAT*

← **Nuremberg Supersprint, 29 June 1986** The TWR Jaguars went well here despite their unsuitability for such a harsh surface, their ground effects making the cars leap around. Eddie Cheever and Derek Warwick finished 2nd and 3rd but Jean-Louis Schlesser in the third car (TWR-J12C-386) qualified 8th and finished in 17th place because of a pit stop for a jammed throttle and the removal of a damaged rear-wheel spat. He is seen here from the crow's nest ahead of Bruno Giacomelli in the Sponsor Guest Team's Lancia LC2-85 (0003) who retired. *LAT*

→ **Brands Hatch 1000km, 20 July 1986** There were approximately 40,000 spectators at Brands Hatch, many no doubt drawn to the TWR Jaguars. Two attended but the driver line-up had been changed, allegedly to increase the team's chances of winning more races. These were Cheever/Brancatelli no.51 and Warwick/Schlesser no.53. Originally the latter were using the no.52 car but it had poorly fitting bodywork which affected the ground effects. This is the no.53 car (TWR -J12C-386) with Warwick on board. They qualified 2nd and 3rd, and both cars contested the lead with Warwick leading the race at 100 laps, but finished respectively 6th and 4th, the cars still subject to niggling problems. Despite their superior handling they also lacked the outright speed of the turbo cars, the Jags reaching 160mph on the pit straight compared to Stuck's 165mph and de Cesaris's 168mph in the Lancia with Boutsen and Ludwig achieving 172mph. Look at the ramshackle pits as they were. *LAT*

Brands Hatch 1000km, 20 July 1986 There were no Rothmans Porsches at Brands Hatch because Weissach had cut back on their race programme. So Bell and Stuck (with Rothmans backing) found another ride with Klaus Ludwig and hired the famous no.7 956B (117) from Reinhold Joest. They finished 2nd having set fastest qualifying time but were delayed by a misfire and fading brakes. Meanwhile, fellow works Porsche driver Bob Wollek was partnered by Mauro Baldi in the carbon-fibre Richard Lloyd Liqui Moly Porsche 962GTi (106B), the successor of Nigel Stroud's original Richard Lloyd Porsche 956B (106B), that was 4th fastest in qualifying but had the speed, better/lesser fuel consumption and Keith Greene as team manager. They won by four laps with Stuck waiting for the flag having run out of fuel. In the background is the South bank and just look at the wonderful view that was had by the spectators. *LAT*

Brands Hatch 1000km, 20 July 1986 Lancia had retired their racing team, but Gianni Mussato's Sponsor Geest Lancia LC2-85 (0003) had been uprated to 1986 spec by Lancia. The drivers were Andrea de Cesaris and Bruno Giacomelli and they qualified 5th fastest, briefly led the race but retired with a gearbox problem on lap 156. This is de Cesaris with the John Bartlett Racing with Goodmans Sound Bardon DB1 Ford Cosworth DFV C200 (01) (Donovan/Cohen-Olivar/Leim) millimetres away at Druids. A very quick and sometimes erratic F1 regular from 1980 till 1994 (208 starts) for many teams, de Cesaris never won a GP. After retiring he became a successful currency broker in Monte Carlo but in 2005 he raced in the Grand Prix Masters series for retired F1 drivers. He was killed when he lost control of his motorcycle on the Grande Raccordo Anulare freeway near Rome. Andrea de Cesaris, 31 May 1959 – 5 October 2014. *LAT*

Brands Hatch 1000km, 20 July 1986 The Bardon DB1 née Arundel C200 was created by Scorpion Racing Services for Edward, Earl of Arundel. It had an unsuccessful time in 1984/85 and was bought by Bartlett in 1986. At Brands Hatch the Goodmans Sound and Croxley Script-sponsored Bardon was driven by Robin Donovan, Max Cohen-Olivar and Kenneth Leim, finishing 18th and last. Bartlett sold it to the aptly named Anton Sobriquet in 1987 who was actually Tony Smedley, FF and later F3 racer. He was our late lamented friend David McKinney's accountant in period, whose knowledge of most things motor racing, especially Maserati 250Fs, was biblical. *LAT*

⬆ Brands Hatch 1000km, 20 July 1986 The meeting was disrupted by four full-course yellows caused by assorted C2 cars, which upset the continuity of the race to the detriment of some entrants. Approaching Paddock Hill bend are the no.66 Cosmik Racing Promotions March 84G Porsche (3) of Tiff Needell and owner Costas Los, the no.17 Brun Motorsport Porsche 962C (Brun/Sigala) and Richard Cleare's March 85G Porsche (6) that he shared with James Weaver and French racer Lionel Robert. They finished 9th, retired and retired respectively. Cleare's March was purchased from American John Kalagian and entered at Le Mans where they won the IMSA GTP class but subsequently there were only retirements including here. *LAT*

➡ Brands Hatch 1000km, 20 July 1986 Ray Mallock and David Leslie were the C2 victors at Brands Hatch in the Ecosse C286 Rover, but further down the ladder were Duncan Bain and David Andrews in the Roy Baker Tiga GC286 Ford Turbo (335) which is listed as having a Cosworth DFL engine. They finished 13th overall and 5th in C2. *LAT*

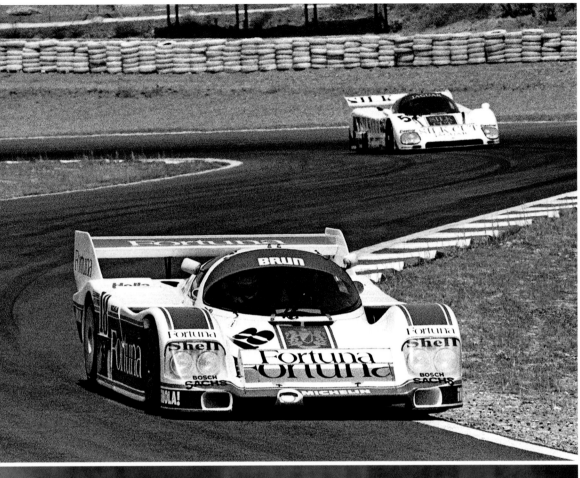

Jerez 360km, 3 August 1986 Porsche were again absent whilst Wollek, Mass and Bell had crossed the Atlantic to participate in the Sears Point IMSA race. Not just Weissach either: there were only 17 starters which included three TWR Jaguars that qualified 2nd, 3rd and 4th. These managed to collide with each other at the first corner of the first lap, Warwick hitting Brancatelli who in turn was hit by Cheever. Warwick ended up in the gravel whilst the other two pitted and Larrauri in one of the two Walter Brun entries took the lead and stayed there to the end with co-driver Jésus Pareja in the Porsche 962C (115). Brun in the older 956 (106), which he shared with Frank Jelinski, finished 2nd and the Warwick/ Lammers Jaguar finished 3rd two laps adrift. The winning car is followed by one of the three Jaguars of which two retired with broken driveshafts. *LAT*

Nürburgring 1000km, 24 August 1986 This race was a case of '*Listen to the rhythm of the falling rain…*' with apologies to the Cascades' 1962 song *Rhythm of the Rain*. The Brun 962C driven by Thierry Boutsen was the fastest qualifier with the boss as co-driver ahead of Stuck in the Rothmans Porsche in 2nd place and Bob Wollek 3rd fastest in the other Rothmans Porsche. On race day the weather was so bad that it was stopped after 22 laps by which time Stuck, unaware of a pace-car period after an accident in the murky, pouring rain, hit teammate Mass. Also out were the three Brun cars. The race was restarted and was won by the Sauber C8 Mercedes 86-C8-02 of Thackwell/Pescarolo, the New Zealander having led in the first part. Here is Thackwell racing through the wet stuff whilst TWR had another poor showing with all three cars out, two during the race and one during practice. *LAT*

Spa 1000km, 15 September 1986 Walter Brun's Porsche 962C (117) driven by Thierry Boutsen and Frank Jelinski started from pole and won the race, despite the attentions of the factory Porsches, the Joest Porsches, the RLR Liqui Moly Porsche and TWR Jaguars. Once again it was all about the fuel restrictions. Bell in the Rothmans 962C was told to back off by Peter Falk and had to make do with 3rd place. Also affected were the winning car and Warwick's TWR Jaguar. *LAT*

Spa 1000km, 15 September 1986 The Jaguars were slightly off the pace of the faster Porsche 962s in qualifying, but in the wet race they were potential winners. The no.51 car of Cheever/Schlesser was delayed by a windscreen soaked in oil from the Rothmans Mass/Wollek car and finished 5th. However, on the final lap Derek Warwick, with Jan Lammers, in the no.52 Jaguar XJR-6 (TWR -J12C-386) caught up with Thierry Boutsen whose Porsche was cutting out with a near empty tank as they approached La Source. Warwick dived inside to take the lead just yards from the finish when the Jaguar spluttered and died whilst the Porsche suddenly burst into life and took the flag with a very angry Warwick coasting over the line 0.8 of a second behind. *LAT*

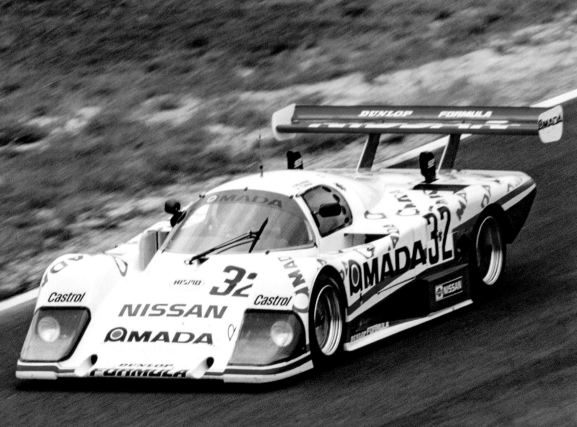

Spa 1000km, 15 September 1986 The C2 category had become increasingly important and at Spa there were 15 starters of which one was the Argo JM (Jo Marquart) Zakspeed Turbo. Marquart had been a designer at McLaren and his Argo cars became very popular and very successful in 1985 in the 'Camel Lights' class in America. However, in Europe the teams had less money and less sponsorship, which compromised their potential. Norwegian rally-cross winner Martin Schanche was partnered here with Irish racer David Kennedy who had competed in many classes from FF to briefly F1. They were 3rd fastest in C2 but retired on lap 98 with a broken gearbox. The winner of the C2 class was the Ecurie Ecosse Ray Mallock/Marc Duez Ecosse C286 Rover (003), a lap ahead of Gordon Spice/Ray Bellm in the former's Spice SE86C Ford Cosworth DFL. *LAT*

Fuji 1000km, 5 October 1986 After the strife and minor success of actually finishing 16th at Le Mans, Nissan's next FIA Championship race was in Japan. This is the Nismo Sport R86V 86G-6 which finished 11th at Fuji driven by Masahiro Hasemi and Takao Wada. They qualified 5th, just 0.006 slower than the Hoshino Racing R86V (Hoshino/Nakaka), and finished 11th with the Hoshino car 10th. They should have been further up the race results but apparently did not know how to optimise the FIA fuel-consumption diktats. The winners were Barilla/Ghinzani in Joest's famous Porsche 956B (117) from Jelinski/Dickens in Brun's Porsche 956 (104) and the TWR Jaguar XJR-6 of Cheever/Warwick. *LAT*

ENTRANTS

7-Eleven/Roush Racing
– Ford Mustang (Roush)
Scott Pruett (USA) DAY, SEB
Klaus Ludwig (D) DAY
Bruce Jenner (USA) DAY, SEB

Team 22
– Royale RP40 Mazda
Paul Corazzo (USA) SEB
Ed Flemke (USA) SEB
Tom Hessert (USA) SEB

901 Racing (Peter Uria)
– Porsche 911 Carrera RSR
Peter Uria (USA) DAY, SEB
Larry Figaro (USA) DAY, SEB
Jack Refenning (USA) DAY, SEB

ADA Engineering
– Gebhardt JC843
Ford Cosworth DFL
Evan Clements (GB) MZA, SIL, LM, BH,
    JER, NUR, SPA, FUJ
Ian Harrower (GB) MZA, SIL, LM, BH
    (DND), JER, NUR, SPA, FUJ
Tom Dodd-Noble (GB) LM

Advan Sports/Nova Engineering
– Porsche 962 C
Kunimitsu Takahashi (J) FUJ
Kenji Takahashi (J) FUJ

Bob Akin Motor Motor Racing
– Porsche 962
Hans-Joachim Stuck (D) DAY, SEB
Bob Akin (USA) DAY (DND), SEB
Jo Gartner (A) DAY (DND), SEB

Alderman Nissan
– Nissan 280ZX
Bob Leitzinger (USA) DAY
Mike Carder (USA) DAY
Louis Baldwin (USA) DAY
Steve Alexander (USA) DAY

Gaston Andrey Racing
– Alba AR2 Ferrari
Roger Andrey (USA) SEB
Bob Herlin (USA) SEB
Rick Mancuso (USA) SEB
Carlo Facetti (I) SEB
Martino Finotto (I) SEB
Ruggero Melgrati (I) SEB

Ares Sports
– Tiga GT285 Mazda
Ron Canizares (USA) SEB
Bill Jacobson (USA) SEB
Howard Katz (USA) SEB

AT & T
– Royale RP40 Buick
Don Bell (USA) DAY
Terry Wolters (USA) DAY
Craig Carter (USA) DAY

All American Racers (Dan Gurney)
– Toyota Celica Turbo
Dennis Aase (USA) DAY, SEB
Chris Cord (USA) DAY, SEB

Alpha Cubic Racing Team
– Porsche 956 B
Noritake Takahara (J) FUJ
Chiyomi Totani (J) FUJ
Kenji Tohira (J) FUJ

Auto Beaurex Motorsport
– Toyota 85C Dome
Naoki Nagasaka (J) FUJ
Steven Andskar (S) FUJ (DND)
Kazuo Mogi (J) FUJ
Hideshi Matsuda (J) FUJ
Naoki Nagasaka (J) FUJ

Automobile Louis Descartes
– ALD 02 BMW
Jacques Heuclin (F) MZA, SIL, LM, BH,
    NUR, SPA
Louis Descartes (F) MZA(DND), SIL, LM,
    BH, NUR, SPA
Hubert Striebig (F) NUR, SPA

Al Bacon Racing – Mazda RX-7
Al Bacon (USA) DAY, SEB
Bill Scott (USA) DAY, SEB
Dennis Krueger (USA) DAY, SEB

Roy Baker Promotions/RBR Racing
–Tiga GC285 Ford Cosworth BDT,
Tiga GC286 Ford Cosworth BDT
David Andrews (GB) DAY, LM, BH, JER,
    NUR, SPA, FUJ
Steve Phillips (USA) DAY
Duncan Bain (GB) DAY, LM (DND), BH,
    NUR, FUJ
Costas Los (GR) SEB
Dudley Wood (GB) SEB, MZA (DND)
Thorkild Thyrring (DK) MZA, LM, NOR,
    BH, JER, NUR, SPA
Mike Allison (USA) LM
Val Musetti (GB) LM, BH
Tom Frank (USA) LM
Michael Hall (AUS) LM (DND), SPA (DND)
Nick Nicholson (USA) LM
John Sheldon (GB) LM, NOR, BH (DND),
    JER (DND), SPA
David Palmer (GB) BH, JER
Max Cohen-Olivar (MA) JER, NUR
    (DND), SPA
'Pierre Chauvet' (Friedrich Glaz) (A) JER
John Williams (GB) SPA
Les Blackburn (GB) SPA
Roy Baker (GB) FUJ
Rudi Thomann (F) FUJ

Rick Balderson – Chevrolet Monza
Bill Gardner (USA) SEB
John Greene (USA) SEB
Steve Noffke (USA) SEB

John Bartlett Racing with
Goodmans Sound – Bardon DB1
Ford Cosworth DFL
Max Cohen-Olivar (MA) SIL, BH
Kenneth Leim (S) SIL, BH, NUR, SPA, FUJ
Nick Adams (GB) SIL (GB), LM, JER
Richard Jones (GB) LM
Robin Donovan (GB) LM, BH, JER, FUJ
David Mercer (GB) NUR, SPA
Ian Kahn (GB) SPA
Yoshiyuki Ogura (J) FUJ

Roland Bassaler
– Sauber SHS C6 BMW
Dominique Lacaud (F) LM, BH, NUR
Yvon Tapy (F) LM
Roland Bassaler (F) LM, BH, NUR
Pascal Pessiot (F) BH

Bayside Disposal Racing
(Bruce Leven) – Porsche 962
Bob Wollek (F) DAY, SEB
Derek Daly (IRL) DAY
Bruce Leven (USA) DAY, SEB (DND)
Paolo Barilla (I) SEB

Bo-And Racing
– Lola T600 Chevrolet
Bard Boand (USA) DAY
Richard Anderson (USA) DAY
Mike Allen (USA) DAY

Bob's Speed Products
– Pontiac Firebird (Python),
Buick Skyhawk
Del Russo Taylor (USA) SEB
Mike Hackney (USA) SEB
Arvid Albanese (USA) SEB
Bob Lee (USA) SEB
Bill Julian (USA) SEB
Timothy S. Lee (USA) SEB
Jim Saxon (USA) SEB

Rick Borlase
– Porsche 934
Rick Borlase (USA) SEB
Jim Torres (USA) SEB
Michael Hammond (USA) SEB

Brooks Racing (Brooks Fryberger)
– Ford Thunderbird
Leo Franchi (USA) DAY
Steve Gentile (USA) DAY
Rick Knoop (USA) DAY

Brun Motorsport
– Porsche 962,
Porsche 962 C, Porsche 956
Thierry Boutsen (B) DAY, MZA, SIL,
    LM, NOR, BH, NUR (withdrawn due to
    weather), SPA
Oscar Larrauri (RA) DAY, MZA, SIL,
    LM, BH, JER, NUR (withdrawn due to
    weather), SPA, FUJ
Drake Olson (USA) MZA
Jésus Pareja (E) MZA, SIL, LM, BH,
    JER, NUR (withdrawn due to weather),
    SPA, FUJ
Massimo Sigala (I) MZA, SIL, LM, BH,
    SPA
Walter Brun (CH) MZA, SIL, LM, NOR,
    BH, JER, NUR (DND withdrawn due to
    weather), SPA
Frank Jelinski (D) SIL, LM, BH, JER,
    NUR, SPA, FUJ
Joël Gouhier (F) LM
Didier Theys (F) LM, SPA
Alain Ferté (F) LM
Stanley Dickens (SWE) NUR (DND
    withdrawn due to weather), FUJ

Bud Light Corvette
– Chevrolet Corvette C4
(Linderfer)
Craig Rubright (USA) SEB
Greg Walker (USA) SEB (DND)
Nort Northam (USA) SEB (DND)

Burdsall-Newsome Racing
– Tiga GT285 Mazda
Peter Welter (USA) DAY, SEB
Roy Newsome (USA) DAY, SEB
Tom Burdsall (USA) DAY, SEB

Carma FF – Alba AR6 Ferrari,
Alba AR6 Carma
Martino Finotto (I) DAY, SIL, SPA
Ruggero Melgrati (I) DAY, SIL (DND), SPA
Almo Coppelli (I) DAY
Carlo Facetti (I) SIL, SPA (DND)

Cara International Racing
– LM 06C Toyota
Franz Konrad (A) FUJ
Akio Morimoto (J) FUJ

Case Racing
– Porsche 924 Carrera GTR
Dave Panaccione (USA) DAY, SEB
Ron Case (USA) DAY (DND), SEB

C C R (Clayton Cunningham)
– Mazda RX-7 Fabcar
Bob Reed (USA) DAY, SEB
Tom Kendall (USA) DAY, SEB
John Hogdal (USA) DAY, SEB

Central 20 Racing Team
– March 85G Nissan
Haruhito Yanagida (J) FUJ
Takamasa Nakagawa (J) FUJ

Certified Brakes (Jim Downing)
– Argo JM19 Mazda
Jim Downing (USA) DAY, SEB
John O'Steen (USA) DAY, SEB
John Maffucci (USA) DAY, SEB

Chamberlain Engineering
– TigaTS85 Hart Turbo
Gareth Chapman (GB) MZA, BH,
    SPA, FUJ
Will Hoy (GB) MZA, BH, SPA, FUJ
Dan Murphy (USA) BH
Mike Sanders (GB) FUJ

Richard Cleare Racing
– March 85G Porsche
Franz Konrad (A) SIL
Richard Cleare (GB) SIL, LM, BH (DND),
    NUR (DND), SPA
Lionel Robert (F) LM, BH
Jack Newsum (USA) LM
James Weaver (GB) BH
David Leslie (GB) NUR (accident), SPA

Richard Conte Buick Hawk
– March 85G Buick
John Paul, Jr (USA) DAY, SEB
Chip Ganassi (USA) DAY
Ivan Capelli (I) DAY
Whitney Ganz (USA) DAY, SEB
Ken Madren (USA) DAY, SEB
Bob Lobenberg (USA) DAY (DND)

Cosmik Racing
– March 84G Porsche
Costas Los (GR) MZA (drove whole
    race), SIL, LM, NOR, BH, JER, NUR,
    SPA, FUJ
Jan Thoele (D) MZA (DNS)
John Graham (CDN) SIL (DND)
Neil Crang (AUS) LM
Raymond Touroul (F) LM
Tiff Needell (GB) BH, JER, SPA, FUJ
Volker Weidler (D) NUR

CRT Contracting
Corporation (Ken Bupp)
– Chevrolet Camaro (Riggins)
Ken Bupp (USA) SEB
Guy Church (USA) SEB
E.J. Generotti (USA) SEB

Clayton Cunningham (CCR)
– Mazda RX-7 Fabcar
Bob Reed (USA) DAY, SEB
Tom Kendall (USA) DAY, SEB
John Hogdal (USA) DAY, SEB

Team Dallas
– Porsche 911 Carrera RSR
Jack Griffin (USA) SEB
Bobby Hefner (USA) SEB
Skip Winfree (USA) SEB)

Deco Sales Associates
– ArgoJM16 Buick
Brent O'Neill (USA) SEB
Steve Shelton (USA) SEB
Don Courtney (USA) SEB

Derichs Rennwagenbau
– Zakspeed C1/8 Ford
Cosworth DFL
Jan Thoelke (D) NOR

Dingman Brothers Racing
– Pontiac Firebird
Steve Millen (NZ) DAY
Elliot Forbes-Robinson (USA) DAY, SEB
Tommy Riggins (USA) DAY, SEB

Dome Motorsport
– Toyota 86C Turbo
Eje Elgh (S) LM, FUJ
Beppe Gabbiani (I) LM, FUJ
Toshio Suzuki (J) LM

Dyson Racing
– Porsche 962
Drake Olson (USA) DAY
Price Cobb (USA) DAY
Rob Dyson (USA) DAY

Ecurie Ecosse – Ecosse C286
Rover, Ecosse C285 Ford
Cosworth DFL
Ray Mallock (GB) SIL, LM, BH, NUR,
    SPA, FUJ
Mike Wilds (GB) SIL, LM
Les Delano (USA) LM
Andy Petery (USA) LM
John Hotchkis (USA) LM
David Leslie (GB) LM, BH
Marc Duez (B) NUR, SPA, FUJ

Eurospec Imports
– Chevrolet Camaro
Carlos Munoz (USA) SEB
Carlos Migoya (USA) SEB
Luis Albiza (USA) SEB

Jean-Claude Ferrarin – Isolia 02 B36
(Chevron) Ford Cosworth DFV
Philippe Mazué (F) NUR, SPA
Jean-Claude Ferrarin (F) NUR (DND),
    SPA

John Fitzpatrick Racing/
Danone Porsche Racing
– Porsche 956B, Porsche 962 C
Emilio de Villota (E) MZA, SIL, LM, JER,
    NUR, SPA
Fermin Velez (E) MZA, SIL, LM, JER,
    NUR, SPA
Philippe Alliot (F) LM
Paco Romero (E) LM, JER
Michel Trollé (F) LM
George Fouché (ZA) LM
Derek Bell (GB) NOR
Adrian Campos (E) JER (DND)

Folgers/Motorcraft
– Ford Mustang (Roush)
Bill Elliot (USA) DAY
Ricky Rudd (USA) DAY
Kyle Petty (USA) DAY
Ken Schrader (USA) DAY

From A Racing (Nova Engineering)
– Porsche 956
Jirou Yoneyama (J) FUJ
Hideki Okada (J) FUJ
Tsunehisa Asai (J) FUJ

Gebhardt Motorsport – Gebhardt JC853 Ford Cosworth DFL
Frank Jelinski (D) MZA
Stanley Dickens (S) MZA, SIL, LM, NOR, BH
Max Payne (GB) SIL, BH
Pierre de Thoisy (F) LM
Jean-François Yvon (F) LM
Nick Adams (GB) BH
Walter Lechner (A) NUR
Ernst Franzmaier (A) NUR

Global American – BMW M1
Steve Cohen (USA) DAY
David Christian (USA) DAY
Tom Congleton (USA) DAY

Global Racing – Mazda RX-7
Carlos Ruesch (RA) SEB
Hugo Gralia (USA) SEB (*DND*)
Alan Andrea (USA) SEB (*DND*)
John Clark (USA) SEB (*DND*)

B.F. Goodrich (Jim Busby) – Porsche 962
Derek Warwick (GB) DAY
Darin Brassfield (USA) DAY, SEB
Jim Busby (USA) DAY, SEB
Jochen Mass (D) DAY
Jan Lammers (NL) DAY
John Morton (USA) DAY, SEB

Graff Racing – Rondeau M482 Ford Cosworth DFL
Marc Menant (F) LM
Jean-Philippe Grand (F) LM
Jacques Goudchaux (F) LM

Group 44 – Jaguar XJR-7
Vern Schuppan (AUS) DAY, SEB
Brian Redman (GB) DAY, SEB
Hurley Haywood (USA) DAY, SEB
Bob Tullius (USA) DAY, SEB
Claude Ballot-Léna (F) DAY, SEB
Chip Robinson (USA) DAY, SEB

Dave Heinz Imports – Chevrolet Corvette (Dillon)
Dave Heinz (USA) DAY, SEB
Steve Zwiren (USA) DAY, SEB
Don Yenko (USA) DAY, SEB
Jerry Thompson (USA) DAY

Henn's Swap Shop Racing – Porsche 962
A.J. Foyt (USA) DAY, SEB
Arie Luyendyk (NL) DAY
Danny Sullivan (USA) DAY
Preston Henn (USA) DAY
Drake Olson (USA) SEB

Hi-Tech Racing – Porsche 935 M16
Miguel Morejon (C) DAY
Joe Varde (USA) DAY
Tico Almeida (USA) DAY

Team Highball – Mazda RX-7 (Highball)
Amos Johnson (USA) DAY, SEB
Dennis Shaw (USA) DAY, SEB
Jack Dunham (USA) DAY, SEB

Highlands County Racing – Pontiac Firebird
William Boyer (USA) SEB
Steve Roberts (USA) SEB
Mike Rand (USA) SEB
Robby Unser (USA) SEB

Holbert Racing – Porsche 962
Al Holbert (USA) DAY, SEB
Derek Bell (GB) DAY, SEB
Al Unser, Jr (USA) DAY, SEB

Hoshino Racing – Nissan R86V March
Kazuyoshi Hoshino (J) FUJ
Osamu Nakako (J) FUJ

Hotchkis Racing – March 83G Porsche
Jim Adams (USA) DAY, SEB
Costas Los (GR) DAY
John Hotchkis (USA) DAY, SEB
John Kalagian (USA) SEB

Arthur Hough Pressings/ Ark Racing – Ceekar 83J-1 Ford Cosworth BDX
Chris Ashmore (GB) SIL
Rudi Thomann (F) SIL
Mike Kimpton (GB) SIL (*DND*)

Teak Hunt Racing (Tom Hunt) – Mazda RX-7
Tom Hunt (USA) DAY, SEB
James Shelton (USA) DAY, SEB
Paul Romano (USA) DAY
Russ Boy (USA) DAY (*DND*)

Team Ikuzawa – Toyota 86C (Dome)
Kenny Acheson (GB) FUJ
Michael Roe (IRL) FUJ (*DND*)

Import Restorations (Charlie Gibson) – Pontiac Firebird (Watson)
Paul Reisman (USA) DAY
Bob Hebert (USA) DAY
Tom Gaffney (USA) DAY
Richard Stone (USA) DAY

Joest Racing/Momo Joest Racing/ Blaupunkt Joest Racing/Sachs Joest Racing – Porsche 962, Porsche 956 B, Porsche 956
Paolo Barilla (I) DAY, MZA, SIL, LM, BH, SPA, FUJ
Randy Lanier (USA) DAY, SEB (*DND*)
Gianpiero Moretti (I) DAY (*DND*), SEB
'John Winter' (Louis Krages) (D) SEB (*DND*), MZA, LM, NOR, BH, NUR (*DND withdrawn due to weather*), SPA, FUJ
Klaus Ludwig (D) MZA, LM, NOR, BH, SPA
Marc Duez (B) MZA
John Morton (USA) SIL, LM
George Follmer (USA) SIL, LM
Kenper Miller (USA) LM
Danny Ongais (USA) NOR
Hans-Joachim Stuck (D) BH
Derek Bell (GB) BH
Piercarlo Ghinzani (I) NUR, FUJ
Kris Nissen (DK) NUR, SPA, FUJ
Vern Schuppan (AUS) SPA
Harald Grohs (D) FUJ

Walter Johnston – Pontiac Firebird
Ken Bupp (USA) DAY
John Hayes-Harlow (GB) DAY
Del Russo Taylor (USA) DAY

Jolly Club – Alba AR6 Carma
Carlo Facetti (I) MZA
Martino Finotto (I) MZA

K & P Racing (Karl Keck) – Chevrolet Corvette (Pratt)
William Wessel (USA) DAY
Mark Kennedy (USA) DAY
David Fuller (USA) DAY, SEB
Karl Keck (USA) DAY
Mark Montgomery (USA) SEB

Kelmar Racing – Tiga GC85 Ford Cosworth DFL
Pasquale Barberio (I) MZA, SIL, BH, JER, NUR
Jean-Pierre Frey (CH) MZA
Maurizio Gellini (I) SIL, BH, JER, NUR
John Nicholson (NZ) SIL, BH

Jerry Kendall – Porsche 935
Jerry Kendall (USA) SEB
Dave White (USA) SEB
Werner Frank (USA) SEB

Kendall Racing – Lola T616 Mazda, Porsche 935
Paul Lewis (USA) DAY, SEB
Chuck Kendall (USA) DAY (*DND*), SEB
Tom Kendall (USA) DAY (*DND*)
Max Jones (USA) DAY (*DND*), SEB

Kouros Racing Team – Sauber C8 Mercedes Benz
John Nielsen (DK) MZA, SIL, LM
Henri Pescarolo (F) MZA, SIL, LM, NUR, SPA
Mike Thackwell (NZ) SIL, LM, NUR, SPA
Dieter Quester (A) LM
Christian Danner (D) LM

Kryder Racing – Nissan 280ZX
Reed Kryder (USA) SEB
Tom Palmer (USA) SEB
Todd Morici (USA) SEB

Latino Racing – Porsche 934, Porsche 911
Kikos Fonseca (CR) DAY, SEB
Luis Mendez (DR) DAY, SEB
'Jamsal' (Enrique Molins) (ES) DAY, SEB
Mauricio DeNarvaez (CO) SEB

Lee Racing – Chevrolet Corvette GTP/Lola T711
Lew Price (USA) DAY, SEB (*DND*)
Jim Mullen (USA) DAY, SEB
Matt Whetstine (USA) DAY
Carson Baird (USA) SEB (*DND*)

Leeward Racing – March 82G Chevrolet
Jim Leeward (USA) DAY
Bill Adam (CDN) DAY
Chip Mead (USA) DAY

Leon Brothers Racing – March 85G Porsche
Al Leon (USA) DAY
Jim Fitzgerald (USA)
Harald Grohs (D) DAY
Art Leon (USA) DAY (*DND*)

Lion Rampant – Mazda RX-7
Chaunce Wallace (USA) SEB
Van McDonald (USA) SEB
Kevin Bruce (USA) SEB

Liqui Moly Equipe (Richard Lloyd) – Porsche 956
James Weaver (GB) SIL, SPA
Klaus Niedzwiedz (D) SIL, NUR, FUJ
Mauro Baldi (I) LM, BH, NUR, SPA, FUJ
Price Cobb (USA) LM
Rob Dyson (USA) LM
Bob Wollek (F) NOR, BH

Ricardo Londono – Pontiac Firebird
Diego Montoya (CO) DAY
Albert Naon, Jr (USA) DAY
Carlos Migoya (USA) DAY

Lucas Truck Services – Chevrolet Camaro (Riggins)
Robert Peters (CDN) DAY
Kent Painter (USA) DAY (*DND*)
Tom Nehl (USA) DAY (*DND*), SEB
Scott Gaylord (USA) DAY (*DND*), SEB
Jim Fortin (USA) SEB

Mandeville Auto Tech – Mazda RX-7 (Chassis Dynamics)
Roger Mandeville (USA) DAY, SEB
Danny Smith (USA) DAY, SEB
Diego Febles (PR) DAY

Martini Racing – Lancia LC2/85
Andrea de Cesaris (I) MZA, SIL
Alessandro Nannini (I) MZA, SIL

Mazdaspeed – Mazda 757
David Kennedy (IRL) SIL, LM, FUJ
Takashi Yorino (J) SIL, LM, FUJ
Yoshimi Katayama (J) SIL, LM (*DND*), FUJ
Youjirou Terada (J) SIL, LM (*DND*), FUJ
Mark Galvin (IRL) LM
Pierre Dieudonné (B) LM, FUJ

Team Memorex (Walter Brun) – Porsche 962 C
Frank Jelinski (D) NOR

MHR Racing (Marty Hinze) – Porsche 935 K3
Marty Hinze (USA) SEB
Jack Newsum (USA) SEB
Tom Blackaller (USA) SEB

Mid O Racing/Rusty Jones /Don Marsh) – Argo JM16 Mazda
Ron Pawley (USA) DAY, SEB
Don Marsh (USA) DAY, SEB (*DND*)
Kelly Marsh (USA) DAY, SEB

MK Motorsport – BMW M1
Pascal Witmeur (B) LM
Michael Krankenberg (D) LM, NUR
Jean-Paul Libert (B) LM
Helmut Gall (D) NUR
Harald Becker (D) NUR

Morgan Performance – Tiga GT286 Buick
Charles Morgan (USA) DAY, SEB
Logan Blackburn (USA) DAY, SEB
David Simpson (USA) DAY

Morrison Cook Motorsport (Tommy Morrison) – Chevrolet Corvette
Jack Baldwin (USA) DAY
Bob McConnell (USA) DAY, SEB
Tommy Morrison (USA) DAY, SEB
Don Knowles (USA) DAY, SEB
Ron Grable (USA) DAY, SEB
John Heinricy (USA) DAY, SEB
Bobby Carradine (USA) DAY, SEB

MSB Racing – Argo JM19 Mazda
Dave Cowart (USA) DAY
Kenper Miller (USA) DAY
Jim Fowells (USA) DAY

Roy Newsome Racing – Mazda RX-7
Richard Stevens (CDN) DAY
Luis Sereix (USA) DAY
Roy Newsome (USA) DAY
Dale Kreider (USA) DAY

Nissan Motorsport – Nissan R86V March, Nissan R85V March
Kazuyoshi Hoshino (J) LM
Keiji Matsumoto (J) LM
Aguri Suzuki (J) LM
James Weaver (GB) LM
Masahiro Hasemi (J) LM, FUJ
Takao Wada (J) LM, FUJ

Obermaier Racing – Porsche 956
Fulvio Ballabio (I) MZA, SIL, LM, BH, JER, NUR
Richard Hamann (D) MZA
Jürgen Lässig (D) SIL, LM, NOR, BH, JER, NUR, SPA
Dudley Wood (GB) SIL, LM, BH, JER, SPA (*DND*)
Harald Grohs (D) NUR
Hervé Regout (B) SPA (*DND*)

OMR Engines – Chevrolet Camaro (Stock Car Products)
Oma Kimbrough (USA) DAY
Chris Gennone (USA) DAY, SEB
Hoyt Overbagh (USA) DAY, SEB
Pieter Baljet (CDN) DAY
Ric Moore (CDN) SEB

Patrick Oudet/Patrick Oudet/ Vetir Racing – Rondeau M382 Ford Cosworth DFL
Jean-Claude Justice (F) LM, SPA
Patrick Oudet (F) LM, SPA

Outlaw Racing – Argo JM19 Mazda
Frank Rubino (USA) DAY, SEB
Ray Mummery (USA) DAY, SEB
John Schneider (USA) DAY
Reggie Smith (USA) SEB (*DND*)

Oz Racing (Ba-Tsu) – MCS March 84C Mazda
Kenji Seino (J) FUJ
Mutsuo Kazama (J) FUJ
Syuuji Fujii (J) FUJ

Peerless Racing – Chevrolet Camaro (Peerless)
Jack Baldwin (USA) SEB
Jim Miller (USA) SEB

Person's Racing – Nissan R86V March
Aguri Suzuki (J) FUJ
Keiji Matsumoto (J) FUJ

Porsche AG – Porsche 961, Porsche 962 C
Claude Ballot-Léna (F) LM
René Metge (F) LM
Hans-Joachim Stuck (D) NOR

Porsche Kremer Racing/ SAT Porsche
Kremer Team – Porsche 962 C,
Porsche 956
Jo Gartner (A) MZA, SIL, LM (*fatal accident*)
Klaus Niedzwiedz (D) MZA
Tiff Needell (GB) SIL
Sarel van der Merwe (ZA) LM
Kunimitsu Takahashi (J) LM
Pierre Yver (F) LM
  (*withdrawn after Gartner's accident*)
Max Cohen-Olivar (MA) LM
  (*withdrawn after Gartner's accident*)
Hubert Striebig (F) LM
  (*withdrawn after Gartner's accident*)
James Weaver (GB) NOR
Franz Konrad (A) NOR
James Weaver (GB) NUR
Alessandro Nannini (I) NUR (*withdrawn*)
Bruno Giacomelli (I) SPA, FUJ
Volker Weidler (D) SPA, FUJ

Primagaz/Primagaz Team Cougar
  – Cougar C12 Porsche
Pierre-François Rousselot (F) SIL
Yves Courage (F) SIL, LM
Pierre-Henri Raphanel (F) LM
Alain De Cadenet (GB) LM

R & H Racing – Porsche 911
Rainer Brezinka (CDN) SEB
Rudy Bartling (CDN) SEB
John Centano (CDN) SEB

Raintree Corporation
  – Ford Mustang (Roush)
Lee Mueller (USA) DAY
Maurice Hassey (USA) DAY, SEB
Lanny Hester (USA) DAY, SEB

Rinzler Motor Racing
  – Tiga GT285 Mazda
Mike Brockman (USA) DAY
Steve Durst (USA) DAY
Deborah Gregg (USA) DAY
Jim Trueman (USA) DAY

Road Circuit Technology – Pontiac
  Firebird, Chevrolet Camaro
Les Delano (USA) DAY, SEB
Andy Petery (USA) DAY
Jeremy Nightingale (GB) SEB
Patty Moise (USA) SEB

Lucien Rossiaud – Rondeau M379 C
  Ford Cosworth DFV
Noël del Bello (F) LM, BH, SPA
Bruno Sotty (F) LM, BH, SPA
Lucien Rossiaud (F) LM, BH, SPA

Rothmans Porsche – Porsche 962 C
Hans-Joachim Stuck (D) MZA, SIL, LM,
  NUR, SPA, FUJ
Derek Bell (GB) MZA, SIL, LM, NUR
  (*DND*), SPA, FUJ
Jochen Mass (D) MZA, SIL, LM, NUR, SPA
Bob Wollek (F) MZA, SIL, LM, NUR, SPA
  (*DND*), SPA
Al Holbert (USA) LM, FUJ
Vern Schuppan (AUS) LM
Drake Olson (USA) LM
Henri Pescarolo (F) FUJ

Roush Racing/Roush/Folger's/
  Motorcraft – Ford Mustang
Tim Coconis (USA) DAY, SEB
Fernando Robles (DR) DAY
Chris Marte (DR) DAY, SEB
Bill Elliot (USA) SEB
Ricky Rudd (USA) SEB

S-P Racing (Gary Auberlen)
  – Porsche 911 Carrera RSR
Karl Durkheimer (USA) DAY, SEB
Gary Auberlen (USA) DAY, SEB
Cary Eisenlohr (USA) DAY, SEB
Peter Jauker (USA) DAY, SEB

SARD (Shin Kato)
  – SARD Toyota MC86X
Syuuroku Sasaki (J) FUJ
David Sears (GB) FUJ

Martin Schance Racing
  – Argo JM19 Zakspeed
Martin Schanche (N) MZA, LM (*DND*),
  NOR, BH, JER, NUR (*DND*), SPA, FUJ
Birger Dyrstad (N) MZA
Torgye Kleppe (N) LM, BH (*DND*), JER,
  NUR (*DND*), FUJ
Martin Birrane (IRL) LM
'Pierre Chauvet' (Friedrich Glaz) (A) NUR
David Kennedy (IRL) SPA

Ernst Schuster
  – Porsche 936C
Siegfried Brunn (D) MZA, SIL, LM,
  NUR (*DND*)
Ernst Schuster (D) MZA, SIL, LM,
  NOR, NUR
Rudi Seher (D) LM, NUR (*DND*)

Shafer Racing – Chevrolet Camaro
  (Banjo's Performance)
George Shafer (USA) SEB
Joe Maloy (USA) SEB
Bill McVay (USA) SEB

Shizumatsu Racing – Mazda 737C
Seisaku Suzuki (J) FUJ
Tetsuji Shiratori (J) FUJ
Kaneyuki Okamoto (J) FUJ

Silk Cut Jaguar – Jaguar XJR-6 TWR
Eddie Cheever (USA) MZA, SIL, LM, NOR,
  BH, JER, NUR, SPA, FUJ
Derek Warwick (GB) MZA, SIL, LM, NOR,
  BH, JER, NUR, SPA, FUJ
Gianfranco Brancatelli (I) MZA, SIL, LM,
  BH, JER, NUR (*DND*), SPA, FUJ
Jean-Louis Schlesser (F) MZA, SIL, LM,
  NOR, BH, JER (*DND*), NUR (*DND*),
  SPA, FUJ
Hurley Hayward (USA) LM
Hans Heyer (D) LM, NUR (*DND*)
Brian Redman (GB) LM
Win Percy (GB) LM
Martin Brundle (GB) JER (*DND*)
Jan Lammers (NL) JER, NUR, SPA, FUJ

Simms-Romano Enterprises
  – Mazda RX-7
Paul Romano (USA) SEB
Jim Freeman (USA) SEB
James Nelson (USA) SEB

Simpson Engineering (Robin Smith)
  – Simpson C286 Ford Cosworth
Richard Jones (GB) SIL
Stefano Sebastiani (I) SIL, BH (*DND*)
Robin Smith (GB) SIL, BH
Vivian Candy (IRL) BH (*DND*)

Skoal Bandits (Buz McCall)
  – Chevrolet Camaro (Timmons)
Buz McCall (USA) DAY, SEB
Pancho Carter (USA) DAY, SEB
Jim Mueller (USA) DAY
Tom Sheehy (USA) DAY, SEB
Walt Bohren (USA) SEB

Spice Engineering – Spice SE86C
  Ford Cosworth DFL
Gordon Spice (GB) MZA, SIL, LM, BH,
  JER, NUR, SPA, FUJ
Ray Bellm (GB) MZA, SIL, LM, BH, JER,
  NUR, SPA, FUJ
Jean-Michel Martin (F) LM

Spirit Racing – Chevrolet Camaro
Wally Dallenbach, Jr (USA) SEB
Tommy Byrne (IRL) SEB

Sponsor Guest Team (Gianni
  Mussato) – Lancia LC2/85
Bruno Giacomelli (I) NOR
Andrea de Cesaris (I) BH
Bruno Giacomelli (I) BH

STS-Mike Meyer Racing – Royale
  RP40/Argo JM16 Mazda
Jim Rothbarth (USA) DAY, SEB
Jeff Kline (USA) DAY, SEB
Mike Meyer (USA) DAY, SEB

Sunrise Racing – Chevrolet Camaro
Jeff Loving (USA) SEB
James Lee (USA) SEB (*DND*)

Techno Racing/Luigi Taverna
  – Alba AR3 Ford Cosworth DFL
Luigi Taverna (I) MZA, LM, BH, SPA (*DND*)
Mario Sala (I) MZA (*DND*)
Tony Palma (I) LM, BH
Marco Vanoli (I) LM
Daniele Gasparri (I) BH
Piercarlo Ghinzani (I) SPA
Gianpiero Lauro (I) SPA (*DND*)

Texas Enterprises/US Tobacco
  – Oldsmobile Calais
Terry Labonte (USA) DAY, SEB
Harry Gant (USA) DAY (*DND*)
Phil Parsons (USA) DAY (*DND*), SEB
Benny Parsons (USA) SEB

Tiga Team – Tiga GC286 Ford
  Cosworth DFL Turbo
Tim Lee-Davey (GB) BH, NUR, SPA, FUJ
Neil Crang (AUS) BH, NUR, SPA
Richard Piper (GB) FUJ

Toyota Team Tom's
  – Toyota 86C (Dome)
Geoff Lees (GB) LM, FUJ
Satoru Nakajima (J) LM, FUJ
Masanori Sekiya (J) LM, FUJ
Toshio Suzuki (J) FUJ
Hitoshi Ogawa (J) FUJ
Kaoru Hoshino (J) FUJ

Trust Engineering – Porsche 956
Vern Schuppan (AUS) FUJ
George Fouché (ZA) FUJ
Keiichi Suzuki (J) FUJ

Turbo Concepts – Porsche 911
Herman Galeano (USA) SEB
Christian Jacobs (USA) SEB
Pedro Cardenas (USA) SEB

Van Every Racing
  – Chevrolet Camaro (Riggins)
Ash Tisdelle (USA) DAY, SEB
Lance Van Every (USA) DAY (*DND*), SEB
Rusty Bond (USA) DAY (*DND*), SEB

'Victor' – Porsche 935
'Victor' (Victor Coggiola) (I) MZA
Tony Palma (I) MZA

Victor Zakspeed Team – Zakspeed
  C1/8 Ford Cosworth DFL
Jochen Dauer (D) NOR

Xtra Super Food CNT (Diman Racing)
  – Royale RP40 Porsche
Mandy Gonzalez (PR) DAY
Ernesto Soto (YV) DAY
Basilio Davila (PR) DAY
Diego Montoya (CO) DAY

WM (Welter/Meunier) Secateva
  – WM P86 Peugeot Turbo,
  WM P83B Peugeot Turbo
François Migault (F) LM
Jean-Daniel Raulet (F) LM
Michel Pignard (F) LM
Claude Haldi (CH) LM
Pascal Pessiot (F) LM
Roger Dorchy (F) LM

Walker Racing
  – Chevrolet Corvette (Linderfer)
Nort Northam (USA) DAY
Greg Walker (USA) DAY
Craig Rubright (USA) DAY

White/Allen Porsche (John Higgins)
  – Fabcar CL Porsche
John Higgins (USA) SEB
Chip Mead (USA) SEB
Howard Cherry (USA) SEB

Whitehall Rocketsports
  (Paul Gentilozzi) – Oldsmobile
  Toronado (Rocketsports)
Bob Bergstrom (USA) DAY, SEB
Gene Felton (USA) DAY, SEB (*DND*)
Paul Gentilozzi (USA) DAY, SEB (*DND*)
Tom Winters (USA) SEB (*DND*)

Jens Winther – URD C83 BMW
Jens Winther (DK) SIL, LM, BH, NUR, SPA
David Mercer (GB) SIL, LM, BH
Lars-Viggo Jensen (DK) LM
Angelo Pallavicini (I) NUR, SPA

Wonzer Racing/Gary Wonzer
  – Porsche 911, Porsche 911
  Carrera RSR
John Hofstra (USA) SEB
Charles Slater (USA) SEB
Mick Robinson (USA) SEB
Gary Wonzer (USA) SEB
Miguel Pagan (PR) SEB
Bruce Dewey (USA) SEB
Tom Cripe (USA) SEB

RESULTS

Daytona 24 Hours,
1/2 February, USA
Started 66, finished 17
1st Holbert USA)/Bell (GB)/Al Unser, Jr
(USA)/Boutsen Porsche 962
2nd Foyt (USA)/Luyendyk (USA)/Sullivan
(USA)/Henn (USA) Porsche 962
3rd Warwick (GB)/Brassfield (USA)/Busby
(USA)/Mass (D) Porsche 962

Sebring 12 Hours, 22 March, USA
Started 76, finished 29
1st Akin (USA)/Stuck (D)/Gartner (A)
Porsche 962
2nd Brassfield (USA)/Morton (USA)/Busby
(USA) Porsche 962
3rd Holbert (USA)/Bell (GB)/Al Unser, Jr
(USA) Porsche 962

Monza Supersprint
20 April, Italy
Started 27, finished 18
1st Stuck (D)/Bell (GB) Porsche 962C
2nd de Cesaris (I)/Nannini (I) Lancia
LC2/85
3rd Sigala (I)/Brun (CH) Porsche 956

Silverstone 1000km, 5 May,
Great Britain
Started 32, finished 21
1st Warwick (GB)/Cheever (USA) Jaguar
XJR-6
2nd Bell (GB)/Stuck (D) Porsche 962C
3rd Gartner (A)/Needell (GB) Porsche 962C

Le Mans 24 Hours, 31 May/1 June
France
Started 50, finished 23
1st Stuck (D)/Bell (GB) Holbert (USA)
Porsche 962C
2nd Larrauri (RA)/Pareja-Mayo (E)/Gouhier
(F) Porsche 962C
3rd Folmer (USA)/Morton (USA)/Miller
(USA) Porsche 956

Nuremburg Supersprint, 29 June,
Germany
Started 24, finished 19
1st Ludwig (D) Porsche 956B
2nd Cheever (USA) Jaguar XJR-6
3rd Warwick (GB) Jaguar XJR-6

Brands Hatch 1000km, 20 July
Great Britain
Started 30, finished 18
1st Wollek (F)/Baldi (I) Porsche 956GTI
2nd Stuck (D)/Bell (GB)/Ludwig (D)
Porsche 956B
3rd Boutsen (B)/Jelinski (D) Porsche 956

Jerez Supersprint, 3 August,
Spain
Started 17, finished 11
1st Larrauri (RA)/Pareja-Mayo (E)
Porsche 962C
2nd Brun (CH)/Jelinski (D) Porsche 956
3rd Warwick (GB)/Lammers (NL)/Schlesser
(F) Jaguar XJR-6

Nürburgring 1000km, 24 August
Germany
Started 31, finished 14
(Race stopped after 22 laps due to
accidents caused by wet weather and
restarted as a two-part race; total
distance covered 121 laps (550km)
1st Thackwell (NZ)/Pescarolo (F) Sauber
Mercedes-Benz C8
2nd Baldi (I)/Niedzwiedz (D) Porsche
956GTI
3rd de Villota (E)/Velez (E) Porsche 956B

Spa 1000km, 15 September,
Belgium
Started 33, finished 23
1st Boutsen (B)/Jelinski (D) Porsche 962C
2nd Warwick (GB)/Lammers (NL)
Jaguar XJR-6
3rd Bell (GB)/Stuck (D) Porsche 962C

Fuji 1000km, 5 October
Japan
Started 40, finished 31
1st Barilla (I)/Ghinzani (I) Porsche 956B
2nd Jelinski (D)/Dickens (SWE)
Porsche 956
3rd Cheever (USA)/Warwick (GB)
Jaguar XJR-6

1987

JAGUAR ON TOP WHILST PORSCHE RENEGES

Porsche firstly decided to run a limited presence in the WSPC, then they went for a two-car team for the season, but at the Norisring they announced their departure, leaving the Porsche customer teams to face the now unbeatable TWR Jaguars.

Weissach was busy developing an F1 engine for McLaren, producing an Indycar (with a March-based chassis) and the ongoing IMSA series. Of these the latter and the accompanying Group-C cars were the least media exposed and therefore dismissed. Also FISA were allegedly not happy with Group C. Why is not officially known although one could guess even before considering the rise and rise of F1.

Either way it was a convenient reason to pull out, but as we shall see they were still in evidence at Le Mans, which they duly won again together with a 2nd place at Jarama, a 3rd and retired at Jerez, 2nd and 6th at Monza, 3rd and 4th at Silverstone and retired at the Norisring. However, the Richard Lloyd 962C GTi won here, driven by Mauro Baldi, but the season was a near whitewash as TWR Jaguar won eight of the ten FIA races to take the Team Championship whilst their driver Raul Boesel won the Drivers' title.

Jaguar enjoyed the benefit of a larger 6,995cc engine, which gave a modest increase in power and increased torque plus a host of other updates, and a new Kevlar Dunlop tyre. Also tried was a short-tail body for Le Mans. It was both infuriating and ironic that they won so many races but not the one they really wanted for the sake of history, Le Mans.

Nissan and Toyota graced Le Mans with not much to show for it plus, of course, the annual Japanese round at Fuji, where the first Japanese car home was a Nissan in 16th place. Mazda, however, were successful at Le Mans, winning the IMSA class.

Another IMSA entry was Porsche's ill-fated 961, its second outing here, and despite a significant increase in power and larger wheels/tyres it was a dud and caught fire after an accident resulting in its demise.

Sauber Mercedes continued to improve but transmission problems intruded, although they were impressive at Le Mans. However, inadequate funding limited the team to just five races. This left the French Primagaz Compétition Cougar C20 as the only other viable C1 car, which finished 3rd at the Sarthe.

In the C2 class Spice Engineering beat Ecurie Ecosse, a reverse of their 1986 season with Kelmar Racing 3rd but a very long way behind. The rest of the C2 grid was either unreliable and/or not quick enough. One such being Martin Schanche's fast Argo JM19B which had seven pole positions out of nine in class but was badly let down by the Zakspeed engine.

At Daytona Al Holbert's Porsche 962C with Chip Robinson, Derek Bell and Al Unser Jr won the race whilst at Sebring Holbert and Robinson finished 2nd after leading until a turbo failure, which allowed Bruce Leven's Bayside Disposal 962 driven by Hans-Joachim Stuck and Jochen Mass to win.

Fuji 1000km, 27 September 1987 Pre-race Ray Mallock, David Leslie, Mike Wilds and Marc Duez seem quite happy about it all at Fuji. However, appearances can be misleading. On the grid Mallock's car (no.102) had a redundant ECU which lost him two laps whilst the other car was mishandling. Additionally, both cars were lacking downforce due to their flat-bottomed design. They finished 14th and 15th and 2nd and 3rd in C2 behind the pre-eminent Spice Engineering SE87C, which had won the C2 Team Championship to consolidate Gordon's Drivers' Championship. *LAT*

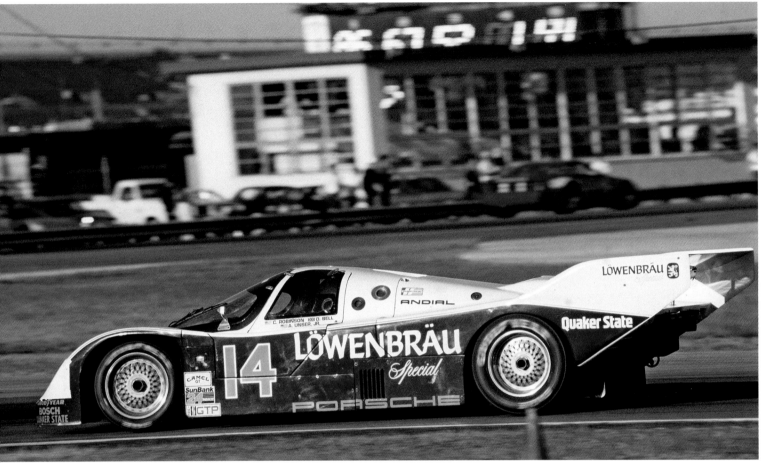

Daytona 24 Hours, 1 February 1987 For the third year in succession Al Holbert's team of Chip Robinson, Derek Bell, Al Unser Jr and Al himself (but only for two hours on the Sunday) in the Porsche 962C (103) found themselves in a duel with A.J. Foyt who entered his Porsche 962 (Holbert Racing 4) for himself, Al Unser and Danny Sullivan. They spent the majority of the race within a lap or so of each other with the Holbert car leading, but with the end in sight Foyt's engine broke on lap 724 although they still finished 4th. The Holbert car on Sunday is on its way to 1st place after 753 laps. Second place fell to Walter Brun's Porsche 962 (128) driven by Oscar Larrauri, Gianfranco Brancatelli and Massimo Sigala after 745 laps and fastest race lap with Rob Dyson's 962 (120) 3rd for Dyson, Price Cobb and Vern Schuppan. *LAT*

Daytona 24 Hours, 1 February 1987 There were two Ford Mustang GTP cars at Daytona, entered by Zakspeed USA for Whitney Ganz/David Hobbs/Gianpiero Moretti and the Roush Racing car for Scott Pruett/Pete Halsmer/Tom Gloy. The former was marginally faster and had a stockblock fuel-injected 6-litre Ford V8 whilst the British-built Roush car, seen here, had a slightly larger-capacity engine with a giant four-choke carburettor. They qualified 11th and 13th and retired on lap 328 (engine) and lap 120 (suspension) respectively. *Revs*

⬆ **Daytona 24 Hours, 1 February 1987** Group 44 entered their XJR-7 (5) at Daytona for Tullius, Hurley Haywood and John Morton and they qualified 7th. The car weighed 930kg (2,050 lbs) and its 5,993cc Jaguar V12 engine gave 600 or 650bhp @7,500 rpm, depending upon whom you believe. It ran as high as 2nd place briefly but retired after 216 laps due to overheating. It is followed by the Greg Walker Racing Chevrolet Corvette driven by Nort Northam, Scott Lagasse and Dennis Krueger that retired seven laps later with engine problems. *Revs*

➡ **Daytona 24 Hours, 1 February 1987** Tom Juckette with Bill McDill and Mike Laws were 25th in the Chevrolet Camaro (Dillon) but not classified at Daytona. The car was entered by McDill and finished 9th in the IMSA GTO class. Juckette together with his brothers owned and operated Witt & Juckette Construction Company and Juckette Management Services, for the development and management of nursing homes. He was a competitor in the SCCA (Sports Car Club of America) and IMSA amongst other clubs and had 17 consecutive starts at the Daytona 24 Hours. Thomas Freeman Juckette, born 3 July 1940, died 17 January 2005 of leukaemia. *Revs*

⬆ **Sebring 12 Hours, 21 March 1987** Amongst the omnipotent Porsche 962s, the Camaros, Mustangs et al. was this outrageous-looking device, the no.18 PAS Pontiac entered by Jeff Beitzel. The drivers were Tim Evans, Andy Pilgrim, Doug Goad and Terry McKenna. British racer Andy Pilgrim went on to become a successful Corvette and Cadillac racer from 1999 to 2013. PAS (Prototype Automotive Services) built roll cages and other racing parts, while Beitzel was an ex-Ford SVO engineer who had connections at General Motors. He built the car with a non-turbo Iron Duke Pontiac 2.4-litre engine, which was too slow to qualify in the 'Lights' class. Beitzel or Bietzel (both versions are online) much later married Gretchen Rossi, one of the stars of the *Real Housewives of Orange County* programme and died of leukaemia in September 2008. *Revs*

⬅ **Sebring 12 Hours, 21 March 1987** Californian Elliott Forbes-Robinson was a motor-racing polymath who won in many series including the American Le Mans Series (ALMS), Super Vee, Trans-Am Series, Can-Am, IMSA GTU and the World Challenge. He was driving a Porsche 962 with Brian Redman and Chris Kneifel for Primus Motorsport and they finished 3rd. Here he is talking to one of the crew chiefs pre-race. *Revs*

→ **Sebring 12 Hours, 21 March 1987** Jochen Mass and Bobby Rahal drove Bruce Leven's Porsche 962 (121) to victory at Sebring but they were lucky. The 2nd-placed Holbert Racing 962 for Chip Robinson and Al Holbert was the quicker car and was leading with about 90 minutes left when it blew a turbo, which cost it 11 minutes. Then the Leven car had electrical problems but managed to hang on, winning by two laps. Also potential winners were A.J. Foyt's 962 for himself, Sullivan and Haywood, but this tangled with a Mazda during a pit stop, and Price Cobb's 962, driven by Cobb and Vern Schuppan, which crashed with brake failure on lap 123 with Schuppan driving. *LAT*

↓ **Sebring 12 Hours, 21 March 1987** As a consequence of growing airport traffic Sebring's 5.2-mile circuit was reduced to 4.11 miles although its rough, bumpy surface was still in evidence. Protofab Engineering began in 1983 and their Chevrolet Camaro was driven by Greg Pickett and Tommy Riggins at Sebring. They finished an impressive 5th overall and 1st in the GTO class. Pickett is the only driver to win a race in four decades of Trans-Am racing and shares with Mario Andretti the distinction of winning a major professional race in five successive decades. Riggins began racing on dirt ovals in 1967 then later in NASCAR Busch Grand National races before taking to road racing with a successful career that including two Drivers' Championships. He had four IMSA GT victories and two in Camel Lights, and years later in 2003 he won Grand-Am's Rolex Series GTS class Drivers' Championship. *LAT*

Jarama 360km, 22 March 1987
Historically, Jarama is remembered
for the Battle of Jarama (6 February
– 27 February 1937), an attempt
by General Francisco Franco's
Nationalists to remove the
Republican lines along the river
Jarama, east of Madrid, during the
Spanish Civil War. Neither side won.
Fifty years on, two new Jaguar XJR-
8s took on a lone Weissach Porsche
962C and four customer cars plus the
Richard Lloyd, Nigel Stroud-designed
962 variant. The rather sparse grid is
obvious (17 starters) and Stuck in the
works Porsche was at the back of the
grid due to a lean fuel mixture. Eddie
Cheever leads away with Lammers
in the other Jaguar following and the
rest spread out behind them. *LAT*

Jarama 360km, 22 March 1987
One Ecurie Ecosse C286 Ford
Cosworth DFL appeared at Jarama,
for Ray Mallock and David Leslie.
Suddenly they were off the pace of
most of the C2 class who had moved
on, most notably the Team Lucky
Strike Argo JM19B Zakspeed and the
Spice SE86C. Nevertheless, Mallock/
Leslie finished 11th overall and
2nd in C2 behind the Velez/Spice
SE86C. Mallock is no doubt checking
out something as a team member
approaches the car, and note that the
driver's door has been removed. *LAT*

Jarama 360km, 22 March 1987
Walter Brun and the Kremers entered
three and two cars respectively at
Jarama. One Brun car for the boss
and Jelinski was new and had a
Thompson chassis, as did the two
Kremer 962Cs for Volker Weidler (D)
and Kris Nissen (DK) and the Spanish
pair of Emilio de Villota/Paco
Romero, who finished 4th and 10th
respectively. Romero is on the left
here and this is what John Fitzpatrick
had to say about him: "In several
races I ran a Spanish pay-driver,
Paco Romero. His brothers were
gambling people in Puerto Banus,
and we had Casino Marbella on the
car. He'd pay for his drive, about
£70,000 a race and more for Le Mans,
by giving me a brown paper bag full
of dirty 5,000-peseta notes. In the end
he got shot." *LAT*

◄ **Jarama 360km, 22 March 1987** John Watson and Jan Lammers won at Jarama from the Stuck/Bell works Porsche with Jaguar teammates Cheever/Boesel 3rd who had a probable fuel-pickup problem. In his final stint Watson backed off to save fuel, allowing the Porsche with Bell driving to catch him up and causing much consternation in the Walkinshaw ranks. However, after the race Watson was unperturbed, having kept an eye on the Porsche, and he crossed the line 1.6 seconds ahead with 8 litres of fuel still on board compared to the 3 litres that Bell had. The damage to the offside of the XJR-8 (TWR-J12C-187) was possibly caused by a slower Palmer in the Liqui Moly Porsche who nudged the Jaguar twice when Watson was trying to pass him. *LAT*

◄ **Jerez 1000km, 29 March 1987** The organisers insisted that FISA rules required an obligatory 1,000km race after a sprint event in the same country (this was a misinterpretation of the rules). So Jerez would be a 6-hour, 1,000km race and the C1 class were allocated an appropriate fuel amount. However, it was not possible to reach the 1,000km within 6 hours at this slow, twisty circuit. Tom Walkinshaw was concerned that this would give the turbocharged cars a 10% fuel advantage as the 6-hour distance would be about 890km. This was ignored. Meanwhile, 130-octane Avgas fuel was supplied to the entrants rather than the obligatory four-star pump fuel so the teams were told to throw away the Avgas by the organisers who would then provide the four-star rubbish. Anyway, Norwegian Martin Schanche and Will Hoy look happy enough here, Schanche's Argo JM19B Zakspeed being the fastest C2 car in qualifying. *LAT*

→ **Jerez 1000km, 29 March 1987**
This time the no.4 Jaguar XJR-8 (TWR-J12C-287) of Cheever/ Boesel won the race despite being bumped by the Tecno Alba AR3 and here it is rounding the corner before the pits, chasing Jochen Mass in the Rothmans Porsche 962C (007). This retired with gearbox failure, but the faster of the two Porsches (now using an improved, lighter PDK gearbox) of Stuck/Bell finished 3rd. The track was very bumpy and many cars suffered. F1 driver Cheever was lucky to win the race as he forgot to sign in (this was not used in F1) and of course the organisers failed to warn him in practice. Instead, afterwards they disqualified him from the race but on appeal with the signatures of all the team managers he was reinstated but with a $5,000 fine plus a $3,000 fine for the team. Shameful and just what you would expect really. *LAT*

→ **Jerez 1000km, 29 March 1987** This gives an indication of just how hot and barren Jerez was on the day and the Liqui Moly Britten Lloyd Porsche 962C GTi was abandoned due to a gearbox gremlin after 27 laps. In the background the Mallock/ Leslie Ecosse passes by en route to 2nd in the C2 class and what looks like blue solar panels are presumably seating for the paying classes who fancied a bit of heat stroke to improve their tans. *LAT*

↑ **Jerez 1000km, 29 March 1987** The C2 category was won by the Spice Engineering Spice SE86C of Gordon Spice and Fermin Velez. They finished 7th on the road and 37 seconds ahead of the Mallock/Leslie Ecosse C286. Both cars had suffered delays, the Spice with a broken solenoid bracket switch and the Ecosse with fading brakes. However, the Schanche/Hoy Lucky Strike Argo JM19 Zakspeed (116) seen here was the fastest C2 car but it stopped early with a split intercooler pipe and then later on a puncture, a suspension failure (bumpy circuit) and ultimately a catastrophic engine failure. *LAT*

← **Monza 1000km, 12 April 1987** The first lap and the usual suspects clamber for the first chicane. On the right Boesel in the TWR Jaguar looks to pass Stuck in the Rothmans Porsche whilst behind a long line of C1 cars follow on. There are ten Porsches in sight and two Jaguars. Stuck set the fastest qualifying time in the Weissach 962C he shared with Bell, with Larrauri 2nd in Brun's 962 and Wollek 3rd fastest in the second works car. However, once again there was controversy regarding AGIP's fuel supply with eight Porsches suffering engine blow-ups in practice. This was perhaps the consequence of running commercial-grade fuel for cars with electronic management systems more appropriate for high-octane use. As ever, the Jaguars were slower with Lammers 4th and Boesel 5th during qualifying but omnipotent in the race. *LAT*

→ Monza 1000km, 12 April 1987
Amongst the C2 class was the Charles Ivey Racing Tiga GC287 Porsche Turbo (332) driven by Mark Newby and Dudley Wood. It was last but one in qualifying sadly and retired on lap 67 with engine problems. Tigas were prolific everywhere and anywhere with a variety of engines and specifications, but ultimately Howden Ganley's creation would shut down in 1989. *LAT*

↓ Monza 1000km, 12 April 1987
Despite two spins, one by Jan Lammers and the other by Raul Boesel, the Lammers/Watson XJR-8 (TWR-J12C-187) won the race by two laps from the Stuck/Bell Porsche 962C (008). Unfortunately for the team, 2nd-placed Boesel's off came only six laps before the finish and he ended up in a gravel trap unable to escape. This was the third TWR victory in a row and more was to come. The XJR-8s now had a 7-litre engine giving over 700bhp, which they needed to beat the turbocharged 962s. Stuck/Bell were 2nd with the Brun Motorsport 962C of Frank Jelinski/Jésus Pareja/Oscar Larrauri 3rd. *LAT*

Silverstone 1000km, 10 May 1987 Raul Boesel in the Jaguar XJR-8 (TWR-J12C-287) is leading Wilds in the Swiftair Ecosse C286 (003) and the other two Jaguars at Silverstone. One of these is the Brundle/Nielsen Le Mans version, which was 10mph faster on the straight bits but a trifle unruly around the bendy bits due to lack of downforce. At Silverstone Boesel was teamed with Eddie Cheever and won the race just 6 seconds ahead of the Lammers/Watson XJR-8, which apparently had an oily windscreen that slowed it down in the late afternoon sun. The 'works' Porsches were 1st and 3rd on the grid, but in race trim they could not stay with the Sauber and Jaguars. Additionally, the 962s had a new Motronic management chip and were being cautious following the Monza fiasco. The Stuck/Bell 962C (008) finished 3rd, one lap behind the two Jaguars, whilst Wilds/Dumfries in the Swiftair Ecosse finished 8th overall and 2nd in the C2 class, beaten by their teammates Mallock/Leslie in no.102 just visible at the back of the queue. *LAT*

Silverstone 1000km, 10 May 1987 Mike Thackwell was a stunning driver who did not fit into the culture of F1. He made an aborted start at the 1980 Canadian GP at the age of 19 years and subsequent attempts all failed for a variety of reasons beyond his control. However, he was successful in F2 despite breaking his left heel in a testing accident at Thruxton in a Ralt Honda, which wrecked his 1981 season. He rejoined Ralt Honda in 1983 and finished runner-up to teammate Jonathan Palmer and then convincingly won the European F2 series in 1984. At Silverstone the Sauber C9 was 2nd fastest in qualifying and led the race from Cheever's Jaguar but it didn't last. Firstly, Thackwell's pace increased the Mercedes' fuel consumption, then its engine started to misfire and on lap 108 the rear suspension collapsed. Note his very blue eyes and the SALVATION ARMY sticker on his helmet. *LAT*

Le Mans, 13/14 June 1987

TWR Jaguar had won four races in a row and had high hopes of making this a fifth. They entered three XJR-8 LM-bodied cars for Eddie Cheever/Raul Boesel/Jan Lammers no.4, Jan Lammers/Win Percy no.5 and Martin Brundle/John Nielsen no.6. No.6 retired with a broken valve spring (or cracked cylinder head according to others) whilst contesting the lead with the Stuck/Bell 962C; no.4 finished 5th after many problems: gearbox fire, no fuel pressure, losing the tail, which was replaced, then another stop on circuit and a broken suspension strut. No.5 began to vibrate on Mulsanne, then a tyre burst and the car became airborne at 200mph plus, somersaulted high into the trees and then landed back on the track, sliding down the road on its side and roof wearing a hole in the car and also Win's helmet. Amazingly he was unharmed and many years later told the author that he would have died but for Tony Southgate's supremely strong and rigid tub which Southgate said could have been repaired. A stark contrast to the Porsches in period. *LAT*

Le Mans, 13/14 June 1987

There were yet more fuel problems at Le Mans with four customer Porsche 962s suffering burnt-out pistons, apparently due to the wrong fuel/electronic chip combination. Porsche AG entered three 962Cs for Stuck/Bell, Wollek/Mass/Schuppan and the Schuppan/Cobb with Canadian racer Kiers Nierop car. However, Cobb crashed this car in practice whilst Bob Wollek got as far as lap 16 when the burnt-out piston syndrome struck. Due to this melange of mishaps Nierop was moved across to the 961 (see next image). Following the failed onslaught of TWR the Stuck/Bell/Holbert 962C (006) seen here won (it was Bell's 5th and final Le Mans win) by 20 laps from the Jürgen Lässig/Pierre Yver/Bernard de Dryver Primagaz Porsche 962C (130). *LAT*

Le Mans, 13/14 June 1987 Despite its obvious flaws Porsche continued to waste money on the 961 project but this was its end. A year on had seen an increase in power (to 680bhp) and 19in wheels/tyres, yet it was slower than in 1986 and started 31st on the grid. The drivers were René Metge, Claude Haldi and the aforementioned Kees Nierop. Late Sunday morning the car was running 11th when Nierop missed a sticking gear approaching Indianapolis and spun into the barriers. He managed to limp away but Porsche's Norbert Singer was watching via an in-car camera and told Nierop to stop and get away from the car as it was on fire. He did and the 961 was burnt out. *LAT*

Le Mans, 13/14 June 1987 Gordon Spice's C2 career carried on its winning ways at Le Mans and he shared the car with Fermin Velez and Philippe de Henning. They were briefly compromised by a puncture and later an oil leak and were engaged in a duel with the Mallock/Leslie/Duez Swiftair Ecosse, but this had a gearbox problem. The Spice finished 6th overall and 1st in C2 whilst the Ecosse finished 8th overall and 2nd in C2. *LAT*

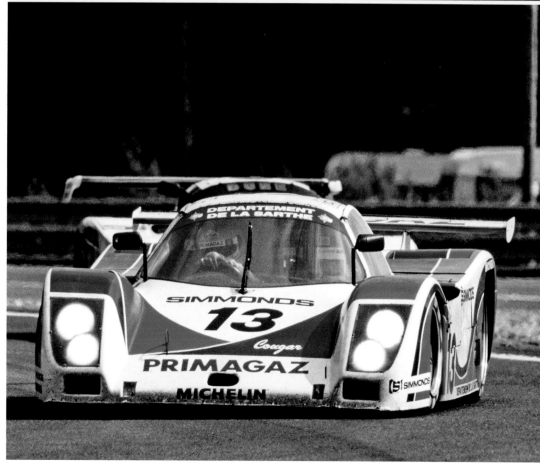

↑ **Le Mans, 13/14 June 1987** Mazdaspeed entered two IMSA 757s at Le Mans for Yoshimi Katayama/Yojiro Terada/Takashi Yorino and David Kennedy/Pierre Dieudonné/Mark Galvin. The latter finished a magnificent 7th overall after some problems including a broken wishbone whilst this car retired very early on with engine failure. Compared to its chubby-looking predecessor, the new car looks much better with its generic Porsche 962 body style. *LAT*

→ **Le Mans, 13/14 June 1987** F3000 racer Pierre-Henri Raphanel, Hervé Regout and Yves Courage qualified 6th at Le Mans in the Cougar C20 (C12-01), an update of the C12. Its former 2.6-litre Porsche engine was replaced by a 2.8-litre twin-turbo unit and chassis, suspension, brakes, intercoolers et al. were revised. There were few problems en route and the car (which had been clocked at the Le Mans test day at 229mph) finished 3rd with entrant/owner Yves Courage driving the final stint only, as was appropriate. *LAT*

↑ **Le Mans, 13/14 June 1987** Of the other contenders at Le Mans both the Sauber C9s retired: the Dumfries/Ganassi no.62 car (87-C2-09) was running in the first six but its gearbox broke on lap 37 after Champcar racer 'Chip' Ganassi took over, whilst the no.61 C9 for Thackwell/Pescarolo and Hideki Okada retired with transmission woes, the Japanese driver not getting to drive the car. A small consolation was Dumfries' fastest race lap. Following is one of the Swiftair Ecosse C286s. Also in the doldrums were the Nissan and Toyota entries, all retired. *LAT*

↗ **Nuremberg 200 miles, 28 June 1987** The Norisring round was twice the distance of its 1986 race and it was per se a Porsche benefit as befits its location. The race was won by the Richard Lloyd GTi Porsche 962C (106B), which had gone up in flames at Le Mans but was now back together with new running gear and engine. Mauro Baldi won the first heat and Jonathan Palmer finished 2nd in the second heat. Here Baldi is millimetres behind the Thackwell Sauber C9, which was retired in Heat 1 due to the excessive heat after 40 laps and did not participate in Heat 2. However, Baldi lost the lead to Lammers' TWR Jaguar on lap 35, but this retired seven laps later with a transmission problem. *LAT*

➡ **Nuremberg 200 miles, 28 June 1987** Fastest car/driver in qualifying at the Norisring was Hans-Joachim Stuck with the factory Porsche 962C (009) in the Dunlop Shell livery. He was hit by Larrauri's Brun Porsche in Heat 1 but classified 2nd much to the amazement of most team managers who were not convinced by the timekeepers. In Heat 2 co-driver Derek Bell retired with engine troubles. *LAT*

↑ **Nuremberg 200 miles, 28 June 1987** Eddie Cheever finished 13th in Heat 1 with the TWR Jaguar XJR-8 (TWR-J12C-287) due to low fuel pressure, but in Heat 2 Raul Boesel drove the car to 1st place after Klaus Ludwig in the Blaupunkt-Joest Porsche, who had dominated the heat, was disqualified for having an oversized fuel tank. It had been driven to 3rd place in Heat 1 by Frank Jelinski. *LAT*

← **Brands Hatch 1000km, 26 July 1987** There had been rumours at the Norisring that Porsche were withdrawing their factory cars from the championship. At Brands Hatch it was the reality and TWR faced the customer cars. Stuck/Bell were entered by Reinhold Joest but Stuck could go no faster than 4th in qualifying with the no.7 Porsche 962C (129), seen here approaching Paddock Hill Bend. They were the first real Porsche, finishing 4th, but were well beaten by Richard Lloyd's honeycomb special 962 driven by Mauro Baldi and Johnny Dumfries who qualified 3rd and finished 2nd in the race. *LAT*

Brands Hatch 1000km, 26 July 1987 The Chamberlain Engineering Spice SE86C had a Brian Hart 418T 4-cylinder 1,873cc 88x77mm DOHC engine with a Holset turbocharger giving 500bhp with a 2.25-bar boost. It was very fast with Nick Adams driving it but reliability was a serious problem and Adams/Foulston finished 15th as noted above having been 9th fastest in qualifying. The SE86C was a good-looking car compared to most of the other C2 machinery as can be seen here in profile. *LAT*

Brands Hatch 1000km, 26 July 1987 Raul Boesel in the no.4 Jaguar XJR-8 (TWR J12C-287) dives inside the Brun Torno Porsche 962C (002BM) driven by the 5th-placed Jochen Mass/Oscar Larrauri. The Jaguars were the quickest cars but they had to try hard to beat Richard Lloyd's special 962, Boesel spinning at Paddock at one point, but eventually Boesel/Nielsen won the race by just 1 minute 53 seconds. The Lammers/Watson Jaguar finished 3rd due to a wheel bearing failure which cost them nine laps. *LAT*

↑ **Nürburgring 1000km, 30 August 1987** Rothmans and Blaupunkt Joest Porsches, Kouros Sauber, TWR Jaguar and the RLR Liqui Moly Porsche were the front runners here and for once it wasn't raining. The RLR car for Mauro Baldi and Jonathan Palmer was fastest qualifier but in the race it did not feature, finishing 5th. Instead it was the Bell/Stuck Rothmans Joest Porsche 962C (004-104), a previous works car, that was the first Porsche home, finishing 2nd after others retired. Notice something? The lack of spectators. *LAT*

↗ **Nürburgring 1000km, 30 August 1987** Two Kouros Sauber Mercedes C9s were entered but the no.62 car (Dumfries/Reuter) suffered an accident during practice. This left the no.61 Sauber C9 Mercedes (87-C9-01), to be driven by Mike Thackwell, Johnny Dumfries and Henri Pescarolo, which qualified 3rd. This, together with the Joest Blaupunkt Porsche (Wollek/Ludwig), led the race but both retired, on lap 138 and lap 117 respectively, with broken gearboxes. *LAT*

→ **Nürburgring 1000km, 30 August 1987** TWR entered Eddie Cheever/Raul Boesel and Jan Lammers/John Watson and they qualified 2nd and 4th. The former won but the latter retired with an engine failure, but that was good enough because it gave TWR the Teams' Championship. This is Cheever (Edward McKay Cheever Jr, born 10 January 1958) who raced in F2, F1 (1977–1989 with 132 starts) and later the CART series, Indy Racing League, winning the 1998 Indianapolis 500 and much else. *LAT*

Spa 1000km, 13 September 1987 The race started dry but by lap 44 Spa was in drizzling mode; then it stopped but back it came on lap 49. Before this meteorological sabotage Mike Thackwell in the claimed 700bhp plus Sauber C9 (who had started 1st on the grid and also set fastest race lap) and Jonathan Palmer in the unique Britten/Lloyd 962 were pulling away from the Jaguar/Porsche cabal. Alas Thackwell had to stop due to a loose seat, not once but three times to ameliorate his problem, which cost the team 9 minutes and any hope of winning the race. Instead Thackwell with ex-Jaguar driver Jean-Louis Schlesser finished 7th, and here is the meteoric New Zealander giving it the beans as they say. *LAT*

Spa 1000km, 13 September 1987 The year had not been kind to Martin Schanche's Lucky Strike Zakspeed-powered Argo JM19B (116), an inappropriate sponsor's name perhaps as it was anything but and a waste given the car's speed. At Spa co-driver Will Hoy set the fastest C2 qualifying (its seventh of the season) and race laps. They were 14th overall and 5th in C2, handicapped by an electrical fault that required seven batteries to finish the race. Meanwhile, Fermin Velez and Gordon won the C2 class in the Spice SE87C, and they were C2 World Champions – in Spice's case this was his third consecutive title. *LAT*

⬆ **Spa 1000km, 13 September 1987** …and the winner was Raul Boesel. The other occupants of the no.6 TWR Jaguar XJR-8 (TWR-J12C-387) were Martin Brundle and the seat-hopping Johnny Dumfries and between them they helped win the Drivers' Championship for Boesel. This was the proverbial icing on the cake following TWR's Team Championship victory at the Nürburgring. Lammers/Watson finished 2nd, but the race was interrupted by a rain storm and shortened by three laps, which prevented the third Jaguar of Cheever/Nielsen from catching and passing the slowing Brun Porsche 962C of Mass/Larrauri that was occupying 3rd place. *LAT*

➡ **Fuji 1000km, 27 September 1987** Johnny Dumfries was partnered by Raul Boesel again and they finished 2nd at Fuji, 56 seconds behind the Lammers/Watson Jaguar XJR-8. It was the eighth victory for the team who were of course Team Championship winners to match Boesel's drivers' cup. Dumfries was the no.2 with Senna at Lotus in 1986 – never a good idea, the Brazilian having already seen off Derek Warwick because he was too quick. After this he concentrated on sports-car racing bar a brief return to F3000 in 1988. John Colum Crichton-Stuart, 7th Marquess of Bute (born 26 April 1958), styled Earl of Dumfries before 1993 who prefers to be known as John Bute. *LAT*

Fuji 1000km, 27 September 1987 The Jaguar 1/2 at Fuji was perhaps predictable although the cars started 5th and 10th in qualifying, the Porsche 962s and a Nissan R86V (which was fastest) having the advantage of high-boost engines but not in the race. Almost as predictable was the failure of the C1 Nissans and Toyota-powered cars to survive a long-distance race. However, the Toyota Tom's Team Toyota 87C no.36 (Geoff Lees, Alan Jones, Masanori Sekiya) held 1st place for quite a while but retired on lap 100 with an electrical fault. *LAT*

Fuji 1000km, 27 September 1987 This is the Walter Brun 962C (115) of Jochen Mass and Oscar Larrauri that finished 4th having challenged the Lloyd car, which finished 3rd (Baldi/Thackwell), until a broken brake line intruded according to *Autosport*. It was a disenchanted Thackwell's final race having left the Kouros Sauber team post Spa apart from a one-off F3000 drive at Pau in 1988. However, the Kremer Leyton House 962C driven by Volker Weidler/Kris Nissen would have finished 4th but for the still-constant threat of fuel starvation caused by the regulations. It ran out on its final lap at the last corner and although Nissen crossed the line on the ignition switch he was over the 400% rule and the car was non-classified. *LAT*

ENTRANTS

**901 Racing
– Porsche 911 Carrera RSR**
Peter Uria (USA) DAY, SEB
Larry Figaro (USA) DAY, SEB
John Hayes-Harlow (GB) DAY
Kyle Rathbun (USA) DAY, SEB
Jack Refenning (USA) SEB

**ADA Engineering – Gebhardt JC843
Ford Cosworth DFL, ADA 02
(Gebhardt)**
Mike Wilds (GB) JAR, JER
Ian Harrower (GB) JAR, JER, BH
Tiff Needell (GB) BH

Advan Alpha Nova – Porsche 962 C
Kunimitsu Takahashi (J) FUJ
Kenny Acheson (GB) FUJ
Kazuo Mogi (J) FUJ

Bob Akin Motor Racing – Porsche 962
Hans-Joachim Stuck (D) DAY
James Weaver (GB) DAY, SEB
Bob Akin (USA) DAY, SEB
Steve Shelton (USA) SEB

**All American Racers (Dan Gurney)
– Toyota Celica Turbo**
Chris Cord (USA) DAY, SEB
Steve Millen (NZ) DAY
Ricky Rudd (USA) DAY, SEB
Jerrill Rice (USA) DAY, SEB
Juan-Manuel Fangio II (RA) DAY, SEB
Willy T. Ribbs (USA) SEB

**Alpha Cubic Racing Team (Renoma)
– Porsche 962 C**
Naoki Nagasaka (J) FUJ
Chiyomi Totani (J) FUJ
Hitoshi Ogawa (J) FUJ

**Altman Bros Motor Racing
– Porsche 914/6**
Mark Altman (USA) SEB
Gary Altman (USA) SEB
Tim Selby (USA) SEB

**Gaston Andrey Racing
– Alba AR2 Ferrari, Tiga GT286
Ferrari, Alba AR6 Ferrari**
Roger Andrey (USA) DAY, SEB
Angelo Pallavicini (CH) DAY
Uli Bieri (CDN) DAY
David Loring (USA) SEB
Willy Lewis (USA) SEB
Martino Finotto (I) SEB
Ruggero Melgrati (I) SEB
Pietro Silva (I) SEB

**Ares Sports
– Tiga GT286 Buick**
Steve Phillips (USA) SEB
Ron Canizares (USA) SEB (*DND*)
Howard Katz (USA) SEB (*DND*)

**Ark Racing with Arthur Hough
– Ceekar 83J-1 Ford Cosworth DFV**
Lawrie Hickman (GB) BH, SPA
Max Payne (GB) BH (*DND*), SPA
Chris Ashmore (GB) SPA

**Aspen Inn (Dick Greer)/Dick Greer
Racing – Mazda RX-7**
Mike Mees (USA) DAY, SEB
Dick Greer (USA) DAY, SEB
John Finger (USA) DAY, SEB

**Auto Beaurex Motorsport
(Kiyoshi Fukui) – Tom's 86C Toyota**
Kaoru Hoshino (JPN) FUJ
Will Hoy (GB) FUJ

**Automobiles Louis Descartes/
Louis Descartes – ALD 02 BMW,
ALD 03 BMW**
Dominique Lacaud (F) JER, MZA, SIL, LM,
NUR, SPA
Gérard Tremblay (F) JER, MZA, SIL, LM,
BH, NUR, SPA
Louis Descartes (F) JER, LM, NUR, SPA
Jacques Heuclin (F) MZA, LM, SPA
Sylvain Boulay (F) SIL, LM
Michel Lateste (F) LM
Rudi Thomann (F) BH
Jean-Claude Ferrarin (F) BH
Thierry Lecerf (F) SPA
Bruno Sotty (F) SPA

Al Bacon Racing – Mazda RX-7
Al Bacon (USA) DAY, SEB
Rod Millen (NZ) DAY
Bob Reed (USA) DAY, SEB

**Roy Baker Racing/Cosmik/
Roy Baker Racing – Tiga GC286
Ford Cosworth DFL, Tiga GC286
Ford Cosworth BDT**
Costas Los (GR) DAY, JAR, JER
John Schneider (USA) DAY
David Andrews (GB) DAY, SIL, LM, BH,
NUR, SPA, FUJ
Pasquale Barberio (I) JAR, JER
Val Musetti (GB) MZA
Rudi Thomann (F) MZA
Max Cohen-Olivar (MA) SIL, NUR
John Sheldon (GB) SIL
Robert Peters (CDN) SIL, LM
Mike Allison (USA) LM
Mike Kimpton (GB) BH, SPA
Jeremy Rossiter (GB) BH
Chris Ashmore (GB) NUR
Patrick de Radigues (F) FUJ

**Ball Brothers Racing
(Durst/Brockman)
– Spice SC86CL Pontiac**
Steve Durst (USA) DAY, SEB
Mike Brockman (USA) DAY, SEB
Tony Belcher (USA) DAY, SEB
Mark Abel (USA) DAY

**John Bartlett Racing with
Goodmans Sounds – Darbon
DB1/2 Ford Cosworth DFL**
John Bartlett (GB) SIL, NOR (*DND*), SPA
Val Musetti (GB) SIL
Kenneth Leim (S) SIL
Tim Lee-Davey (GB) LM
Raymond Boutinaud (F) LM
Robin Donovan (GB) LM
Rob Wilson (NZ) NOR
Tom Waring (GB) SPA
Giovani Lavaggi (I) SPA

**Roland Bassaler – Sauber
SHS C6 (Thompson-Seger &
Hoffman) BMW**
Jean-François Yvon (F) LM
Herve Bourjade (F) LM
Yves Hervalet (F) LM

**Ba-Tsu Racing
– MCS Guppy Mazda**
Kazuhiko Oda (J) FUJ
Syuuji Fujii (J) FUJ
Ichirou Mizuno (J) FUJ

**Bayside Disposal Racing
(Bruce Leven) – Porsche 962**
Jochen Mass (D) DAY, SEB
Klaus Ludwig (D) DAY
Bobby Rahal (USA) SEB

Karl-Heinz Becker – Lola T600 BMW
Karl-Heinz Becker (D) NOR
Volker Cordlandwehr (D) NOR (*DND*)

Noël Del Bello – Sauber C8 Mercedes
Pierre-Alain Lombardi (CH) LM
Gilles Lempereur (F) LM (*DND*)
Jacques Guillot (F) LM (*DND*)
Jean-Pierre Jaussaud (F) NUR
Noël del Bello (F) NUR
Lucien Rossiaud (F) NUR

**Best House Racing Team
(Le Mans?) – LM-Toyota 07C**
Osamu Nakako (JPN) FUJ
Maurizio Sandro Salo (BR) FUJ

**Bieri Racing (see also Gaston Andrey
Racing) – Alba AR2 Ferrari**
Uli Bieri (CDN) SEB
Angelo Pallavicini (CH) SEB
David Murry (USA) SEB (*DND*)

**Bob's Speed Products (Bob Lee)
– Pontiac Firebird (Python),
Buick Skyhawk**
Ken Bupp (USA) DAY
Guy Church (USA) DAY
Del Russo Taylor (USA) DAY, SEB
Mark Montgomery (USA) SEB
David Fuller (USA) SEB
Bob Lee (USA) SEB
Gary Myers (USA) SEB
Timothy S. Lee (USA) SEB

**British Barn Racing Team
– JTK 62C Ford Cosworth DFL**
Jirou Yoneyama (J) FUJ
Hideshi Matsuda (J) FUJ
Kiyoshi Misaki (J) FUJ

**Britten-Lloyd Racing/Liqui
Moly Equipe – Porsche 962GTI**
Mauro Baldi (I) JAR, JER (*DND*), MZA,
SIL, NOR, BH, NUR, SPA, FUJ
Jonathan Palmer (GB) JAR, JER, SIL, LM,
NOR, NUR, SPA
Bruno Giacomelli (I) MZA
James Weaver (GB) LM
Price Cobb (USA) LM
Johnny Dumfries (GB) BH
Mike Thackwell (NZ) FUJ

**Brooks Racing (Brooks Fryberger)
– Chevrolet Camaro (Protofab)**
Bobby Archer (USA) DAY
Tommy Archer (USA) DAY
Robert Lappalainen (SF) DAY (*DND*), SEB
Leo Franchi (USA) DAY (*DND*)
Kenper Miller (USA) SEB (*DND*)

Henry Brosnaham – Chevrolet Camaro
Henry Brosnaham (USA) SEB
Glen Cross (USA) SEB
Jim Johnson (USA) SEB

Brun Motorsport – Porsche 962 C
Gianfranco Brancatelli (I) DAY, JAR,
JER, MZA
Oscar Larrauri (RA) DAY, JAR, JER, MZA,
SIL, LM, NOR, BH, NUR, SPA, FUJ
Massimo Sigala (I) DAY, JAR, JER, MZA,
SIL, SPA

Frank Jelinski (D) JAR, JER, MZA
Walter Brun (CH) JAR, JER, MZA, SIL,
NOR, BH, NUR, SPA
Jésus Pareja (E) JAR, JER, MZA, SIL, LM,
NOR, BH, NUR, SPA, FUJ
Uwe Schafer (D) SIL, LM, NUR, SPA, FUJ
Michel Trollé (F) LM
Paul Belmondo (F) LM
Pierre de Thoisy (F) LM
Bill Adam (CDN) LM
Scott Goodyear (CDN) LM
Richard Spenard (CDN) LM
Jochen Mass (D) NOR, BH, NUR, SPA, FUJ
Hans-Peter Kaufmann (CH) NUR
Franz Hunkeler (CH) NUR
Manuel Reuter (D) FUJ

**CAR Enterprises (Craig A Rubright)
– Chevrolet Corvette**
Craig Rubright (USA) DAY, SEB
Garrett Jenkins (USA) DAY, SEB
Roy Newsome (USA) DAY, SEB

Carma FF – Alba AR6 Carma
Martino Finotto (I) MZA
Ruggero Melgrati (I) MZA
Pietro Silva (I) MZA

**Paul Canary Racing
– Chevrolet Corvette**
Paul Canary (USA) DAY
Jerry Winston (USA) DAY
Phil Currin (USA) DAY

**Catters Racing Team
– Pontiac Firebird**
Carlos Munoz (USA) SEB
Carlos Catter (USA) SEB
Joe Gonzalez (USA) SEB

**CEE Sport Racing (Dave Ford)
– Tiga GC286 Ford Cosworth BDT**
John Fyda (GB) BH
Laurence Jacobsen (GB) BH, SPA
Stefano Sebastiani (I) BH, SPA
Richard Jones (GB) SPA

**Centurion Auto Transport
– Buick Somerset (Riggins)**
Harold Shafer (USA) SEB
Tom Nehl (USA) SEB
Robert Peters (CDN) SEB

**Certified Brakes Racing (Jim
Downing) – Argo JM19 Mazda**
Jim Downing (USA) DAY
John O'Steen (USA) DAY
John Maffucci (USA) DAY

**Chamberlain Engineering
– Spice SE86C Hart 418T, Spice
SE86C Ford Cosworth DFL**
Nick Adams (GB) MZA, SIL, LM, BH,
NUR, SPA
Costas Los (GR) MZA
Graham Duxbury (ZA) MZA, SIL, LM, FUJ
Richard Jones (GB) LM, BH
John Nicholson (NZ) BH
Jean-Louis Ricci (F) BH, FUJ
Olindo Iacobelli (USA) BH, FUJ
John Fulston (GB) BH
Bob Juggins (GB) NUR
Ian Kahn (GB) SPA, FUJ

Chambers Racing – Mazda RX-7
Dennis Chambers (USA) DAY, SEB
Mike Meyer (USA) DAY
Tom Burdsall (USA) SEB
Chaunce Wallace (USA) SEB

**Guy Church (see also Sentry Bank
Equipment) – Mazda RX-7**
Guy Church (USA) SEB
Tom Hunt (USA) SEB
E.J. Generotti (USA) SEB

**Clayton Cunningham Racing
– Mazda RX-7**
Max Jones (USA) DAY, SEB
Bart Kendall (USA) DAY, SEB
Tom Kendall (USA) DAY, SEB

**Richard Cleare Racing
– March 85G Porsche**
James Weaver (GB) SIL
Andrew Gilbert-Scott (GB) SIL
Richard Cleare (GB) SIL

**Cumberland Valley Racing
– Mazda RX-7**
Doug Mills (CDN) SEB
Richard Oakley (USA) SEB

**Manfred Dahm Racing
– Argo JM19 Porsche**
Peter Fritsch (D) LM, NUR
Teddy Pilette (B) LM (*DND*)
Jean-Paul Libert (B) LM (*DND*)
Kenneth Leim (S) BH, NUR, SPA
Robin Donovan (GB) BH
Dieter Heinzelmann (D) NUR
Patrick de Radigues (B) SPA

**DeAtley Motorsports
– March 85G Chevrolet**
Jerry Brassfield (USA) DAY
Michael Roe (IRL) DAY
John Bauer (USA) DAY
Norton Gaston (USA) DAY

**Diman Racing
– Royale RP40 Porsche**
Mandy Gonzalez (PR) SEB
Manuel Villa (PR) SEB
Luis Gordillo (PR) SEB

**Jim Downing
– Argo JM19 Mazda**
Jim Downing (USA) SEB
John Maffucci (USA) SEB
John O'Steen (USA) SEB

**Dune Motorsport
– Tiga GC287 Austin Rover**
Neil Crang (AUS) MZA, SIL, LM, SPA
Duncan Bain (GB) MZA (*DND*), SIL,
LM, SPA
Jean Krucker (CH) SIL, LM

**Dyson Racing (Rob Dyson)
– Porsche 962**
Price Cobb (USA) DAY, SEB
Rob Dyson (USA) DAY
Vern Schuppan (AUS) DAY, SEB

**Ecurie Ecosse/Swiftair
Ecosse – Ecosse C286 Ford
Cosworth DFL**
David Leslie (GB) JAR, JER, MZA, SIL,
LM, NOR, BH, NUR, SPA, FUJ
Ray Mallock (GB) JAR, JER, MZA, SIL,
LM, NOR, BH, NUR, SPA, FUJ
Mike Wilds (GB) SIL, LM, NOR, BH, NUR,
SPA, FUJ
Johnny Dumfries (GB) SIL
Andy Petery (USA) LM
Les Delano (USA) LM
Marc Duez (B) LM, BH, SPA, FUJ
Win Percy (GB) NOR, NUR

Erie Scientific Racing (Frank Jellinek, Jr) – Badger BB Mazda, Royale RP40 Mazda
John Grooms (USA) DAY, SEB
Tom Bagley (USA) DAY, SEB (*DND*)
Frank Jellinek (USA) DAY, SEB
Augie Pabst (USA) DAY

Essex Racing (Mike Gue) – Tiga GT285 Mazda
Steve Phillips (USA) DAY
Howard Katz (USA) DAY
Ron Nelson (USA) DAY

Finco Racing – Tiga GT285 Mazda
Fin Tomlinson (USA) SEB
Terry Loebel (USA) SEB
Richard Morgan (USA) SEB

A.J. Foyt Enterprises – Porsche 962 (Holbert Fabcar)
A.J. Foyt (USA) DAY, SEB
Al Unser (USA) DAY
Danny Sullivan (USA) DAY, SEB
Hurley Haywood (USA) SEB

From A Racing (Nova Engineering) – Porsche 962 C
Hideki Okada (JPN) FUJ
John Nielsen (DK) FUJ

GP Motorsport/Cosmik (Cosmic) Racing – Tiga GC287 Ford Cosworth DFL
Dudley Wood (GB) SIL, LM, NOR (*DND*), BH, NUR, SPA
Costas Los (GR) SIL, LM, NOR, BH, NUR, SPA, FUJ
Tom Hessert (USA) LM
James Weaver (GB) BH
Chris Hodgetts (GB) FUJ

Gebhardt Racing/Motorsport – Gebhardt JC853 BMW, Gebhardt JC873 Audi
Stanley Dickens (S) DAY
Frank Jelinski (D) DAY
Gary Robinson (USA) DAY, SEB
Greg Hobbs (GB) DAY, SEB
David Hobbs (GB) SEB
Alf Gebhardt (USA) SEB
Günter Gebhardt (D) SPA
Walter Lechner (A) SPA
Ernst Franzmaier (A) SPA

Go Racing (Vince Gimondo) – Oldsmobile Calais
Keith Lawhorn (USA) DAY
Vince Gimondo (USA) DAY
Ken Grostic (USA) DAY

Goral Racing – Porsche 911
Paul Goral (USA) SEB
Rusty Bond (USA) SEB
Larry Figaro (USA) SEB

Graff Racing – Rondeau M482 Ford Cosworth DFL
Jean-Philippe Grand (F) LM
Gaston Rahier (F) LM
Jacques Terrien (F) LM

Grey Eagle Racing – Ford Mustang
Jerry Clinton (USA) SEB
Morris Clement (USA) SEB
Stanton Barrett (USA) SEB

Group 44 (Bob Tullius) – Jaguar XJR-7
Bob Tullius (USA) DAY
Hurley Haywood (USA) DAY
John Morton (USA) DAY

Hugo Gralia – Mazda RX-7
Hugo Gralia (USA) DAY
Dennis Dobkin (USA) DAY
Carlos Padrera (USA) DAY (*DND*)
Secondo Tagliero (USA) DAY (*DND*)

Hendricks Motorsports (Rick Hendrick) – Chevrolet Corvette GTP T710 (Lola)
Sarel van der Merwe (ZA) DAY
Doc Bundy (USA) DAY

Hessert Racing – Tiga GT286 Mazda
Tom Hessert (USA) DAY, SEB (*DND*)
Keith Rinzler (USA) DAY, SEB
Eduardo Dibos (PE) DAY, SEB

Hi-Tech Coating – Chevrolet Camaro (Dillon)
Tom Juckette (USA) DAY, SEB
Bill McDill (USA) DAY, SEB (DND)
Mike Laws (USA) DAY
Richard McDill (USA) SEB

Team Highball (Amos Johnson) – Mazda RX-7
Amos Johnson (USA) DAY, SEB
Dennis Shaw (USA) DAY, SEB
Bob Lazier (USA) DAY

Highlands Racing – Pontiac Firebird
William Boyer (USA) SEB
Steve Roberts (USA) SEB

Holbert Racing – Porsche 962
Chip Robinson (USA) DAY, SEB
Derek Bell (GB) DAY
Al Unser, Jr (USA) DAY
Al Holbert (USA) DAY, SEB

Hotchkis Racing (John Hotchkis Sr) – Porsche 962 (Holbert Fabcar)
John Hotchkis (USA) DAY
Jim Adams (USA) DAY
John Hotchkis, Jr (USA) DAY

Olindo Iacobelli – Royale RP40 Ford Cosworth DFL
Olindo Iacobelli (USA) LM, NUR
Jean-Louis Ricci (F) LM, NUR, SPA
Georges Tessier (F) LM (*DND*), NUR, SPA
Gerard Cardinaud (F) SPA

Italya Sports – Nissan R86V (March-LM) 86G
Anders Olofsson (S) LM
Alain Ferté (F) LM
Patrick Gonin (F) LM

Charles Ivey Racing – Tiga GC287 Porsche
Dudley Wood (GB) JAR, MZA
Mark Newby (GB) JAR, MZA
Ian Taylor (GB) SIL
Pete Lovett (GB) SIL
John Cooper (GB) LM
Tom Dodd-Noble (GB) LM
Maz Cohen-Olivar (MA) LM
John Sheldon (GB) BH, NUR, SPA
Philippe de Henning (F) BH, NUR, SPA

Joest Racing/ Blaupunkt-Joest Racing – Porsche 962C
Sarel van der Merwe (ZA) SEB, LM
'John Winter' (Louis Krages) (D) SEB, MZA, NOR, NUR, SPA, FUJ
Danny Ongais (USA) SEB
Klaus Ludwig (D) MZA, NOR, NUR
Piercarlo Ghinzani (I) MZA
Stanley Dickens (SWE) MZA, NOR
Chip Robinson (USA) LM (*DND*)
David Hobbs (GB) LM (*DND*)
Frank Jelinski (D) LM, NOR, NUR, SPA, FUJ
Hurley Haywood (USA) LM (*DND*)
Stanley Dickens (SWE) LM (*DND*), NUR, SPA
Bob Wollek (F) NOR, NUR, FUJ
Hans-Joachim Stuck (D) BH, NUR, SPA
Derek Bell (GB) BH, NUR, SPA

K & P Racing (Karl Keck) – Chevrolet Corvette (Pratt)
Mark Kennedy (USA) DAY
Karl Keck (USA) DAY
Mark Montgomery (USA) DAY
David Fuller (USA) DAY

Kelmar Racing – Tiga GC85 Ford Cosworth DFL
Maurizio Gellini (I) JER, MZA, SIL, NOR, BH
Ranieri Randaccio (I) JER (*DND*), MZA, SIL, NOR, BH
Vito Veninata (I) JER (*DND*), MZA, SPA
Pasquale Barberio (I) SIL, BH, SPA

Kouros Mercedes/Formel Rennsportclub (Peter Sauber) – Sauber C9 Mercedes
Mike Thackwell (NZ) SIL, LM, NOR, NUR, SPA
Henri Pescarolo (F) SIL, LM, NUR
Hideli Okada (J) LM (*DND*)
Johnny Dumfries (GB) LM, NUR
Chip Ganassi (USA) LM
Manuel Reuter (D) NOR (*DND*)
Jean-Louis Schlesser (F) SPA

Kremer Porsche Racing/Leyton House-Kremer Racing – Porsche 962 C (Thompson)
Volker Weidler (D) JAR, JER, SIL, LM (*DND*), NOR, BH, NUR, SPA, FUJ
Kris Nissen (DK) JAR, JER, SIL, LM, NOR, BH, NUR, SPA, FUJ
Emilio de Villota (E) JAR, JER
Paco Romero (E) JAR, JER
Allen Berg (CDN) SIL
Kunimitsu Takahashi (JPN) LM (*DND*)
George Fouché (ZA) LM, FUJ
Franz Konrad (A) LM, FUJ
Wayne Taylor (ZA) LM

Walter Lechner Racing – Porsche 962 C (Thompson)
Walter Lechner (A) NOR
Ernst Franzmaier (A) NOR (*DND*)

Lucas Truck Service – Oldsmobile Calais
Scott Gaylord (USA) SEB
Luis Albiza (USA) SEB
Kent Stover (USA) SEB (*DND*)

Team Lucky Strike Schance/Schance Racing – Argo JM19 B Zakspeed
Will Hoy (GB) JAR, JER, MZA, LM (*DND*), NOR, BH, NUR, SPA

Martin Schanche (N) JAR, JER, MZA, LM, NOR, BH, NUR, SPA
Robin Smith (GB) LM (*DND*)

MSB Racing – Argo JM19 Mazda
Dave Cowart (USA) DAY
Kenper Miller (USA) DAY
Jim Fowells (USA) DAY

Mandeville Auto Tech – Mazda RX-7
Roger Mandeville (USA) DAY, SEB
Kelly Marsh (USA) DAY, SEB
Danny Smith (USA) DAY
Don Marsh (USA) SEB (*DND*)

Mazdaspeed – Mazda 757
Yoshimi Katayama (J) LM, FUJ
Youjirou Terada (J) LM, FUJ
Takashi Yorino (J) LM, FUJ
David Kennedy (IRL) LM, FUJ
Mark Galvin (IRL) LM
Pierre Dieudonné (B) LM, FUJ

Morrison- Cook Motorsport (Tommy Morrison) – Chevrolet Corvette
Tommy Morrison (USA) DAY, SEB
Richard Ceppos (USA) DAY
Don Knowles (USA) DAY, SEB
Stu Hayner (USA) DAY, SEB
John Heinricy (USA) DAY, SEB
Bob McConnell (USA) DAY, SEB
Bill Adam (CDN) DAY
Bobby Carradine (USA) DAY (*DND*), SEB

Motion Promotions – Argo JM16 Buick
George Petrilak (USA) DAY, SEB
Graham Duxbury (ZA) DAY
Bill Jacobson (USA) DAY
Helmut Silberberger (USA) DAY (*DND*)
Dave Rosenberg (USA) SEB
Bruce MacInnes (USA) SEB

Murray Racing – Pontiac Fiero (Spice) Pontiac
Dick Murray (USA) SEB
Terry Visger (USA) SEB

Mussato Action Car (Giannini Mussato) – Lancia LC2/85
Bruno Giacomelli (I) NOR
Franz Konrad (A) NOR (*DND*)

Nissan Motorsports – R87E (March LM) 87G
Kazuyoshi Hoshino (J) LM, FUJ
Kenji Takahashi (J) LM, FUJ
Keiji Matsumoto (J) LM
Masahiro Hasemi (J) LM, FUJ
Aguri Suzuki (J) LM, FUJ (*DND*)
Takao Wada (J) LM
Dave Scott (GB) FUJ

OMR Engines (Hoyt Overbagh) – Chevrolet Camaro (Stock Car Products)
Gene Felton (USA) DAY, SEB
Oma Kimbrough (USA) DAY
Hoyt Overbagh (USA) DAY
Lee Perkinson (USA) DAY, SEB (*DND*)
Matt Mnich (USA) SEB

Oudet Racing – Tiga GC85 Ford Cosworth DFL
Jean-Claude Justice (F) SIL
Bruno Sotty (F) SIL
Patrick Oudet (F) SIL

Peerless/Hendrick (Rick Hendrick) – Chevrolet Camaro (Peerless)
Jack Baldwin (USA) DAY, SEB
Eppie Wietzes (CDN) DAY, SEB

Performance Technology – Argo JM19 Buick
Brent O'Neill (USA) SEB
John Lloyd (USA) SEB

Person's Racing Team (Nissan Motorsports) – Nissan R86V (March LM)
Takao Wada (J) FUJ
Anders Olofsson (S) FUJ

Piper Capon Automotive – Royale RP40 Ford Cosworth
Richard Piper (GB) BH
Mike Catlow (GB) BH (*DND*)

Primagaz Competition (Yves Courage) – Cougar C20 Porsche, Porsche 962 C
Hervé Regout (B) MZA, SIL, LM
Joël Gouhier (F) MZA
Yves Courage (F) SIL, LM
Pierre-Henri Raphanel (F) LM
Jürgen Lässig (D) LM, NOR, NUR, SPA
Pierre Yver (F) LM, NOR, SPA
Bernard de Dryver (B) LM
Cathy Muller (F) NUR
Bernard de Dryver (B) NUR, SPA

Primus Motorsport – Porsche 962 (Holbert Fabcar)
Brian Redman (GB) DAY, SEB
Chris Kneifel (USA) DAY, SEB
Elliot Forbes-Robinson (USA) DAY, SEB

Protofab Racing – Chevrolet Camaro
Wally Dallenbach, Jr. (USA) DAY
John Jones (CDN) DAY
Tommy Riggins (USA) DAY, SEB
Greg Pickett (USA) DAY, SEB
Darrell Waltrip (USA) DAY
Terry Labonte (USA) DAY

Quality Motorsports – Chevrolet Corvette
Dave Heinz (USA) SEB
Bob Young (USA) SEB

RM Racing – Royale RP40 Mazda
Charles Morgan (USA) DAY, SEB
Chris Gennone (USA) DAY
Jim Rothbarth (USA) DAY, SEB

Raintree Corporation – Ford Mustang (Roush)
Ken Johnson (USA) DAY
Maurice Hassey (USA) DAY
Lanny Hester (USA) DAY

Road Circuit Tech (Les Delano) – Buick Somerset
Andy Petery (USA) DAY
Les Delano (USA) DAY
Craig Carter (USA) DAY

Rothmans Porsche/Porsche AG/ Rothmans Porsche Vern Schuppan – Porsche 962 C Porsche 961
Hans-Joachim Stuck (D) JAR, JER, MZA, SIL, LM, NOR
Derek Bell (GB) JAR, JER, MZA, SIL, LM, NOR, FUJ

Jochen Mass (D) JER, MZA, SIL, LM (*DND*)
Bob Wollek (F) JER, MZA, SIL, LM
Al Holbert (USA) LM
Vern Schuppan (AUS) LM (*DND*)
Claude Haldi (CH) LM
Kees Nierop (CDN) LM
René Metge (F) LM
Geoff Brabham (AUS) FUJ

Roush Racing – Ford Mustang GTP, Ford Mustang
Scott Pruett (USA) DAY, SEB
Pete Halsmer (USA) DAY, SEB
Tom Gloy (USA) DAY, SEB
Bill Elliot (USA) DAY
Lyn St James (USA) DAY, SEB
Scott Pruett (USA) DAY
Deborah Gregg (USA) DAY
Bobby Akin, Jr (USA) DAY, SEB
Scott Goodyear (CDN) DAY
Bruce Jenner (USA) DAY, SEB
Todd Morici (USA) DAY
Gary Baker (USA) DAY

SP Racing (Gary Auberlen) – Porsche 911
Bill Auberlen (USA) DAY, SEB
Karl Durkheimer (USA) DAY, SEB
Dieter Oest (USA) DAY
Gary Auberlen (USA) DAY (*DND*), SEB

S Squared Engineering – Porsche 911 Carrera RSR
Charles Slater (USA) DAY, SEB
Ernie Senator (USA) DAY
Dave Duttinger (USA) DAY, SEB
Rudy Bartling (CDN) SEB

SARD (Shin Kato) – Sard MC87A Toyota
Tsunehisa Asai (J) FUJ
David Sears (GB) FUJ
Syuuroku Sasaki (J) FUJ

Sasco Motorsports – Pontiac Firebird (Watson)
Tom Gaffney (USA) DAY
Paul Reisman (USA) DAY
Richard Stone (USA) DAY
Bob Hebert (USA) DAY

Schader Racing – Mazda RX-7
Steve DePoyster (USA) DAY, SEB
Mike Jocelyn (USA) DAY, SEB
Jim Kurz (USA) DAY, SEB
Bob Schader (USA) DAY, SEB

Scott Schubot/S & L Racing – Tiga GT285 Mazda
Jim Brown (USA) DAY
Scott Schubot (USA) DAY, SEB
Linda Ludemann (USA) DAY, SEB
Lance Jones (USA) SEB

Secateva – WM P86 Peugeot
Jean-Daniel Raulet (F) LM Pascal Pessiot (F) LM (*DND*)
François Migault (F) LM (*DND*) /Philippe Gache (F) LM (*DND*)
Dominique Delestre (F) LM (*DND*)
Roger Dorchy (F) LM

Sentry Bank Equipment (Ken Bupp) – Chevrolet Camaro (Frings)
Ken Bupp (USA) SEB
Guy Church (USA) SEB
Del Russo Taylor (USA) SEB

Shafer Racing – Chevrolet Camaro (Banjo's Performance)
Craig Shafer (USA) SEB
Joe Maloy (USA) SEB
George Shafer (USA) SEB

Shizumatsu Racing – Mazda 737C
Tetsuji Shiratori (J) FUJ
Kaneyuki Okamoto (J) FUJ

Silk Cut Jaguar – Jaguar XJR-8
Eddie Cheever (USA) JAR, JER, SIL, LM, NOR, NUR, SPA
Raul Boesel (BR) JAR, JER, MZA, SIL, LM, NOR, BH, NUR, SPA, FUJ
Jan Lammers (NL) JAR, JER, MZA, SIL, LM, NOR, BH, NUR, SPA, FUJ
John Watson (GB) JAR, JER, MZA, SIL, LM, NOR (*DND*), BH, NUR, SPA, FUJ
John Nielson (DK) MZA, SIL, LM, BH, SPA
Martin Brundle (GB) SIL, LM, SPA
Win Percy (GB) LM
Johnny Dumfries (GB) SPA, FUJ

Simms/Romano – Mazda RX-7
Vance Swifts (CDN) DAY, SEB
John Drew (USA) DAY, SEB
Dean Hall (USA) DAY
Paul Romano (USA) DAY, SEB

Skoal Bandit (Buz McCall) – Chevrolet Camaro (Timmons)
Buz McCall (USA) DAY, SEB
Walt Bohren (USA) DAY, SEB
Paul Dallenbach (USA) DAY, SEB

Spice Engineering/AT&T, Spice Engineering – Spice SE86CL Pontiac, Spice SE86C Ford Cosworth DFL, Spice SE87C Ford Cosworth DFL
Bob Earl (USA) DAY
Don Bell (USA) DAY, SEB
Jeff Kline (USA) DAY, SEB
Fermin Velez (E) JAR, JER, MZA, SIL, LM, NOR, BH, NUR, SPA, FUJ
Gordon Spice (GB) JAR, JER, MZA, SIL, LM, NOR, BH, NUR, SPA, FUJ
Philippe de Henning (F) LM
Ray Bellm (GB) NOR
Nick Adams (GB) NOR

Sunrise Racing – Chevrolet Camaro
Jeff Loving (USA) SEB
Richard Small (USA) SEB
Jan Goodman (USA) SEB (*DND*)

Team Tiga Ford Denmark – Tiga GC287 Ford Cosworth BDT
Thorkild Thyrring (DK) JAR, JER, MZA, LM, NOR, BH, NUR, SPA, FUJ
Leif Lindström (S) JAR, JER, MZA
Ian Harrower (GB) LM
John Sheldon (GB) LM, NOR
Val Musetti (GB) BH
Peter Elgaard (DK) NUR, SPA, FUJ

Techno Racing (Luigi Taverna) – Alba AR3 Ford Cosworth DFL
Jean-Pierre Frey (CH) JER, BH
Oscar Berselli (I) JER, MZA
Luigi Taverna (I) JER, MZA, LM, BH
Pasquale Barberio (I) MZA
Patrick Trucco (F) LM
Evan Clements (GB) LM
Giovanni Lavaggi (I) BH

Jose Thibault – Chevron B36 ROC Talbot
José Thibault (F) LM
André Heinrich (F) LM

Tiga Team (Tim Lee-Davey) – Tiga GC87 Ford Cosworth DFL Turbo
Tim Lee-Davey (GB) NUR, SPA, FUJ
Evan Clements (GB) NUT
Val Musetti (GB) SPA
Tetsua Oota (JPN) FUJ

Toyota Team Tom's – Toyota 87C Dome
Alan Jones (AUS) LM, FUJ
Eje Elgh (S) LM (*DND*), FUJ
Geoff Lees (GB) LM (*DND*), FUJ
Tiff Needell (GB) LM
Masanori Sekiya (J) LM, FUJ
Kaoru Hoshino (J) LM
Ross Cheever (USA) FUJ (*DND*)

Trust Engineering – Porsche 962 C
Vern Schuppan (AUS) FUJ
Keiichi Suzuki (J) FUJ
James Weaver (GB) FUJ

Turbo Concepts – Porsche 911
Miguel Morejon (C) SEB
Herman Galeano (USA) SEB

Uniroyal Goodrich/Busby Racing – Porsche 962
Bob Wollek (F) DAY, SEB
Jim Busby (USA) DAY, SEB
Darin Brassfield (USA) DAY, SEB

URD Junior Team – URD C81/2 BMW
Rudi Seher (D) JAR, JER, MZA, SIL, NOR, BH, NUR
Hellmut Mundas (D) JAR, JER, MZA, SIL, NOR, BH, NUR, FUJ
Dieter Heinzelmann (D) JER, MZA
Rudi Thomann (F) SIL
Sean Walker (GB) BH
Robin Smith (GB) FUJ (*DND*)

Van Every Racing (Lance Van Every) – Chevrolet Camaro (Riggins)
Lance Van Every (USA) DAY
Rusty Bond (USA) DAY
Ash Tisdelle (USA) DAY

Vetir Racing – Tiga GC85 Ford Cosworth DFL
Jean-Claude Justice (F) LM
Bruno Sotty (F) LM
Patrick Oudet (F) LM

Victor-Dauer Racing/Dauer Racing – Porsche 962 C
Jochen Dauer (D) NOR, NUR
Johnny Dumfries (GB) NOR
Harold Grohs (D) NUR

Greg Walker Racing (Jack Wilson) – Chevrolet Corvette
Nort Northam (USA) DAY
Scott Lagasse (USA) DAY
Dennis Krueger (USA) DAY

Chaunce Wallace Racing – Mazda RX-7
Richard Oakley (USA) DAY
Chaunce Wallace (USA) DAY
Doug Mills (CDN) DAY

Western Chemical (Auriga Racing) – Chevrolet Camarao (Riggins)
Robert Peters (CDN) DAY
Tom Nehl (USA) DAY
Kent Painter (USA) DAY

Dave White Racing – Porsche 944 Turbo
Arthur Pilla (USA) SEB
Dave White (USA) SEB (*DND*)
George Drolsom (USA) (*DND*)

White Allen Porsche (John Higgins)/MMG White Allen – Fabcar CL Porsche
Howard Cherry (USA) DAY, SEB
John Higgins (USA) DAY, SEB
James King (USA) DAY
Chip Mead (USA) DAY, SEB
Tom Pumpelly (USA) DAY
Scott Overbey (USA) DAY, SEB
Tim McAdam (USA) DAY (*DND*), SEB
Thomas Schwietz (USA) DAY (*DND*)
Charles Monk (CDN) SEB

Whitehall Rocketsports (Paul Gentilozzi) – Oldsmobile Toronado (Rocketsports), Alba AR5 Oldsmobile
Paul Gentilozzi (USA) DAY, SEB
Irv Hoerr (USA) DAY (*DND*), SEB
Ted Boody (USA) DAY (*DND*), SEB
Paul Lewis (USA) DAY, SEB
Skeeter McKitterick (USA) DAY (*DND*), SEB
Tom Winters (USA) DAY (*DND*), SEB

Bill Wink Racing – Chevrolet Camaro
Bill Wink (USA) DAY
Bill Martin (USA) SEB
Don Erickson (USA) SEB
Tim Evans (USA) SEB

Gary Wonzer Racing – Lola T616 Mazda
Ron Case (USA) SEB
Bruce Dewey (USA) SEB
Buzz Cason (USA) SEB
Nort Northam (USA) SEB

Zakspeed (Zakowski/Moretti) – Ford Mustang Probe
Whitney Ganz (USA) DAY
David Hobbs (GB) DAY
Gianpiero Moretti (I) DAY

RESULTS

Daytona 24 Hours, 1/2 February, USA
Started 69, finished 29
1st Robinson (USA)/Bell (GB)/Al Unser, Jr (USA)/Holbert Porsche 962
2nd Larrauri (RA)/Brancatelli (I)/Sigala (I) Porsche 962
3rd Cobb (USA)/Dyson (USA)/Schuppan (AUS) Porsche 962

Sebring 12 Hours, 21 March USA
Started 74, finished 38
1st Mass (D)/Rahal (USA) Porsche 962
2nd Robinson (USA)/Holbert (USA) Porsche 962
3rd Redman (GB)/Kneifel (USA)/Forbes-Robinson (USA) Porsche 962

Jarama Supersprint, 22 March, Spain. Started 17, finished 14
1st Lammers (NL)/Watson (GB) Jaguar XJR-8
2nd Stuck (D)/Bell (GB) Porsche 962C
3rd Cheever (USA)/Boesel (BR) Jaguar XJR-8

Jerez 1000km, 29 March, Spain Started 20, finished 9
1st Cheever (USA)/Boesel (BR) Jaguar XJR-8
2nd Nissen (DK)/Weidler (D) Porsche 962C
3rd Stuck (D)/Bell (GB) Porsche 962C

Monza 1000km, 12 April, Italy Started 24, finished 12
1st Lammers (NL)/Watson (GB) Jaguar XJR-8
2nd Stuck (D)/Bell (GB) Porsche 962C
3rd Jelinski (D)/Pareja-Mayo (E)/Larrauri (RA) Porsche 962C

Silverstone 1000km, 10 May, Great Britain. Started 26, finished 16
1st Cheever (USA)/Boesel (BR) Jaguar XJR-8
2nd Lammers (NL)/Watson (GB) Jaguar XJR-8
3rd Stuck (D)/Bell (GB) Porsche 962C

Le Mans 24 Hours, 13/14 June, France. Started 48, finished 14
1st Stuck (D)/Bell (GB) Holbert (USA) Porsche 962C
2nd Lässig (D)/Yver (F)/de Dryver (B) Porsche 962C
3rd Raphanel (F)/Regout(F)/Courage (F) Cougar-Porsche C20

Nuremberg 200 miles, 28 June, Germany. Started 27, finished 13
1st Baldi (I)/Palmer (GB) Porsche 962GTI
2nd Jelinski (D)/Ludwig (D) Porsche 962C
3rd Larrauri (RA)/Mass (D) Porsche 962C

Brands Hatch 1000km, 26 July, Great Britain. Started 27, finished 18
1st Boesel (BR)/Nielson (DK) Jaguar XJR-8
2nd Baldi (I)/Dumfries (GB) Porsche 962GTI
3rd Lammers (NL)/Watson (GB) Jaguar XJR-8

Nürburgring 1000km, 30 August, Germany. Started 29, finished 20
1st Cheever (USA)/Boesel (BR) Jaguar XJR-8
2nd Bell (GB)/Stuck (D) Porsche 962C
3rd Mass (D)/Larrauri (RA) Porsche 962C

Spa 1000km, 13 September, Belgium Started 32, finished 22
1st Brundell (GB)/Dumfries (GB)/Boesel (BR) Jaguar XJR-8
2nd Lammers (NL)/Watson (GB) Jaguar XJR-8
3rd Mass (D)/Larrauri (RA) Porsche 962C

Fuji 1000km, 27 September, Japan Started 40, finished 31
1st Lammers (NL)/Watson (GB) Jaguar XJR-8
2nd Boesel (BR)/Dumfries (GB) Jaguar XJR-8
3rd Baldi (I)/Thackwell (NZ) Porsche 962GTI

1988

TWR CELEBRATES WHILST THE REST DO THEIR BEST

Once again there was a fuel issue to hand, this time at Monza, already regarded with some suspicion by the teams. Two weeks before the race the organisers told the teams that they could not afford the latest FISA diktat that demanded a minimum 98.7 RON and had persuaded FISA to accept a 97 RON instead.

This caused considerable consternation in the ranks, especially those with turbo engines and the inconvenient fact that any change in fuel was to be of equal quality, not inferior. So the teams arranged for a tanker with the proper stuff to come to Monza from West Germany. Predictably the organisers had the tanker removed but they were forced to back down, the tanker returned and its contents were accepted as the official fuel for the race.

The season evolved into another British versus German cars. This time it was the Sauber Mercedes C9, and TWR Jaguar won six races whilst Sauber Mercedes managed five, which gave TWR the Teams' Championship and Martin Brundle the Drivers' Championship. Most importantly Jaguars finished 1st, 4th and 16th at Le Mans where they entered five cars and multiple drivers, and they had a new car, the XJR-9, still based upon its predecessors with a low-drag version for Le Mans. It now gave 750bhp and over 600lb ft of torque at 5,500rpm.

Sauber were impressive and they finished 2nd in the Teams' Championship albeit 172 points behind the Walkinshaw cars. They were now Daimler-Benz run and more reliable, their drivers were Jean-Louis Schlesser, Mauro Baldi, Jochen Mass, James Weaver, Stefan Johansson, Kenny Acheson, Philippe Streif and Klaus Niedzwiedz. However, both cars were withdrawn at Le Mans due to a rear Michelin tyre failure at the Mulsanne 'kink' during Wednesday practice, which shattered the rear bodywork. This response was perhaps understandable given the 1955 catastrophe.

Porsche, now almost entirely dependent upon the customer teams, finished 3rd courtesy of Reinhold Joest whilst the factory 962s managed just 75 points and 6th in the championship table, helped by their 2nd and 6th places at Le Mans.

In the C2 class it was Spice winning again in both championships, Gordon Spice sharing the drivers' cup with long-time teammate Ray Bellm. The team had ten 1st places plus a 2nd place, which gave them 390 points. With Ecurie Ecosse departed from C2, the runner-up was Chamberlain Engineering whose Spice SE286C Hart turbo driven by a variety of racers had five DNFs, one 2nd, three 3rds, one 4th and one 5th (185 points). Kelmar Racing finished 3rd on 154 points, the rest far back.

Back in the USA Jaguar arrived at Daytona with their new IMSA-spec XJR-9 and won a race of attrition (Brundle/Boesel/Nielsen) with Cheever/Watson/Dumfries 3rd split by Busby's BF Goodrich Porsche 962 (Wollek/Baldi/Redman).

Forty-seven days later at Sebring Jaguar had one of those days and Hans-Joachim Stuck and Klaus Ludwig in the Bayside Disposal Porsche 962 won by a country mile ahead of John Winter, Frank Jelinski and Paolo Barilla in the Joest 962. The Dyson 962 for Price Cobb/James Weaver finished 3rd.

Jarama 360km, 13 March 1988 Two Spices: the yellow and black GP Motorsport 1987 SE87C Ford Cosworth DFL (003) of Costas Los/Philippe de Henning and the Spice Engineering 1988 SE88C (001) of Thorkild Thyrring/Almo Coppelli. The former retired and the latter finished 11th overall and 3rd in the C2 class. Los had a sore neck from a road accident and a slower co-driver who retired the car on lap 89 with no fuel pressure whilst the Spice car, which was fastest C2 qualifier, had lost fourth gear and later had only third to engage. Unlike the multi-sponsorship on the works car, the GP Motorsport car just had Dianetica, a theory of L. Ron Hubbard who proposed that the human mind is subdivided into three parts: the conscious 'analytical mind', the subconscious 'reactive mind' and the 'somatic mind'. *GPL*

↑ **Daytona 24 Hours, 30/31 January 1988** TWR had opened an American operation run by Tony Dowe, and three new IMSA-specification Jaguar XJR-9s came to Daytona, with 6-litre engines, which were the largest allowed. They were driven by Martin Brundle, Raul Boesel, John Nielsen no.60, Davy Jones, Danny Sullivan, Jan Lammers no.61 and Eddie Cheever, John Watson, Johnny Dumfries no.66. There were eight Porsche 962s, some of them faster than the Jaguars, but eventually wear and tear and contact slowed them down. The no.60 car won ahead of the Busby Porsche 962C (Bob Wollek, Mauro Baldi, Brian Redman) with the no.66 Jaguar 3rd despite an engine problem and being shunted up the rear by Redman. The no.61 Jaguar retired on lap 512 with zero oil pressure. *LAT*

← **Daytona 24 Hours, 30/31 January 1988** ADA Engineering entered their ADA 03 (Ford Cosworth DFV) with four drivers: Wayne Taylor (ZA), Ian Harrower (GB), Ian Flux (GB) and Swede Stanley Dickens. It was sponsored by Virgin Airlines and Swiftsure Yachts and it was very fast, qualifying 15th overall (or 16th according to *Autosport*), but because it was underweight for Camel Lights it raced in the GTP class. Sadly, the car had a complete electrical failure and retired after 88 laps. *LAT*

Daytona 24 Hours, 30/31 January 1988 From left to right: Martin Brundle in 'civvies', a part-hidden Raul Boesel and a large Dane, John Nielsen, celebrate their victory at Daytona with the Castrol Jaguar crew behind them. Personally I prefer the Camel GT lady to Nielsen's left. *LAT*

Jerez 800km, 6 March 1988 No 1000km nonsense this year; the Jerez race was now 800km but had only 23 starters, albeit three more than in 1987. The most important thing was the official Mercedes Sauber C9/88 with sponsorship from their subsidiary AEG Olympia. Driven by Jean-Louis Schlesser, Mauro Baldi and Jochen Mass it had over 800bhp and 700lb ft of torque for qualifying and Schlesser's lap was 2 seconds faster than Brundle's effort in the TWR Jaguar XJR-9. In the race the Jaguars were more competitive but ultimately the Sauber won by 24 seconds from the surviving Watson/Nielsen/Wallace XJR-9. *LAT*

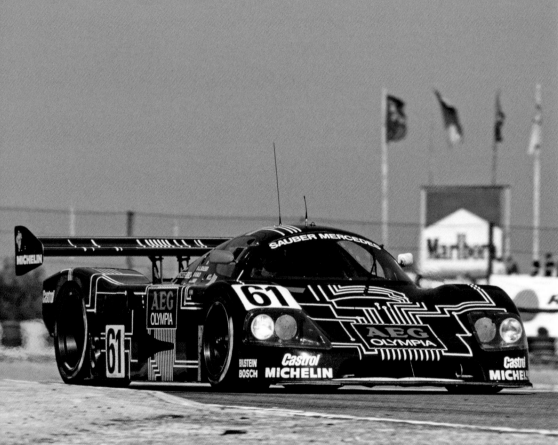

Jerez 800km, 6 March 1988 Behind the Sauber/Jaguar domination the Porsche brigade were outpaced and outraced. Much was expected for the latest iteration of the Richard Lloyd honeycomb chassis 962C GTi (200) driven by James Weaver and Derek Bell. Unfortunately, in first practice it shed a crankcase bolt and the engine was replaced, but this was apparently not as potent as the original, then a Motronics problem intruded and finally a puncture, all of which helped to keep them only 7th fastest. They finished 4th in the race after losing the left-hand door and failing to match the 3rd-placed Joest 962C driven by Ludwig/Wollek. *LAT*

Jarama 360km, 13 March 1988 It was an about face at Jarama with Jaguar beating the Sauber Mercedes 9/88 by a similar margin as at Jerez. The cars were more evenly matched although Schlesser was fastest again in practice but only by five-tenths, in a T-car which nobody protested. To begin with Schlesser pulled away but he had to back off due to his fuel consumption and the Jaguars gradually caught him up. The Sauber lost any chance of winning because its Michelin tyres were not as robust as the more resilient Dunlops on the Jaguars, forcing a second tyre change. So Schlesser/Baldi finished 2nd with the Nielsen/Watson Jaguar 3rd two laps behind. *LAT*

Jarama 360km, 13 March 1988 The first Porsche home was Walter Brun's Lui 962C (002BM) driven by Manuel Reuter and Uwe Schäfer (10 July 1963 – 11 May 2004). They finished 4th two laps behind the winning car. *Lui* (Him in English) was a French adult entertainment magazine created in November 1963 that passed through many different hands and was eventually taken over by Jean-Yves Le Fur in 2013. *LAT*

Sebring 12 Hours, 19 March 1988 An untidy grid not yet lined up properly with remnants of the rain that had started on Friday night and carried on into Saturday morning. Look at the road [*sic*] surface that must have been fun in a 600bhp plus car. *LAT*

← **Sebring 12 Hours, 19 March 1988** Chip Robinson in Al Holbert's Porsche 962 (HR1) was on pole at Sebring but it retired at 142 laps. Instead Bruce Leven's Bayside Disposal Porsche 962 driven by Stuck/Ludwig won, because high entry speed into corners and late braking allied to hard tyres meant that the transmission was not stressed unlike others and they were nine laps ahead of the Joest Racing 962 (116M). This was driven by 'John Winter' (Louis Krages), Frank Jelinski and Paolo Barilla and qualified 9th, benefiting from the high attrition rate. They were compromised by a first-lap tyre change and later a misfire. Here it goes inside of the Protofab Racing Corvette of Tommy Riggins and Greg Pickett, which retired although their teammates (Wally Dallenbach, Jr/John Jones) finished 6th overall and 1st in the GTO class. TWR entered two XJR-9 D Jaguars for Brundle/Boesel/Nielsen, which retired with engine trouble, and Lammers/Jones/Danny Sullivan/Nielsen which finished 7th despite a damaged undertray and a transmission change that cost them 55 minutes. *LAT*

← **Monza 1000km, 10 April 1988** Jean-Lous Schlesser posted fastest qualifying time for the third time in a row despite some tyre problems. He was partnered by Mauro Baldi and Jochen Mass and they made the mistake of racing the Joest Porsches to the detriment of the Sauber's fuel allowance. On the fifth lap Ludwig in the Joest 962C (129) passed Schlesser to lead the race but by lap 15 these two and the Brun Porsche of Larrauri were together. Ultimately the Porsches were also victims of the fuel restrictions, leaving the Sauber Mercedes C9/88 (87-C9-02) to finish 2nd whilst the Ludwig/Wollek Porsche finished 5th. Schlesser leads the pack at the first chicane. *LAT*

⮕ Monza 1000km, 10 April 1988 Gianni Mussato entered the modified ex-works Lancia LC2/88 (0003B) for Andrea de Cesaris and Christian Danner, but it was fickle and suffered from assorted problems including a down-on-power engine, understeer and electrical issues pre-race. Nevertheless, they qualified a respectable 10th but lasted just 11 laps before the turbo blew. Later the car was sold on to Jean-Pierre Frey. *LAT*

⮕ Monza 1000km, 10 April 1988 Aside from the Lucky Strike car there was another Argo JM19C Ford Cosworth DFL at Monza, the pretty blue PC Automotive (Richard Piper) no.191 for Olindo Iacobelli/Martin Birrane/ Richard Piper. It was way off the front runners in C2 and retired on lap 24 with (supposedly) a split fuel tank, leaving Birrane and Piper without a drive. C2 was inevitably the domain of Gordon Spice's Spice SC88C Ford Cosworth DFL, which won the class but others were equally fast albeit not so reliable. The second team Spice car (Coppelli/ Thyrring), the Schanche/ Hoy Argo JM19C and the Adams/Duxbury Chamberlain Engineering Spice SE87C Hart turbo were all a threat until they retired or were too far behind to challenge further. *LAT*

Monza 1000km, 10 April 1988
The Brun Motorsport Porsche 962C (115) was driven to the max by Argentinian Oscar Larrauri aka 'Popi' and Massimo Sigala to take 3rd place. This might be 'Popi' at one of the chicanes and aggressive doesn't really do it justice. The other Brun car (Reuter/Pareja) retired on lap 143 after being hit by Larrauri – whoops. *LAT*

Monza 1000km, 10 April 1988 TWR entered two XJR-9s at Monza for Martin Brundle/Eddie Cheever and Jan Lammers/Johnny Dumfries. Brundle and Lammers set identical lap times for 4th and 5th on the grid and played the waiting game whilst the German cars went all out with dire consequences. The first named won by a lap but Dumfries lost control and ended up in a gravel trap at the Parabolica on lap 113, having done something similar at Jarama. This is Cheever in the XJR-9 (TWR -J12C-588) on the way to victory. *LAT*

→ **Silverstone 1000km, 8 May 1988** A second Sauber C9 appeared at Silverstone, the no.62 (88-C9-030) for Mauro Baldi/James Weaver with Schlesser/Mass in the older car. They qualified 1st and 3rd respectively. On the first lap Cheever and Schlesser were side by side but the Sauber kept its position. On lap 7 Schlesser was held up by a backmarker and Cheever took the lead only for Baldi to usurp him. Here we see Cheever and Baldi caressing each other. This carried on with Cheever slipping back to 3rd whilst the Franco/Italian duo duelled on until Schlesser pitted for fuel. Ultimately the Saubers finished 2nd (no.61) and 3rd (no.62), once again handicapped by the contrived fuel limitations, something that did not hamper the Jaguars so much. Ironically the second Jaguar (Lammers/Dumfries), which had been driven sensibly, ran out of fuel. *LAT*

→ **Silverstone 1000km, 8 May 1988** Derek Bell and Tiff Needell drove the Richard Lloyd Racing honeycomb chassis 962C GTi (200) in its latest livery at Silverstone. Needell set 5th fastest time in qualifying and an impressive Bell overtook Wollek in the Blaupunkt Joest Wollek/Streiff/Hobbs 962C on lap 20. When the Lammers/Dumfries Jaguar ran out of fuel on lap 204, Bell/Needell inherited 4th place. However, they were disqualified for having an oversized fuel tank. This had been checked at Jerez without comment. There was also a fault with the fuel-delivery meter at Silverstone, which was reading about 5% under. So the Blaupunkt Joest 962C (129) Wollek, Streiff and Hobbs inherited 4th place having qualified 4th. The other Joest 962C for Frank Jelinski/Stanley Dickens and 'John Winter' (Louis Krages) finished 5th. *GPL*

Silverstone 1000km, 8 May 1988 Here is the attractive Mazdaspeed Mazda 767 (001) of David Kennedy, Yoshimi Katayama and Yojiro Terada. Its chassis body structure was designed by Nigel Stroud (he of the RLR Porsche clones) and built at Mazdaspeed rather than in Japan. It had a four-rotor engine developing 570bhp and the car qualified 9th and finished 9th although it would have been in the first six but for a delay caused by a fuel-pump problem. *LAT*

Silverstone 1000km, 8 May 1988 In the doldrums was Jean-Pierre Frey (Dollop Racing) in the ex-Mussato Lancia LC2/88, co-driven by Nicola Marozzo who qualified the car in 14th place but it spun off on lap 28 and retired. Alongside is the Olmas GTL200 built by the Olmas Aluminium Company in Turin for Luigi Taverna to replace his Alba AR3 which burnt out in 1987. It had a Kevlar/carbon-fibre monocoque with composite bodywork and a Ford Cosworth DFV or DFL engine and non-started at Monza. At Silverstone it finished 16th and last, and at Le Mans it non-started again after which it disappeared.Behind the Lancia is the Chamberlain Engineering Spice SE86C Hart driven by Nick Adams that retired early on, denying co-driver Ian Khan his ride. *LAT*

Silverstone 1000km, 8 May 1988 The Gordon Spice SE88Cs finished 1st and 2nd in the C2 class with the Thyrring/Coppelli car in 6th place overall and Spice/Bellm 8th after a misfire caused by a burnt-out spark plug, which lost them two laps. However, the fastest C2 car was the immaculate Spice SE87C of Costas Los/Wayne Taylor which was also more fuel efficient. Alas the car was retired with a failed ECU on lap 50. Note that the Spice has a Swiftsure Yacht logo, presumably courtesy of Wayne Taylor who had driven the ADA 03 at Daytona with their sponsorship. *LAT*

Le Mans, 12/13 June 1988 TWR Jaguar went for the jugular at Le Mans with five cars and 14 drivers but it nearly backfired. There were effectively two teams, the regular British/European one and Jaguar's IMSA crew looking after the no.21 and no.22 cars. Here is the TWR Jaguar team including the boss. One thing Jaguar and Porsche did not need to worry about was Team Sauber Mercedes who had withdrawn their cars after Klaus Niedzwiedz suffered a burst Michelin rear tyre on Mulsanne at about 360kph (225mph). He managed not to hit anything or anybody and then drove slowly back to the pits. *LAT*

Le Mans, 12/13 June 1988 Stanley Dickens, 'John Winter' and Franz Konrad are not quite what they seem. Swede Stanley Dickens is the son of a British police officer, hence his British name. His paternal family are descended from the writer Charles Dickens and he is best remembered for his 1989 Le Mans victory. He returned to racing in 2010 and won a round of the Swedish GT series at Ring Knutstorp with Frederik Lestrup. 'John Winter' was a pseudonym for Louis Krages (12 August 1949 – 11 January 2001), a German businessman who hid his racing from his family but was found out when he won at Le Mans in 1985. In 1994 he raced in the German DTM and eventually moved to the USA where he ran a toy business but tragically committed suicide due to depression and business problems. Franz Konrad sometimes raced under a German licence but was Austrian, born in Graz on 8 June 1951. The first two raced with Frank Jelinski and finished 3rd whilst Konrad with David Hobbs and Didier Theys were 5th, both for Reinhold Joest. *LAT*

↑ **Le Mans, 12/13 June 1988** Japanese interest in Le Mans carried on with two Toyota Team Tom's Toyota 88C-Ls for Geoff Lees/Masanori Sekiya/Kaoru Hoshino (no.36) and Paolo Barilla/Hitoshi Ogawa/Tiff Needell (no.37). They qualified 8th and 10th and finished 12th and 24th respectively. The former was delayed by a faulty gear linkage and the latter due to a trip into a Dunlop chicane gravel trap on lap 1 and later another off at Indianapolis, which required repairs, plus more issues thereafter. Their qualifying times were courtesy of high-boost engines but for the race they ran race units. Note the New Man and taka-Q livery as seen originally on Reinhold Joest's Porsches. *GPL*

→ **Le Mans, 12/13 June 1988** Allan Grice, famous Australian Touring Car champion and successful racer in many other categories from 1966 to 2005, was also a politician in the Queensland Parliament (1992–2001). He finished 14th at Le Mans with Win Percy and Mike Wilds despite gearbox problems in the Nissan Motorsports Nissan R88C (87G-2). Their second car retired (Kazuyoshi Hoshino, Takao Wada, Aguri Suzuki) on lap 286 due to a broken exhaust valve. Gricey looks suitably focused as he gets ready for the fray and note the Bob Jane T Marts and SAAS patches. *GPL*

Le Mans, 12/13 June 1988 Also from Japan (or rather the British arm) were the two Mazdaspeed Mazda 767s and a 757. The 767s both developed engine and water-pump problems but finished 17th and 19th whilst the older 757 came in 15th and 2nd, 3rd and 1st in the GTP category respectively. Additionally, Team Le Mans entered the March Nissans that had American V6 engines from Electramotive, but both expired on lap 74 with engine troubles. This is the no.86 car for Anders Olofsson, Lamberto Leoni and Akio Morimoto that qualified 19th. *LAT*

Le Mans, 12/13 June 1988 Looking back to Tertre Rouge, now part of a burgeoning road development, as the three Porsche 962s head up Mulsanne past the famous trees, led by the Leyton House Kremer no.11 driven by Kris Nissen, Harald Grohs and George Fouché. Following are the Camel Brun Motorsport no.4 of Walter Lechner, Franz Hunkeler and Manuel Reuter and the Stuck/Bell/Ludwig 962C. The Kremer car finished 11th and Lechner crashed the Brun car. Look carefully and you can just see a white car emerging from Tertre Rouge at far left. *LAT*

⬆ **Le Mans, 12/13 June 1988** The Shell/Dunlop works Porsche 962C (010) driven by Hans-Joachim Stuck set a searing fastest qualifying lap of 3 min 15.64, which Jaguar declined to challenge. All three 962s and the T car had the latest Bosch Motronic 1.7 engine management system and their 3-litre engines were allegedly producing 800bhp plus in qualifying. They also had an improved underbody and lower rear wing and had reverted to 17in wheels as had the Jaguars. Ludwig, who was tailing the leading Jaguar, went an extra lap before stopping for fuel and the car suddenly stopped at Indianapolis. He managed to trickle back to the pits on the starter motor and occasional surges of fuel, losing two laps and infuriating Stuck and Bell. However, the reserve fuel tank had not worked, but this mishap almost certainly cost Porsche the race. The Andrettis' no.19 finished 6th after water-pump problems and later the loss of a cylinder whilst the Wollek/Schuppan/van der Merwe car retired with engine failure. *LAT*

➡ **Le Mans, 12/13 June 1988** This was the last time Rondeau raced at Le Mans after first appearing here in 1979 with a works car for Ragnotti/Darniche. It is M379 (06) Ford Cosworth DFV or DFL, driven by Swiss racer Pierre-Alain Lombardi and Bruno Sotty (F). It finished 27th in the C2 category but unclassified after many problems including a gearbox rebuild. Lombardi was a former F3 competitor whilst Sotty was a Le Mans regular from 1977 to 1989. As the years went by car sponsorship livery became ever more lurid, as here. *LAT*

↑ **Le Mans, 12/13 June 1988** Also heading for the last corral, albeit in 1989, was the WM-Secateva team now owned by Roger Dorchy. They entered two cars: no.51 for Claude Haldi/Roger Dorchy/Jean-Daniel Raulet in the WM P88 Peugeot and Pascal Pettiot/ Jean-Daniel Raulet in the older P87. The cars had enlarged 2,973.8cc engines claiming over 900bhp and Dorchy reached 405kph (251.65mph) on Mulsanne during practice in the P87. This was apparently the raison d'être for their presence and both cars retired early on with gearbox and overheating problems. They returned in 1989 as P489s and both caught fire in practice, one being withdrawn and the other rebuilt but this went up in flames again and was retired after 110 laps. It was the end of the WM-Secateva team although Peugeot itself would join the new 750kg Group-C category in 1990 with their own car. *LAT*

← **Le Mans, 12/13 June 1988** The C2 class saw another tour de force by BP Spice Engineering who won the C2 category (Spice/Bellm) in the Spice SE88C Ford Cosworth DFL (003) 33 laps ahead of the 2nd-placed ADA Engineering ADA (003) of Jirou Yoneyama (J), Hideo Fukuyama (J) and Ian Harrower (GB). The opposition all collapsed including the faster, older Chamberlain car SE86C with its turbocharged Hart engine that was claimed to produce 650bhp. The dirty, dusty SE88C on Sunday is on its way to the C2 win, its fifth in a row. *LAT*

⬆ **Le Mans, 12/13 June 1988** Jaguar won but it was a hard slog. Two cars retired and two more were handicapped by assorted problems, finishing 4th driven by Derek Daly (IRL), Larry Perkins (AUS) and Kevin Cogan (USA) and 16th with the all American crew of Danny Sullivan, Davy Jones and Price Cobb. They were beaten on sheer speed during qualifying, but in race trim they were on the mark. This is the winning car of Jan Lammers (NL)/Johnny Dumfries (GB)/Andy Wallace (GB), but they were only 2 minutes 36.85 seconds ahead of the Stuck/Bell/Ludwig Porsche after 24 hours. Following is the Daly/Perkins/Cobb no.22. *LAT*

➡ **Brno 360km, 10 July 1988** Just 17 cars started at Brno, with only Joest bothering to attend out of the serious customer teams. It was the first time that a championship race took place in a communist country. However, Sauber and Jaguar were there and Sauber finished 1st (Mass/Schlesser) and 4th (Baldi/Weaver) with TWR Jaguar finishing 2nd (Brundle/Nielsen) and 3rd (Lammers/Dumfries). On lap 10 Baldi had to pit due to a puncture and dropped to 6th, spending the rest of the race catching up, whilst the two Joest cars finished 5th (Wollek/'John Winter'), seen here, and 6th (Konrad/Barth). *LAT*

← **Brands Hatch 1000km, 24 July 1988** Sauber and Joest were qualifying in the ellusive dry patches whilst TWR missed the cut because they were attending to their new 48-valve engine in the Watson/Jones car. As a result the no.2 car of Lammers/Dumfries was the quickest Jaguar in 4th place with Nielsen/Wallace/Brundle 6th and Watson/Jones in a lowly 9th with the ill-handling 48-valve 800bhp car that was predictably top heavy. Lammers in the pit lane awaits the off with another XJR-9 behind him and the no.8 Joest Porsche of Jelinski and 'John Winter' next up. Nearby is Klaus Ludwig with his bright yellow footwear and further back on the pits side is the no.61 Sauber of Baldi/Schlesser which started on pole. Jaguar were fortunate at Brands Hatch with the Sauber's early drama and John Nielsen, Andy Wallace and Martin Brundle won the race by a lap from the still potent Joest Porsche of Bob Wollek and Klaus Ludwig. *LAT*

→ **Brands Hatch 1000km, 24 July 1988** C2 was as ever the domain of Spice Engineering, and Spice/Bellm won here followed on the same lap by the Thyrring/Coppelli car – a nice 1/2 for them – with the older GP Motorsport Spice SE87C of Los/Taylor 3rd. Further down the pecking order was the no.123 Charles Ivey Tiga GC287 Porsche Turbo that finished 12th and last – apparently its Porsche 2.8-litre engine was using far too much fuel. A shame as the Tim Harvey, Chris Hodgetts and Robin Donovan trio were much better than that. *LAT*

Brands Hatch 1000km, 24 July 1988 Two Sauber C9s came to Brands for Mass/Schlesser and Baldi/Weaver, but on lap 8 Steve Hynes in the Roy Baker Racing Tiga GC286 Ford was surrounded by the the Ludwig Porsche and the C9s at Clearways. He made room for Ludwig but went off track and then sideways in front of the Saubers. The Mass car was punted off into the barriers and then hit the Tiga on rebound, whilst Baldi had four flat-spotted tyres. The race was stopped to clear up the mess whilst Mass gave the unfortunate Hynes a bollocking in the RBR pit. This allowed the TWR Jaguar of John Nielsen, Andy Wallace and Martin Brundle to win the race by a lap from the Joest Porsche of Bob Wollek and Klaus Ludwig. Baldi finished 3rd with Schlesser who had replaced Weaver as a result of the accident. Meanwhile, French racer Noël del Bello's older Sauber C8 Mercedes 86-C8-02, shared with Hervé Regout (B) and Bernard Santal (CH), seen here, had qualified 16th but retired with fuel-pump failure on lap 104. *LAT*

Nürburgring 1000km, 3/4 September 1988 It was not only the wet weather that was undesirable but the utterly daft idea of running two 500km races, one on Saturday evening and the other on Sunday afternoon. With the blessing of FISA of course. Worse still, the entrants knew of this but still attended. The organisers also had to borrow lighting from Spa as nobody had thought about the darkness! The no.1 Jaguar XJR-9 (TWR-J12C-588) of Eddie Cheever/Martin Brundle finished 3rd in Heat 1 and 2nd in Heat 2 for a combined result of 2nd place. The Jaguar had been leading in the Sunday race, but apparently a piston burnt out and the car had to be nursed home. This is Cheever having a grass-cutting moment somewhere sometime. *LAT*

Nürburgring 1000km, 3/4 September 1988 Jean Messaoudi's MT Sport Racing Argo JM19C (124) Ford Cosworth driven by himself and Pierre-François Rousselot (F) retired due to a split fuel tank according to period stats. The *Speedy pose d'échappements* logo is in English 'speedy exhaust installation' and was or is a company that does just what it says on the tin. *LAT*

Nürburgring 1000km, 3/4 September 1988 Jean-Louis Schlesser and Jochen Mass won the double 500km at the 'Ring in the no.61 Sauber Mercedes, but their teammates Mauro Baldi and Stefan Johansson in the no.62 car had a miserable time. They finished 7th in Heat 1 with a redundant windscreen wiper and in Heat 2 Baldi lost it on the treacherous surface and hit the Armco twice, damaging the rear suspension, and they were out. *LAT*

→ Nürburgring 1000km, 3/4 September 1988 Walter Brun's cars had a seemingly unending number of sponsors. This one, Hydro Aluminium, is a Norwegian company in Oslo founded in 1947. They have a subsidiary in Geneva, Switzerland and given Brun's Swiss nationality presumably this is who was sponsoring the team. The Porsche 962C (001BM) was driven by Walter Brun and Norwegian Harald Huysman and finished 9th in Heat 1 and 5th in Heat 2 for a combined result of 6th place. *LAT*

↑ **Spa 1000km, 18 September 1988** Once again Spa was wet, and qualifying was a testosterone fest which resulted in Baldi on pole, Lammers 2nd, Schlesser 3rd and Cheever 4th. The conditions suited Lammers and he finished the first lap 5 seconds ahead of Baldi, which increased to 13 seconds by lap 5. Then Lammers pitted with a puncture, allowing the Sauber back into the lead. Thereafter the Saubers were running 1/2, Johansson having been told to let Schlesser (no.61) by which he did whilst the no.62 car had an opaque windscreen caused by an unknown fluid. Nevertheless, Schlesser/Mass were on the way to victory when the No.61 car suffered a broken rear wishbone and lost the lead to Brundle's Jaguar. This was repaired and they fought their way back to 3rd place. *LAT*

↗ **Spa 1000km, 18 September 1988** The Jaguars were just a tad off the Saubers in dry conditions, but in a race of changing fortunes the Lammers/Brundle Jaguar took the lead on lap 121 although the TWR car's Dunlop tyres were spinning up which in turn increased their fuel consumption. Brundle had a significant lead after the Schlesser/Mass problem, but Baldi had refuelled whilst the Jaguar had to stop one more time. This done, Brundle was only 4 seconds behind the Sauber, but the rain increased and the Jaguar's Dunlop inter tyres were too hard for the wet conditions. So Baldi/Johansson won with Lammers/Brundle 2nd and with it the Team Championship cup for TWR. The Cheever/Dumfries XJR-9 retired on lap 49 when Cheever ran out of fuel on track. *LAT*

→ **Spa 1000km, 18 September 1988** Of course Spice engineering won the C2 class at Spa, with the Thyrring/Coppelli car 1st and Spice/Bellm 2nd. Further back the Kelmar Racing Tiga GC288 (366) Ford Cosworth DFL driven by the Italian trio of Ranieri Randaccio, Luigi Taverna and Maurizio Gellini finished 15th and 9th in class. Their sponsorship Amaretto means 'little bitter' in English and Saronno was the town in Lombardy from whence it originated back in the 16th century. It is now marketed as Disaronno. *LAT*

⬆ **Fuji 1000km, 9 October 1988** Car no.50 was the SARD MC88S Toyota for Martin Donnelly, Jochen Dauer and Syuuroku Sasaki, which is apparently advertising Y 1,000,000 prize money from the VICTORY CIRCLE CLUB SPORTS NIPPON NEWSPAPERS. This was about £6,700 in 1988. SARD was Sigma Advanced Racing Development, specialising in motorsport as well as producing aftermarket performance parts for Toyota automobiles. The car qualified 29th (out of 35 starters) and retired on lap 109 due to gearbox failure. *LAT*

⬅ **Fuji 1000km, 9 October 1988** Mount Fuji with its menacing mountain and crumbling 4.47km track was holding its final FIA sports-car round. Thirty-five cars started and surprisingly 22 finished. Jaguar, Sauber and a lone factory Porsche were among the 25 C1-class entrants whilst the C2 brigade numbered seven. This is the Andrettis' Le Mans works 962C (008) with OMRON backing driven by Ludwig and Price Cobb with the Cosmik Spice SE87C Ford Cosworth DFL (003) of Costas Los and American Tom Hessert following. Ludwig/Cobb finished 2nd in the final Porsche factory race in period and the Cosmik led C2 until the drivers were exhausted and they finished 13th overall and 2nd in class to the Thyrring/Coppelli Spice SE88C. *LAT*

Fuji 1000km, 9 October 1988 Both Saubers – Mass, Schlesser and newcomer Kenny Acheson and Baldi with Philippe Streiff – were very fast but troubled, the former with a malfunctioning electronic sensor and the other crashed by Baldi when a front brake disc shattered and blew the tyre. The Lammers Jaguar also had a tyre failure and ended in the barriers, but the Brundle/Cheever XJR-9 (TWR-12C-588) won the race by one lap from the OMRON Porsche. This made Martin Brundle the winner of the Drivers' Championship ahead of Jean-Louis Schlesser. Cheever cuts inside the no.32 Nissan (Masahiro Hasemi/Aguri Suzuki), which finished 12th after qualifying 2nd. *LAT*

Fuji 1000km, 9 October 1988 Andrew Gilbert-Scott and Swede Steven Andskar (who finished 4th in the 1994 Le Mans 24 Hours) drove the Auto Beaurex Motorsport Toyota 87C with an old Dome chassis and 4-cylinder 2.1-litre turbo, which broke its transmission during the morning practice. This required a new gearbox but the race was even more disappointing, Gilbert-Scott retiring on lap 6 with suspension failure. This might be the moment here with one of the Saubers arriving on the scene. Gilbert-Scott is best remembered for his F3000 career from 1986 to 1991, but he also drove for TWR Jaguar in 1989, later returning to Japan for F3000 and touring cars. His final race appears to have been at the 1997 Le Mans, driving a McLaren F1 GTR. *LAT*

ENTRANTS

901 Racing (Peter Uria)
– Porsche 911 Carrea RSR
Peter Uria (USA) DAY, SEB
Jack Refenning (USA) DAY
Larry Figaro (USA) DAY, SEB
Rusty Scott (USA) DAY
Skip Winfree (USA) SEB

ADA Engineering
– ADA 03 Ford Cosworth DFL
Wayne Taylor (ZA) DAY
Ian Harrower (GB) DAY, LM
Ian Flux (GB) DAY
Stanley Dickens (S) DAY
Steve Kempton (GB) JER
Dudley Wood (GB) JER, JAR
Johnny Herbert (GB) JER
John Sheldon (GB) JAR, BH
Tom Dodd-Noble (GB) SIL
Stefano Sebastiani (I) SIL
Colin Pool (GB) SIL
Jirou Yoneyama (J) LM
Hideo Fukuyama (J) LM
'Pierre Chauvet' (Friedrich Glaz) (A) BH
Tim Lee-Davey (GB) BH
Arthur Abrahams (AUS) SAN
John Smith (AUS) SAN

Advan Alpha Nova
(Nova Engineering)
– Porsche 962C
Kunimitsu Takahashi (J) FUJ
Kazuo Mogi (J) FUJ

All American Racing (Dan Gurney)
– Toyota Celica Turbo
Chris Cord (USA) DAY, SEB
Dennis Aase (USA) DAY, SEB
Steve Millen (NZ) DAY
Willy T. Ribbs (USA) DAY, SEB
Rocky Moran (USA) DAY
Juan-Manuel Fangio II (RA) DAY, SEB

Bobby Allison Racing
– Buick Somerset (Allison)
Bobby Allison (USA) DAY
Clifford Allison (USA) DAY
Dick Danielson (USA) DAY

Gaston Andrey Racing
– Alba AR2 Ferrari,
Alba AR6 Ferrari,
Tiga GT286 Ferrari
Angelo Pallavicini (CH) DAY, SEB
Paolo Guatamacchi (I) DAY, SEB
Uli Bieri (CDN) DAY, SEB
Tommy Johnson (USA) DAY
Martino Finotto (I) DAY, SEB
Pietro Silva (I) DAY
Guido Daccò (I) DAY, SEB
Ruggero Melgrati (I) SEB

Apenn Inn (Dick Greer)
– Mazda RX-7 (Chassis Dynamics)
Dick Greer (USA) DAY, SEB
Mike Mees (USA) DAY, SEB
John Finger (USA) DAY, SEB
Matt Mnich (USA) SEB

AT&T Spice Engineering
– Spice SE87L Pontiac
Don Bell (USA) DAY, SEB
Charles Morgan (USA) DAY, SEB
Costas Los (GR) DAY
Charles Morgan (USA) SEB
Hendrik ten Cate (NL) SEB

Auto Beaurex Motorsport
(Kiyoski Fukui)
– Toyota 87C (Dome)
Andrew Gilbert-Scott (GB) FUJ
Steven Andskar (S) FUJ

Automobiles Louis Descartes/
Louis Descartes
– ALD 03 BMW, ALD 04 BMW
Gérard Tremblay (F) JER, MZA, SIL, LM,
BRN, BH, NUR, SPA
Sylvain Boulay (F) JER, LM
Louis Descartes (F) JER, JAR, SIL, LM,
BRN, NUR, SPA, SAN
Jacques Heuclin (F) JAR, MZA, LM, SPA
Domonique Lacaud (F) MZA, SIL, LM,
NUR, SPA
Max-Cohen Olivar (MA) MZA
Pierre Yver (F) MZA
Michel Lateste (F) SIL, LM, BH, SAN
Del Bennett (GB) BH
David Mercer (GB) SPA

Al Bacon Performance
– Mazda RX-7
(Chassis Dynamics)
Al Bacon (USA) DAY, SEB
Bob Reed (USA) DAY, SEB
John Hogdal (USA) DAY
Amos Johnson (USA) SEB

Roy Baker Racing
– Tiga GC286 Ford
Cosworth DFL
Mike Allison (USA) DAY, LM
Stephen Hynes (USA) DAY, LM, BH, SPA
Chris Ashmore (GB) DAY, SIL
Lon Bender (USA) SEB, BRN
Albert Naon, Jr (USA) SEB
Mike Kimpton (GB) SIL, BRN
David Andrews (GB) SIL, LM
John Bartlett (GB) BH, SAN
Max Cohen-Olivar (MA) BH, SPA
John Sheldon (GB) NUR
Neil Crang (AUS) NUR
Val Musetti (GB) SPA
Michael Hall (AUS) SAN

Ball Bros. Racing
(Durst/Brockman)
– Spice SE88P Pontiac
Steve Durst (USA) SEB
Mike Brockman (USA) SEB
Jeff Kline (USA) SEB

Rudy Bartling
– Porsche 911
Rudy Bartling (CDN) SEB
Rainer Brezinka (CDN) SEB
Fritz Hochreuter (CDN) SEB

Roland Bassaler
– Sauber SHS C6 BMW
Jean-François Yvon (F) LM
Remy Pochauvin (F) LM
Roland Bassaler (F) LM

Bayside Motorsport (Bruce Leven)
– Porsche 962
Hans-Joachim Stuck (D) DAY, SEB
Klaus Ludwig (D) DAY, SEB
Sarel van der Merwe (ZA) DAY

Bob's Speed Products (Bob Lee)
– Pontiac Firebird (Python)
Del Russo Taylor (USA) SEB
Bob Lee (USA) SEB
Gary Myers (USA) SEB
Mark Montgomery (USA) SEB

Briody Racing
– March 84G Buick Turbo
John McComb (USA) DAY
Jim Briody (USA) DAY
Bob Nagel (USA) DAY

Bobby Brown Racing
– Tiga GT286 Buick
Ron Nelson (USA) DAY, SEB
Bobby Brown (USA) DAY, SEB
Billy Hagan (USA) DAY, SEB
Sterling Marlin (USA) DAY (DND)

British Barn Racing
– JTK 63C (Tom's)
Ford Cosworth DFL
Hideo Fukuyama (J) FUJ
Jirou Yoneyama (J) FUJ
Kiyoshi Misaki (J) FUJ

Brun Motorsport/Torno/Camel
Brun Motorsport/Repsol Brun
Motorsport – Porsche 962C
Gianfranco Brancatelli (I) DAY
Oscar Larrauri (RA) DAY, JER, JAR,
MZA, NUR, SPA
Massimo Sigala (I) DAY, JER, JAR,
MZA, LM
Manuel Reuter (D) JER, JAR, MZA, LM,
NUR, SPA
Uwe Schäfer (D) JER, JAR, MZA, LM,
NUR
Jésus Pareja (E) JER, JAR, MZA, LM,
NUR
Walter Brun (CH) JER, JAR, MZA,
NUR, SPA
Walter Lechner (A) LM
Franz Hunkeler (CH) LM
Harald Huysman (B) NUR

Car Enterprises (Craig Rubright)
– Chevron Camaro (Dillon)
Bill Wesel (USA) DAY
Craig Rubright (USA) DAY, SEB
Garrett Jenkins (USA) DAY
Kermit Upton (USA) SEB

Cars and Concepts Inc
– Chevrolet Beretta
Tom Kendall (USA) SEB
Max Jones (USA) SEB

Chamberlain Engineering
(Hugh Chamberlain)
– Spice SE88C Ford Cosworth
DFL, Spice SE86C Hart
Claude Ballot-Léna (F) JER, JAR, MZA,
SIL, LM, BRN, BH, NUR, SPA, FUJ,
SAN (DND)
Jean-Louis Ricci (F) JER, JAR, MZA, SIL,
LM, BRN, BH, NUR, SPA, FUJ, SAN
Graham Duxbury (ZA) JER, MZA (DND)
Nick Adams (GB) JER (DND), MZA, SIL,
LM, BRN, BH, NUR, SPA, SAN
Ian Kahn (GB) SIL (DND), FUJ
Jean-Claude Andret (F) LM (DND)
Richard Jones (GB) LM, NUR, SPA
Martin Birrane (IRL) LM, BH
Paul Stott (GB) BRN
John Williams (GB) NUR, SPA
Arthur Abrahams (AUS) FUJ
Dan Murphy (USA) FUJ
Andrew Miedecke (AUS) SAN

Clayton Cunningham Racing
– Mazda RX-7
Bart Kendall (USA) DAY, SEB
Johnny Unser (USA) DAY
Tom Frank (USA) DAY, SEB

John Morton (USA) DAY
Parnelli Jones (USA) DAY
P.J. Jones (USA) DAY

Cumberland Valley Racing
(Chaunce Wallace/Richard
Oakley) – Mazda RX-7
Richard Oakley (USA) DAY, SEB
Matt Mnich (USA) DAY
Doug Mills (CDN) DAY, SEB

Data-Gas/ Hi Tech Racing (Bill
McDill) – March 84G Pontiac
Richard McDill (USA) DAY, SEB
Tom Juckette (USA) DAY, SEB
Bill McDill (USA) DAY, SEB

Victor Dauer Racing
– Porsche 962C
Jochen Dauer (D) NUR
Franz Konrad (A) NUR

Walter Lechner Racing
– Porsche 962C
Walter Lechner (A) SPA
Ernst Franzmaier (A) SPA
Jochen Dauer (D) SPA

Di-Tech Buick(George Petrilak)
– Argo JM16 Buick
Rex McDaniel (USA) SEB
George Petrilak (USA) SEB
Scott Livingston (USA) SEB

Diman Racing
– Royale RP40 Porsche
Mandy Gonzalez (PR) DAY
Skip Winfree (USA) DAY
Manuel Villa (PR) DAY
John Schneider (USA) DAY

Dollop Racing (Antonio Ferrari)
– Argo JM19B Motori Moderni,
Lancia LC2/88 Ferrari
Jean-Pierre Frey (CH) JER, JAR, MZA,
SIL, LM, BRN, NUR
Nicola Marozzo (I) JER, JAR, MZA (DND),
SIL (DND), LM
Ranieri Randaccio (I) LM
Paolo Giangrossi (I) BRN, NUR

Downing/Atlanta(Jim Downing)
– Argo JM19 Mazda
Howard Katz (USA) DAY, SEB
Hiro Matsushita (J) DAY, SEB
Jim Downing (USA) DAY, SEB

Dyson Racing
– Porsche 962
Price Cobb (USA) DAY, SEB
James Weaver (GB) DAY, SEB
Rob Dyson (USA) DAY
Vern Schuppan (AUS) DAY

Erie Scientific
(Frank Jellinek)
– Argo JM16 Mazda
John Grooms (USA) DAY
Tom Bagley (USA) DAY
John Fergus (USA) DAY
Frank Jellinek (USA) DAY

Escort Porsche
(Karl Durkheimer)
– Porsche 911 Carrera RSR
Karl Durkheimer (USA) DAY, SEB
Monte Shelton (USA) DAY
Jim Torres (USA) DAY, SEB
Nort Northam (USA) DAY

Essex Racing Service (Mike Gue)
– Tiga GT286 Chevrolet,
Tiga GT286 Mazda
David Simpson (USA) DAY
Tom Hessert (USA) DAY, SEB
David Loring (USA) DAY, SEB
Ron McKay (USA) DAY
Bill Jacobson (USA) DAY, SEB
Jim Brown (USA) DAY, SEB
John Schneider (USA) SEB

FAI Automotive (Sean Walker)
– Tiga GC287 Ford Cosworth DFL
Sean Walker (GB) SIL, BH
Paul Stott (GB) SIL, BH
Evan Clements (GB) SIL
Ian Flux (GB) BH

Ferrea Racing (Luis Sereix)
– Chevrolet Camaro (Howe)
Luis Sereix (USA) SEB
Daniel Urrutia (USA) SEB

Florida Fixtures (Guy W. Church)
– Mazda RX-7
Russ Church (USA) DAY
Daniel Urrutia (USA) DAY
E.J. Generotti (USA) DAY
Dennis Vitolo (USA) DAY

A J Foyt Racing/Copenhagen
– Porsche 962 (Holbert/Fabcar)
A.J. Foyt (USA) DAY, SEB
Al Unser, Jr (USA) DAY
Elliot Forbes-Robinson (USA) DAY
Hurley Haywood (USA) SEB

From A Racing (Nova Engineering)
– Porsche 962C
Hideki Okada (J) FUJ
Stanley Dickens (S) FUJ

Full Time Racing (Kal Showket)
– Dodge Daytona
Kal Showket (USA) DAY, SEB
Dorsey Schroeder (USA) DAY (DND), SEB
Phil Currin (USA) DAY (DND)
Neil Hanneman (USA) DAY
Bruce MacInnes (USA) SEB

GP Motorsport/Cosmik
– Spice SE87C Ford
Cosworth DFL
Costas Los (GR) JER, JAR, MZA, SIL,
LM, BRN, BH, NUR, SPA, SAN
Philippe de Henning (F) JER, JAR, MZA
(DND), SAN
Wayne Taylor (ZA) SIL (DND), LM, BH,
NUR, SPA
Evan Clements (GB) LM, BRN

Gebhardt Motorsport
– Gebhardt JC873 Audi/Weigel
Hellmut Mundas (D) MZA, NUR
Günter Gebhardt (D) MZA (DND)
Rudi Seher (D) MZA (DND), NUR
Stefan Neuberger (D) NUR

Graff Racing (Jean-Phillipe Grand)
– Spice SE86C Ford Cosworth DFL
Jean-Philippe Grand (F) LM
Jacques Terrien (F) LM
Maurice Guenoun (F) LM

Group 44 (Bob Tullius)
– Jaguar XJR-7
Bob Tullius (USA) DAY
Whitney Ganz (USA) DAY
Hurley Haywood (USA) DAY

**HP Racing (Herbert S. Parks)
– March 86G Buick**
Doc Bundy (USA) SEB
Whitney Ganz (USA) SEB
Bill Cooper (USA) SEB

**HRG Associates
(Hebert/Reisman/Gafney)
– Pontiac Firebird (Watson)**
Bob Hebert (USA) DAY
Paul Reisman (USA) DAY
Andy Strasser (USA) DAY

**Hendrick Motorsports
(Rick Hendrick)
– Chevrolet Corvette GTP (Lola)**
Sarel van der Merwe (ZA) SEB
Elliot Forbes-Robinson (USA)
 SEB

**Team Highball
(Amos Johnson)
– Mazda RX-7 (Highball)**
Amos Johnson (USA) DAY, SEB
Dennis Shaw (USA) DAY, SEB
Bob Lazier (USA) DAY

**Highlands Racing Team
– Pontiac Firebird**
Steve Roberts (USA) SEB
J. Kurt Roehrig (USA) SEB

**Holbert Racing
– Porsche 962 (Holbert)**
Al Holbert (USA) DAY, SEB
Chip Robinson (USA) DAY, SEB
Derek Bell (GB) DAY

**Hotchkis Racing
(John Hotchkis Sr.)
– Porsche 962 Fabcar**
Jim Adams (USA) DAY, SEB
John Hotchkis, Jr (USA) DAY, SEB
John Hotchkis, Sr (USA) DAY, SEB

**Huffaker Racing
(Joe Huffaker, Jr)
– Spice SE86CL Pontiac**
Terry Visger (USA) DAY, SEB
Paul Lewis (USA) DAY, SEB
Jon Woodner (USA) DAY, SEB

**Italya Sport Team Le Mans
– March 88S Nissan**
Toshio Suzuki (J) LM
Michel Trollé (F) LM
Danny Ongais (USA) LM
Anders Olofsson (S) LM, FUJ
Lamberto Leoni (I) LM
Akio Morimoto (J) LM
Takao Wada (J) FUJ

**Charles Ivey Racing
– Tiga GC287 Porsche**
Wayne Taylor (ZA) JER, JAR, MZA
Tim Harvey (GB) JER JAR, MZA (DND),
 SIL, LM, BH
Duncan Bain (GB) SIL
Chris Hodgetts (GB) SIL, LM, BH
John Sheldon (GB) LM
Robin Donovan (GB) BH

**Jiffy Lube Firebird
(Durst/Brackman)
– Spice SE86CL Pontiac**
Steve Durst (USA) DAY
Mike Brockman (USA) DAY
Bob Earl (USA) DAY
Gary Belcher (USA) DAY

**Joest Racing/Blaupunkt
Joest Racing
– Porsche 962C**
Bob Wollek (F) JER, JAR, MZA, SIL,
 BRN, BH, NUR, SPA, FUJ
Klaus Ludwig (D) JER, JAR, MZA,
 BRN, BH
Frank Jelinski (D) JER, JAR, SEB, MZA,
 SIL, LM, BH, NUR, SPA, FUJ
'John Winter' (Louis Krages) (D) JER,
 JAR, SEB, MZA, SIL, LM, BRN, BH,
 NUR, SPA, FUJ
Paolo Barilla (I) SEB, NUR, SPA (DND)
Phillipe Streif (F) SIL
David Hobbs (GB) SIL, LM
Stanley Dickens (S) SIL, LM
Didier Theys (B) LM
Franz Konrad (A) LM, BRN
Jürgen Barth (D) BRN
Harald Grohs (D) FUJ

**Kalagian Racing
(John Kalagian)
– Porsche 962 (Holbert)**
Jim Rothbarth (USA) DAY, SEB
Bernard Jourdain (MEX) DAY,
 SEB (DND)
Michel Jourdain (MEX) DAY
Rob Stevens (USA) DAY

**Kelmar Racing – Tiga GC288
Ford Cosworth DFL, Tiga GC85
(RAM) Ford Cosworth DFL**
Pasquale Barberio (I) JER, JAR, MZA,
 SIL, BRN, NUR, SPA
Vito Veninata (I) JER, JAR, MZA (DND),
 SIL, BRN, BH, NUR, SPA, FUJ
Ranieri Randaccio (I) JER, JAR, MZA
 (DND), SIL, BRN, BH, NUR, SPA,
 FUJ, SAN
Paolo Ciafardoni (I) JER
Maurizio Gellini (I) JER, BRN, BH,
 NUR, SPA
Stefano Sebastiani (I) SPA, SAN
Luigi Tavena (I) SPA

**Lamas Motor Racing
(Lorenzo Lamas)
– Fabcar CL Porsche**
Jack Newsum (USA) DAY, SEB
Howard Cherry (USA) DAY, SEB
Tim McAdam (USA) DAY, SEB
John Higgins (USA) DAY
Charles Monk (CDN) DAY, SEB
Perry King (USA) DAY
Lorenzo Lamas (USA) DAY, SEB
Chip Mead (USA) SEB

**Latino Racing
– Porsche 911Carrera RSR**
Luis Mendez (DR) SEB
Kikos Fonseca (CR) SEB

**Tim Lee-Davey/Team Davey
– Tiga GC88 Ford Cosworth DFL
Turbo, Porsche 962C**
Tim Lee-Davey (GB) LM, NUR, SPA,
 FUJ, SAN
Tom Dodd-Noble (GB) LM (DND), NUR,
 SPA, FUJ
Peter Oberndorfer (D) NUR
Katsunori Iketani (J) FUJ
Neil Crang (AUS) SAN

**Leitzinger Racing
– Nissan 300ZX**
Bob Leitzinger (USA) DAY
Chuck Kurtz (USA) DAY
Butch Leitzinger (USA) DAY

**Jack Lewis Enterprises
– Porsche 911 Carrera RSR**
Bob Beasley (USA) DAY
Steve Volk (USA) DAY
Jack Lewis (USA) DAY

**Pierre-Alain Lombardi
– Rondeau M379C Ford
Cosworth DFV, Spice SE86C
Ford Cosworth DFL**
Pierre-Alain Lombardi (CH) MZA, LM,
 NUR, SPA
Silvio Vaglio (CH) MZA
Rolando Vaglio (CH) MZA
Bruno Sotty (F) LM, NUR, SPA
Thierry Lecerf (F) SPA

**Richard Lloyd Racing
– Porsche 962C/GTI**
James Weaver (GB) JER
Derek Bell (GB) JER, SIL, SPA
Tiff Needell (GB) SIL
David Hobbs (GB) NUR
Martin Donnelly (GB) NUR, SPA

**Team Lucky Strike Schanche
– Argo JM19C Ford
Cosworth DFL**
Will Hoy (GB) JER, JAR, MZA, SIL, BH
Martin Schanche (N) JER, JAR, MZA, SIL
 (DND), LM, BH
Robin Smith (GB) LM
Robin Donovan (GB) LM
'Pierre Chauvet' (Friedrich Glaz) (A)
 NUR, SPA
Robin Smith (GB) NUR, SPA
John Sheldon (GB) SPA

**Luigi Taverna Techno Racing
– Olmas GLT-200 Ford
Cosworth DFV**
Luigi Taverna (I) SIL
Fabio Magnani (I) SIL
Roberto Ragazzi (I) SIL

**MSB Racing (Jim Fowells)
– Argo JM19 Mazda**
Dave Cowart (USA) DAY
Jim Fowells (USA) DAY
Ray Mummery (USA) DAY
Mike Meyer (USA) DAY

**MT Sport Racing
– Argo JM19C Ford
Cosworth DFL**
Pierre-François Rousselot (F) LM, NUR,
 SPA, SAN
Jean Messaoudi (F) LM, NUR, SPA, SAN
Jean-Luc Roy (F) LM

**Mandeville Auto Tech
– Mazda RX-7
(Chassis Dynamics)**
Roger Mandeville (USA) DAY, SEB
Kelly Marsh (USA) DAY, SEB
Don Marsh (USA) DAY, SEB

**Mardi Gras Racing (Rene Azcona)
– Porsche 911 Carrera RSR**
Colin Richard (GB) DAY
Rene Azcona (USA) DAY
Bob Copeman (USA) DAY

**Martinelli/Scott
(Jack Refenning)
– Porsche 911 Carrera (RSR?)**
Jack Refenning (USA) SEB
Rusty Bond (USA) SEB
Freddy Baker (USA) SEB

**Walter Maurer
– Maurer C87 BMW Turbo**
Walter Maurer (D) NUR, SAN
Helmut Gall (D) NUR, SAN
Edgar Dören (D) NUR

**Mazdaspeed
– Mazda 767**
David Kennedy (IRL) SIL, LM, FUJ
Youjirou Terada (J) SIL, LM, FUJ
Yoshimi Katayama (J) SIL, LM, FUJ
Marc Duez (B) LM
David Leslie (GB) LM
Takashi Yorino (J) LM, FUJ
Will Hoy (GB) LM
Hervé Regout (B) LM
Pierre Dieudonné (B) LM, FUJ

**Memorex Telex Racing (Günther
Gebhardt) – Porsche 962C
(Thompson)**
Tiff Needell (GB) FUJ
Gianpiero Moretti (I) FUJ (DND)
Harald Huysman (B) FUJ (DND)

**Tom Milner Racing – Ford Mustang
Probe (Zakspeed)**
Bruce Jenner (USA) DAY
Scott Goodyear (CDN) DAY
Arie Luyendyk (NL) DAY
Tom Gloy (USA) DAY
Calvin Fish (USA) DAY
Thomas Schwietz (USA) DAY

**Momo Racing (Moretti/Dawson)
– March 86G Buick**
Steve Phillips (USA) DAY, SEB (DND)
Jeff Andretti (USA) DAY
Michael Roe (IRL) DAY, SEB
Gianpiero Moretti (I) DAY, SEB
Paolo Barilla (I) DAY (DND)
Tom Gloy (USA) SEB
Didier Theys (B) SEB (DND)

**Motion Promotion
– Argo JM16 Buick**
George Petrilak (USA) DAY
Rex McDaniel (USA) DAY
Bruce MacInnes (USA) DAY

**Mussato Action Car
(Bruno Mussato)
– Lancia LC2-88 Ferrari**
Andre de Cesaris (I) MZA
Christian Danner (D) MZA (DND)

**Nissan Motorsports
– Nissan R88C March LM)**
Kazuyoshi Hoshino (J) LM, FUJ
Takao Wada (J) LM, FUJ
Aguri Suzuki (J) LM, FUJ
Allan Grice (AUS) LM, FUJ
Win Percy (GB) LM
Mike Wilds (GB) LM
Kenji Takahashi (J) FUJ
Masahiro Hasemi (J) FUJ

**Patrick Oudet Vetir Racing
– Tiga GC85 Ford Cosworth DFL**
Jean-Claude Ferrarin (F) BH
Dominique Lacaud (F) BH
Patrick Oudet (F) SPA
Jean-Claude Ferrarin (F) SPA
Pascal Witmeur (B) SPA

**Overbagh Motor Racing (Hoyt
Overbagh) – Chevrolet Camaro
(Stock Car Products)**
Oma Kimbrough (USA) DAY

Hoyt Overbagh (USA) DAY
Chris Gennone (USA) DAY
David Kicak (USA) DAY

**PC Automotive (Piper/Capon)
– Argo JM19C Ford Cosworth DFL**
Olindo Iacobelli (USA) MZA, SIL, LM, BH,
 NUR, SPA
Martin Birrane (IRL) MZA (DND)
Richard Piper (GB) MZA (DND), SIL,
 BH, NUR, SPA
Alain Ianetta (F) LM
John Graham (CDN) LM

**Person's Racing Team (Le Mans)
– March 88S Nissan**
Toshio Suzuki (J) FUJ
Akio Morimoto (J) FUJ (DND)

**Phoenix Race Cars
– Phoenix JG2 Chevrolet**
John Gunn (USA) SEB
Gary Belcher (USA) SEB (DND)

**Marco Polo Motorsports
– Pontiac Fiero**
Dan Ripley (USA) SEB
Alan Freed (USA) SEB
Keith Rinzler (USA) SEB

**Porsche AG/Omron Porsche AG
– Porsche 962C**
Hans-Joachim Stuck (D) LM
Klaus Ludwig (D) LM, FUJ
Derek Bell (GB) LM
Bob Wollek (F) LM
Vern Schuppan (AUS) LM
Sarel van der Merwe (ZA) LM
Mario Andretti (USA) LM
Michael Andretti (USA) LM
John Andretti (USA) LM
Pryce Cobb (USA) FUJ

**Porsche Kremer Racing/
Kenwood Kremer/Leyton
House Kremer – Porsche 962C
(Thompson), Cougar C12 Ford
Cosworth DFL**
Kris Nissen (DK) JAR, SIL, LM
Volker Weidler (D) JAR, MZA,
 NUR, FUJ
Bruno Giacomelli (I) MZA, LM,
 FUJ
Harold Grohs (D) SIL, LM
Kunimitsu Takahashi (J) LM
Hideki Okada (J) LM
George Fouché (ZA) LM
Manuel Reuter (D) FUJ
Oscar Larrauri (RA) FUJ
Naoki Nagasaka (J) FUJ
Kaoru Hoshino (J) FUJ
Masahiko Kageyama (J) FUJ

**Primagaz Compétition/Courage
Compétition (Yves Courage)
– Cougar C20B Porsche,
Cougar C22 Porsche**
Pierre-Henri Raphenal (F) MZA,
 LM
Roberto Ravaglia (I) MZA
Michel Ferté (F) LM
François Migault (F) LM
Paul Belmondo (F) LM
Ukyou Katayama (J) LM
Jürgen Lässig (D) LM
Pierre Yver (F) LM
Dudley Wood (GB) LM
Max Cohen-Olivar (MA) LM
Patrick de Radigues (B) LM

Protofab Polyvoltac (Jack Roush)/
Protofab Racing – Chevrolet
Corvette (Protofab)
Greg Pickett (USA) DAY, SEB
John Jones (CDN) DAY, SEB
Tommy Riggins (USA) DAY, SEB
Tommy Archer (USA) DAY
Chip Mead (USA) DAY
Bill Adam (CDN) DAY
Wally Dallenbach, Jr (USA) SEB

Puleo Racing
– Pontiac Firebird (Python)
Steve Zwiren (USA) DAY
Mark Montgomery (USA) DAY
Anthony Puleo (USA) DAY

Roush Racing – Mercury Merkur
XR4Ti, Mecury Capri
Kenper Miller (USA) DAY
Bobby Akin (USA) DAY
Paul Gentilozzi (USA) DAY
Scott Pruett (USA) DAY, SEB
Paul Miller (USA) DAY
Pete Halsmer (USA) DAY, SEB
Mark Martin (USA) DAY
Lyn St James (USA) DAY, SEB
Deborah Gregg (USA) DAY, SEB
Andy Petery (USA) DAY, SEB
Les Delano (USA) DAY, SEB
Craig Carter (USA) DAY, SEB

S & L Racing (Schubott/Ludemann)
– Spice SE88P Buick
Jim Miller (USA) DAY, SEB
Linda Ludemann (USA) DAY, SEB
Scott Schubot (USA) DAY, SEB

SP Racing (Gary Auberlen)
– Porsche 911 Carrera (RSR?)
Gary Auberlen (USA) DAY, SEB
Adrian Gang (USA) DAY, SEB
Cary Eisenlohr (USA) DAY
Bill Auberlen (USA) DAY, SEB

SARD (Shin Kato)
– SARD MC88S Toyota
Martin Donnelly (GB) FUJ
Jochen Dauer (D) FUJ
Syuuroku Sasaki (J) FUJ

Team Sauber Mercedes
– Sauber Mercedes C9-88
Jean-Louis Schlesser (F) JER, JAR, MZA,
SIL, BRN, BH, NUR, SPA, FUJ, SAN
Mauro Baldi (I) JER, JAR, MZA, SIL,
BRN, BH, NUR, SPA, FUJ, SAN
Jochen Mass (D) JER, MZA, SIL, BRN,
BH, NUR, SPA, FUJ, SAN
James Weaver (GB) SIL, BRN
Stefan Johansson (S) NUR, SPA, SAN
Kenny Acheson (GB) FUJ
Phillipe Streiff (F) FUJ

Secateva – WM P87 Peugeot,
WM P88 Peugeot
Claude Haldi (CH) LM
Jean-Daniel Raulet (F) LM
Roger Dorchy (F) LM
Pascal Pessiot (F) LM

Sentry Bank Equipment (Ken Bupp)
– Chevrolet Camaro (Frings)
Ken Bupp (USA) DAY, SEB
Jack Boxstrom (CDN) DAY
Kent Painter (USA) DAY, SEB
Guy Church (USA) DAY, SEB
Robert Peters (CDN) SEB

Team Shelby (Carroll Shelby)
– Dodge Daytona
Tim Evans (USA) DAY, SEB
Jack Broomall (USA) DAY, SEB
Garth Ullom (USA) DAY, SEB
Neil Hanneman (USA) DAY

Shizumatsu Racing
– Mazda 757
Tetsuji Shiratori (J) FUJ
Syuuji Fujii (J) FUJ
Terumitsu Fujieda (J) FUJ

Silk Cut/Castrol Jaguar
(Tom Walkinshaw)
– Jaguar XJR-9
Martin Brundle (GB) DAY, JER, JAR,
SEB, MZA, SIL, LM, BRN, BH, NUR,
SPA, FUJ, SAN
Raul Boesel (BR) DAY, SEB (DND), LM
John Nielsen (DK) DAY, JER, JAR, SEB,
LM, BRN, BH
Danny Sullivan (USA) DAY, SEB, LM
Davy Jones (USA) DAY, SEB, LM
Jan Lammers (NL) DAY, JER, JAR, SEB,
MZA, SIL, LM, BRN, BH, NUR, SPA,
FUJ, SAN
Eddie Cheever (USA) DAY, JER, JAR,
MZA, SIL, NUR, SPA, FUJ, SAN
John Watson (GB) DAY, JER, JAR, LM
Johnny Dumfries (GB) DAY, JER, JAR,
MZA, SIL, LM, BRN, BH, NUR, SPA
(DND), FUJ (DND), SAN
Andy Wallace (GB) JER, LM, BH
Henri Pescarolo (F) LM
Price Cobb (USA) LM
Derek Daly (IRL) LM
Larry Perkins (AUS) LM
Kevin Cogan (USA) LM

Simms Romano Racing
– Mazda RX-7
Steve Burgner (USA) DAY
Paul Romano (USA) DAY, SEB
Bill Colom (USA) DAY
Jeff Green (USA) DAY
Bill McVey (USA) SEB
Robert Seaman (USA) SEB
William Hornack (USA) SEB

Skoal Bandit Racing
(Buz McCall) – Chevrolet
Camaro (Riggins)
Buz McCall (USA) DAY, SEB
Paul Dallenbach (USA) DAY, SEB
Max Jones (USA) DAY
Jack Baldwin (USA) DAY, SEB

Spice Engineering /BP Spice
Engineering – Spice SE88C
Ford Cosworth DFL
Thorkild Thyrring (DK) JER, JAR,
MZA, SIL, LM, BRN, BH, NUR,
SPA, FUJ, SAN
Almo Coppelli (I) JER, JAR, MZA, SIL,
LM, BRN, BH, NUR, SPA
Gordon Spice (GB) JER, JAR, MZA, SIL,
LM, BRN, BH, NUR, SPA, FUJ, SAN
Ray Bellm (GB) JER, JAR, MZA, SIL, LM,
BRN, BH, NUR, SPA, FUJ, SAN
Eliseo Salazar (RCH) LM, SAN
Pierre de Thoisy (F) LM
Eliseo Salazar (RCH) FUJ

Spirit of Brandon
(Henry Brosnaham)
– Chevrolet Camaro (Howe)
Henry Brosnaham (USA) SEB
Kurt Keller (USA) SEB

Swiss Team Salamin
– Porsche 962C
Antoine Salamin (CH) JER, JAR, MZA,
SIL, BRN, BH, NUR, SPA, SAN (DND)
Enzo Calderari (CH) JER
Max Cohen-Olivar (MA) JAR, SIL
Dudley Wood (GB) MZA
Hellmut Mundas (D) SIL
Luigi Taverna (I) BRN
Giovanni Lavaggi (I) BH, NUR, SPA, SAN
Jean-Denis Delétraz (CH) BH

Takefuji Schuppan Racing/Team/
Rothmans Porsche
(Vern Schuppan)
– Porsche 962C (Thompson)
Brian Redman (GB) LM, FUJ
Eje Elgh (S) LM
Jean-Pierre Jarier (F) LM
Derek Bell (GB) FUJ

Ash Tisdelle
– Chevrolet Camaro (Riggins)
Rusty Bond (USA) DAY (DND), SEB
Ash Tisdelle (USA) DAY (DND), SEB
Lance Van Every (USA) DAY (DND), SEB
Nort Northam (USA) SEB

Toyota Team Tom's
– Toyota 88C
Geoff Lees (GB) LM, FUJ
Masanori Sekiya (J) LM, FUJ
Kaoru Hoshino (J) LM
Paolo Barilla (I) LM, FUJ
Hitoshi Ogawa (J) LM, FUJ
Tiff Needell (GB) LM
Keiichi Suzuki (J) FUJ
Stefan Johansson (S) FUJ

Transact Inc (Jeffrey von Braun)
– Argo JM19B Ferrari
Steve Johnson (USA) DAY
Bob Strait (USA) DAY
Geoff Nicol (AUS) DAY

Trust Racing Team
– Porsche 962C/GTI
George Fouché (ZA) FUJ
Vern Schuppan (AUS) FUJ
Sarel van der Merwe (ZA) FUJ

Unigestion Team /Noël del Bello
Racing – Sauber C8 Mercedes
Bernard Santal (CH) SIL, LM, BH
Jacques Guillot (F) SIL
Noël del Bello (F) SIL, LM, BH
Bernard de Dryver (B) LM
Hervé Regout (B) BH

Uniroyal Goodrich (Jim Busby) –
Porsche 962 (Chapman)
Bob Wollek (F) DAY
Mauro Baldi (I) DAY
Brian Redman (GB) DAY

URD Junior Team – URD C82 BMW
Phil Mahre (USA) DAY
Hellmut Mundas (D) DAY
Steve Mahre (USA) DAY (DND)

Veskanda Racing – Veskanda C1
Chevrolet John Bowe (AUS) SAN
Dick Johnson (AUS) SAN

Greg Walker Racing – Chevrolet
Corvette (Linderfer)
Greg Walker (USA) DAY, SEB
King Smith (USA) DAY, SEB
Scott Lagasse (USA) DAY, SEB

Winters/Whitehall
Motorsports (Paul Gentilozzi)
– Spice SE87L Pontiac,
Spice SE88P Pontiac
Skeeter McKitterick (USA)
DAY, SEB
Bill Koll (USA) DAY
Tom Winters (USA) DAY
Claude Ballot-Léna (F) DAY, SEB
Mario Hytten (CH) DAY
Jean-Louis Ricci (F) DAY, SEB
Olindo Iacobelli (USA) DAY

Gary Wonzer Racing
– Lola T616 Mazda
Jonathan Green (USA) DAY
Joseph Hamilton (USA) DAY
Bill Bean (USA) DAY, SEB
Gary Wonzer (USA) DAY, SEB
Mike Cooper (USA) SEB

John Wood Racing
– Alba AR5 Buick
Brent O'Neill (USA) DAY
John Wood (USA) DAY
David Rocha (USA) DAY

RESULTS

Daytona 24 Hours,
30/31 January, USA
Started 79, finished 26
1st Brundle (GB)/Boesel (BR)/Nielsen
(DK) Jaguar XJR-9
2nd Wollek (F)/Baldi (I)/Redman (GB)
Porsche 962
3rd Cheever (USA)/Watson (GB)/
Dumfries (GB) Jaguar XJR-9

Jerez 800km,
6 March, Spain
Started 23, finished 16
1st Schlesser (F)/Baldi (I)/Mass (D)
Sauber Mecedes C9-88
2nd Nielsen (DK)/Watson (GB)/Wallace
(GB) Jaguar XJR-9
3rd Wollek (F)/Ludwig (D)
Porsche 962C

Jarama Supersprint,
13 March, Spain
Started 23, finished 17
1st Cheever (USA)/Brundle (GB)
Jaguar XJR-9
2nd Schlesser (F)/Baldi (I) Sauber
Mercedes C9-88
3rd Nielsen (DK)/Watson (GB)
Jaguar XJR-9

Sebring 12 Hours
19 March, USA
Started 65, finished 37
1st Stuck (D)/Ludwig (D)
Porsche 962
2nd Krages ('John Winter') (D)/
Jelinski (D)/Barilla (I) Porsche 962
3rd Cobb (USA)/Weaver (GB)
Porsche 962

Monza 1000km,
10 April, Italy
Started 26, finished 11
1st Brundle (GB)/Cheever (USA)
Jaguar XJR-9
2nd Schlesser (F)/Baldi (I)/Mass (D)
Sauber Mercedes C9-88
3rd Larrauri (RA)/Sigala (I)
Porsche 962C

Silverstone 1000km
8 May, Great Britain
Started 27, finished 18
1st Cheever (USA)/Brundle (GB)
Jaguar XJR-9
2nd Schlesser (F)/Mass (D) Sauber
Mercedes C9-88
3rd Baldi (I)/Weaver (GB) Sauber
Mercedes C9-88

Le Mans 24 Hours
11/12 June, France
Started 49, finished 27
1st Lammers (NL)/Dumfries (GB)/Wallace
(GB) Jaguar XJR-9
2nd Stuck (D)/Ludwig (D)/Bell (GB)
Porsche 962C
3rd Dickens (S)/Krages ('John Winter')
(D)/Jelinski (D) Porsche 962C

Brno 360km
10 July, Czechoslovakia
Started 17, finished 12
1st Mass (D)/Schlesser (F) Sauber
Mercedes C9-88
2nd Brundle (GB)/Nielsen (DK) Jaguar
XJR-9
3rd Lammers (NL)/Dumfries (GB) Jaguar
XJR-9

Brands Hatch 1000km
24 July, Great Britain
Started 23, finished 13
1st Nielsen (DK)/Wallace (GB)/Brundle
(GB) Jaguar XJR-9
2nd Ludwig (D)/Wollek (F) Porsche 962C
3rd Baldi (I)/Schlessr (F) Sauber
Mercedes C9-88

Nürburgring 1000km
3 September, Germany
Started 30, finished 17
(Run in two heats but stopped at 200
laps due to torrential rain)
1st Schlesser (F)/Mass (D) Sauber
Mercedes C9-88
2nd Cheever (USA)/Brundle (GB) Jaguar
XJR-9
3rd Wollek (F)/Barilla (I) Porsche 962C

Spa 1000km
18 September, Belgium
Started 27, finished 17
1st Baldi (I)/Johansson (S) Sauber
Mercedes C9-88
2nd Lammers (NL)/Brundle (GB)
Jaguar XJR-9
3rd Schlesser (F)/Mass (D)
Sauber C9-88

Fuji 1000km
9 October, Japan
Started 35, finished 22
1st Cheever (USA)/Brundle (GB) Jaguar
XJR-9
2nd Ludwig (D)/Cobb (USA)
Porsche 962C
3rd Jelinski (D)/Krages (John Winter) (D)
Porsche 962C

Sandown Park Supersrint
20 November, Australia
Started 18, finished 14
1st Schlesser (F)/Mass (D) Sauber
Mercedes C9-88
2nd Baldi (I)/Johansson (S) Sauber
Mercedes C9-88
3rd Cheever (USA)/Brundle (GB)
Jaguar XJR-9

1989

SAUBER SCINTILLATES OR RATHER MERCEDES DOES

This time nothing was going to stop Mercedes-Benz from winning the championships, whilst TWR Jaguar began to falter.

Of more concern were two new additions by the FIA that would seriously damage sports/prototype racing. It began with a punitive diktat that would cost any team who did not attend every race $250,000, although there was the FISA option of missing one European race. The second was that any fuel you liked would be acceptable in a new 750kg C1 class as long as you were going to use a normally aspirated 3.5-litre engine.

However, there was a problem of another sort. Full-time uniformed officials, in this instance an administrator and a technical overseer, applied the rules to their maximum, which caused further problems. In TWR's case it required serious bodywork alterations.

The costly fine would come into action *tout de suite* whilst the other ended the C2 class in due course, with Spice Engineering in the vanguard with their 1989 C1 car. This would be Gordon Spice's final racing year and he retired after Le Mans, having had enough and with other priorities building up. Sadly, the true Spice Engineering soon disappeared although the Spice name hung around for several years beyond this.

Only eight venues constituted the 1989 FIA Championship whilst Le Mans had gone solo, a regular occurrence over time. This time it was ownership of television coverage and the Longines/Olivetti timing that were the problems. All the FIA races were run to a 480km distance; they were Suzuka, Dijon, Jarama, Brands Hatch, Nürburgring, Donington, Spa and Mexico. Apparently 1000km was too long.

These were all won by Team Sauber Mercedes except Dijon which fell to the Joest Porsche 962C (011) sprint car driven by Wollek/Jelinski whilst the Saubers finished 2nd and 3rd and the Jaguars both retired. Sauber also won at Le Mans.

TWR Jaguar employed a young Ross Brawn to develop a turbocharged car, which was the XJR-11, as the XJR-9 was now coming to the end of its potential. This started off with promise at Brands Hatch but race reliability was uncertain and the XJR-11s gradually slipped down the field thereafter. One finished 5th and the other retired at Brands, they were 5th and 10th at the Nürburgring, both retired at Donington and Spa, and embarrassingly at Mexico they were replaced by two XJR-9s which did at least finish 5th and 6th. Things improved in 1990/91 but for now they were struggling.

By contrast Sauber Mercedes had a stonking good year and then some. Their driver line-up was Jean-Louis Schlesser, Mauro Baldi, Kenny Acheson, Jochen Mass, Manuel Reuter, Stanley Dickens and Gianfranco Brancatelli.

C2 continued but it was finished prematurely after 1989, the final victors being Chamberlain Engineering ahead of Team Mako and PC Automotive, all British teams.

Jaguar were also suffering in the States with Wollek/Bell/John Andretti winning at Daytona ahead of the TWR Castrol Jaguar XJR-9 D of Cobb/Nielsen/Wallace/Lammers whilst at Sebring the Electramotive Nissan GTP ZX-T of Robinson/Geoff Brabham/Luyendyk finished 1st ahead of the same Jaguar.

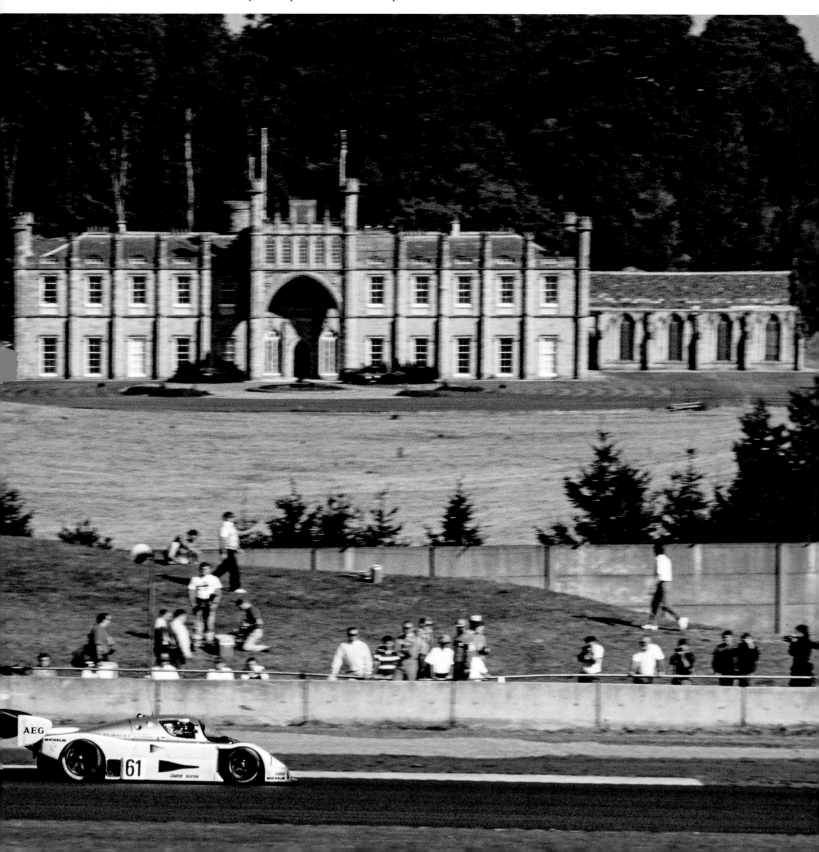

Donington 480km, 3 September 1989 There is a surprising connection between this Donington race and the Second World War. They share the same monthly date, 3 September 1939 and 3 September 1989, 50 years on, plus of course the presence of Mercedes-Benz who raced here together with Auto Union in 1937/38. In the background is Donington Hall, which was owned by the Gillies Shields family from 1902 onwards. In 1931 John Gillies Shields agreed to let Fred Kraner use the roads of the estate to create a motor-racing circuit, Donington Park, which ultimately led to the 1937 and 1938 Donington Grands Prix won by Auto Union. Fast forward to 1989 and here is the no.61 Sauber Mercedes C99/88 88-C9-06 on its way to 2nd place behind its companion no.62 which won the race. *LAT*

← **Daytona 24 Hours, 5/6 February 1989** Daytona began with Bob Holbert driving his late son's two-time Daytona-winning Porsche 962 around the track. At the start of the race Arie Luyendyk in the Electramotive Nissan GTP ZX-T has the no.60 TWR Jaguar XJR-9 D of Jan Lammers for company with the other Nissan ZX-T of Michael Roe behind him. To his right is Larrauri in the Brun 962C with Klaus Ludwig in Leven's Bayside Porsche 962 no.86 beyond and the other two TWR Jaguars behind. The no.66 driven by Derek Daly collided with Roe's Nissan (both drivers blaming each other) and retired whilst the Nissan was withdrawn at 51 laps. The winning no.67 Porsche is at the back of the frame. *LAT*

→ **Daytona 24 Hours, 5/6 February 1989** The GTO class was won by the Roush Racing STROH'S LIGHT Lincoln Mercury Cougar XR-7 driven by Pete Halsmer, Bob Earl, Mark Martin and Paul Stewart, son of Jackie Stewart, who was invited to drive the last stint. They finished 6th overall despite a transmission change and the sister Roush car of Wally Dallenbach, Dorsey Schroeder and Mark Martin following the no.16 here finished 7th after clutch problems. *LAT*

↙ **Daytona 24 Hours, 5/6 February 1989** Electramotive was created by aerospace scientist Don Devendorf and John Knepp in 1975. In 1985, they raced the Lola-designed Lola-Nissan 810, which gradually evolved into the Nissan GTP ZX-T in 1986. By 1988 it was almost wholly Electramotive in design and manufacture and they had many wins with Geoff Brabham who won the IMSA GTP Drivers' Championship. At Daytona Luyendyk, Robinson and Brabham joined by Michael Roe were leading for many hours but retired on lap 453 after losing a valve head. It had never run for more than 3 hours and chief engineer Trevor Harris was pleased that it lasted so long. *LAT*

→ **Daytona 24 Hours, 5/6 February 1989** Tom Milner bought three Probe GTPs from Ford in 1987 and raced them in 1988 sponsored by NTW (National Tyre Warehouse). Milner recalled, "Ford never did anything for us. I think they would rather have liked to have seen the thing disappear… I'd say it was one of the major mistakes of my life… I ran the cars only in 1988." Yet two were entered by Milner for Jean-Pierre Frey, Marty Roth and Albert Naon Jr, who finished 24th in the no.5 car with a 6-litre Ford V8 whilst the no.6 Zakspeed 2.1 turbo engine car retired with electrical problems. Milner had a two-year contract with NTW, but they were taken over by Western Auto and in turn acquired by Sears Roebuck. So he filed a lawsuit for breach of contract and won. *LAT*

Daytona 24 Hours, 5/6 February 1989 The Mazda Motors of America Mazda 757B driven by Yoshima Katayama, Takashi Yorino and Elliot Forbes-Robinson finished 5th despite having to replace an axle. It was entered in the GTP category but having 600bhp from its 4-rotor engine was not enough to challenge the bigger-engined cars. *LAT*

Daytona 24 Hours, 5/6 February 1989 There wasn't much hope in Jim Busby's team at Daytona from Bob Wollek who was driving the long-tailed Miller High Life/BF Goodrich Porsche 962 (108C/CO2). It had many and assorted issues including engine, turbo, electrics, brakes and too much downforce which were all sorted out. John Andretti and Derek Bell with Wollek drove the car as hard as it would go and beat Price Cobb, John Nielsen, Andy Wallace and Jan Lammers who had joined them after his Jaguar, the faster of the two cars, expired. 1st and 2nd were only 82 seconds apart whilst the Brun Motorsports/Kalagian Racing Porsche 962C (002BM) driven by Larrauri, Brun and Stuck, recovering from a knee injury, finished 3rd. *LAT*

Sebring 12 Hours, 18 March 1989 After the relative disappointment at Daytona, Electramotive Engineering won the Sebring 12 Hours with their no.83 Nissan GTP ZX-T (88-01) driven by Robinson, Brabham and Luyendyk. They entered two cars with the same three drivers, but the second car (no.84) lasted only 14 laps when its left rear wheel came adrift with Luyendyk driving. Jaguar were once again 2nd (John Nielsen/Price Cobb) two laps behind the Electramotive Nissan having worn out their brakes trying to stay with it. The other TWR Jaguar, driven by Davy Jones/Jan Lammers, collided with a coasting car and spent many laps in the pits being patched up, eventually finishing 14th, 49 laps behind the winner. *Revs*

Sebring 12 Hours, 18 March 1989 Mike Gue of Essex Racing entered their Spice SE88P Buick V6 for Charles Morgan and Tom Hessert at Sebring and finished 9th and 2nd in the Camel Lights class. They had a successful season and Morgan finished 2nd and Hessert 3rd in the IMSA Camel Lights Championship. *Revs*

Sebring 12 Hours, 18 March 1989 MOMO founder Gianpiero Moretti, Massimo Sigala, Derek Bell and Michael Roe were a Momo/Gebhardt foursome in the Porsche 962 (001GS). They qualified 10th and finished 4th. Roe began racing in 1975 and finished 2nd in the 1978 RAC and Townsend Thoresen FF1600 Championships, and won the Brands Hatch Festival to end the year. He briefly raced in F3, which was unsatisfactory, and later retired but came back in 1983 to race in the Can-Am challenge, which he won in 1984. Later he turned to endurance racing and retired after finishing 17th at the 1990 Le Mans for Nissan Motorsport. *Revs*

Sebring 12 Hours, 18 March 1989 Bruce Leven's Bayside Racing Porsche 962 (139) finished 3rd at Sebring hampered by severe brake problems. It was driven by James Weaver and German-born Dominic Dobson. Up close Sebring's aerodrome road surface looks very punishing, which it was, and in the background are the herd of light aircraft that lived here in perpetuity. Leven's Bayside Disposal team record at Sebring was very impressive: they finished 10th in 1980, 1st in 1981, 5th in 1982, 3rd in 1983, 1st in 1987 and 1st in 1988. *LAT*

Suzuka 480km, 9 April 1989 The first race in the Sports Prototype Championship had 34 starters and two Toyota 89C-Vs at the front, with Geoff Lees/Johnny Dumfries on pole and Hitoshi Ogawa/Paolo Barilla alongside. The no.61 Sauber-Mercedes (Schlesser/Baldi) is marginally in front at the off and will win the race with teammate Kenny Acheson 2nd, who was driving solo as Jochen Mass had contracted an eye infection. This was allowed as long as the driver did not exceed 3½ hours at the wheel. On the left Jan Lammers is going for it but the car ran out of fuel on lap 80 whilst the second Jaguar (Nielsen/Wallace) finished 5th. In the middle is Barilla in one of the Toyotas which finished 6th, but the other one finished 20th following fuel and electrical mishaps. *LAT*

Suzuka 480km, 9 April 1989 The winning car topping up the go juice and note the silver finish, an historic Mercedes feature down the decades and still in use now. What is the man at the front with his foot on the nose of the C9/88 (88-C9-04) pointing at? Presumably Schlesser in the car, whilst at centre bottom Mauro Baldi is removing his left glove. There were 'issues', however, because Acheson was leading and despite Max Welti telling him by radio to let the French/Italian duo by, Kenny apparently couldn't hear him properly. Mercedes were anxious that a two-man team would get 20 drivers' points whilst one, of course, would only get 10. Eventually team manager David Price repeated the request and Acheson responded. *LAT*

Suzuka 480km, 9 April 1989 Only four C2 cars appeared at Suzuka and this one, the Chamberlain Engineering Spice SE86C Hart turbo (Fermin Velez/Nick Adams), won the class but was a lowly 23rd due to a very sedate pace and the wretched fuel limitations. Both the Spice works cars retired with water leaks and electrical issues whilst the Roy Baker Racing Tiga GC289 was disqualified for an assisted start. *LAT*

↑ **Dijon 480km, 21 May 1989** Dijon was a return to former Porsche hegemony with Bob Wollek and Frank Jelinski winning in Reinhold Joest's Porsche 962C (011). It was a case of Goodyears lasting longer than the Michelin rubber. Jaguar meanwhile qualified 7th (Lammers/Tambay) and 9th (Nielsen/Wallace) but both retired. Also in the mix was the Toyota Team Tom's Toyota T88C (Dumfries/Lees) that finished 4th with the two Sauber Mercedes C9s finishing 2nd and 3rd. This is the 3rd-placed Baldi/Acheson C9/88 (88-C9-04) in company with the Nielsen/Wallace Jaguar XJR-9 (TWR-J12C-588). *LAT*

→ **Le Mans 24 Hours, 10/11 June 1989**
There were three Sauber Mercedes C9s at Le Mans, no.63 for Jochen Mass, Manuel Reuter and Stanley Dickens, no.62 for Jean-Louis Schlesser, Jean-Pierre Jabouille and Alain Cudini and no.61 for Mauro Baldi, Kenny Acheson and Gianfranco Brancatelli. The cars were now using the 32-valve M119 engine giving 720bhp @ 7,000rpm. They qualified respectively 11th, 2nd and 1st but finished 1st, 5th and 2nd. There were the usual problems, with the no.62 seen here suffering the most with power loss and body damage. *LAT*

← **Le Mans 24 Hours, 10/11 June 1989** TWR Jaguars arrived with four cars: no.1 for Jan Lammers/Patrick Tambay/Andrew Gilbert-Scott, no.2 for John Nielsen/Andy Wallace/Price Cobb, no.3 for Davy Jones/Derek Daly and Jeff Kline and no.4 for Alan Ferté/Michel Ferté/Eliseo Salazar. The no.1 car was the fastest but all had various problems, with a collision, overheating, gear selection, broken exhausts and so on. Yet Tambay led the race after midnight and the car stayed there until 6.20am on Sunday when its gearbox had to be replaced and later had a spin, nearly hitting the Ferté car. No.1 finished 4th, no.4 8th with Alain Ferté setting fastest lap, no.2 retired (head gasket) and no.3 was out with a valve-spring failure. *GPL*

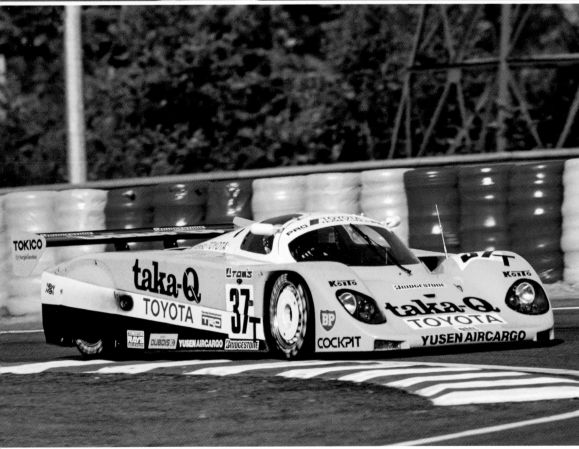

← **Le Mans 24 Hours, 10/11 June 1989** Looking like an ersatz Porsche 962 this is the Toyota Team Tom's Toyota 89C-V (08) of Geoff Lees, Johnny Dumfries and John Watson. It boasted a turbocharged 3.2-litre V8 engine giving 800bhp in qualifying mode and Lees lapped a time of 3m 15.51, but this was with the T-car and did not count. There were two 89CVs entered, the other driven by Paolo Barilla, Hitoshi Ogawa and Ross Cheever, and also a 4-cylinder 88C version (no.38) for Kaoro Hoshino, Didier Artzet and Keeichi Suzuki. They officially qualified 17th, 24th and 25th respectively but all were gone by lap 58, the no.37 in an accident (Dumfries), the no.36 with a broken engine and the no.38 also crashed. *LAT*

→ **Le Mans 24 Hours, 10/11 June 1989** Nissan had ended their March connections and approached Lola to build a new all-composite car for them, the Nissan R89C with a twin-turbo 3.5-litre V8. Three were entered. No.23 (Masahiro Hasemi/Kazuyoshi Hoshino/Toshio Suzuki) started 19th but retired on lap 167 with a cracked cylinder head. The no.24 car was the quickest but Julian Bailey was going flat out from the start and collided with Nielsen's TWR Jaguar on lap 5 and retired with front suspension damage together with a torn-off nose. The third car, driven by Geoff Brabham, Arie Luyendyk and Chip Robinson, lasted 250 laps after surviving brake fade but retired due to an oil leak. This is the Bailey/Blundell/Donnelly car during qualifying with Blundell driving. *LAT*

→ **Le Mans 24 Hours, 10/11 June 1989** Porsches still abounded at Le Mans and this one was something special. It was de facto a 'works' 962C (145) but entered by Joest Racing for Bob Wollek and Hans-Joachim Stuck. Stuck qualified it 5th fastest with a 3-litre race engine after the qualifying special broke. All Joest, Brun and Schuppan cars had water-cooled 3-litre engines. Wollek and Stuck were never out of the first six and spent 6 hours in the lead but were slowed by various problems, a split water hose, an engine fire and a sticking clutch. They finished 3rd but could have won otherwise. *LAT*

◄ **Le Mans 24 Hours, 10/11 June 1989** Despite the 3rd-place finish other Porsches fared badly, the no.14 RLR 962C GTi (200) caught fire on the 23rd hour (lap 339) and burnt out, ditto the Porsche Kremer 962C (CK6) on lap 303 and the Team Schuppan 962C on lap 69. Richard Lloyd also entered his other 962 GTi (201) no.15 for Steven Anskar, David Hobbs and Damon Hill which was apparently lacking all-out speed. They qualified 23rd and were in 9th place in the 14th hour but expired two hours later with engine failure. *LAT*

► **Le Mans 24 Hours, 10/11 June 1989** Following the demise and troubles of the usual C2 suspects, Chamberlain Engineering, Spice Engineering et al., Le Mans veteran Jean-Claude Andruet, Phillip Farjon and Syunji Kasuya finished 14th in Farjon's three-year-old Cougar and C2 winner. It was entered by Courage and renamed CM20LM Porsche. They had driven the car conservatively and even overcame an old Cougar problem, fly-away doors. *LAT*

► **Le Mans 24 Hours, 10/11 June 1989** This was the fifth and final evocation of Aston Martin V8-powered sports prototypes after Nimrod, Nimrod-Ray Mallock, Cheetah and EMKA. Aston Martin with Proteus Technology comprised Peter Livanos, Victor Gauntlett, Richard Williams and Ray Mallock. They made their debut at Dijon having been fined $250,000 by the FIA for missing Suzuka (they had crashed the car during testing at Donington) and hence for not attending every race in the series. Two were entered: no.18 (Costas Los/Brian Redman/Michael Roe) and no.19 (David Leslie/Ray Mallock/David Sears). The cars were not fast enough on Mulsanne (218mph) and the no.19 car retired with electrical troubles whilst no.18 finished 11th. *LAT*

Jarama 480km, 25 June 1989 The FISA option of missing one European race was taken up by Aston Martin, Richard Lloyd Racing, Joest, Mussato Action Car and Mazda at Jarama. Instead some of them went to the well remunerated Norisring. At Jarama Mauro Baldi started 1st in the Sauber C9/88 (87-C9-02) with Schlesser 2nd and Lammers 3rd in the TWR Jaguar. Baldi/Acheson in the no.61 probably would have won but for the loss of brake fluid, which cost three laps to repair, and dropped them to 5th. So Mass/Schlesser won and Lammers/Tambay were 2nd. The no.61 takes the flag. *LAT*

Jarama 480km, 25 June 1989 The no.1 TWR Jaguar XJR-9 (TWR-J12C-588) of Lammers/Tambay and the no.2 XJR-9 (TWR-J12C-688) which finished 5th with the taka-Q Toyota 89C-V (08) of Johnny Dumfries which finished 10th. The Jaguars had crumbling tyres due to the 100-degree (F) temperatures whilst Dumfries drove the entire race, and nearly passed out because of said temperatures, as co-driver Geoff Lees did not drive due to sickness. *LAT*

Jarama 480km, 25 June 1989 Julian Bailey and Mark Blundell drove the Lola-created Nissan R89C-04 to 8th place after qualifying 6th, not for any driver lacking but again due to the extreme heat that was destroying their tyres. This might have been avoided but the Nissan's radio was inoperative and Bailey could not warn the team so when he pitted to hand over to Blundell the crew fitted the same tyres as before. *LAT*

Jarama 480km, 25 June 1989 The Chamberlain Engineering Spice SE89C Ford Cosworth DFL (Fermin Velez/Nick Adams) was the C2 victor. Meanwhile, C2 champions Spice Engineering had taken advantage of the new FISA regulations allowing 3.5-litre C1 cars with a minimum 750kg weight limit compared to the 900kg of the orthodox C1 cars. The Thorkild Thyrring/Wayne Taylor SE89C Ford Cosworth DFZ 3.5 (003) finished 4th overall whilst teammates Eliseo Salazar and Ray Bellm in the no.21 (004), who were marginally quicker in qualifying, retired when their engine caught fire, no doubt another victim of the extreme heat. Gordon Spice, meanwhile, had decided to retire from racing after Le Mans. His other business activities took precedence and he did not want to race anymore. *LAT*

⬅ **Brands Hatch 480km, 23 July 1989** This time the no.61 Baldi/Acheson Sauber C9/88 Mercedes (87-C9-02) won the race on merit whilst the no.62 of Schlesser/Mass ran 2nd until a large piece of rear tyre rubber came adrift and damaged the Sauber's rear suspension. They dropped to 6th place as a result but ultimately finished 3rd after the Jaguar travails. *LAT*

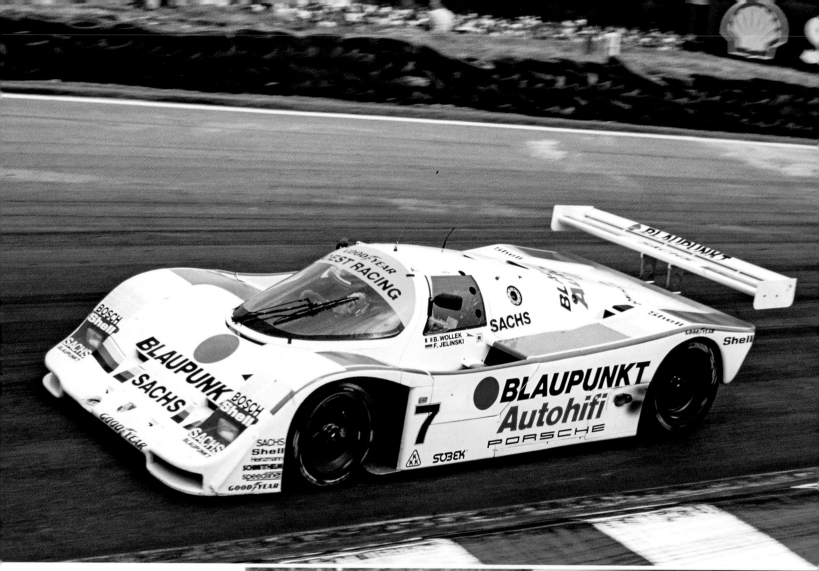

↑ **Brands Hatch 480km, 23 July 1989** There's life in the old dog yet apparently although this Joest Blaupunkt Porsche 962C (145) was the Stuck/Wollek Le Mans car, so not so old. At Brands Hatch it was raced by Wollek and Frank Jelinski where it qualified 6th and finished 2nd after the Jaguar XJR-11s retired and the no.62 Sauber was delayed. *LAT*

→ **Brands Hatch 480km, 23 July 1989** The Protech Aston Martin AMR1 (04) arrived at Brands Hatch having shed some *avoirdupois*, now weighing 920kg, and driven by Ray Mallock and all-round hero and ex-Porsche, Ferrari and much else racer Brian Redman. They qualified a modest 14th just a second shy of the TWR Jaguar XJR-9 of Nielsen/ Wallace and eventually finished 4th, helped by the car's extreme downforce. *GPL*

↑ **Nürburgring 480km, 20 August 1989** Thirty-six cars started the Nürburgring 480km with the omnipresent Saubers in the lead of course. However, back in the melee is the Wollek/Jelinski Blaupunkt Joest Porsche which will lead the race and get to within one lap of the finish and then run out of fuel. What a farce. Behind the Saubers are Andrew Gilbert-Scott in the Nissan R89C, Oscar Larrauri in the red Brun Jägermeister Porsche 962C, the taka-Q Toyota 89C of Johnny Dumfries and at left the no.10 Kremer Porsche CK6 driven by South African George Fouché with Giovanni Lavaggi which will finish 3rd. Further back are the two Jaguar XJR-11s that ended 5th and 10th after assorted problems. *LAT*

↗ **Nürburgring 480km, 20 August 1989** Andrew Gilbert-Scott in the Nissan R89C showed his prowess here, chasing down the Saubers and taking the lead on lap 18 and pulling away. After Bailey took over, their lead grew to 30 seconds but Mass caught up and the Nissan eventually ran out of fuel on lap 103, finishing unclassified. This is Gilbert-Scott ahead of Schlesser at the Coca Cola Kurve with the link road to the old Nordschleife in the background. *LAT*

→ **Nürburgring 480km, 20 August 1989** Irish racer David Kennedy and Belgian Pierre Dieudonné drove the Mazdaspeed Mazda 767B 9001) to 13th overall and 1st in the GTP class despite the fuel restrictions. Kennedy's racing career started with Formula Ford in Ireland in 1972, then F3 in 1977, the Aurora British F1 series in 1978 and later briefly with the Shadow F1 team in 1980. Like so many talented drivers before and after, without the right car and the money it doesn't work. He moved to endurance racing in 1981 and drove for Mazdaspeed from 1984 to 1991 and retired from racing in 1994. *LAT*

↑ **Donington 480km, 3 September 1989** The Sauber Mercedes came to Donington, qualified 1st no.61 and 2nd no.62 and finished 2nd and 1st respectively in the race. Baldi led away whilst Schlesser in the no.62 car became embroiled in a battle with Lammers' Jaguar XJR-11 (189) and Bailey's Nissan. Lammers took 1st twice, but after the first fuel stop co-driver Tambay stopped with a broken distributor drive. Schlesser is just turning into Melbourne corner with Lammers looking to overtake. The other XJR-11 of Wallace/Ferté ran out of fuel on lap 115. Sauber's 1/2 victory guaranteed an already inevitable Team Championship crown for them. *LAT*

↗ **Donington 480km, 3 September 1989** Nissan Motorsports entered only one of their R89Cs at Donington for Julian Bailey and Mark Blundell, and the British duo finished 3rd on the same lap as the winners. This is Blundell followed by one of the Porsche 962s. *LAT*

→ **Spa 480km, 17 September 1989** The two Spice Engineering C1 Spice SE89Cs qualified 8th (Salazar/Bellm) no.21 and 14th (Taylor/Thyrring) no.22, the latter whilst the track was still damp. No.21's engine blew up on lap 53 but no.22 finished 5th ahead of the Joest Porsche 962C (004-104C) of Henri Pescarolo and Jean-Louis Ricci, which took 6th place. Wayne Taylor in the Spice looks like he is about to pass Pescarolo here. *LAT*

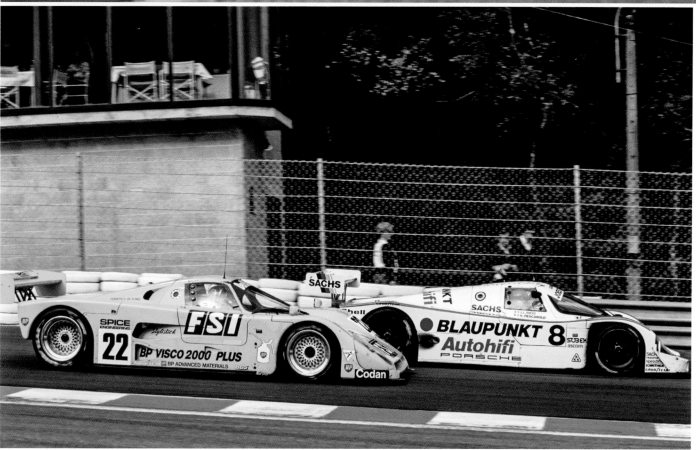

↑ **Spa 480km, 17 September 1989** The Schlesser/Mass Sauber Mercedes C9/88 (88-C9-05) started 6th on the grid and briefly led the race when teammate Baldi pitted. Thereafter the duo were in 2nd place but on the last lap Schlesser found himself running out of fuel. An obviously distressed Jean-Louis was no doubt thinking about his winning the Drivers' Championship, meanwhile another victory for the fuel regulations. As for the TWR Jaguar XJR-11s neither finished, the Lammers/Tambay car retiring on lap 16 with a blown turbo and the Nielsen/Wallace car on lap 26 with an electrical problem, and both Tambay and Wallace did not get to drive. *LAT*

↗ **Spa 480km, 17 September 1989** Somebody decided that this year there would be a rolling start from the bus stop to La Source. Amazingly nothing too dramatic occurred although Lammers connected with Baldi and the Armco but both survived. Tiff Needell in the RLR Porsche 962C GTi (201) is followed by Jari Nurminem in the Tiga Race Team Tiga GC289 (372) which had won the C2 class at Donington. At the rear is Didier Bonnet's Tiga GC289 (possibly 373) driven by Patrick Oudet and Gérard Tremblay. The RLR Porsche retired on lap 15 with engine failure, Nurminem lasted 36 laps before the electrics gave up whilst the Oudet/Tremblay Tiga finished 20th and 8th in C2. *LAT*

→ **Spa 480km, 17 September 1989** The lone Nissan Motorsport Nissan R89C 01 (Bailey/Blundell) was running a lean chip for the race in deference to the fuel restrictions, but in qualifying it was full on and Bailey qualified 7th after his best lap was hindered by a C2 car. They had been using cross-ply front tyres and radial rears for some time but although these worked in the dry, in the wet they were not so good. No.23 cuts inside the Mazdaspeed David Kennedy/Pierre Dieudonné Mazda 767B (001) which finished 9th and 1st in the GTP category. Towards the end of the race the Nissan was in 4th position, but Schlesser's final-lap retirement handed it 3rd place. *LAT*

Mexico 480km, 29 October 1989 The Sauber twins are away in front and it is now simply a case of who will win the Drivers' Championship. Mauro Baldi had just pipped Schlesser to pole by 0.094 of a second, the third-fastest being Dumfries in the Toyota 89C-V, but he was 1.5 seconds slower than Baldi's time. In the race a stoppage caused confusion and Schlesser was 6.5 seconds ahead of his teammates when he stopped for fuel and driver change on lap 39. However, Acheson having replaced Baldi on lap 37 soon caught and passed Mass in the no.62, but on lap 47 Kenny overdid it and crashed, thus Jean-Louis was the new World Champion driver. *LAT*

Mexico 480km, 29 October 1989 Behind the Sauber, Larrauri and Huysman brought the Repsol Brun Motorsport Porsche 962C into 2nd place with Jelinski/Pescarolo 3rd in the Joest Porsche 962C. The RLR Porsche GTi was 4th (Bell/ Needell) whilst 5th and 6th were occupied by the TWR Jaguar XJR-9s (Wallace/Ferte and Lammers/Tambay) in place of the disappointing XJR-11s. One lap behind them in 8th place was the Redman/Leslie Aston Martin AMR1 (05). It had been progressively lightened, had carbon brakes, clutch and titanium components allied to a 6.3-litre Callaway engine, giving a quoted 750bhp. It was a satisfactory end to their season but Ford now had a stake in Aston Martin and Jaguar, and the future was uncertain. *LAT*

1989 Teams, drivers and results

ENTRANTS

901 Racing (Peter Uria)
– Porsche 911
Jack Refenning (USA) DAY, SEB
Rusty Scott (USA) DAY
Freddy Baker (USA) DAY, SEB
Peter Uria (USA) DAY, SEB

A & R Auto Electric
(Anthony Puleo) – Chevrolet
Camaro (Bemco)
Wayne Akers (USA)
Kent Painter (USA)
Anthony Puleo (USA)
David Donner (USA)

ADA Engineering – ADA 02B
(Gebhardt) Ford Cosworth DFL
Lawrence Bristow (GB) LM
Ian Harrower (GB) LM
Colin Pool (GB) LM

Aspen Inn (Dick Greer)
– Mazda RX-7 (Chassis Dynamics)
Dick Greer (USA) DAY, SEB
Mike Mees (USA) DAY, SEB
John Finger (USA) DAY, SEB

Aston Martin (Proteus Technology)
– Aston Martin AMR1 (Courtalds)
David Leslie (GB) DIJ, LM, BH, NUR,
  DON, SPA, MEX
Brian Redman (GB) DIJ, LM, BH, NUR,
  DON, SPA, MEX
Costas Los (GR) LM
Michael Roe (IRL) LM, DON, SPA
David Sears (GB) LM, DON
Ray Mallock (GB) LM
Stanley Dickens (S) SPA

Al Bacon Performance
– Mazda RX-7
(Chassis Dynamics)
Al Bacon (USA) DAY
Bob Reed (USA) DAY
Rod Millen (NZ) DAY

All American Racers (Dan Gurney)
– Toyota 88C Dome
Drake Olson (USA) DAY, SEB
Chris Cord (USA) DAY, SEB
Steve Bren (USA) DAY, SEB

Al Bacon Performance
– Mazda RX-7
(Chassis Dynamics)
Al Bacon (USA) SEB
Bob Reed (USA) SEB

Roy Baker Racing/Roy Baker
Racing/GP Motorsport
– Tiga GC289 Ford Cosworth DFL,
Spice 87C Ford Cosworth DFL
John Sheldon (GB) SUZ (*DSQ*)
Leif Lindström (S) SUZ (*DSQ*)
Dudley Wood (GB) DIJ, LM, BH, NUR,
  DON, SPA (*DNS*)
Philippe de Henning (F) DIJ (*DND*), LM,
  BH, NUR, DON, SPA, MEX
Evan Clements (GB) LM
Chris Hodgetts (GB) MEX

Ball Bros Racing (Durst/Brockman)
– Spice SE88P Buick
Steve Durst (USA) DAY, SEB
Jay Cochran (USA) DAY, SEB
Mike Brockman (USA) DAY, SEB
Tony Belcher (USA) DAY

Bayside Motorsports/Texaco
Havoline Star (Bruce Leven)
– Porsche 962
Bruce Leven (USA) DAY
Rob Dyson (USA) DAY
Dominic Dobson (USA) DAY, SEB
John Paul, Jr (USA) DAY
Klaus Ludwig (D) DAY
James Weaver (GB) DAY, SEB
Sarel van der Merwe (ZA) DAY

Bieri Racing (Uli Bieri)
– Tiga GT286 Ferrari
Martino Finotto (I) DAY, SEB
Paolo Guatamacchi (I) DAY, SEB
Uli Bieri (CDN) DAY, SEB

Bob's Speed Products (Bob Lee)
– Pontiac Firebird (Python)
Del Russo Taylor (USA) SEB
Mark Montgomery (USA) SEB

Carlos Bobeda Racing
– Tiga GT286 Mazda
Tomas Lopez (MEX) SEB
Albert Rocca (USA) SEB
Carlos Bobeda (USA) SEB

Didier Bonnet – ALD 05 BMW,
Tiga GC289 Ford Cosworth DFL
Gérard Tremblay (F) JAR, BH, NUR,
  DON, SPA
Jean-Claude Justice (F) JAR (*DND*),
  BH, NUR
Joel Aulen (F) DON
Patrick Oudet (F) SPA, MEX
Gérard Cuynet (F) MEX

Brun Motorsports/Repsol Brun
Motorsports/Hydro Aluminium
Brun Motorsports/Hydro-Eterna
Watches Brun Motorsports –
Porsche 962 C (Thompson)
Oscar Larrauri (RA) DAY, SUZ, DIJ, LM,
  JAR, NUR, DON, SPA, MEX
Walter Brun (CH) SUZ, DIJ, LM, BH,
  BH, DON, SPA, MEX
Hans-Joachim Stuck (D) DAY
Harald Huysman (B) SUZ, DIJ, LM, JAR,
  BH, NUR, DON, SPA (*CAR DQ*), MEX
Juha Varjosaari (SF) SUZ (*DND*)
Jésus Pareja (E) SUZ, DIJ, LM, JAR, BH,
  NUR, DON, SPA, MEX
Maurizio Sandro Sala (BR) SUZ, LM
Stanley Dickens (S) DIJ, JAR, DON
Akihiko Nakaya (J) LM
Sarel van der Merwe (ZA) LM
Harald Grohs (D) LM
Roland Ratzenberger (A) LM, SPA
Walter Lechner (A) LM, BH
Uwe Schäfer (D) LM, BH, NUR, DON
  (*DND*), SPA (*CAR DQ*)
Dominique Lacaud (F) LM
Franz Konrad (A) LM, BH, NUR
Rudi Seher (D) LM
Andres Vilarino (E) LM

Budweiser Racing (Craig Rubright)
– Chevrolet Camaro (Dillon)
Craig Rubright (USA) DAY
Jean-Paul Libert (B) DAY
Kermit Upton (USA) DAY

Buick/Quaker State (Schubot/
Ludemann) – Spice SE88P Buick
Linda Ludemann (USA) DAY
Scott Schubot (USA) DAY
John Williams (GB) DAY

Ken Bupp – Chevrolet Camaro (Frings)
Ken Bupp (USA) SEB
Robert Peters (CDN) SEB

Caribbean Sol (Dale Kreider)
– Buick Somerset (Riggins)
Jack Boxstrom (CDN) DAY
Dale Kreider (USA) DAY
Mark Porcaro (USA) DAY
Carson Hurley (USA) DAY

Castrol Jaguar Racing/Silk
Cut Jaguar (Tom Walkinshaw)
– Jaguar XJR-9D, Jaguar XJR-9
LM, Jaguar XJR-11
Jan Lammers (NL) DAY, SEB, SUZ, DIJ,
  LM, JAR, BH, NUR, DON, SPA, MEX
Davy Jones (USA) DAY, SEB, LM
Raul Boesel (BR) DAY
Price Cobb (USA) DAY, SEB
John Nielsen (DK) DAY, SEB, SUZ, DIJ,
  LM, JAR, BH, NUR, DON
Andy Wallace (GB) DAY, SUZ, DIJ, LM,
  JAR, BH, NUR, DON, SPA (*DND*), MEX
Derek Daly (IRL) DAY
Martin Donnelly (GB) DAY
Patrick Tambay (F) DAY, SEB, DIJ, LM,
  JAR, BH, NUR, DON, SPA (*DND*), MEX
Andrew Gilbert-Scott (GB) LM
Price Cobb (USA) LM
Derek Daly (IRL) LM
Jeff Kline (USA) LM (*DND*)
Alain Ferté (F) DON, MEX

Chamberlain Engineering
– Spice SE86C Hart, SE89C
Ford Cosworth DFL
Fermin Velez (E) SUZ, DIJ, LM, JAR, BH,
  NUR, DON, SPA, MEX
Nick Adams (GB) SUZ, DIJ, LM, JAR, BH,
  NUR, DON, SPA, MEX
Luigi Taverna (I) LM, JAR, BH, NUR,
  DON, SPA
John Hotchkis, Jr (USA) LM
John Hotchkis (USA) LM
Richard Jones (GB) LM
John Williams (GB) JAR, BH, NUR, DON
Hendrick ten Cate (NL) SPA
Tomas Lopez (MEX) MEX
Quirin Bovy (B) MEX

Chateau Souverain/Bill McDill
– Chevrolet Camaro (Dillon)
Richard McDill (USA) DAY, SEB
Robert Whitaker (USA) DAY
Bill McDill (USA) DAY, SEB

Guy Church – Mazda RX-7
Guy Church (USA) SEB
E.J. Generotti (USA) SEB
Louis D'Agostino (USA SEB

Courage Competition
(Yves Courage)
– Cougar C22S Porsche,
Cougar C22LM Porsche,
Cougar C20B Porsche
Pascal Fabre (F) SUZ, DIJ, LM, JAR,
  BH, NUR, DON, SPA, MEX
Alessandro Santin (I) SUZ
Jean-Louis Bousquet (F) DIJ, LM
Patrick Gonin (F) LM
Bernard de Dryver (B) LM, JAR
Bernard Santal (CH) LM
Jirou Yoneyama (J) LM
Takao Wada (J) LM
Akio Morimoto (J) LM
Anders Olofsson (S) LM
Jean-Claude Andruet (F) LM
Philippe Farjon (F) LM
Syunji Kasuya (J) LM
Hervé Regout (F) BH, NUR,
  DON, SPA
Oscar Manautou (MEX) MEX

Cunningham Racing
(Clayton Cunningham)
– Nissan 300ZX Turbo
John Morton (USA) SEB
Steve Millen (NZ) SEB

Dauer Racing
– Porsche 962 C
Jochen Dauer (D) SUZ, DIJ, BH (*DND*),
  NUR, SPA (*car withdrawn*)
Franz Konrad (A) SUZ, DIJ
Will Hoy (GB) BH, NUR

Team Davey (Tim Lee-Davey)/Team
Davey (Omron Racing Team/Vern
Schuppan) – Porsche 962 C
Tim Lee-Davey (GB) SUZ, DIJ, LM, JAR,
  BH, NUR, SPA (*DND*), MEX
Jürgen Barth (D) SUZ
Vern Schuppan (AUS) SUZ, SPA
Eje Elgh (S) SUZ
Pete Oberndorfer (D) DIJ
Tom Dodd-Noble (GB) LM
Katsunori Iketani (J) LM
Max Cohen-Olivar (MA) JAR
Desiré Wilson (ZA) BH
Heinz-Jörgen Dahmen (D) NUR (*DND*)
Alfonso Toledano (MEX) MEX

Louis Descartes/Automobiles
Louis Descartes – ALD 04 BMW,
ALD C289 Ford Cosworth DFL,
ALD 06 BMW, ALD C289 Ford
Cosworth DFL
Alain Serpaggi (F) DIJ, LM, BH, NUR
  (*DND*), SPA, MEX
Louis Descartes (F) DIJ (*DND*), LM, BH
  (*DND*), DON
Yves Hervalet (F) LM
Marc Fontan (F) NUR, DON (*DND*),
  SPA, MEX
François Wettling (F) SPA
Thierry Lecerf (F) SPA

Diman Racing
– Royale RP40 Porsche
Tato Ferrer (PR) DAY
Rolando Falgueras (PR) DAY
Manuel Villa (PR) DAY
Mandy Gonzalez (PR) DAY

Electramotive Engineering (Don
Devendorf) (See also Nissan
Motorsport) – Nissan GTP ZX-T
(Chapman) (*SECOND CAR WITH
SAME DRIVERS AT DAYTONA AND
SEBRING*)
Arie Luyendyk (NL) DAY, SEB
Chip Robinson (USA) DAY, SEB
Geoff Brabham (AUS) DAY, SEB
Michael Roe (IRL) DAY

Jack Engelhardt
– Badger BB Mazda
Max Schmidt (USA) DAY
Todd Brayton (USA) DAY
Rusty Schmidt (USA) DAY
Jack Engelhardt (USA) DAY

Equipe Alméras Frères
(see also Porsche Alméras
Montpellier) – Porsche 962 C
Jacques Alméras (F) LM
Jean-Marie Alméras (F) LM
Alain Ianetta (F) LM

Erie Scientific (Frank Jellinek, Jr)
– Argo JM16 Mazda
John Grooms (USA) DAY
John Fergus (USA) DAY
Frank Jellinek (USA) DAY
Charles Monk (CDN) DAY (*DND*)

Essex Racing (Mike Gue)
– Tiga GT288 Buick
Charles Morgan (USA) DAY, SEB
John Morrison (GB) DAY
Tom Hessert (USA) DAY, SEB
Reggie Smith (USA) SEB
Michael Dow (USA) SEB
Monte Shalett (USA) SEB

Fabcar American Racing
– Fabcar GTP Chevrolet
Tim McAdam (USA) DAY
Bill Adam (CDN) DAY
Chip Mead (USA) DAY

Far Western Bank Canada
Shoes (Carlos Bobeda)
– Tiga GT286 Mazda
Tony Adamowicz (USA)
Albert Rocca (USA)
Tomas Lopez (MEX)
Aurelio Lopez (MEX)

Fastcolor Images (Bob Leitzinger)
– Nissan 240SX (Leitzinger)
Bob Leitzinger (USA) DAY
Chuck Kurtz (USA) DAY
Butch Leitzinger (USA) DAY

France Prototeam
– Spice SE88C Ford Cosworth DFL,
Argo JM19C Ford Cosworth DFL
Almo Coppelli (I) SUZ, DIJ, BH
Bernard Thuner (CH) SUZ (*DND*), DIJ,
  LM, JAR, BH, NUR, DON, SPA, MEX
Henri Pescarolo (F) DIJ
Alain Ferté (F) DIJ
Pierre de Thoisy (F) LM
Raymond Touroul (F) LM
Jean Messaoudi (F) LM
Pierre-François Rousselot (F) LM

Thierry Lecerf (F) LM
Claude Ballot-Léna (F) JAR, BH, NUR, DON, SPA
Costas Los (GR) BH
Jean Messaoudi (F) MEX

Full Time Racing (Joe Varde)
– Dodge Daytona
Tommy Riggins (USA) DAY
Joe Varde (USA) DAY
Kal Showket (USA) DAY

GT Motorsport (Tommy Johnson)
– Tiga GT285 Mazda
David LaCroix (USA) DAY
David Seabroke (CDN) DAY
Buzzy Smith (USA) DAY
Tommy Johnson (USA) DAY

BF Goodrich/Miller High Life/
Busby Racing (Jim Busby)
– Porsche 962 (Chapman),
Porsche 962 (Holbert/Fabcar)
Bob Wollek (F) DAY, SEB
Derek Bell (GB) DAY, SEB
John Andretti (USA) DAY, SEB
Mario Andretti (USA) DAY
Michael Andretti (USA) DAY

Graff Racing (Jean-Philippe Grand)
– Spice SE89C Ford Cosworth DFV
Jean-Philippe Grand (F) LM
Remy Pochauvin (F) LM
Jean-Luc Roy (F) LM

Gulfwind Marine (Daniel Urrutia)
– Chevrolet Camaro (Howe),
(Southern Racing)
Daniel Urrutia (USA) DAY, SEB
Gene Whipp (USA) DAY, SEB (DND)
Gary Smith (USA) DAY, SEB (DND)
Jack Swanson (USA) DAY

Ken Hendrick Racing
– Oldsmobile Toronado
Ken Hendrick (USA) SEB
Dan Gallant (USA) SEB (DND)

Team Highball (Amos Johnson)
– Mazda RX-7 (Highball)
Amos Johnson (USA), SEB
Dennis Shaw (USA), SEB
Bob Lazier (USA)
Paul Lewis (USA) SEB

Fitz Hochreuter – Porsche 911
Rudy Bartling (CDN) SEB
Rainer Brezinka (CDN) SEB
Fritz Hochreuter (CDN) SEB

Hotchkis Racing (John Hotchkis, Sr)
– Porsche 962 Fabcar
John Hotchkis (USA) DAY, SEB
Jim Adams (USA) DAY, SEB
John Hotchkis, Jr (USA) DAY, SEB

Huffaker Racing (Joe Huffaker, Jr)
– Spice SE86CL Pontiac, Pontiac
Fiero
Dan Marvin (USA) DAY, SEB
Alan Freed (USA) DAY
Mike Allison (USA) DAY
Scott Liebler (USA) DAY

George Robinson (USA) DAY, SEB
Bart Kendall (USA) DAY, SEB
Johnny Unser (USA) DAY, SEB
Bob Lesnett (USA) SEB

Alex Job – Porsche 911
Terry Wolters (USA) DAY
Chris Kraft (USA) DAY, SEB
Rusty Bond (USA) DAY, SEB
Alex Job (USA) DAY, SEB

Joest Racing/Blaupunkt Sachs Joest
Racing – Porsche 962C (Joest)
Frank Jelinski (D) DAY, SEB, SUZ, DIJ, LM, BH, NUR, DON, SPA, MEX
Claude Ballot-Léna (F) DAY, SUZ (DND), DIJ, LM
Jean-Louis Ricci (F) DAY, SEB, SUZ, DIJ, LM
Bob Wollek (F) SEB, SUZ, DIJ, LM, BH, NUR, DON, SPA, MEX (car DQ)
Pierre-Henri Raphanel (F) LM
'John Winter' (Louis Krages) (D) LM
Henri Pescarolo (F) LM, BH, NUR, DON, SPA, MEX
Hans-Joachim Stuck (D) LM
Jean-Louis Ricci (F) BH, NUR, DON, SPA

Bernard Jourdain – Porsche 962
(Holbert)
Bernard Jourdain (MEX) DAY
Oscar Manautou (MEX) DAY
Allen Berg (CDN) DAY
Andres Contreras (MEX) DAY

Jay Kjoller – Porsche 911
Jay Kjoller (USA) DAY, SEB
Patrick Mooney (USA) DAY, SEB
Robin Boone (USA) DAY
Bob Dotson (USA) DAY
Steve Volk (USA) SEB

Kennedy Groves
– Tiga GT285 Mazda
Fred Phillips (USA) DAY
Ron McKay (USA) DAY
Randy Pobst (USA) DAY (DND)

Kryder Racing (Reed Kryder)
– Nissan 300ZX
Reed Kryder (USA) DAY, SEB
Zoltan Polony (USA) DAY
Brian Goodwin (USA) DAY
Craig Shafer (USA) DAY
John Gimble (USA) SEB
Frank del Vecchio (USA) SEB

Leitzinger Racing – Nissan 240ZX
Bob Leitzinger (USA) SEB
Butch Leitzinger (USA) SEB
Chuck Kurtz (USA) SEB

Richard Lloyd Racing (Cabin
Racing)/(Trust Engineering)
Richard Lloyd Racing
– Porsche 962 C/GTI
Derek Bell (GB) SUZ, DIJ, LM, BH, NUR, DON, MEX
Tiff Needell (GB) SUZ, DIJ, LM, BH, NUR, DON, SPA, MEX
George Fouché (ZA) SUZ
Steven Andskar (S) SUZ , SPA
James Weaver (GB) LM, BH

Steven Andskar (S) LM
David Hobbs (GB) LM
Damon Hill (GB) LM
David Hunt BH

Pierre-Alain Lombardi/Lombardi
(Essex Racing) – Spice SE86C Ford
Cosworth DFL, Spice SE88P Buick
Pierre-Alain Lombardi (CH) DIJ, LM, BH, NUR, DON, SPA
Bruno Sotty (F) DIJ, LM, BH, NUR (DND), DON, SPA (DND)
Fabio Magnani (I) LM
Carlos Guerrero (MEX) MEX
Aurelio Lopez (MEX) MEX

MSB Racing – Argo JM19 Mazda
Dave Cowart (USA) DAY
Scott Brayton (USA) DAY
Mike Meyer (USA) DAY
Jim Fowells (USA) DAY

Team Mako (John McNeil) – Spice
SE88C Ford Cosworth DFL
Don Shead (GB) DIJ, LM
James Shead (GB) DIJ, JAR (DND), BH, NUR, DON, SPA
Robbie Stirling (CDN) LM, JAR, BH, NUR, DON, SPA
Ross Hyett (GB) LM
Andres Contreras (MEX) MEX
Giovanni Aloi (MEX) MEX

Mazda Motors of America
(Mazdaspeed) – Mazda 767B
Yoshimi Katayama (J) DAY, SUZ
Takashi Yorino (J) DAY, SUZ
Elliot Forbes-Robinson (USA) DAY
Tetsuya Oota (J) SUZ
Yougiro Terada (J) SUZ (DND)

Mazdaspeed – Mazda 767B
David Kennedy (IRL) DIJ, LM, BH, NUR, DON, SPA, MEX
Pierre Dieudonné (B) DIJ, LM, BH, NUR, DON, SPA, MEX
Chris Hodgetts (GB LM
Takashi Yorino (J) LM
Hervé Regout (B) LM
Elliot Forbes-Robinson (USA) LM
Youjirou Terada (J) LM
Marc Duez (B) LM
Volker Weidler (D) LM

Mandeville Auto Tech (Roger
Mandeville) – Mazda RX-7
(Chassis Dynamics)
Roger Mandeville (USA) DAY, SEB
Kelly Marsh (USA) DAY, SEB
Brian Redman (GB) DAY

Mazda USA/Atlanta (Jim Downing)
– Argo JM19 Mazda
Howard Katz (USA) DAY, SEB
Jim Downing (USA) DAY, SEB
John O'Steen (USA) DAY, SEB
John Maffucci (USA) DAY

Luis Mendez – Porsche 911 Carrera
RSR
Luis Mendez (DR) SEB
Mandy Gonzalez (PR) SEB
Tato Ferrer (PR) SEB

Tom Milner Racing (Tom Milner)
– Ford Probe GTP (Zakspeed)
Jean-Pierre Frey (CH) DAY
Marty Roth (CDN) DAY
Albert Naon, Jr (USA) DAY
Tom Pumpelly (USA) DAY
Ruggero Melgrati (I) DAY
Jack Baldwin (USA) DAY

Motorcraft (Jack Roush)
– Mercury Capri (Roush)
Bob Zeeb (USA) DAY
Jeff Purner (USA) DAY
Bobby Akin (USA) DAY

Motorsports Marketing
(John Higgins)
– Fabcar CL Porsche
John Higgins (USA) DAY, SEB
Lorenzo Lamas (USA) DAY, SEB
Buddy Lazier (USA) DAY
Justus Reid (USA) DAY
Charles Monk (USA) SEB
Chip Mead (USA) SEB

Mussato Action Car (Gianni
Mussato) – Lancia LC2/89 Ferrari
Andrea de Cesaris (I) DIJ
Franco Scapini (I) DIJ (DND), DON, SPA (DQ push start on grid)
Bruno Giacomelli (I) BH, NUR, DON, SPA (DND see Scapini), MEX
Massimo Monti (I) BH, NUR
Enrique Contreras (MEX) MEX

Juan Carlos Negron – Mazda RX-7
(Highball)
Juan Negron (PR) SEB
Chiqui Soldevilla (PR) SEB
Luis Gordillo (PR) SEB

Nissan Motorsport International/
Nissan Motorsports International
(Cabin Racing with Le Mans)
– Nissan R88C (March),
Nissan R89C (Lola)
Kazuyoshi Hoshino (J) SUZ, LM
Toshio Suzuki (J) SUZ, LM
Masahiro Hasemi (J) SUZ, LM
Anders Olofsson (S) SUZ
Takao Wada (J) SUZ
Akio Morimoto (J) SUZ
Julian Bailey (GB) DIJ, LM, JAR, BH, NUR, DON, SPA, MEX
Mark Blundell (GB) DIJ, LM (DND), JAR, DON, SPA, MEX
Martin Donnelly (GB) LM (DND)
Geoff Brabham (AUS) LM
Chip Robinson (USA) LM
Arie Luyendyk (NL) LM
Andrew Gilbert-Scott (GB) BH (DND), NUR

Brent O'Neill – Argo JM19 Buick
Brent O'Neill (USA) SEB
Steve Shelton (USA) SEB
Don Courtney (USA) SEB (DND)

Obermaier Primagaz/From A Racing
(Nova Engineering)/Obermaier
Primagaz – Porsche 962 C
Akihiko Nakaya (J) SUZ
Harald Grohs (D) SUZ

Jürgen Lässig (D) DIJ, LM, JAR, BH, NUR, SPA, MEX
Pierre Yver (F) DIJ, LM, JAR, BH, NUR, SPA, MEX (DND)
Paul Belmondo (F) LM

Oftedahl Racing
(Gordon Oftedahl)
– Buick Somerset
Ric Moore (CDN) DAY
Pieter Baljet (CDN) DAY
Randy McDonald (CDN) DAY

Overbagh Motor Racing (Hoyt
Overbagh) – Chevrolet Camaro
(Stock Products)
Oma Kimbrough (USA) DAY
Robert Kahn (USA) DAY
Hoyt Overbagh (USA) DAY
Robert Siegal (USA) DAY (DND)
Robert Peters (CDN) DAY (DND)

Overton Autosport
(John Overton)
– Mazda RX-7
Lance Stewart (USA) DAY, SEB
Ron Cortez (USA) DAY, SEB
Jeff Alkazian (USA) DAY
Chet Fillip (USA) DAY

PC Automotive (Piper/Capon)
– Spice SE88C Ford Cosworth
DFL, ADA 02B (Gebhardt) Ford
Cosworth DFL
Richard Piper (GB) DIJ, JAR, BH, NUR, DON, SPA, MEX
Olindo Iacobelli (USA) DIJ, JAR, BH (DND), NUR, DON, SPA, MEX

Phoenix Race Cars
– Phoenix JG2 Chevrolet
John Gunn (USA) SEB
Chip Mead (USA) SEB (DND)
Gary Belcher (USA) SEB (DND)

Porsche Alméras Montpellier/
Advan Alpha Nova (Nova
Engineering)/ Porsche Alméras
Montpellier (See also Equipe
Alméras Frères) – Porsche 962 C
Kunimitsu Takahashi (J) SUZ
Stanley Dickens (S) SUZ
Jacques Alméras (F) DIJ, JAR, BH, NUR, SPA, MEX
Jean-Marie Alméras (F) DIJ, JAR, NUR, SPA, MEX

Porsche Kremer Racing/
Porsche Kremer Racing/
Leyton House – Porsche 962
CK6/88 and CK6/89
Bruno Giacomelli (I) SUZ, LM
Giovanni Lavaggi (I) SUZ (DND), LM, JAR, NUR, DON, SPA
Masanori Sekiya (J) SUZ
Hideki Okada (J) SUZ
Kunimitsu Takahashi (J) LM
George Fouché (ZA) LM, JAR, NUR, DON, SPA
Hideki Okada (J) LM
Masanori Sekiya (J) LM
Manuel Reuter (D) MEX
Franz Konrad (A) MEX

Porto Kaleo Team (Tiga/Kelmar Racing Patrick Oudet)/ Port Kaleo/ Noël del Bello/Porto Kaleo Team (Roy Baker) – Tiga GC288 Ford Cosworth DFL, Tiga GC289 Ford Cosworth DFL

Maurizio Gellini (I) DIJ
Jari Nurminen (SF) DIJ
Pasquale Barberio (I) DIJ, JAR, NUR, DON (DND), SPA, MEX
Jean-Claude Justice (F) LM
Noël del Bello (F) LM
Jean-Claude Ferrarin (F) LM
Ranieri Randaccio (I) DIJ, JAR, NUR, DON, SPA, MEX
Stefano Sebastiani (I) LM, BH, DON, SPA
Vito Veninata (I) LM, BH
Robin Smith (GB) LM
Mike Kimpton (GB) DON
Jean-Pierre Frey (CH) SPA

Powell Equipment – Chevrolet Corvette

John Jones (CDN) SEB
Hunter Jones (CDN) SEB
Richard Andison (CDN) SEB

Red Lion Racing – BMW 325i

Mike Graham (USA) SEB
Dave Russell (USA) SEB
Alan Crouch (USA) SEB

Paul Reisman – Chevrolet Camaro (Watson)

Paul Reisman (USA) DAY
Bob Hebert (USA) DAY (DND)
Tom Gaffney (USA) DAY (DND)
Doug Mills (CDN) (DND)

Road Circuit Technology – Mercury Capri (Roush)

Andy Petery (USA) DAY, SEB
Les Delano (USA) DAY, SEB
Craig Carter (USA) DAY, SEB

Rocketsports (Paul Gentilozzi) – Oldsmobile Cutlass

Scott Pruett (USA) DAY
Jerry Clinton (USA) DAY
Les Lindley (USA) DAY
Paul Gentilozzi (USA) DAY (DND)

S & L Racing/Buick/Quaker State (Schubot/Ludemann) – Spice SE88P Buick

Linda Ludemann (USA) DAY, SEB
Scott Schubot (USA) DAY, SEB
John Williams (GB) DAY
Tom Blackaller (USA) SEB

SP Racing (Gary Auberlen) – Porsche 911 Carrera

Gary Auberlen (USA) DAY
Bill Auberlen (USA) DAY
Cary Eisenlohr (USA) DAY
Monte Shelton (USA) DAY

Thomas Sapp – Chevrolet Corvette C4

Tim Morgan (USA) SEB
Marcus Opie (USA) SEB
Peter Morgan (USA) SEB
Charles Bair (USA) SEB

Team Sauber Mercedes – Sauber C9/88

Jean-Louis Schlesser (F) SUZ, DIJ, LM, JAR, BH, NUR, DON, SPA, MEX
Mauro Baldi (I) SUZ, DIJ, LM, JAR, BH, NUR, DON, SPA, MEX
Kenny Acheson (GB) SUZ (Solo drive allowed, see Mass below), DIJ, LM, JAR, BH, NUR, DON, SPA, MEX
Jochen Mass (D) SUZ (DNS due to eye infection), DIJ, LM, JAR, BH, NUR, DON, SPA, MEX
Gianfranco Brancatelli (I) LM
Jean-Pierre Jabouille (F) LM
Alain Cudini (F) LM
Manuel Reuter (D) LM
Stanley Dickens (S) LM

Team Schuppan – Porsche 962 C

Will Hoy (GB) LM
Jean Alesi (F) LM
Dominic Dobson (USA) LM
Vern Schuppan (AUS) LM
Eje Elgh (S) LM
Gary Brabham (AUS) LM

Secateva – WM P489 Peugeot

Pascal Pessiot (F) LM
Jean-Daniel Raulet (F) LM
Philippe Gache (F) LM

Skoal Bandit Racing (Buz McCall) – Chevrolet Camaro (Peerless)

Tom Kendall (USA) DAY
Max Jones (USA) DAY, SEB
Buz McCall (USA) DAY, SEB
Jack Baldwin (USA) DAY

Charles Slater – Porsche 911

Charles Slater (USA) SEB
Kenneth Brady (USA) SEB
Norm Dupont (USA) SEB

Spice Engineering – Spice SE89C Ford Cosworth DFZ

Eliseo Salazar (RCH) SUZ, JAR, BH, NUR, DON, SPA, MEX
Ray Bellm (GB) SUZ (DND), DIJ, LM, JAR, BH, SPA, MEX (DND)
Thorkild Thyrring (DK) SUZ, DIJ (DND), LM, JAR, BH, NUR, DON, SPA, MEX
Wayne Taylor (ZA) SUZ (DND), DIJ, LM, JAR, BH, NUR (DND), DON, SPA
Costas Los (GR) DIJ
Lyn St James (USA) LM
Gordon Spice (GB) LM
Tim Harvey (GB) LM, NUR DON
Bernard Jourdain (MEX) MEX

Spice Engineering USA – Spice SE88P Pontiac

Dieter Quester (A) DAY
Costas Los (GR) DAY, SEB
Jeff Kline (USA) DAY, SEB

Spirit of Brandon (Ken Bupp) – Chevrolet Camaro (Frings)

Steve Burgner (USA) DAY
Ken Bupp (USA) DAY
Henry Brosnaham (USA) DAY
Robert Peters (CDN) DAY
Mark Montgomery (USA) DAY

Stroh's Light Cougar/Roush Racing (Jack Roush) – Lincoln Mercury Cougar XR-7

Wally Dallenbach, Jr (USA) DAY, SEB
Dorsey Schroeder (USA) DAY, SEB
Mark Martin (USA) DAY
Pete Halsmer (USA) DAY, SEB
Bob Earl (USA) DAY, SEB
Paul Stewart (GB) DAY

Swiss Team Salamin (Ba Tsu)/ Swiss Team Salamin/Swiss Team Salamin Walter Lechner Racing School– Porsche 962 C

Kazuo Mogi (J) SZ
Kenji Takahashi (J) SUZ
Antoine Salamin (CH) DIJ, BH, NUR, DON, SPA
Max Cohen-Olivar (MA) DIJ, NUR, DON, SPA
Walter Lechner (A) DIJ
Ernst Franzmaier (A) DIJ
Giovanni Lavaggi (I) BH

Taymay Inc. (Frank E. Everett) – Spice SE86CL Pontiac

Parker Johnstone (USA) DAY
Frank Everett (USA) DAY
Ron Nelson (USA) DAY

Tiga Racing Team – Tiga GC289 Ford Cosworth DFL

Jari Nurminen (SF) SUZ, JAR, DON, SPA, MEX
Luigi Taverna (I) SUZ
Max Cohen-Olivar (MA) LM
John Sheldon (GB) LM, BH, NUR
Robin Donovan (GB) LM
Mario Hytten (CH) JAR, BH
Stephen Hynes (USA) NUR
Tony Trevor (GB) DON
Carlo Rossi (I) SPA (DND)
Oscar Hidalgo (MEX) MEX

Torno/Momo/Gebhardt(Moretti/ Gebhardt) – Porsche 962 C

Massimo Sigala (I) DAY, SEB
Mauro Baldi (I) DAY
Gianpiero Moretti (I) DAY, SEB
Stanley Dickens (S) DAY
Michael Roe (IRL) SEB
Derek Bell (GB) SEB

Toyota Team Tom's/ Toyota Team Tom's (Shin Kato) – Toyota 89C-V, Toyota 88C

Geoff Lees (GB) SUZ, DIJ, LM, JAR (DND due to injury), NUR, SPA
Johnny Dumfries (GB) SUZ, DIJ, LM, JAR, BH, NUR, DON, SPA, MEX
Hitoshi Ogawa (J) SUZ, LM
Paolo Barilla (I) SUZ, LM
Roland Ratzenberger (A) SUZ
Keiichi Suzuki (J) SUZ
Ross Cheever (USA) LM
John Watson (GB) LM BH, DON, MEX
Kaoru Hoshino (J) LM
Didier Artzet (F) LM
Keiichi Suzuki (J) LM (DND)

Transact Inc. (Jeffrey von Braun) – Argo JM19 B Ferrari

Tom Phillips (USA) DAY

Steve Johnson (USA) DAY
Bob Lesnett (USA) DAY

Chaunce Wallace/Lion Rampant Racing – Chevrolet Camaro (Riggins)

Jim Burt (USA) DAY
Nort Northam (USA) DAY
Chaunce Wallace (USA) DAY, SEB
Ferdinand de Lesseps (F) SEB
Luis Sereix (USA) SEB
Hervé Regout (B) SEB

Whitehall Motorsports (Roy Roach) – Spice SE87L Pontiac Cosworth

Jim Rothbarth (USA) DAY (Fuel pump failure on pace lap)
Mike Ciasulli (USA) DAY (See above)
Kenper Miller (USA) DAY (See above)
Gene Felton (USA) DAY (See above)

Gary Wonzer Racing – Lola T616 Mazda

Bill Bean (USA) DAY, SEB
Michael Dow (USA) DAY
Gary Wonzer (USA) DAY, SEB (DND)
Nort Northam (USA) SEB (DND)
Bruce Westcott (USA) SEB (DND)

RESULTS

**Daytona 24 Hours, 5/6 February, USA
Started 67, finished 26**

1st Wollek (F)/Bell (GB)/Andretti (USA) Porsche 962
2nd Cobb (USA)/Nielsen (DK)/Wallace (GB)/Lammers (NL) Jaguar XJR-9
3rd Larrauri (RA)/Brun (D)/Stuck (D) Porsche 962 C

**Sebring 12 Hours,18 March, USA
Started 53, finished 32**

1st Robinson (USA)/Brabham (AUS)/ Luyendyk (NL) Nissan GTP ZX-T
2nd Nielsen (DK)/Cobb (USA) Jaguar XJR-9
3rd Weaver (GB)/Dobson (USA) Porsche 962

**Suzuka 480km, 9 April, Japan
Started 34, finished 25**

1st Schlesser (F)/Baldi (I) Sauber-Mercedes C9/88
2nd Acheson (GB) Sauber-Mercedes C9/88
3rd Wollek (F)/Jelinski (D) Porsche 962 C

**Dijon 480km, 21 May, France
Started 36, finished 25**

1st Wollek (F)/Jelinski (D) Porsche 962 C
2nd Schlesser (F)/Mass (D) Sauber-Mercedes C9/88
3rd Baldi (I)/Acheson (GB) Sauber-Mercedes C9/88

Le Mans 24 Hours, 10/11 June, France. Started 55, finished 19

1st Mass (D)/Reuter (D)/Dickens (S) Sauber-Mercedes C9
2nd Baldi (I)/Brancatelli (I)/Acheson (GB) Sauber-Mercedes C9
3rd Bob Wollek (F)/Hans-Joachim Stuck (D) Porsche 962 C

**Jarama 480km
25 June, Spain
Started 23, finished 19**

1st Schlesser (D)/Mass (D) Sauber-Mercedes C9/88
2nd Lammers (NL)/Tambay (F) Jaguar XJR-9
3rd Larrauri (RA)/Pareja (E) Porsche 962 C

**Brands Hatch 480km
23 July, Great Britain
Started 36, finished 22**

1st Baldi (I)/Acheson (GB) Sauber-Mercedes C9/88
2nd Wollek (F)/Jelinski (D) Porsche 962 C
3rd Schlesser (F)/Mass (D) Sauber-Mercedes C9/88

**Nürburgring 480km
20 August, Germany
Started 36, finished 22**

1st Schlesser (F)/Mass (D) Sauber-Mercedes C9/88
2nd Baldi (I)/Acheson (GB) Sauber-Mercedes C9/88
3rd Fouché (ZA)/Lavaggi (I) Porsche 962 CK6

**Donington Park 480km
3 September, Great Britain
Started 33, finished 18**

1st Schlesser (F)/Mass (D) Sauber-Mercedes C9/88
2nd Baldi (I)/Acheson (GB) Sauber-Mercedes C9/88
3rd Bailey (GB)/Blundell GB Nissan R89C

**Spa 480km, 17 September, Belgium
Started 38, finished 22**

1st Baldi (I)/Acheson (GB) Sauber-Mercedes C9-88
2nd Wollek (F)/Jelinski (D) Porsche 962 C
3rd Bailey (GB)/Blundell (GB) Nissan R89C

**Autódromo Hermanos Rodríguez 480km, 29 October, Mexico
Started 31, finished 23**

1st Schlesser (F)/Mass (D) Sauber-Mercedes C9/88
2nd Huysman (B)/Larrauri (RA) Porsche 962 C
3rd Jelinski (D)/Pescarolo (F) Porsche 962 C

Over a protracted period in the 1970s sports-car racing per se had been in the doldrums, at least on this side of the Atlantic.

Generally speaking, this was the consequence of the CSI who decided to ban the 5-litre behemoths of Porsche and Ferrari after 1971, thus losing some of the drama and aesthetics. Instead the prototype Ferraris, Alfa Romeos, Matras, Mirages, Lolas et al. were 3-litre pseudo F1 cars, very quick but lacking the brute force of their predecessors. As the 1970s drew to a close the situation was pretty dire with little or no serious works cars and lacklustre races, but things would improve significantly in the forthcoming decade.

Porsche were on a different tack and continued to develop the 911, which also ran in the Sports 3-litre class with the prototypes, whilst their once almost invincible 908 was now obsolete and underpowered but still reliable. However, Weissach did enter and win at Le Mans in 1976/77 with their 936 Turbo whilst the 911 strain evolved into the 930/934/935 cars that continued on into the 1980s to great effect.

With the advent of the next decade two years were spent racing with leftovers and few factory cars, Jean Rondeau won at Le Mans and Jöst entered a Porsche-approved 936 clone as a 908/80 turbo car which finished 2nd. In 1981 Ickx/Mass drove a works Porsche 936 to victory, but this was a stopgap before something far more potent appeared in 1982: the Porsche 956.

Thereafter the 956s reigned supreme. They were more powerful, more reliable and generally much faster than their counterparts until Walkinshaw's TWR Jaguar team arrived. So now the cars were fantastically powerful but as ever officialdom could not contain its control gene and subjected the Group-C cars to a fuel-limitation diktat as noted elsewhere that continued on through the years.

The 956 was replaced by the 962 and continued to win but less frequently as the TWR Jaguars improved whilst Peter Sauber's Sauber Mercedes C8 evolved into the C9, which was now under the control of Mercedes-Benz. They finished second to TWR in 1988 and won the championships with relative ease in 1989. There were, of course, many other smaller teams, especially in the C2 category, most of which were rarely winning, the stand-out team being Spice Engineering.

It was a given that things would change again and they did in the 1990s whilst it is worth noting that the days of open-top two-seaters had died out in the early 1980s after Lancia had joined the coupé crowd in 1983. As for the drivers, there were some tragic accidents but overall the ever-increasing safety rules helped save lives that in earlier times would have been lost. The standard of said racers was impressive with exception, including many in the small private teams.

Back in the USA things were different under IMSA rules, but even here the Porsche clan were top of the tree for much of the decade with the Al Holbert, Bob Akin, Bruce Leven, Preston Henn, Bob Garretson et al. winning consistently at Daytona and Sebring.

With hindsight the 1980s turned out to be rather better than they might have been, but the shadow of F1 was forever present and one suspects that the amount of sponsorship at the top end of the sports/prototype grids was not popular with certain vested interests.

Time and Two Seats Book II (Motorsport
Research Group, 1999) by János L. Wimpfenn

*Tony Southgate: From Drawing Board to Chequered
Flag* (MRP Publishing, 2010) by Tony Southgate

Kings of the Nürburgring: Der Nürburg-Ring: 1925–1983
(Transport Bookan Publications, 2005) by Chris Nixon

*Sebring: The Official History of America's Great Sports
Car Race* (David Bull Publishing, 1995) by Ken Breslauer

*Le Mans: The Official History of the World's Greatest Motor Race
1980–89* (Haynes Publishing, 2012) by Quentin Spurring

Jaguar at Le Mans: Every Race, Car and Driver, 1950–1995
(Haynes Publishing, 2001) by Paul Parker

Prototypes: The History of the IMSA GTP Series (David
Bull Publishing, 2000) by J. A. Martin and Ken Wells

Endurance Racing 1982–1991 (Osprey Publishing 1992)
by Ian Briggs

Fitz: My Life at the Wheel (Autosports Marketing
Associates Ltd) by John Fitzpatrick

Additionally, period *Autosport, Motor Sport* and latter-day
Octane publications were sourced for which my thanks
and appreciation.

Aase, Dennis 41
Abarth 268C engine 128
Acheson, Kenny 170, 264-65, 270, 272
ADA (Anglo Dutch American) 128, 184, 228, 242
Adamowicz, Tony 13, 128
Adam, Bill 41
Adams, Jim 40, 102, 161
Adams, Nick 217, 264, 271
Akin, Bob 17, 48, 64, 178
Alba Engineering
  AR2 109, 122
  AR3 207
  AR6 158
Alboreto, Michele 16, 43, 78, 81, 89, 94
ALD (Automobiles Louis Descartes) 169
Alderman, George 120
Aldridge, Geoff 66
All American Grand Touring (AAGT) 38
Allam, Jeff 96, 105
Alliot, Philippe, 101
Ambrosio, Franscesco 18
Andial Racing 14
André Chevally Racing (ACR) 22,28
Andretti, John 177
Andretti, Mario 72, 121, 203
Andretti, Michael 72, 101, 121
Andrews, David 166
Andruet, Jean-Claude 158, 268
Andskar, Steven 251
Apple Computers Inc. 38
Argo 194, 198, 205-06, 208, 220, 233, 246
Ashmore, Chris 166
Aston Martin 68, 74, 82, 88, 96, 116, 280
  AMR1 280
  Owners Club 82
  Proteus Technology 268, 273
Attwood, Richard 127
Auto Beaurex Motorsport 251
Autofarm 8, 9, 23
Automobile Club d'Italia (ACI) 30

Bailey, Julian 267, 270, 272, 276
Bailey, Len 55, 88, 96
Baird, Carson 120
Baker, Roy 106, 149
Baker, Wayne 92
Baldi, Mauro 79, 124, 128, 149, 165, 189, 198, 214, 216, 229, 232, 235, 242, 246, 264-65, 270, 272
Balestre, Jean-Marie 66, 116
Ballot-Léna, Jean-Claude 25, 91, 128, 161, 177, 185
Barbour, Dick 18, 26
Bardon DB1 190

Barilla, Paolo 89, 107, 124, 128, 156, 178, 183, 194
Barth, Jürgen 21, 24, 50, 77
Bartlett, John 102
Bassaler, Roland 161
Bayside Disposal Racing 42, 232, 263
Bedard, Patrick 41
Beitzel, Jeff 202
Bell, Derek 17, 30, 46, 50, 64, 77, 80, 95, 97, 110, 128, 141, 174, 177, 180, 183, 200, 214, 230, 235, 263
Bellm, Ray 125, 134, 174, 179, 226
Bellof, Stefan 97-98, 110, 116, 141, 146, 151, 161, 165
BF Goodrich 124, 131
Blundell, Mark 271, 276
BMW
  M1 10, 24, 36, 46, 70, 100
  Procar M1 17
BMW M1 Procar Series 12, 36
Boesel, Raul 207-08, 210, 216-18, 221, 229
Bohren, Walt 127
Bond, Colin 141
Bosch Motronic engine management system 8-9, 122, 210, 241
Bourgoignie, Claude 53
Boutsen, Thierry 50, 95, 134, 136, 148, 165, 192-93
Brabham, Geoff 259, 261
Brabham, Jack 138
Brancatelli, Gianfranco 180
Brands Hatch Racing 14
Bratenstein, Raine 12
Brawn, Ross 256
Broadley, Eric 44, 68
Brooks, Richard 77
Brumos-Porsche 25
  935-77A 18
Brundle, Martin 147, 164, 221, 226, 229, 246, 251
Brun Motorsport 18,100, 137, 151, 174, 184, 191-93, 205, 217, 222, 230, 234, 247
Brunn, Siegfried 10, 16, 30, 46
Brun, Walter 7, 63, 88, 98, 122, 205, 247
Bundy, Doc 128
Busby, Jim 12, 124, 260
Bussi, Christian 79

Calderari, Enzo 70
Canon Racing 100, 133-134, 159, 165, 170
Capoferri M1 18
Capoferri, Marco 10, 18
Carr, Steve 9
Carter, Maurice 40
Castrol Denmark (Team) 70
Ceekar 83J-1 166

Central Racing Team 110, 138
Chamberlain Engineering 217, 264, 271
Chamberlain, Joe 13
Chamberlain, John 13
Charles Ivey Racing 8, 9, 53, 117, 134-35, 209
Chasseuil, Guy 49
Cheetah
  G603 106
  G604 162
Cheever, Eddie 16, 18, 180, 183, 188, 205-06, 210, 216, 218, 234-35, 246, 251
Chevrolet
  Camaro 37, 38, 76, 203
  Corvette 13, 201
  Monza Turbo 40
Chevron B36 14
Cleare, Richard 8-9, 23, 65, 94, 96, 105, 168
Cluxton, Harley 72
Cobb, Price 203, 250
Cohen-Olivar, Max 190
Constanzo, Alfred 140
Conte, Phil 120
Conte Racing 120
Cooke Racing 72
Cooper, John 53
Coppelli, Almo 227
Cord, Chris 40
Coudere, Alain 102
Cougar 7, 88
  C12 185
  C20 7, 198, 213
  CM20LM 268
Courage, Yves 7, 185, 213
Cowart, Dave 17, 118
Craft, Chris 50, 117
Crang, Neil 40, 125, 134, 140

Dale, Mike 90
Danner, Christian 233
Dare-Bryan, Val 8-9, 168
Datsun
  280ZX 120
  Fairlady 80
Dauer, Jochen 175
Dave Kent Racing 38
Dawson, Ian 44, 66
de Cadenet, Alain 10, 21, 22, 55, 117, 185
De Cadenet-Lola LM 10, 21
de Cesaris, Andrea 45, 180, 190, 233
de Dryver, Bernard 79
de Henning, Philippe 212, 227
del Bello, Noël 244
DeNarvaez, Mauricio 41, 65, 118, 121
Descartes, Louis 169
de Thoisy, Pierre 184
de Villota, Emilio 36, 44, 66, 175, 205
Dick Barbour Racing 14
Dickens, Stanley 184, 238
Dieudonné, Pierre 12, 274
Dini, Spartaco 21
Dobson, Dominic 263

Dome 156
  85C-L Toyota 157
  Zero 53
Dominelli, Jerry David 72, 116
Donnington Hall 257
Donovan, Robin 190
Dorchy, Roger 69, 76, 102, 158, 242
Dören, Edgar 11, 44, 130
Dorset Racing 56
Downe, Viscount 68, 74, 82, 96, 116, 127
Downing, Jim 18
  A Driving Passion, Gordon Kirby 72
Dron, Tony 8, 23, 45, 65, 94, 98
Duez, Marc 178, 194, 198
Duffield, David 130
Dumfries, Johnny 138, 170, 216, 218, 221, 266, 270
Duxbury, Graham 121
Dykstra, Lee 90, 177

Ecurie Ecosse (team) 130, 158, 163, 174, 194, 205
Edwards, Guy 36, 44, 134
Electramotive Engineering 259, 261
El Salvador Racing 118
EMKA Productions 46
  Aston Martin C83/1 88, 96
  Aston Martin C84/1 159, 168
Essex Racing 261
Evans, Bob 50, 68, 159
Evans, Tim 202

Fabi, Teo 83, 94
Fabre, Pascal 102
Facetti, Carlo 36, 44-45, 93, 109
Farjon, Phillip 268
Fassler, Paul 93
Faure, Nick 159
Felton, Gene 77
Ferrari 6
  308 GTB Turbo 36, 44-45
  250 GTO 21
  365 GTB/4 13
  512 BB/LM 12, 21, 25, 118
Ferrari Club Italia 21
Ferrari, Enzo 21
Ferté, Alain 127
Ferté, Michel 130
Feurstenau, Brian 90
Field, Ted 18, 42,54
Finotti, Martino 36, 44, 93, 109, 122
Fiorio, Cesare 10
Firestone Tire & Rubber 38
FISA 62, 198, 206
Fitzpatrick, John 7, 22, 26, 54, 72, 83, 88, 109, 133-34, 136-37, 141, 175, 205
Follmer, George 183

Forbes-Robinson, Elliot 260
Ford
  C100 55, 67, 71, 80-82, 88, 107
  Capri 23, 48
  Mustang 38, 200
  Probe GTP 259
Ford-Cosworth DFL 44, 56, 65-67, 69, 72, 76, 80, 102, 106-07, 127, 158, 179, 184, 205, 227, 246, 271
Ford-Cosworth DFV 18, 22, 53, 55, 79, 128, 130
Fornage, Dominique 158
Fouché, George 169, 175, 240
Foushee, Lanky 177
Fowler, Peter 139
Foyt, A.J. 91, 148, 177, 200
Franchi, Carlo see 'Gimax'
Francia, Giorgio 30, 43, 56, 66, 70, 89, 107
Francisci, Claudio 18
Frey, Jean-Pierre 236
Frings, Dennis 76
Frisselle, Brad 18
fuel regulations 151, 157, 194, 222, 232, 235, 278, 284

Gaillard, Patrick 105
Galica, Divina 14, 134
Gall, Helmut 83
Gallo 18
Galvin, Mark 168
Ganley, Howden 72, 125, 209
Garcia, Tony 101, 120
Garretson, Bob 38, 56, 64-65
Gartner, Jo 174, 183, 186
Gauld, Graham 130
Gauntlett, Victor 68
Gebhardt Motorsport 137, 140, 184
General Motors 179
Gil Baird Techspeed Racing 134
Gilbert-Scott, Andrew 251, 274
'Gimax' (Carlo Franchi) 18, 93
Ghinzani, Piercarlo 18, 43, 67, 76, 80, 89, 94, 194
Giacomelli, Bruno 188, 190
Ginther, Richie 82
Goad, Doug 202
Goddard, Geoff 45
Gouhier, Joël 184
Gozzi, Adriano 93
GP Motorsport 227
Graemiger, Charles (Chuck) 106, 162
Graham, John 90, 162
Grano, Umberto 70
Greene, Keith 186, 189
Gregg, Deborah 118
Gregg, Peter 18, 118
Gregg Walker Racing 201
Grice, Allan 139, 238

Grid C8 S1 66
Grid Team Lola 36, 44, 54
Grob, Ian 12
Grob, Ken 12
Grohs, Harald 46, 74, 83, 97, 100, 122, 240
Group 44 (team) 18, 41, 88, 90, 116, 128, 161, 177, 201
GS Tuning 36
GTi Engineering 7, 45, 88, 122, 133-34, 153, 159, 165, 170, 189, 198, 207, 213, 230, 235, 268, 278
Gue, Mike 261

Hagan, Billy Jo 37, 77
Haldi, Claude 158, 212
Halsmer, Pete 91
Hamilton, Robin 90
Hansen, Peter 70
Harrier RX83C 106
Harris, Trevor 259
Harrop, Ron 139
Hasemi, Masahiro 194
Hayje, Johan 124
Haywood, Hurley 18, 42, 77, 101, 161, 177
Heimrath, Ludwig 164
Heimrath, Ludwig Jr 164
Heini Mader (racing components) 36, 162, 179
Henn, Preston 12, 17, 88, 91, 116, 130
Henn's Thunderbird Swap Shop (team) 12, 14, 88, 130, 148, 177
Herd, Robin 12
Hesketh Engineering 55
Hessert, Tom 261
Heuclin, Jacques 74, 169
Heyer, Hans 74, 83, 109, 121, 128, 164, 166
Hickman, Lawrie 31
Hill, Graham 82
Hinze, Marty 92
Hobbs, David 46, 66, 72, 83, 177
Holbert, Al 17, 42, 77, 95, 101, 174, 178, 198, 200, 203, 232
Holbert, Bob 95, 259
Holbert Racing 177, 203, 232
Holland, Don 94
Holup, Gerhard 11, 44
Honegga, Pierre 23
Horsmann, John 72
Hoshino, Kaoro 157
Hoshino, Kazuyoshi 169
Hoshino Racing 169
Howey, Clark 40
Howey Farms 40
Hoy, Will 206, 208, 220
Hudson Wire Company 17
Hutchins, Mark 23
Huysman, Harald 247
Hynes, Steve 244

Ian Taylor Racing 14
Ickx, Jacky 26, 50, 68, 77, 83, 88, 165, 180

IMSA (International Motor Sports Association) 12, 62, 116, 121
Interscope Racing 14, 18, 42, 54
iRacing 14

Jaguar 7, 183, 198, 242, 280
    XJR-5 7, 88, 90, 116, 128
    XJR-5B 161
    XJR-6 146-147, 163-164, 180, 193
    XJR-7 177, 201
    XJR-8 205-07, 208, 210-211, 216-17, 221
    XJR-9 7, 226, 228, 232, 234, 244, 246, 251, 256, 259, 270
    XJR-11 7, 256, 272-73, 276, 278, 280
Jaussaud, Jean-Pierre 7, 26, 76, 106
Jelinski, Frank 105, 137, 162, 193, 205, 265, 273
Jenner, Bruce 12
Jensen, Lars-Viggo 70
Jenvey, Richard 31
Joest Racing 10, 69, 72, 80, 88, 109, 116, 156, 174, 178, 189, 216, 218, 226, 242
    Porsche 908/80 10, 26, 46, 49-50, 74
    Porsche 935J 14
    Porsche 936C 74, 80, 83
    Porsche 956 95, 97, 109, 146, 183
    Porsche 956B 134, 156, 180
    962C 216, 218, 265, 267, 273
Joest (Jöst), Reinhold 7, 10, 16, 24, 26, 46, 49-50
Johansson, Stefan 121, 246
Johnson, Dick 139
Jolly Club (racing team) 16, 36, 44-45, 93, 109
Jones, Alan 97, 166
Jones, Brad 139
Jones, Davy 177
Jones, Richard 56
Jordan, Eddie 46
Juckette, Tom 201

Kalagian, John 8
Kasuya, Syunji 268
Katayama, Yoshimi 105, 236, 260
Keegan, Rupert 134, 140
Kegel Enterprises 38
Kelleners, Helmut 70
Kelly, Jim 41
Kelmar Racing 248
Kendall, Chuck 41
Kennedy, David 194, 236, 274
Kent-Cooke, Ralph 80, 102

Kessel, Loris 106, 162
Klausler, Tom 38
Kline, Jeff 38
Knoop, Rick 12, 91, 124
Koch, Dale 40
Koll, Bill 38
Konrad, Franz 238
Korten, Michael 12
Kouros 7
Kouros Sauber Mercedes
    C8 7
    C9 218-20
Kouros Sauber Mercedes C8 174
Krages, Louis 156, 178, 238
Kreepy Krauly (team) 121
Kremer (Brothers) 7, 36, 49, 55, 74, 88, 105, 146, 164, 174, 186
    Porsche 917 36, 49, 55
    Porsche 935 K3 18, 22, 26
    Porsche 956 97, 101
    Porsche 962 183
    Porsche 962C 186
    CK5-01 8
    CK5-82 98, 105
    CK5-83 105
Kremer, Erwin 94
Kroesemeijer, Kees 164

Labonte, Terry 37
Lacaud, Dominique 161
Lafosse, Jean-Louis 53
Lammers, Jan 100, 134, 153, 166, 193, 205-06, 209, 218, 244, 259, 276
Lancia (Corse) 6, 10, 18, 31, 36, 45, 52, 67, 80, 116, 124, 138, 166, 190
    Beta Montecarlo 10, 16, 18, 43, 45, 54
    LC1 67, 71, 78, 80, 82-83
    LC2 89, 94, 106-07, 124-25, 128, 133, 151, 154, 157, 165-166, 180, 188, 190, 233, 236
    Mussato Action Car 6
Lanfranchi, Tony 134
Lanier, Randy 92
Lapeyre, Xavier 49
Larrauri, Oscar 18, 122, 184, 217, 222, 234
Lässig, Jürgen 11, 44, 97
Lateste, Michel 74
Leclère, Michel 18
Lees, Geoff 68, 252, 266, 270
Leim, Kenneth 190
Leoni, Lamberto 240
Leslie, David 130, 158, 168, 191, 199, 205
Leven, Bruce 18, 42, 232, 263
Lincoln Mercury Cougar XR-7 259
Liqui Moly (team) 174, 189, 207

Lloyd, Richard (Richard Lloyd Racing) 7, 45, 134, 153, 159, 174, 189, 198, 214, 216-17, 230, 235, 268, 278
LM Bellancauto (Rome Ferrari Dealer) 21
Lobenberg, Bob 120
Lola
    T286 28
    T297 56
    T380 10, 18, 56
    T600 36, 44, 54, 56, 88, 120
    T610 67, 102
    T616 Mazda 124, 131
Lola-Nissan 810 259
Lombardi, Maria Grazia 'Lella' 14, 29, 31, 43, 56
Lombardi, Pierre-Alain 241
Los, Costas 8, 191, 227
Lotus Esprit S1 31
Lucchini Corse 93
    BMW S280 93
Lucchini, Giorgio 93
Ludwig, Klaus 23, 55, 67, 80, 107, 131, 156, 178, 232, 244, 250
Luyendyk, Arie 259, 261

Mallock, Ray 68, 82, 88, 96, 127, 130, 158, 190, 194, 199, 205, 273
Mamers, Max 50
Mandeville Racing 18
Mandeville, Roger 18
Marazzi, Roberto 30
March 8, 186
    82G 64-65, 72, 88
    83G 88, 92, 118
    84G 121, 191
    85G 8, 169, 177, 186, 191
    M1C 12
Marozzo, Nicola 236
Martini Racing 44, 71, 107, 124, 154
Martin, Jean-Michel 7, 74, 80
Martin, Philippe 38, 74, 80
Martin, Tony 121
Maserati 6
Mass, Jochen 23, 46, 48, 50, 77, 134, 154, 161, 170, 183, 203, 207, 217, 222, 229, 232, 244, 246
Matthews, Derek 166
Mazda
    RX-7 10, 18, 23, 38, 90, 105
Mazda Motors of America 260
    757B 260
Mazdaspeed 12, 88
    717C 88, 105
    757 213, 240
    767 236, 240
    767B 274, 278
McCaig, Hugh 130
McFarlin, Rob 38
McGriff, Hershel 77
McKenna, Terry 202

McKitterick, Skeeter 17
McLaren North America 38
Meldeau, Mike 93
Mena, Alfredo 118
Mendez, Charles 41
Mercedes-Benz 7, 198, 256-57, 264-65, 284
    C9 7, 264-65
    450SLC 139
Mercer, David 153
Merl, Volkert 16, 109, 122
Messaoudi, Jean 246
Metge, René 185, 212
Meunier, Michel 28
Miedecke, Andrew 141
Migault, François 69
Miller, Jack 118
Miller, Kenper 17, 118
Mirage M12 72
Momo Porsche 79
Montoya, Diego 101
Moretti, Gianpiero 41, 66, 78, 263
Morgan, Charles 261
Morimoto, Akio 240
Morton, John 13, 38, 120, 183
Motorsport Marketing 92
Mueller, Lee 38
Mullen, Jim 92, 127
Muller, Cathy 140
Müller, Herbert 36, 46
Mussato, Gianni 233
My Life at the Wheel, John Fitzpatrick 133

Nakajima, Satoru 157
Nannini, Alessandro 128, 149, 166, 180
Naon, Albert 101
NART (North American Racing Team) 54
Needell, Tiff 74, 96, 159, 168, 183, 191, 235, 278
Negline, Michael 8
Nierop, Kees 92, 212
Nève, Patrick 12
Newby. Mark 209
Newey, Adrian 64, 92
Newsome, Jack 9
Niedzwiedz, Klaus 48, 50, 80, 107, 238
Nielsen, John 179, 183
Nimrod Aston Martin 68, 74, 82, 88, 96, 116, 127
    NRA/C2 68, 118
    C2B 96
Nissan 186, 194
    GTP ZX-T 259, 261
    LM03 Fairlady Z 110, 138
    R86V 86G-6 194
    R89C 267, 271-72, 274, 276, 278
Nissen, Kris 205, 240
Nova Engineering Japan 88

Obermaier Racing 88, 97
Obrist, Albert 16
O'Connor, Geoff 9, 94
Odor, Jan 31
Oftedahl Racing 93

Olofson, Anders 240
Olson, Drake 90, 178, 183
Ongais, Danny 18, 42
Ono, Masao 53
O'Rourke, Steve 46, 88, 96, 159, 168
Osella
   BMW PA7 18
   BMW PA8 14, 29, 30
   BMW PA9 36, 43, 56, 70, 93
Osella, Enzo 14

Pallavicini, Angelo 40
Palmer, Jonathan 100, 134, 136, 153, 159, 165, 214
Pareja, Jésus 184
PAS Pontiac 202
Patrese, Riccardo 16, 71, 83, 89, 94, 124, 149, 151, 154, 165-66, 180
Paul Jr, John 130
Paul Sr, John 17, 21
Payne, Max 166
PC Automotive 233
Percy, Win 211
Performance Motorcar 118
Pescarolo, Henri 55, 66, 69, 74, 76, 83, 131, 134, 179, 183, 218
Pessiot, Pascal 158
Phillips, Jack 9
Phillips, Simon 54
Pickett, Greg 203, 232
Piedade, Domingos 79
Pignard, Michel 50, 69, 102, 158
Pilgrim, Andy 202
Pinske, Lothar 67
Piquet, Nelson 24, 36
Plankenhorn, Axel 97
Pontiac
   Fiero 179
   Firebird 93
Pope, Steve 93
Porsche 6-7, 8, 36, 49, 77, 88, 101, 133, 138, 174, 192, 198, 284
   908/03 16, 24, 30, 46
   908/80 10, 26, 46, 49-50
   911 Carrera RSR 41
   911 SC 38
   917 36, 49
   924 Carrera 8, 25, 45
   934 9, 23, 40, 65, 92, 94
   935/78-81 72, 79
   935-80 42
   935 (GTX) 21
   935 J 14, 41
   935 K3 17, 18, 42, 44, 53-54, 56, 64, 70, 72, 80
   935 K4 83
   935L 91
   936 26, 50
   936/81 50, 53
   936C 74, 80, 83
   956 7, 8, 18, 77, 80, 88, 95, 98, 100, 109-10, 116, 122, 125, 130-31, 135, 169
   956B 137, 153, 159, 165, 170, 178, 180

962 8, 130-31, 134, 177-178, 183, 203, 232
961 185, 198, 212, 240, 260, 263
962C 151, 156, 170, 180, 184-87, 191-93, 198, 200, 205-208, 211, 214, 216-17, 230, 234-35, 240-41, 247, 250, 267-68, 278
Poulsen, Jörgen 70
Pozzi, Charles 25, 54
Preece, Dave 82
Price, Lew 120
Protofab Engineering/ Racing 203, 232
Pryce, Tom 18

Quester, Dieter 124, 177

Racing Associates 14
Racing Beat 91
Ragnotti, Jean 53
Rahal, Bobby 38, 46, 49, 56, 65, 177, 203
Ramirez, Carlos 93, 118
Ransom, Sue 140
Raphanel, Pierre-Henri 185, 213
Raulet, Jean-Daniel 50, 69, 102, 158
Ray, Lester 106
Raymond, Martin 14
Re-Car Racing 139
Red Lobster (team) 17, 118
Redman, Brian 21, 26, 38, 128, 161, 177, 273
Reed, Bob 91
Regout, Hervé 213, 244
Rennod Racing 54
Reuter, Manuel 162, 230
Richard Cleare (RC) Racing 8-9, 168
Riggins, Tommy 203, 232
Rise, Giuseppe 66
Robert, Lionel 9
Robinson, Barry 8, 134
Robinson, Chip 161, 177, 200, 203, 232, 261
Rocca, Marco 14
Roe, Michael 263
Röhrl, Walter 16, 46, 50
Romano, Baptiste 140
Romero, Paco 205
Rondeau, Jean 7, 10, 26, 66, 76, 130,158
Rondeau (racing team) 26, 53, 69, 76, 88, 116, 127, 241
   M379 26, 53, 102, 241
   M382 66, 76, 79
   M482 69, 102, 127
Rosberg, Keke 100
Rosche, Paul 29
Rossiter, Jeremy 149
Rothmans Porsche 95, 133, 135, 137, 146, 154, 164, 170, 174, 180, 183, 189, 207-08, 218
Roush Racing 200, 259
Rousselot, Pierre-François 246
Rover SD1 8
Rude, Kathy 38

Salmon, Mike 68, 96, 127
SARD (Sigma Advanced Racing Developments) 250
Sardou, Max 12, 69, 127
Sauber 88, 198, 242, 256-57, 284
   BMW SHS C6 6, 63, 65, 79, 81-82, 88, 161
   BMW Italia M1 70
   C7 101
   C8 179, 183, 192, 244
   C9 210, 218-20, 226, 229, 235, 238, 244, 264-65, 270, 272, 276, 278
Sauber, Peter 7, 36
Saulnier, Serge 50
Schäfer, Uwe 230
Schanche, Martin 194, 198, 206, 208
Schlesser, Jean-Louis 164, 180, 187-88, 229-30, 232, 246, 264, 274, 276, 278, 280
Schmidt, Helmut 161
Schnitzer 63
Schornstein, Dieter 45, 122
Schuppan, Vern 50, 77, 101, 169, 177, 183, 203
Schwarz, George 137
Scorpion Racing Services 190
Scuderia Mirabella 89, 107
Scuderia Supercar Bellancauto 54
Scuderia Torino Corse 29
Sebring, Ken Breslauer 92
Seger & Hoffman Aerospace 7
Sekiya, Masanori 157, 252
Senna, Ayrton 133
Servanin, François 102
Shadow Racing 18
Shafer, Carl 93
Sheldon, John 40, 127
Shell Sport F1 series 14
Shelton, Steve 118
Shelton, Tom 118
Sigala, Massimo 18, 122, 234, 263
Silk Cut (sponsor) 180
Silman, Roger 163
Singer, Norbert 161, 212
Skip Barber Racing 14
Skoal Bandit 134-36
Smedley, Tony 190
Smith, Glen 128
Smith, Paul 149
Smith, Pete 41
Smith, Vicki 118
Smith-Haas, Margie 94, 140
Sobriquet, Anton 190
Soper, Steve 105
Soto, Ernesto 23
Sotty, Bruno 241
Southgate, Tony 146, 163, 211
Spice, Gordon 7, 81, 125, 140, 163, 174, 179, 208, 212, 220, 226, 256, 271

Spice Engineering 7, 81, 146, 198-99, 208, 227, 236, 242, 244, 248, 256, 271, 276, 284
Spice-Tiga Racing 125, 134, 140, 158, 163
Steckkönig, Günter 25
Stiff, Fred 66
Stirano, Giorgio 122
St James, Lyn 90
Stommelen, Rolf 24
Stratagraph (racing team) 37, 76
Striebig, Hubert 74
Stroud, Nigel 136, 236
Stuck, Hans-Joachim 24, 36, 63, 82, 98, 122, 137, 156, 161, 180, 183, 187, 205, 208, 214, 232, 241, 267
Surer, Marc 67, 80, 82, 153, 164
Suzuki, Keiichi 169, 252

Takahashi, Kunimitsu 186
Tapy, Yvon 161
Taylor, Wayne 276
Terada, Yojiro 105, 236
Thackwell, Mike 147, 164, 183, 192, 210, 214, 218
Thatcher, Mark 14, 29
Theys, Didier 102
Thoelke, Jan 137
Thompson, Bryan 139
Thompson, John 55
Thompson, Steve 134
Thorby, Andrew 44
Thyrring, Thorkild 227
Tide & Mosler (team) 118
Tiga Racing 8, 72, 209
Time and Two Seats, Janos L. Wimpfenn 6
Tom's Team (Toyota) 157, 222, 238, 252, 265-66
   Toyota 89C-V 263, 266
Trisconi, François 28
Triumph TR8 18, 41
Trueman, Jim 65,118
Truffo, Duilio 70
Trust Racing Team 169
Tullius, Bob 41, 88, 90, 116, 128, 161, 177
Turner, Stuart 81
Twitchen, Peter 8-9
TWR (Tom Walkinshaw Racing) Jaguar 146-47, 163, 166, 174, 180, 183, 186, 188, 192-93, 198, 208-09, 216, 218, 221, 226, 228, 232, 234, 238, 242, 248, 256, 266, 270, 272, 284

Ultramar Team Lola 67, 102
Ungar, Ernst 74
Ungar Racing Developments (URD) 74
   C81 BMW 74, 83
   C83 BMW 153
Unser, Al 148
Unser, Al Jr 174, 177, 200

Valentine, Richard J. 13, 40

Spice Engineering 7, 81,

van der Merwe, Sarel 121, 186
Velez, Fermin 175, 208, 212, 220, 264, 271
Velga Racing Team 46
Vestey, Paul 117
Violati, Fabrizio 21
von Bayern, Leopold 100

Wada, Takao 110, 138, 194
Walger, Leon 56
Walkinshaw, Tom 7, 163, 206
Warwick, Derek 105, 109, 180, 183, 188, 193
Watson, John 128, 156, 177, 206, 209, 218, 266
Weaver, James 105, 159, 230, 263
Weidler, Volker 205
Welter, Gérard 28
Weralit Racing 44
Whittington Brothers 14, 18
Whittington, Dale 50
Wietzes, Eppie 40
Wilds, Mike 130, 158, 199
Williams, Frank 18
Williams, Tom 77
Wilson, Desiré 10, 21, 22
Wimpfenn, Janos L. 6
Winkelhock, Manfred 48, 55, 67, 80, 146, 153, 161, 164
'Winter, John' (Louis Krages) 156, 178, 238
Winther, Jens 70, 100, 153
WM Peugeot/Secateva 28, 50, 69, 76, 88, 158, 242
   P79/80 28
   P81 50
   P82 69
   P83 102, 159
   P87 242
   P88 242
Witmeur, Pascal 79
Wolf, Tracy 40
Wolff, Bill 128
Wollek, Bob 49, 55, 74, 83, 91, 95, 109, 124, 128, 148-49, 151, 153-54, 165, 180, 189, 260, 265, 267, 273
Wolters, Terry 92
Wood, Dudley 53, 134, 149, 209
Woods, Jerry 26
Woods, Roy 17
Woodward, David 9
World Endurance Championship 8
   for Drivers 62, 67
   for Makes 62, 67

Yanagida, Haruhito 110, 138
Yorino, Takashi 105, 260
Yvon, Jean-François 184

Z&W Enterprises 23
Zakowski, Erik 23, 55, 107
Zakspeed 23, 48, 55, 88
Zakspeed USA 200
Zorzi, Renzo 10, 18